THE SOHO BIBLIOGRAPHIES

VIII

HENRY JAMES

Henry James by John S. Sargent, 1912

A BIBLIOGRAPHY OF
HENRY JAMES

THIRD EDITION

LEON EDEL

AND

DAN H. LAURENCE

REVISED WITH THE ASSISTANCE OF

JAMES RAMBEAU

CLARENDON PRESS · OXFORD
1982

Oxford University Press, Walton Street, Oxford OX2 6DP
London Glasgow New York Toronto
Delhi Bombay Calcutta Madras Karachi
Kuala Lumpur Singapore Hong Kong Tokyo
Nairobi Dar es Salaam Cape Town
Melbourne Auckland
and associates in
Beirut Berlin Ibadan Mexico City Nicosia

Published in the United States by
Oxford University Press, New York

First published 1957
Second edition 1961
Third edition 1982

British Library Cataloguing in Publication Data
Edel, Leon
A bibliography of Henry James.—3rd. ed.—(Soho
bibliographies)
I. Title   II. Laurence, Dan H.   III. Series   016.813'4
Z8447
ISBN 0–19–818186–8

Printed in Great Britain by
Richard Clay (The Chaucer Press) Ltd, Bungay, Suffolk

This book is gratefully dedicated to
LE ROY PHILLIPS
and to those who helped us build upon his foundations
SIMON NOWELL-SMITH
ALLAN WADE
EDNA KENTON

CONTENTS

ILLUSTRATIONS

ABBREVIATIONS

HJ   Henry James (1843–1916).

HJ Sr   Henry James Sr. (1811–1882).

WJ   William James (1842–1910).

BAL   Jacob Blanck, *Bibliography of American Literature*,
                  Vol. 5. New Haven, 1969.

Brussel   I. R. Brussel, *Anglo-American First Editions: Part
                  II: West to East 1786–1930*. London and New
                  York, 1936.

Carter   John Carter, *A.B.C. for Book-Collectors*. London, 1952.

Collamore   H. Bacon Collamore, donor of the Collamore col-
                  lection of James material in the Colby College
                  Library.

Gibson & Arms   William M. Gibson and George Arms, *A Biblio-
                  graphy of William Dean Howells*. New York, 1948.

Harlow   Virginia Harlow, *Thomas Sergeant Perry: A Bio-
                  graphy*. Durham, N.C., 1950.

Kramer   Sidney Kramer, *A History of Stone & Kimball and
                  Herbert S. Stone & Co.* Chicago, 1940.

Lubbock   Percy Lubbock, ed., *The Letters of Henry James*,
                  2 vols. London, 1920; New York, 1920.

Muir   Percy H. Muir, *Points 1874–1930: Being Extracts
                  from A Bibliographer's Note-Book*. London, 1931.

Phillips   Le Roy Phillips, *A Bibliography of the Writings of
                  Henry James*. New York, 1930.

Randall   David A. Randall, formerly of Scribner's, now of
                  the Lilly Library, Indiana University.

Ransom   Will Ransom, *Private Presses and Their Books*.
                  London, 1929.

Sadleir   Michael Sadleir, *XIX Century Fiction: A Biblio-
                  graphical Record Based on His Own Collection*,
                  2 vols. London, Berkeley and Los Angeles, 1951.

INTRODUCTION

In 1904 Le Roy Phillips, a graduate of Amherst College
and member of a Boston book firm, wrote to Henry James
to announce his plan for a bibliography of the novelist's
work. He asked him for his help, particularly in identifying
a considerable body of unsigned writings in periodicals.
The answer was as candid as it was inevitable. Authors,
wrote James, "in general do not find themselves interested
in a mercilessly complete resuscitation of their writings."
There were always "too many that they desire to forget and
keep buried."

> This leads them to watch with some detachment the
> process of digging up. They of course cannot prevent it
> and must accept all manner of consequence—but they
> must at least keep their hands from the pick-axe and the
> spade. My own impression is that I have hitherto got off
> well and have been very little bibliographized, for I have
> escaped positively knowing of anything of the sort, and
> I have certainly escaped contributing to it.

He might have added words to the effect that he had made
matters as difficult as possible for his future bibliographers
by coyly speaking of publications which "nothing would
induce me now to name" or by alluding, in his prefaces, to
stories "printed elsewhere", without naming the "elsewhere."

This wilful mystification has made James for years a
bibliographical "case" entirely different from the authors of
a few limited, well-polished works, or those who have
proudly fathered all they have written. In certain of James's
stories of writers, the fictional authors speak of their books
as children. James quite clearly considered some of his to be

11

illegitimate. This doubtless provokes a feeling of exaspera-
tion as the literary genealogist struggles with the great
family tree, but it does make for a certain irresistible
fascination in the hunt. Yet even if Henry James had been
more precise, the bibliographical burden would have been
extremely heavy: the sheer quantity of his writings, the
anonymity of so many of his reviews and essays, the confusion resulting from publication in many places and with
many publishers, the piracies, the multiple revisions and re-
revisions, the publication since his death of many of his
letters in widely scattered volumes, the very accidents of
publication—such as the reversal of two chapters in *The
Ambassadors*—the unravelling of all this has made for a
difficult if engrossing task.

This bibliography tells the story of what happened to the
writings of Henry James after they left his busy work-table
to be set up in type and published in magazine and book.
The story of their inception is to be found in James's notebooks, and there is a more self-conscious and intricately-
woven record in the prefaces which he wrote for the New
York Edition. The chronicle of the intermediate stage—the
author's descent into the market-place, manuscript in hand,
to drive his bargains with editors and publishers—belongs
elsewhere. We are concerned here with the final stage only.
This book, its compilers believe, contains the fullest account
yet set down, descriptive and historical, of the physical form
in which the novelist's works and ephemeral writings were
given to the world.

Henry James wrote for more than half a century and for
the printing presses on both sides of the water. His French
predecessor—and model—Honoré de Balzac had but one
publishing world to deal with in the creation of his *Comédie
Humaine*, and that within the tight literary boundaries of the
French capital. The American novelist, in an era of copyright
chaos, before the advent of the literary agent, negotiated

and published in three literary capitals: Boston, New York and London. He bargained stiffly: he demanded his price and usually received it. He lived by his pen for some three decades before he began to make use of a comparatively small inheritance. Artists, he explained to a young contemporary, had to be realists. They had to earn their bread and butter from month to month, and to that end had no right to disdain the "pot-boiler"—which represented, wrote James, "in the lives of all artists, some of the most beautiful things ever done by them." This explains why Henry James kept turning out, with his left hand, as it were, articles, reviews, short stories, while with his right he was producing his great novels. A magazine wanted an article on whether there was a life after death? He would write it providing his price was met. A preface to an edition of Shakespeare's *Tempest*? This could be written with the same facility as articles on the speech and manners of American women. The "producing" James is a formidable figure to conjure with, as the contents of this volume reveal.

Just how remarkable his productivity was may be judged by his output during 1878, the year in which he was leading an extremely active social life in a London that had newly discovered him and was treating him as a literary lion. This was the year in which he recorded, for the edification of the family circle in Cambridge, that he dined out a hundred and seven times. But late dinners and social calls, and the elaborate rituals of Victorian London, did not prevent him from seeing through the press *French Poets and Novelists*, *The Europeans*, *Daisy Miller* and the revised *Watch and Ward*. He also revised *The American* during that crowded year for British publication, prepared the two-volume edition of tales, *Daisy Miller and Other Stories*, and the American issue of *An International Episode*. This was not all. He contributed a total of thirty-six stories, articles, reviews and notes to periodicals on both sides of the water. And all this without benefit of secretary or typewriter; it was still the era of longhand and gaslight, and James worked in his small rooms in Bolton Street, always reading his own proofs; in addition he maintained a correspondence during this period, both professional and friendly, which in itself could fill a large volume.

An author who produced on Henry James's scale was not likely to keep the account-book of himself. Arnold Bennett, another prolific writer, but more of a journalist than James, used to total up the statistical record of his fertility at the end of each year and note in his journal the number of words he had written. Henry James would have considered such book-keeping a waste of time. He lost track of his productions early in life. If he returned to his essays in the periodicals it was only to "promote" them, by a process of careful revision, to the more permanent pages of a book. During the ten-year apprenticeship that preceded the publication of his first books, James had gained such a head start that ever after he had a comfortable back-log of his writings from which to assemble a volume whenever the occasion offered. Year after year James used to put out two, three, or four books within the twelvemonth, running always the risk of creating a glut in his own somewhat limited market. His brother, William James, who worked for a decade preparing his *Psychology*, recorded his amazement in his letters. How did Henry achieve such literary legerdemain? The novelist's answer might be summarized quite simply: he enjoyed writing, he was a happy producer; indeed his essay on Flaubert's letters contains a constant cry of surprise at Flaubert's doleful "torment of style."

Early in the 1880's James became aware of the sinister forces of bibliography. In his forty-second year, when he had been writing for almost a quarter of a century, he dipped back into the old *Atlantic* and *Galaxy* issues to recover some of his earliest tales. He selected fourteen, a sufficient number to make up a sizable Victorian "three-decker," to which he gave the title *Stories Revived*. The reserve supply was far from exhausted; indeed enough tales remained uncollected to fill four more volumes which came out at various times after James's death. The revision of *Stories Revived* is drastic. Names of characters are changed, whole scenes are rewritten, every page shows signs of re-touching. "It had come to the writer's knowledge," James explained in a one-paragraph foreword, "that they [the stories] were being to some extent 'hunted up,' and there seemed to be good reasons for anticipating further research by re-introducing them."

Le Roy Phillips completed his bibliography in 1906, and it was published during that year in the fine typography of Bruce Rogers. This volume, for the first time, disclosed the extent of Henry James's ephemeral writings. In 1930, a decade and a half after James's death, the long labour of love was brought up-to-date by Mr Phillips in the augmented *Bibliography of the Writings of Henry James*, a volume now out of print, which has been the substantial cornerstone of Jamesian scholarship to this day. He had seen the need for a bibliography at the right moment, and he was able to discover (in the still-extant account-book of the *Nation*, carefully kept by Wendell Phillips Garrison, and since preserved in the New York Public Library) a record of the payments made to Henry James by the journal for his writings. This made possible identification of most of the anonymous contributions. Today it is possible to confirm many of these, and add certain others, from the novelist's letters to his parents, where there are frequent allusions to his writings. With very few exceptions* most of the original attributions were correct; and it was possible for us to add others from these sources and from evidence

---

* These exceptions are: "The Manners of the Day in Paris," *Nation* VI (23 January 1868) 73–74, which is by William James, and "The Progress of Anthropology," *Nation* VI (6 February 1868) 113–115, which Ralph Barton Perry identified as by William James. William's

found in certain volumes of Henry James's library (unfortunately dispersed before we could exhaust all the data it had to offer).

"The expediency of discovering and bringing out from their obscurity the earliest of the unsigned critical notes and reviews was only too apparent," Mr Phillips wrote in his enlarged bibliography. "Recalling the search of twenty-five years ago and the diminishing number of those who, from their private knowledge, could give assistance, I doubt the likelihood of a 'resuscitation' so 'mercilessly complete,' if we had waited until a later date."

Yet even when Mr Phillips had completed his task, the never-ending process of bibliographical research, as he well knew, went on. His discoveries stimulated others. In 1934 the late Edna Kenton, who had been following independent bibliographical courses, produced a notable list of additions which she published in the Henry James issue of *Hound and Horn*. On his side the late Allan Wade, a bibliographer of Yeats and editor of James's dramatic essays, had unearthed the first appearance of a series of tales and articles in British periodicals not hitherto noted, which he communicated to Dr Edel, who on his side had come upon still further material in his editing of James's plays and the writing of his biography of the novelist. I. R. Brussel's *Anglo-American First Editions, Part Two: West to East 1786–1930*, with its comprehensive section on James, had appeared in 1936. By

---

letters to Henry show that the novelist on occasions retouched and edited these writings of his brother's. The error in ascribing these papers to Henry James arose from the fact that payment for them was made to him and so recorded in the *Nation's* account-books. The article on J. Foxcroft Cole, *Atlantic Monthly* XXXIII (May 1874) 629–630, also seems wrongly attributed by Phillips. James could not have seen the art exhibition here described since he was abroad at the time. In addition to the above, we find the novelist listed as receiving payment for an article on "The Labor Campaign" in the *Nation* of 1 September 1870. We do not believe it to be from his pen, although it may have been written by his father.

the time of the Henry James centenary in 1943 it was clear that a sufficiently large body of new material existed to warrant the planning of a new bibliography. This was begun at that time by Dr Edel and was focused largely upon the unearthing and listing of James's writings, so as to render the Phillips bibliography more complete. There remained, however, the difficult task of collating all the editions, tracking down translations, and extending the research to publishers' files. The major part of this task was undertaken by Mr Laurence.

As a result of his inspection of first editions in the Library of Congress and the British Museum, the Houghton Library at Harvard, the Yale University Library, the notable collections formed by H. B. Collamore (now at Colby College in Waterville, Maine), C. Waller Barrett and Simon Nowell-Smith, as well as many other private collections, each collation is based on an examination of at least twelve copies—except, obviously, where fewer copies are extant. Where a reported copy could not be personally examined, a full collation was sent to the library or collector for comparison. Such instances, however, were rare.

Surviving records of firms which published James were consulted and, where extant, stock and cost books were examined. Where the firm was no longer in existence the search was carried with considerable success to printing houses and binderies. Date of publication was never taken as final from any single source. This bibliography records the exact number of copies delivered by the printer when that figure is a small one, for instance 95, or 280. Where the printings were larger, the "overs" and "unders" were eliminated in favour of the publisher's *ordered* number of copies, given in round figures (that is 1500 rather than 1520, 3000 rather than 2970). In the listing of first impressions these have been referred to as "first editions"—meaning *first impression of the first edition*. A clear distinction has been drawn wherever possible between the often misused "issue"

17

and "state." Edges are described as "trimmed" and "untrimmed," never "rough-trimmed." All variant bindings detected are listed, as well as variant end-papers; doubtless other variants will turn up. Binder's fly-leaves have been recorded when noted; their insertion frequently appears to have been inconsistent.

When they seem to be significant, "freaks" are described; no reference is made to solitary instances of copies bound without free end-papers, copies bound uniquely by the printer, or other oddities which occasionally turn up in the market. Nor has any attempt been made to record dust-jackets except in two pertinent instances.

Where there are disagreements on the Olympus of bibliography we have simply followed the guidance of one of our bibliographical mentors that "bibliographical expression shouldn't be made more complicated than some people find it. . . . The bibliographer works not for a select, esoteric few, but also for the poor struggling bookseller in Chillicothe and the librarian in Peru, Indiana." To this end, signatures have been collated where necessary as singletons ($[1]^1$, $[*]^1$), rather than the Bowers - prescribed $[\chi^1]$ which seems to us to offer no advantage and which might be confusing to the uninitiated.

Since American and British bibliographers seem to be seldom in agreement on book size, we have accepted the size (Small 8vo; Square 4to) given by the publishers in advertisements at time of publication. The describing of styles and colours of cloth continues to defy standardization. Some American bibliographers have sought to arrive at conformity in cloth-identification by use of manufacturers' sample-book letters ("T" or "G" cloth, for instance). This has not appeared to us to be very helpful, and we have tended to lean upon the sample illustrations and descriptions in Michael Sadleir's *XIX Century Fiction*. On the other hand, where colour is concerned, we have hesitated to accept such British exoticisms as "Auricula

Purple" and "Cossack Green" and have quite simply described the colours as they appeared to us in broad daylight. *Rust red, olive brown, salmon pink* may not stand all tests, but they function adequately for such readers as are not wholly colour-blind. Where we encountered variant bindings of the same basic colour, but with differences in shading, we on occasion appealed for help to the sex which daily distinguishes colour-variations in clothing, jewellery and household goods.

As to the ever-present question concerning measurement of title-leaves—metric or inch-scale?—we accepted the opinion of the majority of British and American dealers and collectors we consulted. There is no doubt that the metric system *theoretically* meets international needs. But where this book will most be used the inch-scale seemed to us to be preferred. We have met this preference.

Wherever possible we have indicated whether Henry James revised his texts, without however going into detail, this being clearly a matter for textual scholarship rather than for bibliography. Failure on our part to mention revision must not be assumed to mean that no revision is to be found in the particular book or article. James was an inveterate "revisionist," and most scholars know by now that it is perilous to quote any passage of James's without collating all texts.

Our collations have focused primarily upon those volumes which the novelist himself saw through the press and then upon the relevant posthumous works. We have supplied also a check-list of books containing Henry James's letters and extracts from letters, and while this is comprehensive we do not pretend that it is exhaustive. The section on foreign translations, while inevitably the least definitive in a bibliography, is broader than we expected when this work was first launched. It was made possible by assistance given in all parts of the world—the assignment of staff librarians to conduct Mr Laurence through closed stacks to aid his search and provide ready translation; the arrangements made by the Swedish Consul to have books delivered to New York from the Royal Library in Stockholm; the gifts of books from publishers in both Europe and South America; the detailed answers to questionnaires by staffs of libraries in Eastern Europe; the generous efforts of Professor Makoto Sangu of Tokyo, who first unearthed and described the Japanese translations, and then sent copies of the works for personal examination. Such international scholarly co-operation has served to insure that the list of translations is basically accurate and representative. It has served also to emphasize anew that where books and culture are concerned fewer frontiers exist than might be imagined.

Although the roles of the collaborators were distinctly defined from the first—Dr Edel bringing to the book his long saturation in Jamesian scholarship and Mr Laurence being involved in all the technicalities of modern bibliography—the final work is a collaboration for which we take joint responsibility. Our data assembled, we worked it over together, step by step. In this task we have had the singular good fortune to be able to draw upon the counsel of Mr Simon Nowell-Smith, the learned and witty compiler of *The Legend of the Master* and former librarian of the London Library. To him this book owes much more than can be stated in a mere acknowledgment. Our manuscript was to have been reviewed also by Allan Wade, an indefatigable bibliographer who was one of the most sensitive of Jamesians, as readers of *The Scenic Art* know. It will always be a matter of deep regret to us that he did not have occasion to do so before his sudden death during the summer of 1955.

This volume is offered in the firm belief that the bibliographer is a very special kind of literary historian—one who is justified in interpreting his role as broadly as possible. To that end we have drawn freely upon the vast body of

Jamesian documentation for any data which might make for a richer and fuller story of the work. If this is not quite the *histoire des œuvres* which the Vicomte de Spoelberch de Lovenjoul compiled for the *Comédie Humaine* of Balzac, it is perhaps a work which may pave the way for a history of the particular human comedy which the American novelist brought into being.

Our debt to the many who helped in various ways is signalled in the acknowledgment, in an enumeration which cannot, unfortunately, convey the degree of assistance given. We would like here, however, to express our gratitude to Mr Rupert Hart-Davis, who insisted that the time was ripe for a bibliography and who kept us at our task. We owe a special debt of gratitude to Mr William James, the novelist's nephew, for the use of the James family correspondence, and both of us wish to express our special thanks to Professor William A. Jackson, the librarian of the Houghton Library at Harvard, for his unfailing courtesy and his generous assistance.

LEON EDEL
New York University
DAN H. LAURENCE

Bibliography involves so many minute bits of information that the task of improving a published work and bringing it up to date seems endless. Grateful for the reception of this book from the first, we have tried to rectify such errors and omissions as we have discovered, or which kind readers have pointed out to us. Committed as we both have been to other large scholarly tasks, we were fortunate to be able to enlist a young specialist in Henry James, Professor James Rambeau of the Pennsylvania State University, as a "co-reviser." He has provided us with valuable assistance in the preparation of this new edition.

We have taken into account the researches of the late Jacob Blanck in his James section of the *Bibliography of American Literature*. He very kindly communicated to us most of his new findings. In a certain sense the *BAL* can be consulted as complementary to our work; where we are in disagreement with it we have indicated by cross-reference possible alternate interpretations. Given the wide scope of his undertaking, Mr Blanck drew for his James section on a comparatively limited number of library sources: our nets perforce had to be cast more widely. Thus we offer more variants than can be accounted for in a compendium such as the *BAL*. We are also grateful to Mr Wayne C. Paton and Professor George Monteiro for their help.

We have not attempted to bring the translations section up to date. The *Index Translationum* of UNESCO, issued annually since 1948, now provides this information for those interested. We have also adhered to our original intention of not listing the many recent reprints of James's novels and tales as "first separate edition." We have tried to remain as "definitive" as possible, time having demonstrated that the core of this book remains unchallengeable. We hope it will continue to serve both scholars and book-lovers interested in James's works and their publishing history.

L.E.
D.H.L.

A. ORIGINAL WORKS

First edition:

A | PASSIONATE PILGRIM, | AND OTHER TALES. | BY |
HENRY JAMES, JR. | [publisher's device] | BOSTON: |
JAMES R. OSGOOD AND COMPANY, | LATE TICKNOR &
FIELDS, AND FIELDS, OSGOOD, & CO. | 1875.

$(7\frac{7}{16} \times 4\frac{13}{16})$: gathered and signed in 12's,* [i]^2 1–20^{12} 21^6; signed also
in 8's, [A]^8 B–I^8 J^8 K–U^8 V^8 W^8 X–2E^8, pp. 496. 12mo.

Contents: binder's fly-leaf at front; [1–2], title, on verso copyright
notice and imprint, "University Press: Welch, Bigelow, & Co., | Cam-
bridge."; [3–4], contents, verso blank; [5–6], divisional fly-title, verso
blank; [7]–496, text; binder's fly-leaf at back.

Issued in (*a*) green, (*b*) deep purple, (*c*) terra-cotta, and (*d*) dark
rust-brown sand-grain or fine-cross-ribbed cloth, bevelled edges,
single-rule frame within single-wide-rule border in blind on front and
back covers, lettering and outer wide-rule and inner narrow-rule at
top and bottom in gilt on spine; brown end-papers; all edges trimmed.

Published 31 January 1875, at $2, the first printing consisting of 1500
copies. Approximately 400 copies, bound in 1878 and later, bear the
Houghton Osgood & Co. imprint on spine, or are cased uniformly
with A16b, bearing imprint of Houghton, Mifflin & Co. on spine.

No separate English edition. Copies of the American edition were imported and offered for sale at 10/6. These copies were hand-stamped,
beneath publisher's imprint on title-page, "London: Trübner & Co."
or "London: Trübner and Co. 57 & 59 Ludgate Hill."

On 4 March 1873 HJ's father wrote to him that he had discussed
with J. R. Osgood publication of "a selection from your tales."
Osgood offered 15 per cent royalty if HJ paid for the plates, or 10 per
cent on sales after the first thousand, if Osgood covered all costs. The
father offered to pay for the stereotyping. HJ, then abroad, wrote to

---

* Sig. 21, however, appears in gathering 20. cf. Simon Nowell-Smith, "Signatures in Some Nineteenth Century Massachusetts Duodecimos: a Query." *The
Library*, 5th Series, III, No. 1 (June 1948), 58–62.

his mother 24 March 1873: "I value none of my early tales enough to bring them forth again, and if I did, should absolutely need to give them an amount of verbal retouching which it would be difficult out here to effect." He added that he wished to issue instead a volume "of tales on the theme of American adventurers in Europe, leading off with the *Passionate Pilgrim*." (HJ, *Letters*, I, 1974, p. 357.) When the book was finally issued James did not pay for the plates, but did so for the volume of travel sketches that followed.

CONTENTS

There are extensive revisions in most of the tales between serial and book publication.

A Passionate Pilgrim
> First appeared in the *Atlantic Monthly*, March–April 1871.

The Last of the Valerii
> First appeared in the *Atlantic Monthly*, January 1874.

Eugene Pickering
> First appeared in the *Atlantic Monthly*, October–November 1874.

The Madonna of the Future
> First appeared in the *Atlantic Monthly*, March 1873.

The Romance of Certain Old Clothes
> First appeared in the *Atlantic Monthly*, February 1868.

Madame de Mauves
> First appeared, under the title "Mme. de Mauves," in the *Galaxy*, February–March 1874.

A2 TRANSATLANTIC SKETCHES 1875

a. *First edition:*

TRANSATLANTIC SKETCHES. | BY | HENRY JAMES, JR. | [publisher's device] | BOSTON: | JAMES R. OSGOOD AND COMPANY, | LATE TICKNOR & FIELDS, AND FIELDS, OSGOOD, & CO. | 1875.

$(7\frac{7}{16} \times 4\frac{3}{4})$: gathered and signed in 12's, 1–16^{12} 17^{10}; signed also in 8's, [A]^8 B–I^8 J^8 K–U^8 V^8 W^8 X–Y^8 [Z]^2, pp. vi, [7]–404. 12mo.

Contents: binder's fly-leaf at front; [i–ii], recto blank, on verso advertisement of title "By the Same Author"; [iii–iv], title, on verso copyright notice and imprint, "University Press: Welch, Bigelow, &

Co., | Cambridge."; [v]–vi, contents; [7]–401, text; at bottom of p. 401 imprint, "Cambridge: Electrotyped and Printed by Welch, Bigelow, & Co."; [402], blank; [403–404], blank leaf; binder's fly-leaf at back.

Issued in (a) rust-brown, (b) dark green, and (c) purple fine-cross-ribbed or sand-grain cloth, bevelled edges, single-rule frame within single-wide-rule border in blind on front and back covers, lettering and outer wide-rule and inner narrow-rule at top and bottom in gilt on spine; brown-coated end-papers; all edges trimmed.

Published 29 April 1875, at $2, the first printing consisting of 1500 copies. Printed from the author's own plates. An indeterminate number of copies of the first impression was issued, after 1883, with the Houghton Mifflin & Co. imprint on spine.

No separate English edition. Copies of the American edition were imported, in June 1875, and offered for sale at 10/6. These copies were hand-stamped, beneath publisher's imprint on title-page, "London: Trübner & Co." or "London: Trübner and Co. 57 & 59 Ludgate Hill."

CONTENTS

Numerous revisions and some insertions between serial and book publication. The first 72 lines of *Swiss Notes*, for example, constitute newly-inserted material.

Chester
    First appeared in the *Nation*, 4 July 1872.
Lichfield and Warwick
    First appeared in the *Nation*, 25 July 1872.
North Devon
    First appeared in the *Nation*, 8 August 1872.
Wells and Salisbury
    First appeared in the *Nation*, 22 August 1872.
Swiss Notes
    First appeared in the *Nation*, 19 September 1872.
From Chambéry to Milan
    First appeared in the *Nation*, 21 November 1872.
From Venice to Strasburg
    First appeared in the *Nation*, 6 March 1873, with Strasburg spelled "Strassburg."
The Parisian Stage
    First appeared in the *Nation*, 9 January 1873.
A Roman Holiday
    First appeared in the *Atlantic Monthly*, July 1873.

A. ORIGINAL WORKS

Roman Rides
First appeared in the *Atlantic Monthly*, August 1873.

Roman Neighborhoods
First appeared in the *Atlantic Monthly*, December 1873.

The After-Season in Rome
First appeared, under the title "The After-Season at Rome," in the *Nation*, 12 June 1873.

From a Roman Note-Book
First appeared in the *Galaxy*, November 1873.

A Chain of Cities
First appeared, under the title "A Chain of Italian Cities," in the *Atlantic Monthly*, February 1874.

The St. Gothard
First appeared, under the title "An Autumn Journey," in the *Galaxy*, April 1874.

Siena
First appeared in the *Atlantic Monthly*, June 1874.

The Autumn in Florence
First appeared in the *Nation*, 1 January 1874

Florentine Notes
First appeared, in eight parts, in the *Independent*, 1874, under the following titles: "Florentine Notes," 23 and 30 April, 21 May; "A Florentine Garden," 14 May; "Old Italian Art," 11 June; "Florentine Architecture," 18 June; "An Italian Convent," 2 July; "The Churches of Florence," 9 July.

Tuscan Cities
First appeared in the *Nation*, 21 May 1874.

Ravenna
First appeared in the *Nation*, 9 July 1874.

The Splügen
First appeared, under the title "A Northward Journey," in the *Independent*, 20–27 August 1874.

Homburg Reformed
First appeared in the *Nation*, 28 August 1873.

Darmstadt
First appeared, under the title "An Ex-Grand-Ducal Capital," in the *Nation*, 9 October 1873.

In Holland
First appeared in the *Nation*, 27 August 1874.

In Belgium
First appeared in the *Nation*, 3 September 1874.

A. ORIGINAL WORKS

b. *First Continental edition, revised* (1883):

FOREIGN PARTS | BY | HENRY JAMES | AUTHOR OF |
"DAISY MILLER," "THE PORTRAIT OF A LADY,"
ETC. | AUTHORIZED EDITION. | LEIPZIG | BERNHARD
TAUCHNITZ | 1883.

($6\frac{7}{16} \times 4\frac{5}{8}$): [1]^8 2–20^8, pp. 320, followed by 16-page catalogue of advertisements. 16mo.

Contents: [1–2], series half-title and volume number, on verso list of books "By the Same Author"; [3–4], title, verso blank; [5–6], "Note" by Henry James, verso blank; [7–8], contents; [9]–318, text; [319–320], imprint, "Printing Office of the Publisher.," verso blank; catalogue dated July 1883.

Issued in the Tauchnitz "Collection of British Authors" (see F7), of which this was Vol. 2164.

Published 1883, at M. 1.60.

James's note, p. [5], reads: "The papers in this volume, reprinted from periodicals were collected and published in Boston in the year 1875, under the name of *Transatlantic Sketches*. For this 'Tauchnitz edition' the name has been changed and the sketches have been revised." Four complete essays, and portions of a fifth, included in the earlier volume, are omitted, these being: "The Parisian Stage," "The After-Season in Rome," "The Autumn in Florence," "The Splügen," and Parts II, VI, VII and VIII of "Florentine Notes."

A3   RODERICK HUDSON   1875

a. *First edition:*

RODERICK HUDSON. | BY | HENRY JAMES, JR. | [publisher's device] | BOSTON: | JAMES R. OSGOOD AND COMPANY, | LATE TICKNOR & FIELDS, AND FIELDS, OSGOOD, & CO. | 1876. [1875]

($7\frac{5}{16} \times 4\frac{3}{4}$): gathered in 12's, [unsigned: a^2 A–U^{12} X^2]; signed in 8's, [i]^2 1–30^8 31^2, pp. iv, 484. 12mo.

Contents: binder's fly-leaf at front; [i–ii], title, on verso copyright notice and imprint, "Riverside, Cambridge: | Stereotyped and Printed by | H. O. Houghton and Company."; [iii–iv], contents, verso blank; [1]–482, text; [483–484], blank; binder's fly-leaf at back.

A. ORIGINAL WORKS

Issued in (*a*) green patterned-sand-grain and (*b*) deep rust-brown and (*c*) terra-cotta fine-bead-grain cloth, bevelled edges, single-rule frame within single-wide-rule border in blind on front and back covers, lettering and outer wide-rule and inner narrow-rule at top and bottom in gilt on spine; brown-coated end-papers; all edges trimmed.

Published November 1875, at $2, the first (and only) printing consisting of 1500 copies. Announced as "just ready" in *Publishers' Weekly*, 20 November 1875, three days after the first copies had been delivered by the binder. Copies have been noted with Houghton, Osgood imprint on spine.

No separate English edition of this text. Copies of the American edition were imported, in January or February 1876, and offered for sale at 10/6. Reviewed in the *Academy*, 12 February 1876. These copies were hand-stamped, beneath publisher's imprint on title-page, "London: Trübner & Co." or "London: Trübner and Co. 57 & 59 Ludgate Hill."

First appeared in the *Atlantic Monthly*, January–December 1875. Slight revision between serial and book publication, including division of serial chapter XII into chapters XII and XIII in book. This is the only novel of James's which has chapter-titles and these were eliminated in subsequent editions.

b. *First English edition, revised* (1879):

RODERICK HUDSON. | BY | HENRY JAMES, JR. | IN THREE VOLUMES. | VOL. I. [II.] [III.] | REVISED EDITION. | LONDON: | MACMILLAN AND CO. | 1879.

($7\frac{5}{16} \times 4\frac{7}{8}$): Volume I, [A]^2 B–R^8 S^1, pp. iv, 258, followed by 40 page catalogue of advertisements. Volume II, [A]^1 B–S^8 T^2 U^1, pp. ii, 278. Volume III, [A]^1 B–R^8 S^4, pp. ii, 264. Stapled. Crown 8vo.

Contents: Volume I: [i–ii], title, on verso imprint, "London: | Printed by William Clowes and Sons, | Stamford Street and Charing Cross."; [iii–iv], note on revisions, verso blank; [1]–258, text; catalogue dated May 1879.

Volume II: [i–ii], title-leaf uniform with Vol. I; [1]–277, text; [278], imprint as on p. [ii].

Volume III: [i–ii], title-leaf uniform with Vol. I; [1]–263, text; [264], imprint as on p. [ii].

Issued in dark blue fine-bead-grain cloth, double-rule border and curved-edge panel in black on front cover and in blind on back cover,

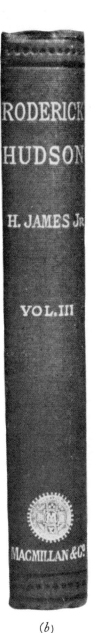

(a)   *(b)*

First English edition 1879: binding variants

PLATE I

A. ORIGINAL WORKS

lettering and publisher's device in gilt and decorative rules at top and bottom in black on spine; brown-coated end-papers; all edges untrimmed (bottom trimmed in some copies).

Published 11 June 1879, at 31/6, the first (and only) printing consisting of 500 copies.

There are two variant binding states noted, for which no priority has been established. In the one, page size measures $7\frac{5}{16} \times 4\frac{7}{8}$, the curved-edge panel in black on front cover measuring $6\frac{1}{16} \times 3\frac{3}{16}$, with a $\frac{9}{16}''$ spacing between inner border and panel. In the other, page size measures $7\frac{3}{16} \times 4\frac{3}{4}$, the panel on front cover measuring $6 \times 3\frac{1}{8}$, with a $\frac{7}{16}''$ spacing between inner border and panel. There are variations, too, in the brasses on spine, particularly in the "L" of "Vol." and the publisher's device, as well as in the style of type in the publisher's imprint (see Plate I).

The note in Volume I, p. [iii], reads: " 'Roderick Hudson' was originally published in Boston, in 1875. It has now been minutely revised, and has received a large number of verbal alterations. Several passages have been rewritten." In addition, the chapter titles are eliminated. The thirteen original chapters are divided into twenty-six.

c. *Later editions (from 1880):*

In May 1880 Macmillan published a one-volume "new edition" of 1500 copies at 6/-, uniform with A4c (*The American*, 1879). The text follows A3b. In 1882 Houghton, Mifflin imported two batches of 250 sheets each and issued them with cancel prelims, bound uniform with A16b (*The Portrait of A Lady*, 1881). In 1888 Macmillan published a yellowback issue, Globe 8vo., of 2000 copies at 2/-.

A4   THE AMERICAN   1877

a. *First edition:*

THE AMERICAN. | BY | HENRY JAMES, JR. | [publisher's device] | BOSTON: | JAMES R. OSGOOD AND COMPANY, | LATE TICKNOR & FIELDS, AND FIELDS, OSGOOD, & CO. | 1877.

($7\frac{3}{8} \times 4\frac{13}{16}$): gathered in 12's [unsigned: A–T^{12} U^{12} (–U$_{12}$)]; signed in 8's, [1]^8 2–29^8 30^8 (–30$_8$), pp. 478. 12mo.

Contents: binder's fly-leaf at front; [1–2], recto blank, on verso advertisement of "Mr. James's Writings."; [3–4], title, on verso copyright notice and imprint, "Riverside, Cambridge: | Stereotyped and Printed by | H. O. Houghton and Company."; [5]–473, text; [474], blank; [475–478], two blank leaves.

Issued in (*a*) rust-brown, (*b*) light green, and (*c*) dark green fine-cross-ribbed cloth, bevelled edges, single-rule frame within single-wide-rule border in blind on front and back covers, lettering and outer wide-rule and inner narrow-rule at top and bottom in gilt on spine; brown-coated end-papers; all edges trimmed.

Published May 1877, at $2, first printing consisting of 1000 copies. The earliest advertisement, headed "New Books," appeared in the *Boston Transcript*, 5 May 1877, two days after first copies had been delivered by the binder.

Bound copies of this edition were imported for the English market in June 1877, and offered for sale at 10/6. These copies were hand-stamped, beneath publisher's imprint on title-page, "London: Trübner & Co." or "London: Trübner and Co. 57 & 59 Ludgate Hill."

First appeared in the *Atlantic Monthly*, June 1876–May 1877. Numerous revisions between serial and book publication.

b. *First English edition (unauthorized, 1877):*

THE AMERICAN. | BY | HENRY JAMES, JR. | [publisher's device] | LONDON: | WARD, LOCK & CO., | WARWICK HOUSE, | DORSET BUILDINGS, SALISBURY SQUARE. [1877]

($6\frac{3}{4} \times 4\frac{1}{2}$): [A]⁸ B–2E⁸, pp. 448. Crown 8vo.

Contents: [1–2], half-title, advertisement on verso; [3–4], title, advertisement on verso; [5]–435, text; at bottom of p. 435 imprint, "Butler & Tanner, The Selwood Printing Works, Frome and London"; [436], blank; [437–448], advertisements, numbered pp. [1]–12.

Issued in multicoloured pictorial boards, lettering and illustration in blue, red, black, tan, and yellow on front cover, advertisement in black on back cover, lettering in black and multicoloured rules and decoration on spine; advertisements on paste-down and both sides of free end-papers; all edges trimmed.

Published December 1877, at 2/-. Noted under "New Publications" in the *Academy*, 8 December 1877; Cambridge copy deposited 18 December 1877.

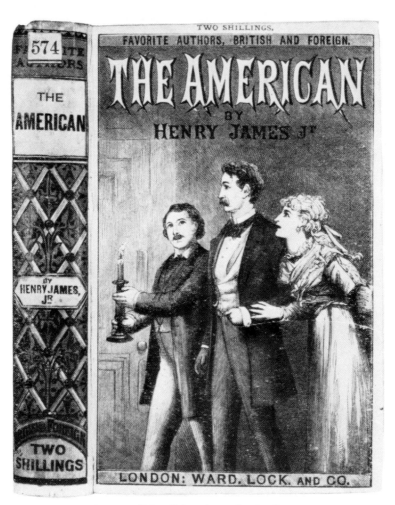

First English edition (unauthorized) 1877

PLATE II

No. 32 in Ward, Lock's "Favorite Authors, British and Foreign" series, published without authorization. In a letter to Elizabeth Boott, 30 January 1878, James spoke of the edition as "vilely printed" and added "there are whole paragraphs omitted." HJ to his mother, 13 January 1878: "Did I tell you it had been reprinted here by Ward & Lock, in the railway library, with a wonderful picture on the cover? But this of course is a piracy, & I get no profit from it." (Unpublished letters, Houghton Library.) (See Plate II.)

Height of page varies considerably in copies examined, ranging from 6⅝ to 6⅞. British Museum copy contains an extra leaf of advertisements tipped in at back: on recto, "Humorous Books", on verso "National Reference Books". This leaf appears in no other copy examined.

Later issued, from the same plates, lacking date on title-leaf, in the "Select Library of Fiction" series, No. 519, in 1888 or 1889, 2/- in paper, 2/6 in red cloth gilt, and in the "Copyright Novel Series," 3/6 in cloth, announced by Ward, Lock, & Bowden in the *English Catalogue*, May 1894.

c. *Second English edition (authorized, 1879):*

THE AMERICAN. | BY | HENRY JAMES, JR. | LONDON: | MACMILLAN AND CO. | 1879.

(7⅜ × 5): [A]⁸ B–Y⁸, pp. 352, followed by 40 page catalogue of advertisements. Crown 8vo.

Contents: [1–2], half-title, on verso publisher's device; [3–4], title, on verso imprint, "Charles Dickens and Evans, | Crystal Palace Press."; [5]–350, text; at bottom of p. 350 imprint, as on p. [4] but in one line; [351–352], advertisements; catalogue dated November 1878.

Issued in dark blue fine-bead-grain cloth, decorative embossed bands in gilt and black across front cover and spine and in blind across back cover, lettered in gilt on spine; brown-coated end-papers; all edges untrimmed (bottom trimmed in some copies).

Published March 1879, at 6/-, the first (and only) printing consisting of 1250 copies. Publisher reports publication date as 11 March 1879. Advertised as available "This Day" in the *Athenaeum*, 15 March.

Some copies lack catalogue of advertisements. Variant green-coated end-papers noted.

A5   FRENCH POETS AND   1878
                 NOVELISTS

a. *First edition:*

FRENCH | POETS AND NOVELISTS. | BY | HENRY JAMES JR. | LONDON: | MACMILLAN AND CO. | 1878. | THE RIGHT OF TRANSLATION AND REPRODUCTION IS RESERVED. [Final line is bracketed]

(7½ × 5): [A]⁴ B–2E⁸ 2F⁴, pp. viii, 440. Crown 8vo.

Contents: [i–ii], half-title, on verso publisher's device; [iii–iv], title, on verso copyright notice; [v–vi], note on serial appearance of contents, verso blank; [vii–viii], contents, verso blank; [1]–439, text; [440], imprint, "London: | R. Clay, Sons, and Taylor, | Bread Street Hill, E.C."

Issued in dark blue smooth-bead-grain cloth, lettered in gilt on spine; white end-papers; all edges untrimmed. For a possible variant binding, see Sadleir, Vol. I, p. 187.

Published 19 February 1878, at 8/6, the first (and only) printing consisting of 1250 copies.

No separate American edition. Bound copies of this edition were imported and sold at $2.50. First advertised in the *New York Tribune*, 2 March 1878.

An error in pagination, "80" for "280," appears throughout the issue.

Macmillan published the book although its reader, John Morley, characterized it as "mediocre . . . honest scribble work and no more." James's introductory "Note" reads: "These Essays originally appeared in several American periodicals. To the seven papers represented by the title the Author has ventured to add five others which have much in common with the subjects of the former."

CONTENTS

Minor revisions in all articles between serial and book publication.

Alfred de Musset
     First appeared in the *Galaxy*, June 1877.
Theophile Gautier
     First appeared, as a review of *Théâtre de Théophile Gautier: Mystères, Comédies, et Ballets*, in the *North American Review*, April 1873.

A. ORIGINAL WORKS

Charles Baudelaire
 First appeared, as a retrospective review-article on *Les Fleurs du Mal*, in the *Nation*, 27 April 1876.

Honoré de Balzac
 First appeared in the *Galaxy*, December 1875.

Balzac's Letters
 First appeared, as a review of *Correspondance de H. de Balzac, 1819–1850*, in the *Galaxy*, February 1877.

George Sand
 First appeared in the *Galaxy*, July 1877.

Charles de Bernard and Gustave Flaubert
 First appeared, as part of an article "The Minor French Novelists," in the *Galaxy*, February 1876.

Ivan Turgénieff
 First appeared, as a review of Turgenev's *Frühlingsfluthen* and *Ein König Lear des Dorfes*, in the *North American Review*, April 1874.

The Two Ampères
 First appeared in the *Galaxy*, November 1875.

Madame de Sabran
 First appeared, under the title "The Letters of Madame de Sabran," in the *Galaxy*, October 1875.

Mérimée's Letters
 First appeared, under the title "The Letters of Prosper Mérimée," in the *Independent*, 9 April 1874.

The Théâtre Français
 First appeared in the *Galaxy*, April 1877.

b. *First Continental edition* (1883):

FRENCH | POETS AND NOVELISTS. | BY | HENRY JAMES, | AUTHOR OF | "DAISY MILLER," "THE POR-TRAIT OF A LADY," | ETC. ETC. | AUTHORIZED EDITION. | LEIPZIG | BERNHARD TAUCHNITZ | 1883.

($6\frac{7}{16} \times 4\frac{1}{2}$): [i]⁴ 1–21⁸ 22⁴, pp. viii, 344. 16mo.

Contents: [i–ii], series half-title, on verso list of works "By the Same Author"; [iii–iv], title, verso blank; [v–vi], "Note," verso blank; [vii–viii], contents, verso blank; 1–344, text; at bottom of p. 344 imprint, "Printing Office of the Publisher."

Issued uniform with Tauchnitz "Collection of British Authors" (see F7), of which this was Vol. 2181.

Date of publication not determined, probably October 1883. The note on p. [vii] duplicates that of the first edition (see A5a) but the author has added the following sentence: "The present edition, a reprint of a volume published in England, is issued with his [the author's] full assent and under his revision."

c. *Second English edition* (1884):

In January or February 1884 Macmillan published a new edition in the uniform Eversley series, at 4/6, the first printing consisting of 1000 copies, from the Tauchnitz stereotyped plates.

d. *First American edition* (1964). See p. 202.

A6 WATCH AND WARD 1878

First edition:

WATCH AND WARD. | BY | HENRY JAMES JR. | [decorative device] | BOSTON: | HOUGHTON, OSGOOD AND COMPANY. | THE RIVERSIDE PRESS, CAMBRIDGE. | 1878.

$(5\frac{3}{4} \times 4\frac{3}{16})$: [unsigned: $1-14^8$ (-14_8)], pp. 222. 18mo.

Contents: binder's fly-leaf at front; [1–2], title, on verso copyright notice, reservation of rights, and imprint, "University Press: Welch, Bigelow, & Co., | Cambridge."; [3–4], "Note" (dated April, 1878) on serial appearance and revisions, verso blank; [5]–219, text; at bottom of p. 219 imprint, "Cambridge: Electrotyped and Printed by Welch, Bigelow, & Co."; [220], blank; [221–222], blank leaf. Each chapter decorated with a head-piece and an initial letter in small decorative panel; tail-pieces to chapters 1, 9, 10, 11.

Issued in (a) bright green and (b) red-brown diagonal-fine-ribbed cloth, lettering and decorative devices in gilt on front cover, single-rule panel and decorative devices in blind on front and back covers, lettering in gilt and decorative devices with interspersed rules in blind on spine; (a) sun-tan, (b) deep blue, (c) blue-grey, (d) dark brown, and (e) blue-green coated end-papers; all edges trimmed and 'red-stained.

Published 29 May 1878, at $1.25, first printing consisting of 1000 copies. Advertised as being in the "Little Classic" style of format.

In later impressions the final signature reads 14^6.

No separate English edition. Copies of the American edition were imported and offered for sale at 6/6, in June 1878. These copies were hand-stamped, beneath publisher's imprint on title-page, "London:

Trübner & Co." or "London: Trübner and Co. 57 & 59 Ludgate Hill."

First appeared in the *Atlantic Monthly*, August–December 1871. HJ wrote to HJ Sr., 19 April 1878, that Osgood had proposed publication of this first novel, which had not previously appeared in book form, and that HJ had consented as a way of "turning an honest penny. . . . [T]hough very thin, and as 'cold' as an icicle—it will appear pretty enough." (HJ, *Letters*, II, 1975, p. 167.) The note on p. [3] states that the text "has now been minutely revised, and has received many verbal alterations."

A7   THE EUROPEANS   1878

a. *First edition:*

THE EUROPEANS. | A SKETCH. | BY | HENRY JAMES, JR. | IN TWO VOLUMES. | VOL. I. [II.] | LONDON: | MACMILLAN AND CO. | 1878.

$(7\frac{1}{4} \times 4\frac{7}{8})$: Volume I, [A]^2 B–R^8, pp. iv, 256, followed by 40-page catalogue of advertisements. Volume II, [A]^2 B–S^8, pp. iv, 272. Stapled. Crown 8vo.

Contents: Volume I: [i–ii], half-title, on verso publisher's device; [iii–iv], title, on verso copyright notice and imprint, "Bungay: | Clay and Taylor, Printers."; [1]–255, text; [256], blank; catalogue dated June 1878.

     Volume II: prelims uniform with Vol. I; [1]–272, text; at bottom of p. 272 imprint, "Clay and Taylor, Printers, Bungay."

Issued in bright blue sand-grain cloth, double-rule border and curved-edge panel in black on front cover and in blind on back cover, lettering and publisher's device in gilt and decorative rules at top and bottom in black on spine; brown-coated end-papers; all edges untrimmed (fore and/or bottom edges trimmed in some copies).

Published 18 September 1878, at 21/-, the first printing consisting of 250 copies. There were two additional impressions of 250 copies each, in October and November 1878, lacking any imprint to distinguish them from the first issue.

An error has been noted in Volume I, in the chapter numberings of the page heads, rectos only, "IV" appearing for "V" on pp. 171–191 (M$_{6-8}$ N$_{1-8}$), with variations noted in texts examined. There appear to be three states of error: (*a*) pp. 171–191, (*b*) pp. 177–191 only,

(c) pp. 171–175 only (the latter corrected in some copies by scratching out by hand). It is possible that the error appeared only in the first and/or second impressions and was corrected for the second and/or third runs, the (b) and (c) variations of the error resulting from a mixture of gatherings from separate runs.

Variant binding state also noted consists of sheets of the two volumes of the first edition bound into one volume, the binding being uniform with that of the second (one-volume) edition—presumably a remainder binding.

First appeared in the *Atlantic Monthly*, July–October 1878. Numerous minor revisions between serial and book publication.

b. *First American edition:*

THE EUROPEANS. | A SKETCH. | BY | HENRY JAMES, JR. | [publisher's device] | BOSTON: | HOUGHTON, OSGOOD AND COMPANY. | THE RIVERSIDE PRESS, CAMBRIDGE. | 1879. [1878]

($7\frac{7}{16} \times 4\frac{3}{4}$): gathered in 12's [unsigned: A² B–M¹² N¹⁰]; signed in 8's, [i]² 1–17⁸ 18⁶, pp. iv, 284. 12mo.

Contents: binder's fly-leaf at front; [i–ii], blank leaf; [iii–iv], title, on verso copyright notice, reservation of rights, and imprint, "Riverside, Cambridge: | Stereotyped and Printed by | H. O. Houghton and Company."; [1]–281, text; [282], blank; [283–284], blank leaf; binder's fly-leaf at back.

Issued in (a) dark green, (b) bright green, and (c) terra-cotta fine-cross-ribbed cloth, bevelled edges, single-rule frame within single-wide-rule border in blind on front and back covers, lettering and outer wide-rule and inner narrow-rule at top and bottom in gilt on spine; chocolate brown-coated end-papers; all edges trimmed.

Published 12 October 1878, at $1.50, the first printing consisting of 1500 copies.

Although the Macmillan edition preceded the American edition, at least one copy of the latter exists with the Trübner London imprint stamped on the title-page.

c. *Second English edition* (1879):

In April 1879 Macmillan published a one-volume "new edition" of 1000 copies at 6/-, uniform with A4c (*The American*, 1879). The text follows A7a. For Times Book Club remainder binding, see F25.

A. ORIGINAL WORKS

a. *First edition:*

DAISY MILLER │ A STUDY │ BY HENRY JAMES, JR. │ [rule] │
NEW YORK │ HARPER & BROTHERS, PUBLISHERS │
FRANKLIN SQUARE │ 1879 [1878]

(4¾ × 3⅛): [1]⁸ 2–8⁸, pp. 128. 32mo.

Contents: [1]–4, advertisements; [5–6], title, on verso copyright notice; [7]–116, text; [117–128], advertisements.

Issued in pale buff paper wrappers, cut flush, lettering and decorative rules in red and black on front cover, publisher's device in red on front cover, advertisements in black on back cover, lettering and series number in black on spine; advertisements on inner sides of wrappers; all edges trimmed.

Issued simultaneously in green diagonal-fine-ribbed cloth, lettered and blocked on front cover in red and black, uniform with wrappered edition, publisher's device in black on back cover, lettered (minus series number) in (*a*) black or (*b*) red on spine; buff end-papers; all edges trimmed.

Published 1 November 1878, at 20 cents in wrappers, 35 cents in cloth, No. 82 in Harper's Half-Hour Series.

The first issue may be identified by the listing of only 79 titles in the Harper Half-Hour Series advertisements at the front of the book.

First appeared in the *Cornhill Magazine*, June–July 1878. Two unauthorized American periodical appearances preceded this edition: (*a*) *Littell's Living Age*, 6 and 27 July 1878, and (*b*) the *Home Journal* (New York), 31 July, 7 and 14 August 1878.

b. *First English edition* (1879)*:*

DAISY MILLER: A STUDY. │ AN INTERNATIONAL EPISODE. │ FOUR MEETINGS. │ BY HENRY JAMES, JR. │ IN TWO VOLUMES. │ VOL. I. [II.] │ LONDON: │ MAC-MILLAN AND CO. │ 1879. │ RIGHT OF TRANSLATION IS RESERVED. [Final line is bracketed]

(7¼ × 5): Volume I, [A]⁴ B–S⁸, pp. viii, 272. Volume II, [A]⁴ B–R⁸ S⁴, pp. viii, 264, followed by 40 page catalogue of advertisements. Stapled. Crown 8vo.

Contents: Volume I: [i–ii], half-title, on verso publisher's device; [iii–iv], title, on verso imprint, "Bungay │ Clay and Taylor, Printers";

A. ORIGINAL WORKS

[v–vi], "Note" on original publication of tales, verso blank; [vii–viii], contents of Vol. I, verso blank; [1]–271, text; [272], blank.

Volume II: [i–iv], uniform with Vol. I; [v–vi], contents of Vol. II, verso blank; [vii–viii], divisional fly-title, verso blank; [1]–263, text; [264], imprint as on p. [iv]; catalogue dated November 1878. The divisional fly-title on p. [vii] reads "Daisy Miller: A Study", though the volume begins with Chapter III of "An International Episode."

Issued in bright blue sand-grain cloth, double-rule border and curved-edge panel in black on front cover and in blind on back cover, lettering and publisher's device in gilt and decorative rules at top and bottom in black on spine; brown-coated end-papers; all edges untrimmed (bottom trimmed in some copies).

Published 15 February 1879, at 21/-, the first printing consisting of 250 copies. A second impression in March 1879 consisted of an additional 250 copies, lacking any imprint to distinguish them from first issue.

CONTENTS

Volume I:

Daisy Miller
An International Episode
    These two tales had prior book publication in America. (See A8a, A9).

Volume II:
An International Episode (continued)
Four Meetings
    First appeared in *Scribner's Monthly*, November 1877.

c. *Later editions (from 1880):*

In January 1880 Macmillan published a one-volume "new edition," consisting of two printings before publication totalling 1500 copies at 6/-, uniform with A4c (*The American*, 1879). The text follows A8b. For Times Book Club remainder binding, see F24. In March 1883 Harper reprinted *Daisy Miller* as No. 303 in its Franklin Square Library (together with *An International Episode*, *The Diary of A Man of Fifty*, and *A Bundle of Letters*). In 1888 Macmillan published a yellowback issue of A8b, Globe 8vo., of 2000 copies at 2/-. In December 1892 Harper published an edition of *Daisy Miller* and *An International Episode*, illustrated by Harry W. McVickar, 8vo., in a limited issue of 250 copies at $15, boxed, and an ordinary issue at

$3.50, boxed. The two tales were reprinted from the same plates as separate volumes: *Daisy Miller* in 1900 and *An International Episode* in 1902.

A9   AN INTERNATIONAL EPISODE   1879

First edition:

AN INTERNATIONAL EPISODE | BY HENRY JAMES, JR. | AUTHOR OF "DAISY MILLER" ETC. | [rule] | NEW YORK | HARPER & BROTHERS, PUBLISHERS | FRANKLIN SQUARE | 1879

($4\frac{3}{4} \times 3\frac{1}{8}$): [A]⁸ B–I⁸, pp. 144. 32mo.

Contents: [1–4], advertisements; [5–6], title, on verso copyright notice; [7]–136, text; [137–144], advertisements.

Issued in pale buff paper wrappers, cut flush, lettering and decorative rules in red and black on front cover, publisher's device in red on front cover, advertisements in black on back cover, lettering and series number in black on spine; advertisements on inner sides of wrappers; all edges trimmed.

Issued simultaneously in green diagonal-fine-ribbed cloth, lettered and blocked on front cover in red and black, uniform with wrappered edition, publisher's device in black on back cover, lettered (minus series number) in black on spine; buff end-papers; all edges trimmed.

Published 24 January 1879, at 20 cents in wrappers, 35 cents in cloth, No. 91 in Harper's Half-Hour Series. One copy noted contains a contemporary inscription of 15 January 1879, perhaps a pre-publication copy. Publisher's advertisements in three newspapers record the publication date.

The first issue contains an error in type-setting, corrected in later impressions, the last line of p. 44 being repeated at the top of p. 45. All first-issue copies examined contain this error and have advertisements of Bulwer's works on p. [137] and Katharine King's on p. [144]. Later impressions advertise the works of Virginia W. Johnson on p. [137] and those of Mrs Oliphant on p. [144]. There are variant advertisements on the pages between. A copy has been noted, containing the latter state of advertisements, inscribed with the date "1.25.79", but there has been no corroborative evidence to warrant a conclusive assignment of priority.

First appeared in the *Cornhill Magazine*, December 1878–January 1879.

For first English book publication, see A8b.

A10 THE MADONNA OF THE FUTURE 1879

a. *First edition:*

THE | MADONNA OF THE FUTURE | AND OTHER TALES. | BY | HENRY JAMES, JR. | IN TWO VOLUMES. | VOL. I. [II.] | LONDON: MACMILLAN AND CO. | 1879. | THE RIGHT OF TRANSLATION IS RESERVED.

($7\frac{3}{8} \times 5$): Volume I, [A]⁴ B–T⁸, pp. viii, 288. Volume II, [A]⁴ B–Q⁸ R⁴, pp. viii, 248. Stapled. Crown 8vo.

Contents: Volume I: [i–ii], half-title, on verso publisher's device; [iii–iv], title, on verso imprint, "London: | R. Clay, Sons, and Taylor, | Bread Street Hill."; [v–vi], "Note" on original appearance of tales, verso blank; [vii–viii], contents of Vol. I, verso blank; [1]–288, text.

Volume II: [i–iv], uniform with Vol. I; [v–vi], contents of Vol. II, verso blank; [vii–viii], divisional fly-title, verso blank; [1]–245, text; [246], imprint, "R. Clay, Sons, and Taylor, Printers . . ."; [247–248], advertisements.

Issued in dark blue fine-bead-grain cloth, double-rule border and curved-edge panel in black on front cover and in blind on back cover, lettering and publisher's device in gilt and decorative rules at top and bottom in black on spine; brown-coated end-papers; all edges untrimmed.

Published October 1879, at 21/-, the first (and only) printing consisting of 500 copies. Publisher reports publication date as 16 October 1879. The book was advertised as available "This Day" in the *Athenaeum*, 11 October.

Some copies measure $7\frac{1}{2} \times 5$.

A. ORIGINAL WORKS

b. *Later editions (from 1880):*

In April 1880 Macmillan published a one-volume "new edition" of 1000 copies at 6/-, uniform with A4c (*The American*, 1879). The text follows A10a. For Times Book Club remainder binding, see F29. In 1888 Macmillan published a yellowback issue, Globe 8vo., of 2000 copies at 2/-.

A11   CONFIDENCE   1879

a. *First edition:*

CONFIDENCE | BY HENRY JAMES JR. | [publisher's device] | IN TWO VOLUMES | VOL. I. [II.] | LONDON | CHATTO & WINDUS, PICCADILLY | 1880 [1879] | ALL RIGHTS RESERVED

($7\frac{1}{4} \times 4\frac{7}{8}$): Volume I, [A]² B–U⁸ X⁴, pp. iv, 312. Volume II, [A]² B–R⁸, pp. iv, 256, followed by 32 page catalogue of advertisements. Crown 8vo.

Contents: Volume I: [i–ii], half-title, on verso advertisement of "New Novels"; [iii–iv], title, on verso imprint, "London: Printed by | Spottiswoode and Co., New-Street Square | and Parliament Street";

[1]–309, text; at bottom of p. 309 imprint, as on p. [iv]; [310], blank; [311–312], publisher's device, verso blank.

Volume II: [i–iv], uniform with Vol. I; [1]–253, text; at bottom of p. 253 imprint, as on p. [iv]; [254], blank; [255–256], publisher's device, verso blank; catalogue dated December 1879.

Issued in (a) dull olive-brown and (b) dark green smooth cloth, carpet pattern in triangular panel in black on front and back covers, lettered in black on front cover and in gilt on spine; blue-on-white floral-patterned end-papers; all edges untrimmed (bottom trimmed in some copies). Brussel describes both volumes as lacking half-titles, but we have never found this to be the case. He also reverses the pagination of the volumes.

Published 10 December 1879, at 21/-, the first printing consisting of 500 copies.

HJ, dissatisfied with royalty returns from Macmillan, wrote to Chatto & Windus, 27 September 1879, to offer "a short novel," for which he desired to receive "a royalty & a certain sum of money down." Mindful of copyright difficulties, he added: "The novel is to appear in America, but I should naturally make a point of securing copyright in England by slightly anticipating the American publication." (Unpublished letter, Houghton Library.)

First appeared in *Scribner's Monthly*, August 1879–January 1880. Extensive revision between serial and book publication, including the division of the 12 serial chapters into 31 (but into 30 for the American edition).

b. *First American edition* (1880):

CONFIDENCE. | BY HENRY JAMES, JR. | [publisher's device] | BOSTON: | HOUGHTON, OSGOOD AND COMPANY. | THE RIVERSIDE PRESS, CAMBRIDGE. | 1880.

($7\frac{7}{16} \times 4\frac{7}{8}$): gathered in 12's [unsigned: A–O^{12} P^6]; signed in 8's, [1]^8 2–21^8 22^6, pp. 348. 12mo.

Contents: binder's fly-leaf at front; [1–2], blank leaf; [3–4], title, on verso copyright notice and imprint, "University Press: | John Wilson and Son, Cambridge."; [5]–347, text; at bottom of p. 347 imprint, as on p. [4] but in one line with ampersand substituted for "and"; [348], blank; binder's fly-leaf at back.

Issued in (a) red-brown, (b) orange-brown, and (c) dark green fine-cross-ribbed cloth, bevelled edges, single-rule frame within single-wide-rule border in blind on front and back covers, lettering and outer

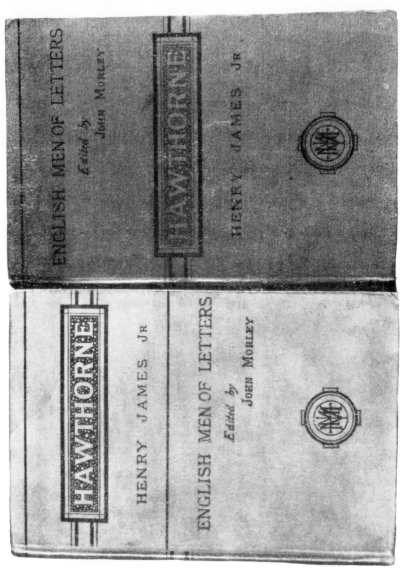

First edition 1879: binding variants (*b*) and (*a*)

PLATE III

wide-rule and inner narrow-rule at top and bottom in gilt on spine; brown-coated end-papers; all edges trimmed.

Published 7 February 1880, at $1.50, first printing 1500 copies.

A later binding state is noted, in dark green cloth, bearing the Houghton, Mifflin & Co. imprint on spine. These copies were bound from sheets of a later impression, but bear no indication that they are not first issue.

c. *Later editions (from 1880):*

In October 1880 Chatto & Windus published a one-volume "new edition," Crown 8vo., of 2500 copies at 3/6, issued in gunmetal-grey cloth, lettered and blocked in gilt and black. The text follows A11a. Remainder sheets were issued in a yellowback edition, post 8vo., at 2/- in August 1881. In September 1882 Chatto & Windus published an issue of 500 copies, from the plates of the one-volume edition, at 3/6 in their Piccadilly Library series. In 1891 Houghton, Mifflin published an issue, from the plates of A11b, in paper wrappers, 16mo., No. 29 in the River-Side Paper Series at 50 cents.

A new edition, "now first edited from the manuscript" by Herbert Ruhm, and containing extracts from the *Notebooks*, was issued in 1962 by Grosset & Dunlap, New York, in the Universal Library.

A12   HAWTHORNE   1879

a. *First edition:*

HAWTHORNE | BY | HENRY JAMES, JUNR. | LONDON | MACMILLAN AND CO | 1879 | THE RIGHT OF TRANSLA-TION AND REPRODUCTION IS RESERVED

($7\frac{1}{4} \times 4\frac{7}{8}$): [A]⁴ B–M⁸ N⁴, pp. viii, 184, followed by 4 inserted pages of advertisements. Crown 8vo.

Contents: [i–ii], series half-title, verso blank; [iii–iv], title, on verso imprint, "London: | R. Clay, Sons, and Taylor, | Bread Street Hill.";
[v]–vi, contents; [vii–viii], fly-title, verso blank; [1]–183, text; [184], imprint as on p. [iv]; double-leaf of advertisements, pp. [1]–4, tipped in at back.

Issued in three variant bindings, for which no priority has been established. The publisher believes all three may have been issued simultaneously: (*a*) Issued in dark crimson smooth-linen-grain cloth, the front cover being lettered and blocked as follows: [rule] | ENGLISH MEN OF LETTERS | EDITED BY | JOHN MORLEY | HAWTHORNE [within panel, against decorative band] | HENRY JAMES JR | [publisher's mono-gram]; single-rule and decorative band in black across back cover and spine, publisher's monogram in cloth colour against black background on back cover, lettered in black on spine; dark blue-green end-papers; all edges trimmed. (See Plate III.)

(b) Issued in yellow-ochre smooth linen-grain cloth, the front cover being lettered and blocked as follows: [rule] | HAWTHORNE [within panel, against decorative band] | HENRY JAMES JR | [rule] | ENGLISH MEN OF LETTERS | EDITED BY | JOHN MORLEY | [publisher's device]; balance of description uniform with (a). (See Plate III.)

(c) Issued in white buckram, lettering and two single-rules in black on white paper label on spine; white end-papers; all edges untrimmed. Page size: $7\frac{1}{2} \times 5$. This issue was called "Library Edition" by the publisher.

Published 12 December 1879, at 2/6, the first printing consisting of 6000 copies. A second impression, in January 1883, consisted of 2000 copies, which contain the imprint "Seventh Thousand" on the verso of title-leaf of all copies.

There are two variant states of advertisements in the first edition. In the first state, the advertisement for the English Men of Letters series, p. 2 of insert double-leaf at back, lists *Hawthorne* as "In Preparation." In the second state, the title is listed among the volumes of the series "Now Publishing." Both states of advertisements are noted in all three variant bindings.

In July 1887 a new impression of 5000 copies was issued, at 1/6 in cloth, 1/- in paper; in December 1887 a cancel title-leaf was inserted in remaining copies, eliminating the "Junr" after the author's name at HJ's specific request. In May 1902 a new impression of 1000 copies was issued, at 2/-, to which an Index was added for the first time.

HJ was invited by John Morley to write this volume especially for the English Men of Letters series. There was no prior serialization.

b. *First American edition* (1880):

HAWTHORNE | BY | HENRY JAMES, JR. | [publisher's device] | NEW YORK | HARPER & BROTHERS, PUB-LISHERS | FRANKLIN SQUARE | 1880

$(7\frac{3}{8} \times 4\frac{7}{8})$: $1-8^{12}$, pp. viii, 184. 12mo.

Contents: binder's fly-leaf at front; [i–ii], blank leaf; [iii–iv], series half-title, verso blank; [v–vi], title, on verso copyright notice and reservation of rights; [vii]–viii, contents; [1]–177, text; [178], blank; [179–184], advertisements; binder's fly-leaf at back.

Issued in dark olive-drab cloth, lettering and small single-rule in red on front cover and spine, publisher's monogram in red on back cover; brown-coated end-papers; all edges trimmed.

Published 15 January 1880, at $1.

There are minor variations in text between English and American editions, suggesting independent proof-readings. "Three or four beautiful talents" in the English edition (p. 3, line 12), for example, reads "Three or four beautiful plants" in the American edition (p. 3, line 8).

James received a flat sum of £100 for the American rights of the book, writing to HJ Sr., 17 January 1880: "I hope indeed it *may* have some success in America—though I know not why I should, since I have none of the profit of it. The whole of this by the pre-arranged conditions of the affair is between the Macmillans & Harpers. So if you see it selling, don't glory, but repine, as the money will all flow into the over-gorged coffers of Bedford St." (Unpublished letter, Houghton Library.) James, however, had actually chosen the flat payment. A letter to Frederick Macmillan, 22 January 1879, reveals: "The amount of the profit of my 'Hawthorne' being uncertain, & the convenience to me of receiving a round sum, down, on the completion of the book, being considered, I prefer, of your two alternatives [the second was a royalty arrangement], the 1st: viz: the £100, covering everything. I shall content myself with a disinterested observation of the sale, whatever it is, that the book may have in the Harpers' hands. Thank you for the choice." (Unpublished letter, Macmillan archives.)

A13   A BUNDLE OF LETTERS   1880

a. *First edition (unauthorized):*

A BUNDLE | OF | LETTERS. | BY | HENRY JAMES, JR. | (REPRINTED FROM THE PARISIAN.) | [decorative rule] | LORING, PUBLISHER, | CORNER BROMFIELD & WASHINGTON STREETS, | BOSTON. [1880]

($6\frac{3}{8} \times 5\frac{1}{4}$): [unsigned: 1–4⁸], pp. 64, stapled or oversewn. Square 16mo.

Contents: [1–2], title, verso blank; [3]–64, text; at bottom of p. 64 imprint, "Rockwell & Churchill, Printers, 39 Arch Street."

Issued in (*a*) pale blue, (*b*) cream white, (*c*) pale pink, and (*d*) pale yellow-green stiff paper wrappers, cut flush, pattern of vertical bands of five rules in red and horizontal bands of five rules in blue on both outer and inner sides of wrappers, lettered in black on front cover, advertisements in black on back cover and inner sides of wrappers; all edges trimmed. Decorative headpiece, p. [3], tailpiece, p. 64, and panelled initial letters to each of the nine sections of the tale.

Published 24 January 1880, at 25 cents. Brussel reports a copy with an 1879 inscription, but the Loring newspaper announcements and James family correspondence establish the later date.

There are three distinct lettering-variants on front cover. The primary state (*a*), determined by examination of numerous early-dated copies,

BY
HENRY JAMES, Jr.,
(*a*) and (*b*)

BY
HENRY JAMES, Jr.
(*c*)

has a comma after "Jr." and author's name is printed in wide-serif letters, narrowly spaced. In the secondary states, (*b*) is identical with (*a*) except for omission of comma, while in (*c*) the author's name is printed in small-serif letters, more widely spaced. There are discrepancies, too, between settings, in the spacing between placements of lettering on front covers, and in the placements of the headings, "Loring's Successful Novels" and "Loring's Successful Books," on the inner front wrapper and outer back wrapper.

The pattern of criss-crossed rules on the wrappers varies considerably between copies, in some of which the blue rules are vertical and the red horizontal, while in others the pattern is entirely eliminated from the inner sides of wrappers. Page size varies also, from $6\frac{3}{16} \times 5\frac{1}{4}$ to $6\frac{7}{8} \times 5\frac{5}{8}$.

This unauthorized publication is discussed in HJ's letters to his parents. "Loring's proceeding is an impudent one," he wrote to his mother, 2 February 1880; "*He has no legal right to republish in any sort of book-form, however small or cheap, any article* contributed to any periodical, anywhere in the world, by an AMERICAN CITIZEN, without the formal leave of that citizen". On 15 February 1880 he wrote to his father, "I am still irate, the more so that you tell me that the thing is selling like Wildfire." He is now satisfied, however, that he has no redress, and finds that his failure to copyright the tale gave Loring the legal right to reproduce it. "But he has no moral right, & his doing so without asking my assent or offering me any profit remains a scandalous & impudent proceeding." He adds, "Will you kindly send me 2 or 3 more of his pamphlets? Since he has issued the thing, I may as well have 'em to give away, & they are very chastely 'gotten up'." (HJ, *Letters*, II, 1975, pp. 269–271.)

First appeared in the *Parisian* (an English-language weekly published in Paris), 18 December 1879.

b. *Second edition (unauthorized):*

[Seaside Library masthead, newspaper style] | SWEET NELLY, MY HEART'S DELIGHT. | BY WALTER BESANT AND JAMES RICE. | AND | A BUNDLE OF LETTERS. | BY HENRY JAMES, JR. [1880]

($12\frac{1}{4} \times 8\frac{1}{4}$), a single unsigned quire of sixteen leaves, pp. 32. 4to.

Contents: "Sweet Nelly, My Heart's Delight" occupies pp. [1]–20, and "A Bundle of Letters" pp. 20–26, followed by 6 pages of advertisements.

The Seaside Library, published by George Munro, was a weekly publication, issued on white newsprint, without wrappers, at 10 cents. This issue was Vol. XXXIV, No. 702, published 23 February 1880, the text being taken from the Loring piracy of a month before.

A14   THE DIARY OF A MAN   1880
              OF FIFTY

First American edition (authorized):

THE | DIARY OF A MAN OF FIFTY | AND | A BUNDLE OF LETTERS | BY | HENRY JAMES, JR. | AUTHOR OF | "DAISY MILLER" "AN INTERNATIONAL EPISODE" ETC. | [decorative rule] | NEW YORK | HARPER & BROTHERS, PUBLISHERS | FRANKLIN SQUARE | 1880

($4\frac{3}{4} \times 3\frac{1}{8}$): [1]^8 2–9^8, pp. 144. 32mo.

Contents: [1]–4, advertisements of Harper's Half-Hour Series; [5–6], title, on verso copyright notice and reservation of rights; [7–8], divisional fly-title, on verso notices uniform with p. [6]; [9]–135, text; [136], blank; [137–144], advertisements.

Issued in pale buff paper wrappers, cut flush, lettering and decorative rules in red and black on front cover, publisher's device in red on front cover, advertisements in black on back cover, lettering and series number in black on spine; advertisements on inner sides of wrappers; all edges trimmed.

Issued simultaneously in green cloth, lettered and blocked on front cover in red-brown and black, uniform with wrappered edition, publisher's device in black on back cover, lettered (minus series number) in red-brown on spine; buff end-papers; all edges trimmed.

Published 9 April 1880, at 25 cents in wrappers, 40 cents in cloth, No. 135 in Harper's Half-Hour Series.

Cloth issue appears in three distinct binding states. In the first, lettering is in red-brown, with titles of both tales on spine. In the second, both titles are lettered in black on spine. In the third, lettering is in orange-red, with only "The Diary of A Man of Fifty" imprinted on spine. No priority has been established.

CONTENTS

The Diary of A Man of Fifty
    This tale had prior book publication in England.
A Bundle of Letters
    First authorized American publication. The text follows that of the serialization in the *Parisian*. See A13 for unauthorized American publications.

A15   WASHINGTON SQUARE   1880

a. *First edition:*

WASHINGTON SQUARE | BY HENRY JAMES, JR. | AUTHOR OF | "DAISY MILLER" "AN INTERNATIONAL EPISODE" ETC. | ILLUSTRATED BY GEORGE DU MAURIER | NEW YORK | HARPER & BROTHERS, FRANK-LIN SQUARE | 1881 [1880]

($6\frac{5}{8}$ × $4\frac{11}{16}$): [1]⁸ 2–17⁸, pp. 272. 16mo.
Contents: binder's fly-leaf at front; [1–2], recto blank, on verso frontispiece illustration; [3–4], title, on verso copyright notice and

reservation of rights; [5–6], list of illustrations, verso blank; [7]–266, text; [267–272], advertisements, numbered pp. [1]–6; binder's fly-leaf at back. Wood-engraved frontispiece and five full-page illustrations on text pages, with tissue guards, reverse sides blank, reckoned in pagination; six smaller illustrations in the text.

Issued in olive-drab diagonal-fine-ribbed cloth, illustration framed within double-rule panel blocked on front cover, lettering in cloth colour and red-brown against gilt panels within crossed triple-rule series of bands in red-brown and gilt on front cover and spine; (*a*) drab tan- or (*b*) dark brown-coated end-papers; all edges trimmed.

Published 1 December 1880, at $1.25.

First appeared in the *Cornhill Magazine*, June–November 1880, and in *Harper's New Monthly Magazine*, July–December 1880. The twelve Du Maurier illustrations were reproduced from the *Cornhill Magazine*. There appear to have been no revisions between serial and book publication, except for a few changes in punctuation.

b. *First English edition* (1881):

WASHINGTON SQUARE | THE PENSION BEAUREPAS | A BUNDLE OF LETTERS | BY HENRY JAMES, JUN. | VOL. I. [II.] | LONDON | MACMILLAN AND CO. | 1881

($7\frac{7}{16} \times 5$): Volume I, [A]⁴ B–R⁸ S⁴ [T]², pp. viii, 268. Volume II, [A]² B–S⁸, pp. iv, 272, followed by 40 page catalogue of advertisements. Crown 8vo.

Contents: Volume I: [i–ii], half-title, on verso publisher's device; [iii–iv], title, verso blank; [v–vi], "Note" on original appearance of tales, verso blank; [vii–viii], divisional fly-title, verso blank; [1]–265, text; at bottom of p. 265 imprint, "Printed by R. & R. Clark, Edinburgh."; [266], blank; [267–268], blank leaf.

Volume II: [i–iv], uniform with Vol. I; [1]–371 [271], text; at bottom of p. 371 [271] imprint, as on p. 265 of Vol. I; [272], blank; catalogue dated December 1879.

Issued in dark blue-green fine-bead-grain cloth, double-rule border and curved-edge panel in black on front cover and in blind on back cover, lettering and publisher's device in gilt and decorative rules at top and bottom in black on spine; (*a*) brown-coated or (*b*) white end-papers; all edges untrimmed.

Published January 1881, at 21/-, the first printing consisting of 500 copies. A second impression, consisting of 250 copies, was issued in

March 1881. The publisher reports publication date as 26 January 1881. The book was advertised as available "Immediately" in the *Athenaeum*, 15 January.

The first impression of Vol. II contains three misnumbered pages, reading 368, 369, and 371, instead of 268, 269, and 271. This error was corrected in the second impression, which was issued in red-brown cloth, with yellow-coated end-papers, and re-cut brasses on spine. The author's name appears as "H. James Jr" on spine of first impression, and as "Henry James, Jun." on spine of second impression. (See Plate IV.) Second impression of Vol. I sometimes lacks final leaf, [T_2]; Vol. II lacks catalogue.

Brussel records an "issue" consisting of first-impression binding on second-impression sheets (i.e. with pagination error corrected) and catalogue dated January 1881 in Vol. II. A copy of this hybrid is in the University of Texas Humanities Research Center. For a possible binding variant, see Sadleir, Vol. I, p. 188.

CONTENTS

Washington Square
 This had prior book publication in America.
The Pension Beaurepas
 First appeared in the *Atlantic Monthly*, April 1879.
A Bundle of Letters
 This had prior book publication in America.

c. *Later editions (from* 1881)*:*

In August 1881 Macmillan published a one-volume edition of 500 copies at 6/-, uniform with A4c (*The American*, 1879). The text follows A15b. In 1889 Macmillan published a yellowback issue, Globe 8vo., of 2000 copies at 2/-.

A16 THE PORTRAIT OF A LADY 1881

a. *First edition:*

THE PORTRAIT OF A LADY | BY | HENRY JAMES, JR., | AUTHOR OF "THE EUROPEANS," ETC., ETC. | IN THREE VOLUMES. | VOL. I. [II] [III.] | LONDON: | MAC-MILLAN AND CO. | 1881. | THE RIGHT OF TRANSLATION AND REPRODUCTION IS RESERVED.

($7\frac{7}{16} \times 4\frac{15}{16}$): Volume I, [A]^2 B–R^8 S^6, pp. iv, 268. Volume II, [A]^2

B–R⁸, pp. iv, 256. Volume III, [A]² B–Q⁸ R⁴, pp. iv, 248, followed by 24 page catalogue of advertisements. Crown 8vo.

Contents: Volume I: [i–ii], half-title, on verso publisher's device; [iii–iv], title, on verso imprint, "Clay and Taylor, Printers, | Bungay, Suffolk."; [1]–266, text; [267–268], blank.

Volume II: [i–iv], uniform with Vol. I ; [1]–253, text; [254], imprint, as on p. [iv]; [255–256], blank. (Title-page of Volume II lacks full stops after "In Three Volumes" and "Vol. II".)

Volume III: [i–iv], uniform with Vol. I; [1]–248, text; at bottom of p. 248 imprint, "Clay and Taylor, Printers, Bungay."; catalogue dated December 1881.

Issued in (a) dark blue and (b) dark blue-green fine-bead-grain cloth, double-rule border and curved-edge panel in black on front cover and in blind on back cover, lettering and publisher's device in gilt and decorative rules at top and bottom in black on spine; brown-coated end-papers; all edges untrimmed.

Published November 1881, at 31/6, the first printing consisting of 750 copies. Publisher reports date of publication as 8 November 1881. Advertisement in the *Athenaeum*, 29 October 1881, announces publication as 4 November. A second impression, consisting of 250 copies, is dated 1882 on title page. A copy of this has been noted with the three volumes bound together in red cloth.

Some copies of the first impression lack catalogue of advertisements at back of Volume III. Others contain catalogue dated April 1881, probably inserted through error or through shortage at the bindery.

First appeared in *Macmillan's Magazine*, October 1880–November 1881, and in the *Atlantic Monthly*, November 1880–December 1881. Minor revisions between serial and book publication.

b. *Second edition, American issue:*

THE | PORTRAIT OF A LADY. | BY | HENRY JAMES, JR. | [publisher's device] | BOSTON: | HOUGHTON, MIFFLIN AND COMPANY. | NEW YORK: 11 EAST SEVENTEENTH STREET. | THE RIVERSIDE PRESS, CAMBRIDGE. | 1882. [1881]

(7⅜ × 4¾): gathered in 12's [unsigned: 1¹ 2–22¹² 23⁸]; signed in 8's, [A]¹ B–2K⁸ 2L⁴, pp. ii, 520. Stapled. 12mo.

Contents: binder's fly-leaf at front; [i–ii], title, on verso copyright notice; [1]–520, text; binder's fly-leaf at back.

Issued in (*a*) light tan and (*b*) forest green diagonal-fine-ribbed cloth, lettering in red-brown and decorative devices and rules in red-brown and gilt on front cover and spine; brown-coated end-papers; all edges trimmed.

Published 16 November 1881, at $2, the first printing consisting of 1500 copies. There were five additional impressions between November 1881 and August 1882, totalling 5000 copies, lacking any imprint to distinguish them from first issue.

First issue is identifiable by a full stop after the imprint, "Copyright, 1881." on p. [ii]. In the second and subsequent impressions the full stop is missing. With the exception of the title-page this edition was presumably printed from a duplicate casting of the plates of A16c.

Two secondary binding states are noted, in dark brown and in grey-green diagonal-fine-ribbed cloth. These binding states frequently have floral-patterned pale tan- or grey-coated end-papers. See *BAL* for additional variant information.

Randall, in collating the first edition for a series of one hundred American first editions, *Publishers' Weekly*, 19 July 1941, read [A]² for the first signature, failing to note first leaf is a binder's fly-leaf and non-conjugate. He also recorded the signatures of this volume as in 8's, although the quires are gathered in 12's.

c. *Second edition, English issue* (1882):

In June 1882 Macmillan published a one-volume "new edition" of 1000 copies at 6/-, uniform with A4c (*The American*, 1879). Text as in A16a.

A17   THE POINT OF VIEW   1882

Pre-publication Copyright edition:

THE POINT OF VIEW | BY | HENRY JAMES, JUN. | NOT PUBLISHED | 1882

$(7\frac{7}{16} \times 4\frac{15}{16})$: [A]² B–D⁸ E⁴ [F]², pp. iv, 60. [8vo]

Contents: [i–ii], half-title, verso blank; [iii–iv], title, verso blank; [1]–59, text; [60], blank.

Issued in blue-grey stiff paper wrappers, cut flush, front cover being a duplication of title-page with addition of single-rule border with heart and star devices at the corners in black; inner sides of wrappers blank; top edge untrimmed, other edges trimmed. Privately printed, at

HJ's expense, in July 1882, by Macmillan and Co., London, for American copyright protection. Brussel appears to have included the wrappers in his pagination.

The copy now in the Collamore collection at Colby is the only one known to be extant. It was discovered by Euan Cox, London bookseller, in 1928, on the front table of a local bookstall.

First published appearance of the tale was in the *Century Magazine*, December 1882, the serial publication including a footnote reproduced on p. [1] of the Copyright edition. This was eliminated in subsequent book appearances of the tale.

A18   DAISY MILLER: A COMEDY   1882

a. *Pre-publication Copyright edition:*

DAISY MILLER | A COMEDY | BY | HENRY JAMES JUN. | NOT PUBLISHED | 1882

$(7\frac{3}{8} \times 4\frac{15}{16})$: [A]^2 B–I^8 K^4 L^2, pp. iv, 140. [8vo]
Contents: [i–ii], half-title, verso blank; [iii–iv], title, on verso cast of characters and list of acts; [1]–139, text; [140], blank.

Issued in blue-grey stiff paper wrappers, cut flush, front cover being a duplication of title-page with addition of single-rule border with heart and star devices at the corners in black; inner sides of wrappers blank; all edges untrimmed.

Privately printed, at HJ's expense, in July 1882, by Macmillan and Co., London, for copyright protection.

Copies as described above are in the Houghton and Colby Libraries. A third copy, in the Library of Congress, is bound in light tan paper wrappers.

First published appearance of the play was in the *Atlantic Monthly*, April–June 1883.

b. *First published edition* (1883):

HENRY JAMES | [rule] | DAISY MILLER | A COMEDY | IN THREE ACTS | [publisher's device] | BOSTON | JAMES R. OSGOOD AND COMPANY | [rule] | 1883

$(7\frac{3}{8} \times 4\frac{3}{4})$: gathered in 6's [unsigned: 1–16^6]; signed in 8's, [i]^1 [1]^8 2–11^8 12^7, pp. ii, 190. 12mo.

Contents: [i–ii], half-title, verso blank; [1–2], recto blank, advertisement on verso; [3–4], title, on verso copyright notice, reservation of rights, and imprint, "Cambridge: | Printed by John Wilson and Son, | University Press."; [5–6], "Dramatis Personae," verso blank; [7]–189, text; at bottom of p. 189 imprint, "Cambridge: University Press, John Wilson & Son."; [190], blank.

Issued in (*a*) wine, (*b*) dark blue, (*c*) dark purple-brown, (*d*) blue-green, (*e*) rose, and (*f*) chocolate brown diagonal-fine-ribbed cloth, single-rule frame within single-wide-rule border in blind on front and back covers, lettering and publisher's device in gilt on spine; white end-papers; all edges trimmed.

Published September 1883, at $1.50, the first printing consisting of 1000 copies. Noted under "Books of the Week," in the *Independent*, 13 September 1883; Library of Congress deposit made the same day.

A variant binding state has been noted, with Ticknor & Company monogram imprinted at foot of spine, in place of J. R. Osgood monogram.

A secondary binding state of the first edition has been noted, in smooth green cloth, lacking the double rule in blind on covers, bearing the Houghton Mifflin & Co. imprint on spine.

A19   THE SIEGE OF LONDON   1883

a. *First edition:*

THE SIEGE OF LONDON, | THE PENSION BEAUREPAS, | AND | THE POINT OF VIEW. | BY | HENRY JAMES, JR. | AUTHOR OF "DAISY MILLER," "THE AMERICAN," | "THE PORTRAIT OF A LADY," ETC. | [publisher's device] | BOSTON: | JAMES R. OSGOOD AND COMPANY. | 1883.

($7\frac{5}{16} \times 4\frac{7}{8}$): gathered in 6's [unsigned: 1–25⁶]; signed in 12's, [i]³ 1–12¹² 13³, pp. vi, 294. 12mo.

Contents: [i–ii], blank leaf; [iii–iv], title, on verso copyright notice, reservation of rights, and imprint, "University Press: | John Wilson and Son, Cambridge."; [v–vi], contents, verso blank; [1–2], divisional fly-title, verso blank; [3]–294, text.

Issued in (*a*) dark purple-brown, (*b*) terra-cotta, (*c*) dark rust-brown, and (*d*) green diagonal-fine-ribbed cloth, single-rule frame within single-wide-rule border in blind on front and back covers, lettering and publisher's device in gilt on spine; white end-papers; all edges trimmed.

Published 24 February 1883, at $1.50, the first printing consisting of 1500 copies. A "Second Edition" was issued in March 1883, consisting of 1000 copies. However, copies of the first impression, bound in 1888 and later, have the Houghton Mifflin & Co. imprint on spine.

CONTENTS

The Siege of London
    First appeared in the *Cornhill Magazine*, January–February 1883.
The Pension Beaurepas
    This tale had prior book publication in England.
The Point of View
    First appeared in the *Century Magazine*, December 1882. See A17 for pre-publication Copyright edition.

b. *First Continental edition* (1884):

THE SIEGE OF LONDON; | THE POINT OF VIEW; | A PASSIONATE PILGRIM. | BY | HENRY JAMES, | AUTHOR OF "DAISY MILLER," "THE AMERICAN," ETC. | AUTHORIZED EDITION. | LEIPZIG | BERNHARD TAUCHNITZ | 1884.

(6 × 4⅜): [1]⁸ 2–18⁸ 19⁴, pp. 296, followed by 16 page catalogue of advertisements. 16mo.

Contents: [1–2], half-title, advertisement on verso; [3–4], title, verso blank; [5–6], Authorization note, on verso Revision note signed "Henry James. December, 1883."; [7–8], contents, verso blank; [9–10], fly-title, verso blank; [11]–294, text; [295–296], imprint, "Printing Office of the Publisher", verso blank; catalogue dated March 1884.

Issued uniform with Tauchnitz "Collection of British Authors" (see F7), of which this was Vol. 2234.

Published Spring 1884, at M. 1.60.

For this edition HJ eliminated *The Pension Beaurepas*, third tale in the American edition, and substituted *A Passionate Pilgrim*, concerning which the note on revision, p. [6], reads: "It is proper to state that the last of the three tales contained in this volume, a story originally

57

published in Boston in 1872, has been, in the matter of language, much altered and amended for reproduction here." This text was used, a year later, in *Stories Revived*.

A20 COLLECTIVE EDITION OF 1883
1883

First collected edition:

1. *The Portrait of A Lady* (Vol. I):

THE | PORTRAIT OF A LADY | BY | HENRY JAMES | IN THREE VOLUMES | VOL. I. | LONDON | MACMILLAN AND CO. | 1883

($6\frac{1}{4} \times 4\frac{1}{8}$): [A]² B–Q⁸, pp. iv, 240. Pott. 8vo.

Contents: [i–ii], half-title, on verso publisher's device; [iii–iv], title, on verso imprint, "Printed by R. & R. Clark, Edinburgh."; [1]–239, text; at bottom of p. 239 imprint, as on p. [iv]; [240], blank.

Issued in royal blue cloth, narrow single-rule frame within wide single-rule border in gilt on front cover and in blind on back cover, lettering and wide outer-rule and narrow inner-rule at top and bottom in gilt on spine; white end-papers; all edges untrimmed.

Issued simultaneously in cream-white stiff paper wrappers, cut flush, lettered in red on front cover and spine, double-rule border in red on front cover, advertisements within single-rule border in red on back cover; inner sides of wrappers blank; all edges trimmed.

The remaining thirteen volumes are uniform with Volume I, except that publisher's imprint on spine varies, some copies reading "Macmillan" and others "Macmillan & Co."

2. *The Portrait of A Lady* (Vol. II): [A]² B–P⁸ Q⁴(–Q₄), pp. iv, 230.
3. *The Portrait of A Lady* (Vol. III): [A]² B–P⁸ [Q]¹, pp. iv, 226.
4. *Roderick Hudson* (Vol. I): [A]² B–O⁸, pp. iv, 208. Advertisements, O₈.
5. *Roderick Hudson* (Vol. II): [A]² B–N⁸ O², pp. iv, 196. Advertisements, O₂.
6. *The American* (Vol. I): [A]² B–N⁸ O⁶, pp. iv, 204.
7. *The American* (Vol. II): [A]² B–O⁸, pp. iv, 208.
8. *Washington Square*: [A]² B–N⁸ O⁶, pp. iv, 204.

9. *The Europeans*: $[A]^2$ B–N^8, pp. iv, 192. Advertisements, N_8.

10. *Confidence*: $[A]^2$ B–Q^8, pp. iv, 240. Advertisements, Q_8.

11. *The Siege of London. Madame de Mauves*: $[A]^4$ B–N^8 $O^4(-O_4)$, pp. viii, 198. This volume contains a blank leaf $[A_1]$ and a table of contents, verso blank, $[A_4]$. Wrappered issue contains a conjugate leaf of advertisements, O_4, lacking in cloth issue.

12. *An International Episode. The Pension Beaurepas. The Point of View*: $[A]^4$ B–O^8 P^4, pp. viii, 216. Advertisements, P_4. Leaves $[A_{1,4}]$ uniform with *The Siege of London*.

13. *Daisy Miller: A Study. Four Meetings. Longstaff's Marriage. Benvolio*: $[A]^4$ B–N^8 O^4 $O2^2$, pp. viii, 204. Advertisements, $O2_2$. Leaves $[A_{1,4}]$ uniform with *The Siege of London*.

14. *The Madonna of the Future. A Bundle of Letters. The Diary of A Man of Fifty. Eugene Pickering*: $[A]^4$ B–M^8 N^4 $N2^2$, pp. viii, 188. Leaves $[A_{1,4}]$ uniform with *The Siege of London*.

Published 13 November 1883, at 1/- in wrappers, 1/6 in cloth, 21/- for the full set in cloth, boxed, the first printing consisting of 5000 copies of each volume.

Concerning this edition James wrote to Frederick Macmillan, 19 April 1883, from Washington, D.C.: "Let me immediately answer your inquiry about my view of the projected new edition of my stories. I like the idea very much, & only make the condition that these books be as pretty as possible. Can you make them really pretty for 18-pence a volume? I should like them to be *charming*, & beg you to spare no effort to make them so. Your specimen page will enlighten me as to this. . . . I hope fortune will favour the enterprise." (HJ, *Letters*, II, 1975, pp. 410–411.)

Advertisements are recorded as existing in only some of the volumes in *A Bibliographical Catalogue of Macmillan & Co.'s Publications from 1843 to 1889* (London and New York, 1891). We have found such advertisements in all volumes listed in this catalogue, save *The Siege of London*. There seems to have been, however, no consistent appearance of the advertisement leaf, which is usually present in the wrappered issue and in the secondary cloth issue as in *Daisy Miller* (see below). It is usually lacking in copies of the first cloth issue. These may have been kept free of advertisement in conformity with HJ's desire for elegance in the volumes.

A secondary binding state has been noted, issued in slightly smaller format ($6 \times 3\frac{7}{8}$), bound in flexible cloth boards in varying colours (salmon, ochre, cream, green, etc.), lettered and ruled, with publisher's devices on front and back covers, in brown. Copies have been reported to us as bound two volumes in one in uniform secondary binding.

The series of volumes was reissued monthly, May 1886 to February 1887, under the title, "Pocket Edition of Mr. Henry James's Novels and Tales," at 2/- in cloth. These copies appear to have been bound uniform with the first cloth issue, but with a later dating on title-page: *Daisy Miller* and *The Madonna of the Future* being dated 1887, the remaining volumes 1886.

CONTENTS

The novels and tales collected in this edition had prior book publication in England, with the following exceptions:

The Point of View
The Siege of London
These tales had prior book publication in America (see A19a).

A21   PORTRAITS OF PLACES   1883

a. *First edition:*

PORTRAITS OF PLACES | BY | HENRY JAMES | LONDON | MACMILLAN AND CO. | 1883

$(7\frac{1}{2} \times 4\frac{15}{16})$: [A]⁴ B–2A⁸ 2B⁴, pp. viii, 376. Crown 8vo.

Contents: [i–ii], half-title, on verso publisher's device; [iii–iv], title, on verso imprint, "Printed by R. & R. Clark, Edinburgh."; [v]–vi, "Note to the English Edition"; [vii–viii], contents, verso blank; [1]–376, text; at bottom of p. 376 imprint, as on p. [iv].

Issued in green-blue smooth cloth, lettered in gilt on spine; white end-papers; all edges untrimmed.

Published 18 December 1883, at 7/6, the first (and only) printing consisting of 1000 copies.

First-issue copies are bound both in shiny surface and dull finish cloths. The author's surname is printed in uniform capitals; the publisher's imprint varies, some copies having uniform capitals, others having an initial letter larger than the rest of the name; the ampersand also varies in size and design, suggesting simultaneous use of more than one brass by the binder.

A secondary "issue" (so termed by Muir), presumed to be a remainder binding, is lettered in a cheaper gilt, with the "J" of "James" on the spine longer than the remaining letters. A photograph of the variants appears in Muir.

A special "Note to the English Edition" explains the early authorship of the papers and their original destination for an American audience.

CONTENTS

Extensive revisions, in most essays, between serial and book publication.

I. *Venice*
> First appeared in the *Century Magazine*, November 1882.

II. *Italy Revisited*
> First appeared as two separate essays, "Italy Revisited" and "Recent Florence," in the *Atlantic Monthly*, April–May 1878.

III. *Occasional Paris*
> First appeared, under the title "Paris Revisited," in the *Galaxy*, January 1878.

IV. *Rheims and Laon: A Little Tour*
> First appeared, under the title "A Little Tour in France," in the *Atlantic Monthly*, January 1878.

V. *Chartres*
> First appeared, under the title "Chartres Portrayed," in the *New York Tribune*, 29 April 1876.

VI. *Rouen*
> First appeared, under the title "Summer in France," in the *New York Tribune*, 12 August 1876.

VII. *Etretat*
> First appeared, under the title "A French Watering Place," in the *New York Tribune*, 26 August 1876.

VIII. *From Normandy to the Pyrenees*
> First appeared in the *Galaxy*, January 1877.

IX. *An English Easter*
> First appeared in *Lippincott's Magazine*, July 1877.
> Listed in contents as on p. 181, but actually starts on p. 183.

X. *London at Midsummer*
> First appeared in *Lippincott's Magazine*, November 1877.

XI. *Two Excursions*
> First appeared, as part of an article titled "Three Excursions," in the *Galaxy*, September 1877.

XII. *In Warwickshire*
> First appeared in the *Galaxy*, November 1877.

XIII. *Abbeys and Castles*
First appeared in *Lippincott's Magazine*, October 1877.

XIV. *English Vignettes*
First appeared in *Lippincott's Magazine*, April 1879.

XV. *An English New Year*
First appeared, under the title "The New Year in England," in the *Nation*, 23 January 1879.

XVI. *An English Winter Watering-Place*
First appeared in the *Nation*, 3 April 1879.

XVII. *Saratoga*
First appeared in the *Nation*, 11 August 1870.

XVIII. *Newport*
First appeared in the *Nation*, 15 September 1870.

XIX. *Quebec*
First appeared in the *Nation*, 28 September–5 October 1871.

XX. *Niagara*
First appeared in the *Nation*, 12–19 October 1871.

b. *First edition, American issue* (1884):

HENRY JAMES | [rule] | PORTRAITS OF PLACES | [publisher's device] | BOSTON | JAMES R. OSGOOD AND COMPANY | [rule] | 1884

$(7\frac{3}{8} \times 4\frac{7}{8})$: gathered in 6's [unsigned: 1–32⁶]; signed in 8's, [A]⁴ B–I⁸ [K]⁸ L–2A⁸ 2B⁴, pp. viii, 376. 12mo.

Contents: [i–ii], half-title, on verso list of works "By the Same Author"; [iii–iv], title, on verso copyright notice, reservation of rights, and imprint, "University Press: | John Wilson and Son, Cambridge."; [v–vi], "Note," verso blank; [vii–viii], contents, verso blank; [1]–376, text.

Issued in (*a*) brown, (*b*) ochre, (*c*) dark blue-green, (*d*) light blue-grey, and (*e*) dull maroon diagonal-fine-ribbed or sand-grain cloth, single-rule frame within single-wide-rule border in blind on front and back covers, lettering and publisher's device in gilt on spine; white end-papers; all edges trimmed.

Published 29 January 1884, at $1.50, the first printing consisting of 1500 copies, from the Macmillan plates.

Editorial "note" lists earlier serial appearances.

c. *First Continental edition* (1884):

The Tauchnitz edition, "Collection of British Authors," Vol. 2276, contains James's authorization note, dated Paris, 14 February 1884.

A. ORIGINAL WORKS

The text is that of the first edition, but Chapters XV–XX are eliminated. (See F7.)

A22   NOTES ON DRAWINGS BY   1884
              GEORGE DU MAURIER

First edition:

NOTES | (NO. 15 OF SERIES) | BY | MR. HENRY JAMES | ON A | COLLECTION OF DRAWINGS | BY | MR. GEORGE DU MAURIER | EXHIBITED | AT | THE FINE ART SOCIETY'S | 148 NEW BOND STREET | 1884

($8\frac{3}{8} \times 5\frac{3}{8}$): [A]⁸ B–D⁸ E¹, pp. 66. [8vo]

Contents: [1–2], recto blank, on verso Du Maurier illustration; [3–4], title, on verso announcement of future exhibition; [5]–17, text by Henry James; [18], blank; [19]–66, catalogue of Du Maurier's drawings; at bottom of p. 66 imprint, "Printed by J. S. Virtue and Co., Limited, City Road, London."

Issued in grey-blue paper wrappers, cut flush, front cover being a duplication of title-page except for addition of imprints, "Exhibition No. 30" and "Price 6d.", in black; advertisements in black on back cover and inner sides of wrappers; all edges trimmed.

Published 23 June 1884, at sixpence, simultaneously with the opening of the exhibition.

A variant imprint at bottom of p. 66 has been noted, reading: "London: Printed by J. S. Virtue and Co., Limited, City Road." This suggests there were two or more printings. No priority has been established.

A23   A LITTLE TOUR IN FRANCE   1884

a. *First edition:*

HENRY JAMES | [rule] | A LITTLE TOUR IN FRANCE | [publisher's device] | BOSTON | JAMES R. OSGOOD AND COMPANY | [rule] | 1885 [1884]

($7\frac{3}{8} \times 4\frac{13}{16}$): gathered in 6's [unsigned: 1–20⁶ 21¹⁰]; signed in 8's, [i]² 1–16⁸, pp. iv, 256. 12mo.

Contents: binder's fly-leaf at front; [i–ii], recto blank, on verso advertisement of "Henry James's Latest Works"; [iii–iv], title, on verso copyright notice, reservation of rights, and imprint, "University Press: | John Wilson and Son, Cambridge."; [1]–255, text; at bottom of p. 255 imprint, "University Press, Cambridge: John Wilson and Son."; [256], blank; binder's fly-leaf at back.

Issued in (*a*) forest-green, (*b*) steel blue, (*c*) grey-green, (*d*) light chocolate-brown, (*e*) royal blue, and (*f*) red-brown diagonal- or vertical-fine-ribbed or fine-sand-grain cloth, single-rule frame within single-wide-rule border in blind on front and back covers, lettering and device in gilt on spine; white end-papers; all edges trimmed.

Published 5 September 1884, at $1.50, the first printing consisting of 1500 copies. Of these, approximately 400 copies, bound after 1885, bear the Houghton Mifflin & Co. imprint on spine.

Some copies lack the border and frame in blind on covers (one copy also lacks publisher's device on spine and has brown-coated end-papers); some lack binder's fly-leaves at front and back.

First appeared, under the title *En Province*, in the *Atlantic Monthly*, July–November 1883, and February, April–May 1884. Numerous revisions between serial and book publication. James used the title "A Little Tour in France" for an article published in the *Atlantic Monthly*, January 1878. When it was included in *Portraits of Places*, 1883, its title was altered to "Rheims and Laon: A Little Tour."

b. *Second edition, ordinary issue* (1900):

A LITTLE TOUR [in red] | IN FRANCE [in red] | BY HENRY | JAMES | WITH ILLUSTRATIONS | BY JOSEPH PENNELL | [publisher's device, in red] | BOSTON AND NEW YORK | HOUGHTON, MIFFLIN AND COMPANY | THE RIVER-SIDE PRESS, CAMBRIDGE [in red] | MDCCCC

(7¾ × 5): [unsigned: 1² 2⁶ 3–24⁸], pp. [2], xiv, 352. Crown 8vo.

Contents: binder's fly-leaf at front; [1–2], half-title, verso blank, not reckoned in pagination; [i–ii], title, on verso copyright notice; [iii]–vii, Preface, signed "H.J.", dated 9 August 1900; [viii], blank; [ix]–x, contents; [xi]–xiii, list of illustrations; [xiv], blank; [1]–2, Introductory note; [3]–345, text; [346], blank; [347]–350, Index; [351], blank; [352], imprint, "The Riverside Press | Electrotyped and Printed by H. O. Houghton & Co. | Cambridge, Mass., U.S.A." Frontispiece, with tissue guard and 43 illustrations tipped in, and 22 illustrations on text leaves.

Issued in dark green cloth, lettering and multi-ruled panels in cream-green and castle ornament blocked in gilt, cream-green, and orange-brown on front cover, lettering in gilt and single-rule border and panels with fleur-de-lys ornament in cream-green on spine; white end-papers; top edge trimmed and gilt, other edges untrimmed.

Published 31 October 1900, as a "Holiday Edition," at $3 in cloth, $5 in half polished morocco, the first printing consisting of 2000 copies. The edition was designed by Bruce Rogers.

A few minor revisions were made in the text. The preface is new and the note labelled "Introductory" is extensively rewritten. In Chapter VII, "Chenonceaux," James altered the name of the inn from Grand Monarque to the Bon Laboureur after receiving a complaint from the landlord that he had misnamed the hostelry.

Sheets of the second edition were later issued, with unaltered title-page date, in the uniform binding of the Park Street Library. The work was also reprinted from the same plates, with new half-title and title-leaf settings, in the Atlantic Monthly Library of Travel (Vol. Three), 1907. A Pocket Edition, printed from the same plates, was published 26 September 1914, bound in leather, the first (and only) printing consisting of 1000 copies.

c. *Second edition, limited issue* (1900):

[Decorative rule, in red] | A LITTLE TOUR | IN FRANCE | BY | HENRY JAMES | [rule, in red] | WITH ILLUSTRATIONS BY JOSEPH PENNELL | [rule, in red] | [publisher's device] | CAMBRIDGE | PRINTED AT THE RIVERSIDE PRESS [in red] | MDCCCC

($8\frac{11}{16} \times 5\frac{7}{8}$): Collation and contents uniform with ordinary issue. Illustrations printed on tissue and tipped into text leaves. Limitation notice added to p. [ii]: "Two hundred and fifty copies printed."

Issued in white linen-finish half buckram, light cobalt blue paper boards, lettering in black and two single-rules and two rows of fleurs-de-lys in red on white paper label on spine; white end-papers; all edges untrimmed.

Published simultaneously with ordinary issue, at $5, the edition being limited to 250 copies.

d. *First English edition, ordinary issue* (1900):

A LITTLE | TOUR IN FRANCE | BY | HENRY JAMES | [illustration] | WITH NINETY-FOUR ILLUSTRATIONS BY | JOSEPH PENNELL | LONDON | WILLIAM HEINE-MANN | 1900

($7\frac{15}{16} \times 5\frac{13}{16}$): [a]⁸ A–R⁸, pp. xvi, 272. Pott. 4to.

Contents: [i–ii], illustrated half-title, on verso list of "Novels by Henry James"; [iii–iv], title, on verso copyright notice; v–viii, "Preface," signed H.J., dated 9 August 1900; ix–xi, contents; [xii], illustration; xiii–xvi, list of illustrations; 1–2, Introductory note; 3–[270], text; at bottom of p. [270] imprint, "Printed by Ballantyne, Hanson & Co. | London & Edinburgh"; [271–272], blank. Frontispiece, with tissue guard, and 43 illustrations tipped in, not reckoned in pagination. 50 additional illustrations on text leaves.

Issued in grey linen-grain cloth, words separated by colon devices in black on front and back covers, publisher's device in black and gilt on front cover, words separated by colon devices and two fleurons in black and publisher's imprint in gilt on spine; white end-papers; top edge trimmed and gilt, other edges untrimmed.

Published late October or early November 1900, at 10/-, the first printing consisting of 1500 copies. Although advertised in the *Athenaeum*, 27 October 1900, as ready "Monday" (29 October), the publisher's stock-book records reveal that first delivery to the trade did not occur until 5 November.

Six copies were bound, in October 1905, in a trial "gift binding," in red half calf, red linen-grain cloth boards, bogus raised bands on spine, lettering and decorative devices in gilt on spine, pink-and-blue marbled end-papers, top edge trimmed and gilt, other edges untrimmed, with an inserted ribbon bookmark. These were later distributed as gifts by the publisher.

e. *First English edition, limited issue* (1900):

($9\frac{13}{16} \times 6\frac{3}{8}$): Collation and contents uniform with ordinary issue, with added limitation notice on p. [ii]: "This Edition on Japanese Vellum consists of One Hundred and Fifty Copies only." Photogravure illustrations are printed on India paper mounted on Japanese and have fly-title tissue guards.

Issued in full white vellum boards, lettered in gilt on front and back covers and spine, publisher's device in gilt on front and back covers, decorative ornaments in gilt on spine; white end-papers; top edge trimmed and gilt, other edges untrimmed.

Published simultaneously with ordinary issue, at £2.

A24   TALES OF THREE CITIES   1884

a. *First edition:*

HENRY JAMES | [rule] | TALES OF THREE CITIES | [publisher's device] | BOSTON | JAMES R. OSGOOD AND COMPANY | [rule] | 1884

($7\frac{3}{8} \times 4\frac{3}{4}$): gathered in 6's [unsigned: i^2 1–30^6]; signed in 8's, [i]^2 [1]^8 2–22^8 23^4, pp. iv, 360. 12mo.

Contents: [i–ii], blank leaf; [iii–iv], title, on verso copyright notice, reservation of rights, and imprint, "University Press: | John Wilson and Son, Cambridge."; [1–2], divisional fly-title, verso blank; [3]–359, text; [360], blank.

Issued in (*a*) dull violet-brown, (*b*) ochre, and (*c*) blue diagonal-fine-ribbed cloth, single-rule frame within single-wide-rule border in blind on front and back covers, lettering and publisher's device in gilt on spine; white end-papers; all edges trimmed.

Published 17 October 1884, at $1.50, the first printing 1500 copies.

A secondary binding state of the first edition has been noted, in green or brown smooth cloth, lettered in gilt on spine, with Houghton Mifflin & Co. imprint on spine. These copies have a binder's fly-leaf at back, and sometimes at front.

The Osgood cost-books, according to *BAL*, record the "pamphlet" printing, for English copyright, of 12 copies of "The Impressions of a Cousin" on 4 September 1883, 12 copies of "Lady Barberina," chapters 1–4, on 5 January 1884, and 12 copies of "Lady Barberina," concluded, on 17 January 1884. Twelve copies of "A New England Winter" were printed on 17 March 1884. No copies of these works in this format have been discovered.

CONTENTS

The Impressions of A Cousin
First appeared in the *Century Magazine*, Nov–Dec 1883.

Lady Barberina
First appeared in the *Century Magazine*, May–July 1884.
A New England Winter
First appeared in the *Century Magazine*, August–September 1884.

b. *First English edition:*

TALES | OF | THREE CITIES | BY | HENRY JAMES |
LONDON | MACMILLAN AND CO. | 1884

(7½ × 4$\frac{15}{16}$): [A]⁴ B–U⁸ X⁴, pp. viii, 312. Crown 8vo.

Contents: [i–ii], blank leaf; [iii–iv], half-title, on verso publisher's device; [v–vi], title, verso blank; [vii–viii], contents, verso blank; [1–2], divisional fly-title, verso blank; [3]–309, text; at bottom of p. 309 imprint, "Printed by R. &. R. Clark, Edinburgh."; [310], blank; [311–312], advertisements.

Issued in dark green smooth cloth, single-rule border in blind on front and back covers, lettering and single-rule at top and bottom in gilt on spine; white end-papers; all edges untrimmed. For a possible variant binding, see Sadleir, Vol. I, p. 187.

Published 18 November 1884, at 4/6, the first (and only) printing consisting of 1500 copies.

The three tales do not appear in the same order as in the American edition, "The Impressions of A Cousin" being moved to the last place in the book.

For Times Book Club remainder binding, see F33.

A25   THE ART OF FICTION   1884

First edition (unauthorized):

WALTER BESANT | [rule] | THE | ART OF FICTION |
BOSTON | CUPPLES, UPHAM AND COMPANY | 1885
[1884]

(7⅝ × 4⅜): [unsigned: 1–5⁸ 6⁶], pp. 92. 12mo.

Contents: [1–2], title, verso blank; 3–85, text; [86], blank; [87–92], advertisements, dated October 1884.

Issued in canary yellow cloth, lettered in black on front cover: WALTER BESANT | AND | HENRY JAMES | [rule] | THE | ART OF FICTION | CUPPLES

UPHAM & CO.; lettered in black on spine; white end-papers; all edges trimmed.

Published November 1884, at 50 cents. Advertised under the heading "Cupples & Upham's New Books," in the *Boston Transcript*, 29 November 1884.

Besant's essay was originally published by Cupples, Upham in paper wrappers, square 12mo, at 25 cents, in August 1884. When the James essay of the same title appeared in *Longman's* a month later, it was set up and bound with the Besant in a new front-cover setting, but the original title-leaf was maintained. In the new edition James's essay occupied pp. 51–85.

The volume was reissued in 1887 or 1888 by the newly-organized firm of Cupples & Hurd, from the original plates, with a new title-leaf imprint. When this firm was dissolved in 1889, the firm of DeWolfe, Fiske & Co. bought the plates, and reissued the volume under its own imprint.

James's essay first appeared in *Longman's Magazine*, September 1884.

A26 THE AUTHOR OF BELTRAFFIO 1885

First edition:

HENRY JAMES | [rule] | THE AUTHOR OF BELTRAFFIO | PANDORA [asterisk] GEORGINA'S REASONS | THE PATH OF DUTY | FOUR MEETINGS | [publisher's device] | BOSTON | JAMES R. OSGOOD AND COMPANY | [rule] | 1885

$(7\frac{3}{8} \times 4\frac{7}{8})$: gathered in 6's [unsigned: $1–30^6$ 31^2]; signed in 8's, $[i]^1$ $[1]^8$ $2–22^8$ 23^5, pp. ii, 362. 12mo.

Contents: [i–ii], recto blank, on verso advertisement of "Henry James's Latest Works."; [1–2], title, on verso copyright notice, reservation of rights, and imprint, "University Press: | John Wilson and Son, Cambridge."; [3–4], contents, verso blank; [5–6], divisional fly-title, verso blank; [7]–362, text; at bottom of p. 362 imprint, as on p. [2], in one line.

Issued in (*a*) dull olive-green, (*b*) ochre, and (*c*) purple-brown cloth, single-rule frame within single-wide-rule border in blind on front and back covers, lettering and publisher's device in gilt on spine; white end-papers; all edges trimmed.

Published February 1885, at $1.50, the first (and only) printing consisting of 1500 copies. Review copies were distributed 30 January 1885. First noted, under "New Books Received," in the *New York Times*, 16 February 1885.

Copies issued after 1885 were bound in olive-green or brown smooth cloth, lacking frame and border in blind on front and back covers, containing binder's fly-leaves at front and back, and bearing the Houghton Mifflin & Co. imprint on spine. Also noted in secondary binding (uniform with A48b), green or brown cloth, with Houghton Mifflin & Co. imprint on spine.

CONTENTS

The Author of Beltraffio
> First appeared in the *English Illustrated Magazine*, June–July 1884.

Pandora
> First appeared in the *New York Sun* (and syndicated), 1 and 8 June 1884.

Georgina's Reasons
> First appeared in the *New York Sun* (and syndicated), 20 and 27 July, and 3 August 1884.

The Path of Duty
> First appeared in the *English Illustrated Magazine*, December 1884.

Four Meetings
> This tale had prior book publication in England (see A8b).

A27   STORIES REVIVED   1885

a. *First edition:*

Volume I:

STORIES REVIVED | IN THREE VOLUMES | VOL. I. | THE AUTHOR OF 'BELTRAFFIO.' PANDORA. | THE PATH OF DUTY. | A DAY OF DAYS. A LIGHT MAN. | BY | HENRY JAMES | LONDON | MACMILLAN AND CO. | 1885

($7\frac{1}{2} \times 4\frac{15}{16}$): [A]^4 B–S^8 T^4, pp. viii, 280. Crown 8vo.

Contents: [i–ii], half-title, on verso publisher's device; [iii–iv], title, on verso imprint, "Printed by R. &. R. Clark, Edinburgh."; [v–vi], "Notice" on original publication and revisions, dated February 1885,

(b)　　　　(a)

First edition 1885 : binding variants

PLATE V

verso blank; [vii–viii], contents of Vol. I, verso blank; [1]–280, text; at bottom of p. 280 imprint, as on p. [iv], but lacking full stop after ampersand.

Volume II:

STORIES REVIVED │ IN THREE VOLUMES │ VOL. II. │ GEORGINA'S REASONS. A PASSIONATE │ PILGRIM. A LANDSCAPE-PAINTER. │ ROSE-AGATHE. │ BY │ HENRY JAMES │ LONDON │ MACMILLAN AND CO. │ 1885

($7\frac{1}{2}$ × $4\frac{15}{16}$): [A]⁴ B–S⁸ T⁴, pp. viii, 280. Crown 8vo.

Contents: [i–ii], blank leaf; [iii–iv], half-title, on verso publisher's device; [v–vi], title, on verso imprint, "Printed by R. & R. Clark, Edinburgh."; [vii–viii], contents of Vol. II, verso blank; [1]–280, text; at bottom of p. 280 imprint, as on p. [vi].

Volume III:

STORIES REVIVED │ IN THREE VOLUMES │ VOL. III. │ POOR RICHARD. THE LAST OF THE VALERII. │ MASTER EUSTACE. │ THE ROMANCE OF CERTAIN OLD CLOTHES. │ A MOST EXTRAORDINARY CASE. │ BY │ HENRY JAMES │ LONDON │ MACMILLAN AND CO. │ 1885

($7\frac{1}{2}$ × $4\frac{15}{16}$): [A]⁴ B–S⁸, pp. viii, 272. Crown 8vo.

Contents: [i–ii], blank leaf; [iii–iv], half-title, on verso publisher's device; [v–vi], title, on verso imprint, "Printed by R. & R. Clark, Edinburgh."; [vii–viii], contents of Vol. III, verso blank; [1]–269, text; [270], blank; [271–272], advertisements.

The three volumes issued uniformly in dark blue fine-bead-grain cloth, double-rule border and curved-edge panel in black on front cover and in blind on back cover, lettering and publisher's device in gilt and decorative rules at top and bottom in black on spine; brown-coated end-papers; all edges untrimmed.

The volumes were published simultaneously on 15 May 1885, at 31/6, the first (and only) printing consisting of 500 copies.

A variant binding state has been noted, issued in dark blue-green sand-grain cloth, the brasses on the spine differing completely from the state described above (see Plate V), with blue-on-white patterned end-papers.

A. ORIGINAL WORKS

The format for the title-leaves was dictated by James, who wrote to the publisher, 28 January 1885: "I recommend printing on the title-page of each volume (in the French manner,) the contents of the same, as on the reverse of this note [Volume I is outlined exactly as later published]. If there were not 3 vols. I should go in for simply enumerating the tales, on the title-page à la française, printing the name of the 1st biggest." (Unpublished letter, Macmillan archives.)

The "Notice" in Vol. I, dated February 1885, states: ". . . these earlier stories have been in every case minutely revised and corrected—many passages being wholly rewritten." None of the stories had appeared previously in England.

CONTENTS

The Last of the Valerii
 This tale had prior book publication in America (see A1).
Master Eustace
 First appeared in the *Galaxy*, November 1871.
The Romance of Certain Old Clothes
 This tale had prior book publication in America (see A1).
A Most Extraordinary Case
 First appeared in the *Atlantic Monthly*, April 1868.

b. *Second edition* (1885):

In November 1885 Macmillan published a two-volume edition of 1000 copies at 6/- per volume, uniform with A4c (*The American*, 1879). Labelled "First Series" and "Second Series," the volumes are identical in content and text with A27a, with some rearrangement of the order of the tales. For Times Book Club remainder binding, see F32.

Sadleir records a one-volume edition of *Stories Revived*, as have booksellers from time to time in their catalogues. This edition, however, does not exist, the volume being the "First Series" volume of the second edition.

A28   THE BOSTONIANS   1886

a. *First edition:*

THE | BOSTONIANS | A NOVEL | BY | HENRY JAMES | IN THREE VOLUMES | VOL I. [VOL. II.] [VOL. III.] | LONDON | MACMILLAN AND CO. | 1886

($7\frac{1}{2} \times 5$): Volume I, [A]^2 B–Q^8 R^2, pp. iv, 244. Volume II, [A]^2 B–P^8 Q^2, pp. iv, 228. Volume III, [A]^2 B–P^8 Q^4 [R]^2, pp. iv, 236. Crown 8vo.

Contents: Volume I: [i–ii], half-title, on verso publisher's device; [iii–iv], title, on verso copyright notice; [1–2], divisional fly-title, verso blank; [3]–244, text; at bottom of p. 244 imprint, "Printed by R. & R. Clark, Edinburgh."

 Volume II: [i–iv], uniform with Vol. I; [1–2], divisional fly-title, verso blank; [3]–226, text; at bottom of p. 226 imprint, "Printed by R. & R. Clark, Edinburgh."; [227–228], advertisements.

 Volume III: [i–iv], uniform with Vol. I; [1]–232, text; at bottom of

p. 232 imprint, "Printed by R. & R. Clark, Edinburgh."; [233–236], advertisements.

Issued in dark blue-green fine-bead-grain cloth, double-rule border and curved-edge panel in black on front cover and in blind on back cover, lettering and publisher's device in gilt and decorative rules at top and bottom in black on spine; brown-coated end-papers; all edges untrimmed.

Published 16 February 1886, at 31/6, the first printing consisting of 500 copies. A second impression, in March 1886, consisted of 100 copies, lacking any imprint to distinguish them from first issue.

On title-page of Volume I a full stop following "Vol" is lacking.

Sadleir records final signature of Vol. III as Q^6, but the two conjugate leaves forming $[R]^2$ are tipped in as a separate insert.

First appeared in the *Century Magazine*, February 1885–February 1886. Numerous minor revisions between serial and book publication.

b. *Second edition* (1886):

THE | BOSTONIANS | A NOVEL | BY | HENRY JAMES | LONDON AND NEW YORK | MACMILLAN AND CO. | 1886

$(7\frac{5}{16} \times 4\frac{7}{8})$: $[A]^2$ B–2F^8 $[2G]^2$, pp. iv, 452. Crown 8vo.

Contents: [i–ii], half-title, on verso publisher's device; [iii–iv], title, on verso copyright notice; [1–2], divisional fly-title, verso blank; [3]–449, text; at bottom of p. 449 imprint, "Printed by R. & R. Clark, Edinburgh."; [450], blank; [451–452], dollar advertisements.

Issued uniform with A4c (*The American*, 1879).

Published May 1886, at 6/-, the first (and only) printing consisting of 5000 copies, divided between domestic and American issues.

Page size varies from $7\frac{5}{16} \times 4\frac{3}{4}$ to $7\frac{3}{8} \times 5$. Amy Lowell's copy, in the Houghton Library, is in blue cloth, but with white end-papers.

A variant binding exists, issued in maroon half cloth, deep pink cloth boards, lettering within single-rule panels in gilt on spine. As this binding appears with great frequency in America, it seems likely that this was the American issue; moreover, all copies examined contain the extra leaf $[2G_2]$ at the back, with dollar advertisements. Copies of the blue cloth issue have been noted both with and without this leaf.

The publisher's records fail to record a separate American issue, but show that 3000 of the original 5000 copies printed were designed for export. The American issue was published 19 March 1886, at $1.75, preceding the English publication of the second edition by nearly two months.

The Macmillan issue of the novel for the American market was the result of a financial entanglement that proved costly to HJ. He had sold serial and book rights to J. R. Osgood for a flat sum of $4,000; American rights were leased for five years, foreign (including British) rights were yielded outright. In May 1885 Osgood's firm failed; HJ discovered he had not only lost the money owed to him by Osgood, but also most of the rights in his book. These were assigned to the Macmillan Company, one of Osgood's creditors. Under a new agreement entered into with the Macmillans for the American distribution, HJ received a straight 15 per cent royalty. His earnings for *The Bostonians*, for both markets plus serialization, came to £492.

A29   THE PRINCESS CASAMASSIMA   1886

a. *First edition:*

THE | PRINCESS CASAMASSIMA | A NOVEL | BY | HENRY JAMES | IN THREE VOLUMES | VOL. I. [II.] [III.] | LONDON | MACMILLAN AND CO. | AND NEW YORK | 1886

$(7\frac{7}{16} \times 4\frac{7}{8})$: Volume I, [A]^2 B–Q^8 R^6, pp. iv, 252. Volume II, [A]^2 B–R^8 S^2, pp. iv, 260. Volume III, [A]^2 B–Q^8 R^2, pp. iv, 244. Crown 8vo.

Contents: Volume I: [i–ii], half-title, on verso publisher's device; [iii–iv], title, on verso copyright notice; [1–2], divisional fly-title, verso blank; [3]–252, text; at bottom of p. 252 imprint, "Printed by R. & R. Clark, Edinburgh."

Volume II: [i–iv], uniform with Vol. I; [1]–257, text; at bottom of p. 257 imprint, "Printed by R. & R. Clark, Edinburgh."; [258], blank; [259–260], advertisements.

Volume III: [i–iv], uniform with Vol. I; [1]–242, text; at bottom of p. 242 imprint, "Printed by R. R. & [sic] Clark, Edinburgh"; [243–244], advertisements.

Issued in dark blue-green fine-bead-grain cloth, double-rule border and curved-edge panel in black on front cover and in blind on back cover, lettering and publisher's device in gilt and decorative rules at top and bottom in black on spine; brown-coated end-papers; all edges untrimmed. In *Gazette of the Grolier Club*, Vol. II, no. 7, February 1947, reference is made to a variant binding.

Published 22 October 1886, at 31/6, the first (and only) printing consisting of 750 copies.

Page size varies from $7\frac{5}{16} \times 4\frac{7}{8}$ to $7\frac{1}{2} \times 5$. Some copies contain green-coated end-papers.

First appeared in the *Atlantic Monthly*, September 1885–October 1886. Minor revisions between serial and book publication.

b. *Later editions* (*from* 1886):

In October 1886 Macmillan printed a one-volume edition of 3000 copies, for both the domestic and American markets. The American issue was published 2 November 1886 at $1.75, and the English issue in August 1887 at 6/-, both uniform with A4c (*The American*, 1879). The text follows A29a. Although the earliest copies bear a title-page imprint: LONDON | MACMILLAN AND CO. | AND NEW YORK | 1886 the appearance of copies imprinted with the date: 1887 | ALL RIGHTS RESERVED suggests that the publisher had the single printing run off with two dates, the first designed for the exported American issue. Some copies dated 1886 contain an 1887 British catalogue of advertisements, though several copies have been noted lacking the catalogue. It is possible that not all copies designed for the American market were actually exported, and that some sheets were incorporated into the English issue.

In 1888 Macmillan published a yellowback issue, Globe 8vo., consisting of two printings of 2000 copies each at 2/-. Sadleir records this as 1889.

A30   PARTIAL PORTRAITS   1888

a. *First edition:*

PARTIAL PORTRAITS | BY | HENRY JAMES | LONDON | MACMILLAN AND CO. | AND NEW YORK | 1888 | ALL RIGHTS RESERVED

$(7 \times 4\frac{11}{16})$: [A]⁶ B–2C⁸ 2D⁴ [2E]², pp. xii, 412. Crown 8vo.

Contents: [i–ii], blank leaf; [iii–iv], half-title, on verso publisher's device; [v–vi], title, on verso copyright notice; [vii–viii], "Notice" on serial publication of contents, verso blank; [ix–x], contents, verso blank; [xi–xii], divisional fly-title, verso blank; [1]–408, text; at bottom of p. 408 imprint, "Printed by R. & R. Clark, Edinburgh."; [409–412], advertisements.

Issued in dark green smooth cloth, single-rule border in blind on front and back covers, lettering and single-rule at top and bottom in gilt on spine; white end-papers; all edges untrimmed.

Published 8 May 1888, at 6/-, the first printing consisting of 2000 copies, divided between domestic and American issues.

Some copies lack blank leaf [A$_1$]. Binding shade varies slightly in several copies examined, suggesting use of different cloths for separate binding orders; no priority established.

Reprinted from the original plates in January 1894, in the Eversley Series, at 5/- (later reduced to 4/-), the first printing consisting of 500 copies.

CONTENTS

I. *Emerson*
First appeared, under the title "The Life of Emerson," in *Macmillan's Magazine*, December 1887.
II. *The Life of George Eliot*
First appeared, under the title "George Eliot's Life," in the *Atlantic Monthly*, May 1885.
III. *Daniel Deronda: A Conversation*
First appeared in the *Atlantic Monthly*, December 1876.
IV. *Anthony Trollope*
First appeared in the *Century Magazine*, July 1883.
V. *Robert Louis Stevenson*
First appeared in the *Century Magazine*, April 1888.
VI. *Miss Woolson*
First appeared, under the title "Miss Constance Fenimore Woolson," in *Harper's Weekly*, 12 February 1887.
VII. *Alphonse Daudet*
First appeared in the *Century Magazine*, August 1883.
VIII. *Guy de Maupassant*
First appeared in the *Fortnightly Review*, March 1888.
IX. *Ivan Turgénieff*
First appeared in the *Atlantic Monthly*, January 1884.
X. *George du Maurier*
First appeared, under the title "Du Maurier and London Society," in the *Century Magazine*, May 1883.

XI. *The Art of Fiction*

This essay had prior (unauthorized) book publication in America (see A25). Revisions between serial and this first authorized book appearance.

b. *First edition, American issue:*

The American issue consisted of exported bound copies of the first edition, uniform title-leaf, with substitution of dollar advertisements on pp. [409–412].

Published 26 May 1888, Globe 8vo, at $1.75. Exact number of copies of this issue not ascertained; the publisher believes there were about 500.

A31   THE REVERBERATOR   1888

a. *First edition:*

THE | REVERBERATOR | BY | HENRY JAMES | IN TWO VOLUMES | VOL. I [II] | LONDON | MACMILLAN AND CO. | AND NEW YORK | 1888 | ALL RIGHTS RESERVED

$(7 \times 4\frac{5}{8})$: Volume I, [A]² B–N⁸, pp. iv, 192. Volume II, [A]² B–O⁸, pp. iv, 208. Globe 8vo.

Contents: Volume I: [i–ii], half-title, on verso publisher's device; [iii–iv], title, on verso copyright notice; [1]–190, text; at bottom of p. 190 imprint, "Richard Clay and Sons, Limited, London and Bungay."; [191–192], advertisements.

Volume II: [i–iv], uniform with Vol. I; [1]–207, text; [208], imprint, "Richard Clay and Sons, Limited, | London and Bungay."

Issued in (*a*) steel blue and (*b*) dark green smooth cloth, bands of five rules in gilt across top and bottom of front cover and spine, publisher's device in blind on back cover, lettered in gilt on spine; blue-black-coated end-papers; all edges untrimmed.

Published June 1888, at 12/-, the first (and only) printing consisting of 500 copies. The publisher reports publication date as 5 June 1888. Advertised in both the 19 and 26 May issues of the *Athenaeum* under the heading "Next week" and as available on 2 June.

First appeared in *Macmillan's Magazine*, February–July 1888. Minor revisions between serial and book publication; the 14 chapters were re-numbered I–VII in each volume.

b. *Second edition, American issue:*

THE | REVERBERATOR | BY | HENRY JAMES | LONDON | MACMILLAN AND CO. | AND NEW YORK | 1888 | THE RIGHT OF TRANSLATION AND REPRODUCTION IS RESERVED

($6\frac{7}{8} \times 4\frac{3}{4}$): [A]² B–P⁸ Q⁴, pp. iv, 232. 12mo.

Contents: [i–ii], half-title, on verso publisher's device; [iii–iv], title, on verso imprint, "Copyright, | 1888, | By Henry James"; [1]–229, text; [230], imprint, "Richard Clay and Sons, Limited, | London and Bungay."; [231–232], blank leaf.

Issued in dark blue diagonal-fine-ribbed cloth, decorative band in gilt across top of front cover and spine, triple-rule in blind across bottom of front and back covers and in gilt across bottom of spine, four rules in blind across top of back cover, lettered in gilt on spine; blue-black-coated end-papers; all edges trimmed.

Published June 1888, at $1.25, the first (and only) printing consisting of 3000 copies. First advertised in the *New York Tribune*, 23 June 1888. The chapters are re-numbered I–XIV.

c. *Second edition, English issue:*

($7\frac{1}{4} \times 4\frac{3}{4}$): Collation and contents uniform with American issue except for imprint on verso of title-leaf, "First Edition (2 vols. Globe 8vo) June 1888. | New Edition 1 vol. Crown 8vo, August 1888." and addition of catalogue dated April 1888.

Issued in dark blue diagonal-fine-ribbed cloth, decorative band at top in gilt and two decorative bands at bottom in blind on front cover and spine, publisher's device in blind on back cover, lettered in gilt on spine; blue-black-coated end-papers; all edges untrimmed.

Published August 1888, at 6/-, the first (and only) printing consisting of 1000 copies. Advertised as "Just ready" in the *Universal Review*, 15 August 1888.

A variant binding state has been noted, uniform with A4c (*The American*, 1879) except for blue-black-coated end-papers.

For Times Book Club remainder binding, see F31.

a. *First edition:*

THE ASPERN PAPERS | LOUISA PALLANT | THE MODERN
WARNING | BY | HENRY JAMES | IN TWO VOLUMES—
VOL. I [II] | LONDON | MACMILLAN AND CO. | AND NEW
YORK | 1888 | ALL RIGHTS RESERVED

$(7 \times 4\frac{3}{4})$: Volume I, [A]^4 B–Q^8, pp. viii, 240. Volume II, [A]^4 B–R^8
S^4, pp. viii, 264. Globe 8vo.

Contents: Volume I: [i–ii], blank leaf; [iii–iv], half-title, on verso
publisher's device; [v–vi], title, on verso copyright notice; [vii–viii],
divisional fly-title, verso blank; [1]–239, text; at bottom of p. 239
imprint, "Printed by R. & R. Clark, Edinburgh"; [240], blank.

 Volume II: [i–ii], half-title, on verso publisher's device; [iii–iv],
title, on verso copyright notice; [v–vi], contents, verso blank; [vii–
viii], "Note" on change of title of second tale, verso blank; [1–2],
divisional fly-title, verso blank; [3]–258, text; at bottom of p. 258 imprint, "Printed by R. & R. Clark, Edinburgh"; [259–264], advertisements.

Issued in steel blue smooth cloth, bands of five rules in gilt across top
and bottom of front cover and spine, publisher's device in blind on
back cover, lettered in gilt on spine; black-coated end-papers; all
edges untrimmed.

Published September 1888, at 12/-, the first (and only) printing
consisting of 650 copies. First advertised, as ready "Immediately," in
the *Athenaeum*, 29 September 1888.

Library of Congress copy contains white end-papers. *BAL* labels
this a sophistication.

CONTENTS

Volume I:

The Aspern Papers
 First appeared in the *Atlantic Monthly*, March–May 1888.

Volume II:

Louisa Pallant
 First appeared in *Harper's New Monthly Magazine*, February
1888.

A. ORIGINAL WORKS

The Modern Warning

> First appeared, under the title "Two Countries," in *Harper's New Monthly Magazine*, June 1888.

b. *Second edition, American issue:*

THE ASPERN PAPERS | LOUISA PALLANT | THE MODERN WARNING | BY | HENRY JAMES | LONDON | MACMILLAN AND CO. | AND NEW YORK | 1888 | ALL RIGHTS RESERVED

$(7\frac{3}{8} \times 4\frac{3}{4})$: [A]^4 B–T^8 U^2, pp. viii, 292. 12mo.

Contents: [i–ii], half-title, on verso publisher's device; [iii–iv], title, on verso copyright notice; [v–vi], contents, on verso "Note" on change of title of third tale; [vii–viii], divisional fly-title, verso blank; [1]–290, text; at bottom of p. 290 imprint, "Printed by R. & R. Clark, Edinburgh."; [291–292], blank.

Issued in dark blue diagonal-fine-ribbed cloth, decorative band at top in gilt and three single-rules at bottom in blind on front cover, four rules at top and three rules at bottom in blind on back cover, lettering and decorative band at top and three rules at bottom in gilt on spine; black-coated end-papers; all edges trimmed.

Published November 1888, at $1.50, the first (and only) printing consisting of 2000 copies. Advertised in the *New York Tribune*, 10 November 1888.

c. *Second edition, English issue* (1890):

Collation and contents uniform with American issue except for 1890 title-page date, added imprint on verso of title leaf: "First Edition (2 Vols. Globe 8vo) 1888 | New Edition (1 Vol. Crown 8vo) 1890", advertisements priced in shillings on pp. [291–292], and catalogue of advertisements, 60 numbered pages, dated August 1890.

Issued in crimson diaper cloth, one wide and one narrow rule at top and bottom in blind on front and back covers and in gilt on spine, publisher's device in gilt on front cover and in blind on back cover, lettered in gilt on spine; white end-papers; all edges untrimmed.

Published October 1890, at 3/6, the first printing consisting of 2000 copies. (Second impression of 1000 copies was not made until 1939.) Advertised in the *Academy*, 25 October 1890.

For Times Book Club remainder binding, see F23.

a. *First edition:*

A LONDON LIFE | THE PATAGONIA | THE LIAR | MRS.
TEMPERLY | BY | HENRY JAMES | IN TWO VOLUMES—
VOL. I [II] | LONDON | MACMILLAN AND CO. | AND
NEW YORK | 1889 | ALL RIGHTS RESERVED

(7 × 4¾): Volume I, [A]⁴ B–S⁸ T⁴ [U]², pp. viii, 284. Volume II,
[A]⁴ B–Z⁸ 2A⁴ [2B]², pp. viii, 364. Globe 8vo.

Contents: Volume I: binder's fly-leaf; [i–ii], half-title, on verso
publisher's device; [iii–iv], title, on verso copyright notice; [v–vi],
contents of Vol. I, on verso "Note" on change of title of fourth tale;
[vii–viii], divisional fly-title, verso blank; [1]–281, text; at bottom of
p. 281 imprint, "Printed by R. & R. Clark, Edinburgh."; [282], blank;
[283–284], advertisements; binder's fly-leaf.

Volume II: binder's fly-leaf; [i–ii], blank leaf; [iii–iv], half-title, on
verso publisher's device; [v–vi], title, on verso copyright notice; [vii–
viii], contents of Vol. II, verso blank; [1–2], divisional fly-title, verso
blank; [3]–361, text; at bottom of p. 361 imprint, "Printed by R. & R.
Clark, Edinburgh."; [362], blank; [363–364], advertisements.

Issued in (*a*) steel-blue and (*b*) dark blue-green smooth cloth, band of
five rules at top and bottom in gilt on front cover and spine, publisher's
device in blind on back cover, lettered in gilt on spine; black-coated
end-papers; all edges untrimmed.

Published April 1889, at 12/-, the first (and only) printing consisting of
500 copies. The publisher reports publication date as March 1889.
The earliest advertisement noted, reading available "Immediately," is
in the *Athenaeum*, 6 April.

Binder's fly-leaves lacking in some copies.

CONTENTS

Volume I:
A London Life
    First appeared in *Scribner's Magazine*, June–September 1888.
Volume II:
The Patagonia
    First appeared in the *English Illustrated Magazine*, August–
    September 1888.
The Liar
    First appeared in the *Century Magazine*, May–June 1888.

Mrs. Temperly
First appeared, under the title "Cousin Maria," in *Harper's Weekly*, 6, 13, and 20 August 1887.

b. *Second edition, American issue:*

A LONDON LIFE | THE PATAGONIA | THE LIAR | MRS. TEMPERLY | BY | HENRY JAMES | LONDON | MACMILLAN AND CO. | AND NEW YORK | 1889 | ALL RIGHTS RESERVED

$(7\frac{3}{8} \times 4\frac{7}{8})$: [A]⁴ B–2A⁸, pp. viii, 368. 12mo.

Contents: [i–ii], half-title, on verso publisher's device; [iii–iv], title, on verso copyright notice; [v–vi], contents, on verso "Note" on change of title of fourth tale; [vii–viii], divisional fly-title, verso blank; [1]–366, text; at bottom of p. 366 imprint, "Printed by R. & R. Clark, Edinburgh"; [367–368], dollar advertisements.

Issued in dark blue diagonal-fine-ribbed cloth, decorative band at top in gilt and two decorative bands at bottom in blind on front cover and spine, publisher's device in blind on back cover, lettered in gilt on spine; black-coated end-papers; all edges trimmed.

Published the week of 29 April 1889, at $1.50, the first (and only) printing consisting of 2000 copies.

Fore and bottom edges of some copies are untrimmed.

c. *Second edition, English issue:*

$(7\frac{3}{8} \times 5)$: Title-page, collation and contents uniform with American issue except for addition of imprint on verso of title-leaf: "First Edition (2 Vols. Globe 8vo) published April 1889 | New Edition (1 Vol. Crown 8vo) May 1889", and six pages of advertisements, pp. [367–372], priced in shillings.

Issued uniform with A32c (*The Aspern Papers*, second edition, 1890).

Published May 1889, at 3/6, the first (and only) printing consisting of 2000 copies. Publisher reports publication date as 10 August, but the work is noted under "Books of the Week" in the *Pall Mall Budget*, 23 May, and in an advertisement during the same month.

For Times Book Club remainder binding, see F28.

d. *First Continental edition* (1891):

Issued, as Vol. 30, in the English Library, Leipzig: Heinemann and

Balestier, 1891, at M. 1.60 or 2 francs. For details of format, see F1.

The second tale, "The Patagonia," was not included in this edition.

A34   THE TRAGIC MUSE   1890

a. *First edition:*

THE TRAGIC MUSE | BY | HENRY JAMES | IN TWO VOLUMES | VOL. I. [II.] | [publisher's device] | BOSTON AND NEW YORK | HOUGHTON, MIFFLIN AND COMPANY | THE RIVERSIDE PRESS, CAMBRIDGE | 1890

($6\frac{15}{16} \times 4\frac{5}{8}$): Volume I, [unsigned: 1^2 $2-27^8$ 28^4], pp. iv, 422, [2]. Volume II, [unsigned: 1^2 $2-29^8$ 30^6], pp. iv, [423]–882. 16mo.

Contents: Volume I: binder's fly-leaf at front; [i–ii], recto blank, advertisement on verso; [iii–iv], title, on verso copyright notice, reservation of rights, and imprint, "The Riverside Press, Cambridge, Mass., U.S.A. | Electrotyped and Printed by H. O. Houghton & Company."; [1]–422, text; [1–2], blank.

Volume II: [i–ii], blank leaf; [iii–iv], title, verso uniform with Vol. I; [423]–882, text; binder's fly-leaf at back.

Issued in (*a*) forest green, (*b*) scarlet, and (*c*) dark blue linen-grain cloth, lettering within single-rule panels, between decorative bands of fine rules, and small ornamental devices in gilt on front cover and spine; white end-papers; all edges trimmed (fore and bottom edges untrimmed in some copies).

Published 7 June 1890, at $2.50, the first printing consisting of 1000 copies.

First appeared in the *Atlantic Monthly*, January 1889–May 1890. Numerous revisions between serial and book publication.

b. *First English edition:*

THE TRAGIC MUSE | BY | HENRY JAMES | IN THREE VOLUMES | VOL. I. [II.] [III.] | LONDON | MACMILLAN AND CO. | AND NEW YORK | 1890 | THE RIGHT OF TRANSLATION AND REPRODUCTION IS RESERVED

($7\frac{1}{8} \times 4\frac{11}{16}$): Volume I, [A]^2 B–Q^8 R^4, pp. iv, 248. Volume II, [A]^2 B–Q^8 R^6, pp. iv, 252. Volume III, [A]^2 B–R^8 S^2, pp. iv, 260. Crown 8vo.

The Tragic Muse.

by

Henry James

London.
Macmillan & Co.
1890.

James's autograph layout for the title-page
of first English edition

A. ORIGINAL WORKS

Contents: Volume I: [i–ii], half-title, on verso publisher's device; [iii–iv], title, on verso imprint: "Richard Clay & Sons, Limited, | London & Bungay."; [1]–248, text; at bottom of p. 248 imprint, as on p. [iv], in one line.

Volume II: [i–iv], uniform with Vol. I; [1]–252, text; at bottom of p. 252 imprint, as on p. [iv], in one line.

Volume III: [i–iv], uniform with Vol. I; [1]–258, text; at bottom of p. 258 imprint, as on p. [iv], in one line; [259–260], blank leaf.

Issued in royal blue diaper cloth, lettered in gilt on front cover and spine, single-rule border in blind on front and back covers, publisher's device and double-rule at top and bottom in gilt on spine; black-coated end-papers; all edges trimmed.

Published June 1890, at 31/6, the first (and only) printing consisting of 500 copies. Brussel assigns priority to this edition on the basis of a listing in the *Publishers' Circular* as issued during the last two weeks in May; the publisher, however, reports June publication, and this is supported by an advertisement announcing publication "shortly," in the *Athenaeum*, 14 June 1890. The first advertisement noting the work as available, under the heading "New Novels," appeared in the *Athenaeum*, 28 June.

c. *Second English edition* (1891):

THE TRAGIC MUSE | BY | HENRY JAMES | LONDON | MACMILLAN AND CO. | AND NEW YORK | 1891 | THE RIGHT OF TRANSLATION AND REPRODUCTION IS RESERVED

$(7\frac{5}{16} \times 4\frac{7}{8})$: [A]² B–2H⁸ 2I⁶, pp. iv, 492, followed by 64 page catalogue of advertisements. Crown 8vo.

Contents: [i–ii], half-title, on verso publisher's device; [iii–iv], title, on verso publication history and imprint, "Richard Clay and Sons, Limited, | London and Bungay."; [1]–488, text; [489–492], advertisements, numbered pp. 1–4; catalogue dated January 1891.

Issued in scarlet diaper cloth, one wide and one narrow rule in blind at top and bottom of front and back covers and in gilt on spine, publisher's device in gilt on front cover and in blind on back cover, lettered in gilt on spine; white end-papers; all edges trimmed (top untrimmed in some copies).

Published February 1891, at 3/6, the first printing consisting of 2000 copies. Earliest advertisement noted in the *Athenaeum*, 7 February

1891. The title was erroneously advertised in the *Athenaeum* and the *Pall Mall Gazette*, throughout February, as *A Tragic Muse*; it was corrected in March advertisements.

Some copies contain sheets of the Colonial issue, being identified by the Colonial volume number, "No. 109.," at the left of the last line on the title-page.

For Times Book Club remainder binding, see F34.

A35   THE AMERICAN: A COMEDY   1891
IN FOUR ACTS

Non-published edition:

THE AMERICAN | A COMEDY IN FOUR ACTS | BY | HENRY JAMES | LONDON | WILLIAM HEINEMANN | 1891 | ALL RIGHTS RESERVED [The final line is bracketed]

($7\frac{3}{16} \times 4\frac{3}{4}$): [a]² A–M⁸, pp. iv, 192. [8vo]
Contents: [i–ii], title, verso blank; [iii–iv], list of characters, verso blank; [1]–191, text; [192], blank.

Issued in blue-grey paper wrappers, cut flush, lettered in black on front cover, inner sides of wrappers blank; top and bottom edge untrimmed, fore edge trimmed.

Privately printed, at James's expense, the first week of September 1891. The pages are set up in the same style as *Theatricals*, with names of characters centered over the speeches in the French manner. James apparently intended to have this type used for a published edition of the play, had it proved a greater success.

A second impression of about 20 copies, two of them interleaved, contained minor textual correction and elimination of "A Comedy" from title-page and front cover; page size: $7\frac{5}{16} \times 4\frac{7}{8}$.

The number of copies printed is undetermined; eight are known to be extant, including one each of the first and second impressions at Houghton, and first impressions at Princeton and Colby.

The play was not published during James's lifetime, its first book appearance being in *The Complete Plays of Henry James*, 1949 (see A95). One authorized quotation appeared in *The Drama Birthday Book*, 1895 (see B14).

A36   THE LESSON OF THE MASTER   1892

a. First edition:

THE LESSON OF THE MASTER | THE MARRIAGES THE
PUPIL | BROOKSMITH | THE SOLUTION SIR EDMUND
ORME | BY | HENRY JAMES | NEW YORK | MACMILLAN
AND CO. | AND LONDON | 1892 | ALL RIGHTS RESERVED
($7\frac{7}{16} \times 5$): A–T^8 [U]^8, pp. vi, 314. 12mo.

Contents: binder's fly-leaf at front; [i–ii], half-title, on verso publisher's device; [iii–iv], title, on verso copyright notice and imprint, "Typography by J. S. Cushing & Co., Boston, U.S.A. | [rule] | Presswork by Berwick & Smith, Boston, U.S.A."; v–[vi], contents, verso blank; 1–302, text; [303–314], advertisements; binder's fly-leaf at back.

Issued in dull blue smooth cloth, lettering and publisher's monogram in black and vertical rule in red-purple on front cover, lettering and publisher's device in gilt on spine, book and wreath ornaments in red-purple on front cover and spine; white end-papers; all edges trimmed.

Published February 1892, at $1, in Macmillan's Dollar Novel Series, the first printing consisting of 2900 copies, divided between domestic and English issues. Advertised as "in the press" in the *New York Times*, 3 February 1892; noted under "Books of the Week" in the *New York Tribune*, 20 February.

Some copies lack binder's fly-leaves.

CONTENTS

The Lesson of the Master
> First appeared in the *Universal Review*, 16 July–15 August 1888.

The Marriages
> First appeared in the *Atlantic Monthly*, August 1891.

The Pupil
> First appeared in *Longman's Magazine*, March–April 1891.

Brooksmith
> First appeared, simultaneously, in *Harper's Weekly* and in *Black and White*, 2 May 1891.

The Solution
> First appeared in the *New Review*, December 1889–February 1890.

Sir Edmund Orme
> First appeared in *Black and White*, Xmas number (issued 25 November) 1891.

b. *First edition, English issue:*

THE LESSON OF THE MASTER | THE MARRIAGES THE
PUPIL | BROOKSMITH | THE SOLUTION SIR EDMUND
ORME | BY | HENRY JAMES | LONDON | MACMILLAN
AND CO. | AND NEW YORK | 1892 | ALL RIGHTS RE-
SERVED

$(7\frac{3}{8} \times 5)$: [a]⁴ A–T⁸, pp. [2], vi, 304, followed by two catalogues of
advertisements. Crown 8vo.

Contents: [1–2], blank leaf, not reckoned in pagination; [i–ii], half-
title, on verso publisher's device; [iii–iv], title, on verso copyright
notice and imprint, uniform with p. [iv] of American issue; v–[vi],
contents, verso blank; 1–302, text; [303–304], blank; catalogue of
advertisements, 4 unnumbered pages, dated 20 February 1892;
44-page catalogue dated December 1891.

Issued in royal blue diaper cloth, decorative band at top in gilt and
two decorative bands at bottom in blind on front cover and spine,
publisher's device in blind on back cover, lettered in gilt on spine;
green-coated end-papers; all edges untrimmed.

Published February 1892, at 6/-, the issue consisting of sheets of the
first American edition. Advertised in the *Athenaeum*, 27 February
1892.

Some copies lack the first (four-page) catalogue of advertisements.

Colonial issue provided sheets of Times Book Club issue (see F44).

A37   THE REAL THING   1893

a. *First edition:*

THE REAL THING | AND OTHER TALES | BY | HENRY
JAMES | NEW YORK | MACMILLAN AND CO. | AND
LONDON | 1893 | ALL RIGHTS RESERVED

$(7\frac{3}{8} \times 5)$: [unsigned: 1–18⁸], pp. x, 278. 12mo.

Contents: [i–ii], half-title, on verso publisher's device; [iii–iv], title,
on verso copyright notice and imprint, "Norwood Press: | J. S.
Cushing & Co.—Berwick & Smith. | Boston, Mass, U.S.A."; [v–vi],

A. ORIGINAL WORKS

"Note" on change of title of second tale, verso blank; vii–[viii], contents, verso blank; [ix–x], divisional fly-title, verso blank; 1–275, text; [276], blank; [277–278], advertisements.

Issued in dull blue smooth cloth, lettering and publisher's monogram in black and vertical rule in red-purple on front cover, lettering and publisher's device in gilt on spine, book and wreath ornaments in red-purple on front cover and spine; white end-papers; all edges trimmed.

Published March 1893, at $1, in Macmillan's Dollar Novel Series, the first printing consisting of 1500 copies, divided between domestic and English issues.

With a single exception, all copies examined contain a cancel title-leaf. An apparently unique copy, discovered by I. R. Brussel and recently added to the Collamore Collection at Colby, contains a first-state title-leaf [1_2], conjugate with [1_7], the copyright on the verso reading: "Copyright, 1892, | By Macmillan & Co." On the cancel title-leaf in the second state the copyright date is altered to 1893.

CONTENTS

The Real Thing
First appeared in *Black and White*, 16 April 1892.
Sir Dominick Ferrand
First appeared, under the title "Jersey Villas," in *Cosmopolitan Magazine*, July–August 1892.
Nona Vincent
First appeared in the *English Illustrated Magazine*, February–March 1892.
The Chaperon
First appeared in the *Atlantic Monthly*, November–December 1891.
Greville Fane
First appeared in the *Illustrated London News*, 17 and 24 September 1892.

b. *First edition, English issue:*

THE REAL THING | AND OTHER TALES | BY | HENRY JAMES | LONDON | MACMILLAN AND CO. | AND NEW YORK | 1893 | ALL RIGHTS RESERVED.

($7\frac{3}{8} \times 5$): [unsigned: 1–18⁸], pp. x, 278, followed by 48 page catalogue of advertisements. Crown 8vo.

Contents: prelims and text uniform with American issue except for reversal of place of publication on title-page and copyright date 1892 on verso; advertisements eliminated from pp. [277–278], which are blank; catalogue dated January 1893.

Issued in (a) royal blue and (b) dark blue diaper cloth, decorative band at top in gilt and two decorative bands at bottom in blind on front cover and spine, publisher's device in blind on back cover, lettered in gilt on spine; green-coated end-papers; all edges untrimmed (bottom edge trimmed in some copies).

Published March 1893, at 6/-, the issue consisting of sheets of the first American edition. Noted in "List of New Books," in the *Athenaeum*, 18 March 1893; advertised in the same publication 25 March.

For Times Book Club remainder binding, see F30.

A38   PICTURE AND TEXT   1893

First edition:

PICTURE [in red] | AND TEXT [in red] | BY | HENRY JAMES | [publisher's device, against cream-buff panel within blind impression] | NEW YORK | HARPER AND BROTHERS [in red] | MDCCCXCIII

($5\frac{7}{8} \times 3\frac{9}{16}$): [i]^4 [ii]^2 (coated stock, inserted between [i$_{1,2}$]) 1–11^8, pp. xii, 176. 16mo.

Contents: [i–ii], blank leaf; [iii–iv], recto blank, on verso portrait of James, with tissue guard bearing facsimile autograph in red; [v–vi], title, on verso copyright notice and reservation of rights; [vii–viii], "Note" on original appearance of essays, verso blank; [ix–x], contents, verso blank; [xi–xii], list of illustrations, verso blank; [1]–175, text; [176], blank. In addition to frontispiece portrait, there are seven illustrations tipped in, not reckoned in pagination; these illustrations are reproduced from *Harper's New Monthly Magazine*, June 1889, where they served as illustration to James's essay, "Our Artists in Europe." Headpiece, p. [1], and decorative initial letter at beginning of each essay.

A. ORIGINAL WORKS

Issued in dark green linen-grain cloth, lettering within decorative panel and all-over torch devices in gilt on front cover, lettering and torch decoration in gilt on spine; white end-papers; all edges trimmed (bottom edge untrimmed in some copies).

Published 2 June 1893, at $1, in Harper's American Essayists.

A "de luxe" binding in white cloth, blocked as above, top edge gilt, was issued at $1.25, possibly simultaneously with ordinary issue, although the earliest inscription date noted is December 1893. The Harper trade annual catalogue for 1894 records a "white and gold" issue of the American Essayists series for sale only in complete sets. Gibson & Arms assign this binding as first issue in the case of Howells's *Criticism and Fiction*, labelling the green binding second issue, but offer no evidence to substantiate the assignment.

Three secondary bindings are noted, the first in green cloth, lettering in red and ornaments blocked in grey; the second in red cloth, lettering and ornaments in black; the third in grey cloth, lettering and ornaments in black, the publisher's imprint on spine differing from the original ornamental brass, being in uniform roman type, $\frac{3}{16}''$ high. A fourth secondary binding, in blue cloth, lettering and ornaments in black, appeared at Parke-Bernet on 7 May 1963.

CONTENTS

Minor revisions in all texts between serial and book publication.

Black and White
>   First appeared, under the title "Our Artists in Europe," in *Harper's New Monthly Magazine*, June 1889.

Edwin A. Abbey
>   First appeared in *Harper's Weekly*, 4 December 1886. Partially reprinted in *A Catalogue of the Drawings by Mr. Edwin A. Abbey for "She Stoops to Conquer,"* 1886 (see B3).

Charles S. Reinhart
>   First appeared in *Harper's Weekly*, 14 June 1890.

Alfred Parsons
>   First appeared as a "Prefatory Note" in *Catalogue of A Collection of Drawings by Alfred Parsons, R.I.*, 1891 (see B7).

John S. Sargent
>   First appeared in *Harper's New Monthly Magazine*, October 1887.

Honoré Daumier
> First appeared, under the title "Daumier, Caricaturist," in the
> *Century Magazine*, January 1890.

After the Play
> First appeared in the *New Review*, June 1889.

A39   THE PRIVATE LIFE   1893

a. *First edition:*

THE PRIVATE LIFE | THE WHEEL OF TIME LORD
BEAUPRE | THE VISITS COLLABORATION | OWEN
WINGRAVE | BY | HENRY JAMES | LONDON | JAMES R.
OSGOOD, MCILVAINE & CO. | 45, ALBEMARLE STREET,
W. | 1893

$(7\frac{1}{2} \times 5)$: A^4 B–X^8 Y^6, pp. viii, 332. Crown 8vo.

Contents: [i–ii], blank leaf; [iii–iv], half-title, verso blank; [v–vi],
title, verso blank; [vii–viii], contents, verso blank; [1–2], divisional
fly-title, verso blank; [3]–331, text; [332], printer's device and imprint,
"Chiswick Press:—C. Whittingham and Co., Tooks Court, |
Chancery Lane."

Issued in royal blue vertical-ribbed cloth, lettering and lily-bud and
flower devices in gilt on front cover and spine; white end-papers; all
edges untrimmed.

Published 3 June 1893, at 5/-, the first (and only) printing consisting of
1000 copies.

CONTENTS

The Private Life
> First appeared in the *Atlantic Monthly*, April 1892.

The Wheel of Time
> First appeared in *Cosmopolitan Magazine*, December 1892–
> January 1893.

Lord Beaupré
> First appeared, under the title "Lord Beauprey," in *Macmillan's
> Magazine*, April–June 1892.

The Visits
> First appeared, under the title "The Visit," in *Black and White*,
> 28 May 1892.

Collaboration

First appeared in the *English Illustrated Magazine*, September 1892.

Owen Wingrave

First appeared in the *Graphic*, Xmas number (issued 28 November) 1892.

b. *First American edition:*

THE PRIVATE LIFE | LORD BEAUPRÉ | THE VISITS | BY | HENRY JAMES | [publisher's device] | NEW YORK | HARPER & BROTHERS PUBLISHERS | 1893

($6\frac{13}{16} \times 4\frac{3}{8}$): [i]² [ii]¹ [1]⁸ 2–14⁸ 15⁶, pp. vi, 236. 16mo.

Contents: [i–ii], blank leaf; [iii–iv], title, on verso copyright notice and reservation of rights; [v–vi], contents, verso blank; [1–2], divisional fly-title, verso blank; [3]–232, text; [233–236], advertisements.

Issued in (*a*) olive green and (*b*) dark green linen-grain cloth, lettering in gilt and triple-rule border and grillework design in silver on front cover and spine, publisher's device in gilt on front cover; white endpapers; top edge trimmed and (*a*) gilt or (*b*) ochre-stained, other edges untrimmed.

Published 15 August 1893, in Harper's American Story Tellers series, at $1. Advertisement, p. [233], erroneously lists price as $1.25.

This edition contains only the first, third, and fourth tales included in the English edition of *The Private Life*. The remaining three tales were collected in a uniform companion volume, *The Wheel of Time* (see A41).

Harper's printed a large quantity of sheets and had these bound in small quantities over a period of time, resulting in many secondary binding states. Among these are noted: (*a*) green linen-grain cloth, lacking grillework design on front cover, lettered in black on front cover, spine unchanged; (*b*) maroon linen-grain or vertical-ribbed cloth, front cover blank, lettering in gilt and grillework designs and rule border in blind on spine; (*c*) olive-green vertical-ribbed or linen-grain cloth, lettered in red on front cover and spine, publisher's device in red on front cover, triple-rule border and grillework design in blind on front cover and spine; (*d*) ochre or light red linen-grain cloth, triple-rule border and grillework design in black on front cover and spine, lettered in black on spine, lettering and publisher's device eliminated from front cover; (*e*) green or red linen-grain cloth, lettered in black on spine, border rules and design eliminated from spine, front cover blank. In all these secondary issues top edge is trimmed but unstained, other edges untrimmed. Page size tends to vary slightly, but is generally $6\frac{5}{8} \times 4\frac{1}{4}$.

A40   ESSAYS IN LONDON AND   1893
ELSEWHERE

a. *First edition:*

ESSAYS IN LONDON | AND ELSEWHERE | BY | HENRY JAMES | LONDON | JAMES R. OSGOOD, MCILVAINE & CO. | 45 ALBEMARLE STREET, W. | MDCCCXCIII | ALL RIGHTS RESERVED

($7\frac{15}{16} \times 5\frac{5}{16}$): [A]⁴ B–X⁸, pp. viii, 320. Post 8vo.

Contents: [i–ii], half-title, verso blank; [iii–iv], title, verso blank; [v–vi], editorial note, verso blank; [vii–viii], contents, verso blank; [1]–320, text; at bottom of p. 320 imprint, "Printed by R. & R. Clark, Edinburgh."

Issued in pale salmon vertical-fine-ribbed cloth, lettered in gilt on front cover and spine, double-rule vertical ornament with decorative leaf-like tips in gilt on front cover; white end-papers; all edges untrimmed (bottom trimmed in some copies).

Published June 1893, at 7/6, the first (and only) printing consisting of 1000 copies. Advertised in the *Academy*, 17 June 1893.

CONTENTS

London
First appeared in the *Century Magazine*, December 1888.
James Russell Lowell
First appeared in the *Atlantic Monthly*, January 1892.
Frances Anne Kemble
First appeared in *Temple Bar*, April 1893.
Gustave Flaubert
First appeared in *Macmillan's Magazine*, March 1893.

Pierre Loti
> First appeared in the *Fortnightly Review*, May 1888.

The Journal of the Brothers de Goncourt
> First appeared in the *Fortnightly Review*, October 1888.

Browning in Westminster Abbey
> First appeared in the *Speaker*, 4 January 1890.

Henrik Ibsen
> I. *On the Occasion of "Hedda Gabler"*
>> First appeared in the *New Review*, June 1891.
> II. *On the Occasion of "The Master-Builder"*
>> First appeared, under the title "Ibsen's New Play," in the *Pall Mall Gazette*, 17 February 1893.

Mrs. Humphry Ward
> First appeared in the *English Illustrated Magazine*, February 1892.

Criticism
> First appeared, under the title "The Science of Criticism," in the *New Review*, May 1891, and in the *Philadelphia Press* and the *New York Herald*, 10 May 1891, under revised titles (see D444).

An Animated Conversation
> First appeared in *Scribner's Magazine*, March 1889.

b. *First American edition:*

ESSAYS IN LONDON | AND | ELSEWHERE | BY | HENRY JAMES | [publisher's device] | NEW YORK | HARPER & BROTHERS PUBLISHERS | 1893

($7\frac{1}{2} \times 5$): [i]⁴ 1–19⁸ [20]⁴, pp. viii, 312. Post 8vo.

Contents: [i–ii], blank leaf; [iii–iv], title, on verso copyright notice and reservation of rights; [v–vi], editorial note, verso blank; [vii–viii], contents, verso blank; [1]–305, text; [306], blank; [307–312], advertisements.

Issued in blue diagonal-fine-ribbed cloth, grillework triangles in four corners in silver on front cover and in blind on back cover, lettering in gilt and grillework ornaments at top and bottom in silver on spine; white end-papers; top edge trimmed, other edges untrimmed.

Published 12 September 1893, at $1.25.

First American edition:

THE WHEEL OF TIME | COLLABORATION | OWEN WIN-
GRAVE | BY | HENRY JAMES | [publisher's device] | NEW
YORK | HARPER & BROTHERS PUBLISHERS | 1893

($6\frac{13}{16} \times 4\frac{3}{8}$): [i]² [1]⁸ 2–13⁸ 14⁶, pp. iv, 220. 16mo.

Contents: [i–ii], title, on verso copyright notice and reservation of
rights; [iii–iv], contents, verso blank; [1–2], divisional fly-title, verso
blank; [3]–220, text.

Issued in dark green linen-grain cloth, lettering in gilt and triple-rule
border and grillework design in silver on front cover and spine,
publisher's device in gilt on front cover; white end-papers; top edge
trimmed and ochre-stained, other edges untrimmed.

Published 26 September 1893, in Harper's American Story Teller
series, at $1.

This edition contains the second, fifth, and sixth tales included in the
English edition of *The Private Life*, the three remaining tales having
been collected in a uniform companion volume comprising the
American edition of *The Private Life* (see A39b).

This edition, like that of its companion volume, is noted in secondary
binding states, issued in (*a*) red linen-grain cloth, triple-rule border
and grillework design in blind on front cover and spine, publisher's
device in blind on front cover, lettered in gilt on front cover and spine;
and (*b*) dark green linen-grain cloth, front cover blank, lettering in red
and grillework design in blind on spine. In both secondary states top
edge is trimmed but unstained, other edges untrimmed. Size is
uniform with first issue.

A42   THEATRICALS   1894

a. *First edition, English issue:*

THEATRICALS | [rule] | TWO COMEDIES | TENANTS
DISENGAGED | BY | HENRY JAMES | LONDON | OSGOOD,
MCILVAINE & CO. | 45 ALBEMARLE STREET | 1894 | ALL
RIGHTS RESERVED

($7\frac{1}{2} \times 5$): [A]⁴ B–X⁸ Y⁴, pp. viii, 328. Crown 8vo.

Contents: [i–ii], half-title, verso blank; [iii–iv], title, on verso advertisement of *Theatricals: Second Series* "In the Press"; [v]–vi, "Note," signed H.J.; [vii–viii], contents, verso blank; [1–2], divisional fly-title, on verso cast of characters of *Tenants*; [3]–325, text; at bottom of p. 325 imprint, "Printed by R. & R. Clark, Edinburgh"; [326], blank; [327–328], advertisement, verso blank.

Issued in yellow-green buckram, lettering and ornamental device in gilt on front cover and spine; white end-papers; all edges untrimmed.

Published June 1894, at 6/-, the first (and only) printing consisting of 1010 copies, of which 550 were exported for the American issue. Advertised "To be published next week," in the *Athenaeum*, 26 May 1894, and noted in the "List of New Books" in the same publication, 9 June.

Both plays included in this volume were unproduced; neither had prior serial appearance.

b. *First edition, American issue:*

This issue consisted of 550 copies of the English edition, uniformly bound, with substituted imprint NEW YORK | HARPER & BROTHERS, PUBLISHERS on title-page, and Harper imprint on spine. Pp. [327–328], blank leaf.

Published June 1894, at $1.75. Publication was probably simultaneous with the English issue, the book being announced as a "forthcoming volume" in the *New York Tribune*, 3 June 1894, and noted under "Books of the Week" in the same publication, 9 June.

A43   GUY DOMVILLE   1894

Non-published edition:

PRINTED—AS MANUSCRIPT— | FOR PRIVATE CIRCU-LATION ONLY. | [rule] | GUY DOMVILLE | PLAY IN THREE ACTS | BY | HENRY JAMES. | [decorative device] | LONDON: | PRINTED BY J. MILES & CO., 195, WARDOUR STREET, | OXFORD STREET, W. | [rule] | 1894.

$(7\frac{3}{16} \times 4\frac{13}{16})$: [A]⁸ B–E⁸, pp. 80. [8vo]

Contents: [1–2], title, verso blank; [3–4], cast of characters, on verso list of acts and scenes; [5]–79, text; [80], blank.

Issued in faded blue paper wrappers, cut flush, front cover duplicating

GUY DOMVILLE

PLAY IN THREE ACTS

BY

HENRY JAMES.

London:
PRINTED BY J. MILES & CO., 105, WARDOUR STREET,
OXFORD STREET, W.

1894.

title-page, lettered in black; inner sides of wrappers blank; all edges trimmed.

Printed October 1894, at James's expense; the exact number of copies is unknown, though the impression was a small one.

Five copies are known to be extant, one each in the Houghton, Huntington, University of Virginia, and Colby libraries, and one in the Lord Chamberlain's archive in the British Library. The Huntington and Colby copies are variants, in that they are interleaved, with holograph corrections and alterations for the use of the cast.

The play was not published during James's lifetime, its first book appearance being in *The Complete Plays of Henry James*, 1949 (see A95). James did, however, permit the publishing of a single quotation in *The Drama Birthday Book*, 1895 (see B14), and nine quotations in *The George Alexander Birthday Book*, 1903 (see B23).

A44 THEATRICALS: SECOND SERIES 1894

a. *First edition, English issue:*

THEATRICALS | SECOND SERIES | THE ALBUM THE REPROBATE | BY | HENRY JAMES | LONDON | OSGOOD, MCILVAINE & CO. | 45 ALBEMARLE STREET | 1895 [1894] | ALL RIGHTS RESERVED

($7\frac{1}{2} \times 5$): [A]⁸ B–2D⁸ [2E]¹, pp. xvi, 418. Crown 8vo.

Contents: [i–ii], half-title, verso blank; [iii–iv], title, verso blank; [v]–xiv, author's "Note"; [xv–xvi], contents, verso blank; [1–2], divisional fly-title, on verso cast of characters of *The Album*; [3]–416, text; at bottom of p. 416 imprint, "Printed by R. & R. Clark, Edinburgh."; [417–418], advertisements, pp. 1–2.

Issued in yellow-green buckram, lettering and ornamental device in gilt on front cover and spine; white end-papers; all edges untrimmed.

Published early December 1894, at 6/-, the first (and only) printing consisting of 1010 copies, of which 550 were exported for the American issue. Noted in "List of New Books" in the *Athenaeum*, 1 December 1894, and advertised as "just published" in the same publication, 8 December.

Both plays included in this volume were unproduced; neither had prior serial appearance.

b. *First edition, American issue:*

This issue consisted of 550 copies of the English edition, uniformly bound, with substituted imprint NEW YORK | HARPER & BROTHERS, PUBLISHERS on title-page, and Harper imprint on spine. Leaf of advertisements, pp. [417–418], eliminated.

Published December 1894, at $1.75. Publication was probably simultaneous with the English issue, the book being advertised as "just published" in the *New York Tribune*, 5 December 1894.

A45   TERMINATIONS   1895

a. *First edition:*

TERMINATIONS [in red] | THE DEATH OF THE | LION .. THE COXON | FUND . . THE MIDDLE | YEARS . . THE ALTAR | OF THE DEAD . . . . . | BY HENRY JAMES | [acorn device] | LONDON: WILLIAM HEINEMANN [in red] | MDCCCXCV

$(7\frac{1}{2} \times 5)$: [a]⁴ A–Q⁸ R², pp. viii, 260, followed by 16 p. of advertisements. Crown 8vo.

Contents: [i–ii], half-title, advertisement on verso; [iii–iv], title, on verso reservation of rights; [v–vi], "Note" on original appearance of tales, verso blank; [vii–viii], contents, verso blank; [1–2], divisional fly-title, verso blank; [3]–260, text; at bottom of p. 260 imprint, "Printed by Ballantyne, Hanson & Co. | London and Edinburgh."; 16 unnumbered and undated pages of advertisements, on lighter stock.

Issued in light blue diagonal-fine-ribbed cloth, lettered in gilt on front cover and spine, four irises in blind on front cover, publisher's device in blind on back cover; white end-papers; all edges untrimmed.

Published 15 May 1895, at 6/-, the first printing consisting of 1000 copies. A second impression, in July 1895, consisted of 500 copies.

———

SPECIAL NOTE ON HEINEMANN EDITIONS:

The Heinemann one-volume editions of James's novels and tales (seven titles in all) follow a general pattern. There are three standard forms:

  (i) Sheets of the first impression of the edition for the domestic market, printed on laid paper, with title-page in red and black, were bound in light blue diagonal-fine-ribbed cloth with *four irises* blocked in blind on front cover. Such titles as went into second or third impressions follow this formula.

(ii) Sheets of these domestic impressions bound up at later dates appear in the same or slightly varying shades of blue diagonal-fine-ribbed cloth, with *nine tulip buds* blocked in blind on front cover and with re-cut brasses for the lettering.

(iii) Sheets of the colonial edition on smooth-coated wove paper, with all-black title-page dated in arabic numerals, were bound up for the domestic market in cheaper quality blue cloth, uniform with (ii) but with brasses again re-cut; these copies usually lack the colonial half-title and the advertisements and are trimmed to $7\frac{1}{4} \times 4\frac{3}{4}''$.

Besides these three standard forms, there are many intermediate variants, such as mixed domestic and colonial sheets; domestic issues in which colonial half-titles have not been eliminated; and two or more sets of brasses on otherwise identical sets of sheets. Many of these are freaks. We have noted all variants which seem significant. (See Plate VII.)

————

The second impression of *Terminations* was issued in both primary and secondary bindings, but may be identified by imprint on verso of title-leaf: "Second Edition | [rule] | First Edition, May 1895". There is some variation in the preliminary leaves.

Of the colonial edition (see F52), 100 sets of sheets were transferred to the domestic market in the third standard binding (see Special Note above). Sadleir notes a copy with two extra blank leaves at front, the first being pasted to the inside front cover; this is obviously one of the aforementioned freak copies.

CONTENTS

The Death of the Lion
> First appeared in the *Yellow Book*, April 1894.

The Coxon Fund
> First appeared in the *Yellow Book*, July 1894.

The Middle Years
> First appeared in *Scribner's Magazine*, May 1893.

The Altar of the Dead
> First appeared here; no prior serialization.

b. *First American edition:*

TERMINATIONS | THE DEATH OF THE LION | THE
COXON FUND | THE MIDDLE YEARS | THE ALTAR OF
THE DEAD | BY | HENRY JAMES | AUTHOR OF "DAISY
MILLER" ETC. | [publisher's device] | NEW YORK |
HARPER & BROTHERS PUBLISHERS | 1895

$(7\frac{1}{4} \times 4\frac{13}{16})$: [i]⁴ 1–15⁸ 16⁴, pp. viii, 248. Post 8vo.

Contents: [i–ii], blank leaf; [iii–iv], title, on verso advertisement, copyright notice, and reservation of rights; [v–vi], "Note" on original
appearance of tales, verso blank; [vii–viii], contents, verso blank;
[1]–242, text; [243–248], advertisements.

Issued in pale green-on-white linen-grain cloth, lettered in gilt on
front cover and spine, three flower-and-leaf ornaments in gilt and
green on front cover, one flower-and-leaf ornament in gilt and green
on spine, publisher's imprint in slightly seriffed lettering, $\frac{1}{8}''$ high, on
spine; white end-papers; all edges trimmed.

Published 18 June 1895, at $1.25.

Advance copies, for copyright deposit, were bound in dark blue cloth,
with title only, in black, on white paper label on spine.

A secondary binding is noted, in pea green linen-grain cloth, lettered
and blocked uniform with first issue except for publisher's imprint,
which is heavily seriffed and $\frac{3}{32}''$ high, and elimination of ornament
on spine.

A46   EMBARRASSMENTS   1896

a. *First edition:*

EMBARRASSMENTS [in red] | THE FIGURE IN THE |
CARPET . . GLASSES . | THE NEXT TIME . . | THE WAY
IT CAME . . | BY HENRY JAMES | [acorn device] | LONDON:
WILLIAM HEINEMANN [in red] | MDCCCXCVI

$(7\frac{1}{2} \times 5)$: [a]⁴ A–Q⁸ R⁴, pp. viii, 264, followed by 32 pages of advertisements. Crown 8vo.

Contents: [i–ii], half-title, advertisement on verso; [iii–iv], title, on
verso reservation of rights; [v–vi], "Note" on original appearance of
tales, verso blank; [vii–viii], contents, verso blank; [1–2], divisional

fly-title, verso blank; [3]–263, text; at bottom of p. 263 imprint, "Printed by Ballantyne, Hanson & Co. | London and Edinburgh"; [264], blank; 32 unnumbered and undated pp. of advertisements on lighter stock.

Issued in light blue diagonal-fine-ribbed cloth, lettered in gilt on front cover and spine, four irises in blind on front cover, publisher's device in blind on back cover; white end-papers; all edges untrimmed.

Published 12 June 1896, at 6/-, the first printing consisting of 1250 copies. A second impression, February 1897, consisted of 250 copies.

The second impression, issued in the second standard binding (see SPECIAL NOTE, p. 101) lacks advertisements at back.

Of the colonial issue, an indeterminate number of sets of sheets was transferred to the domestic market in the third standard binding.

CONTENTS

The Figure in the Carpet
First appeared in *Cosmopolis*, January–February 1896.
Glasses
First appeared in the *Atlantic Monthly*, February 1896.
The Next Time
First appeared in the *Yellow Book*, July 1895.
The Way It Came
First appeared in the *Chap Book*, 1 May 1896, and in *Chapman's Magazine of Fiction*, May 1896.

b. *First American Edition* (1896):

EMBARRASSMENTS | BY | HENRY JAMES | AUTHOR OF "DAISY MILLER," "THE EUROPEANS" | ETC., ETC. | NEW YORK | THE MACMILLAN COMPANY | LONDON: MACMILLAN & CO., LTD. | 1896 | ALL RIGHTS RESERVED

(7$\frac{11}{16}$ × 5$\frac{1}{8}$): [B]⁸ C–X⁸ [Y]⁴, pp. vi, 322. 12mo.

Contents: binder's fly-leaf at front; [i–ii], half-title, on verso publisher's device; [iii–iv], title, on verso copyright notice and imprint, "Norwood Press | J. S. Cushing & Co.—Berwick & Smith | Norwood Mass. U.S.A."; v–[vi], contents, verso blank; [1–2], divisional fly-title, verso blank; 3–320, text; [321–322], advertisements; binder's fly-leaf at back.

Issued in claret linen-grain cloth, single-rule border in blind on front and back covers, lettering and single-rule underscoring the title in gilt on spine; white end-papers; top edge trimmed and gilt, other edges untrimmed.

Published June 1896, at $1.50, the first printing consisting of 1600 copies. Brussel gives this edition priority over the English edition, stating that the publisher reported publication date as 10 June 1896. This, however, was the date of copyright deposit. On 6 June 1896 the book was advertised in *Publishers' Weekly* as "Nearly Ready". On 20 June, the same publication, in its "Notes in Season" column, announced the book as "just ready." It was advertised in the *New York Tribune* on 24 June under "New Novels," no previous listing being noted in its "Books Received" columns. It seems probable, therefore, that English publication on 12 June 1896 was antecedent to the American.

Two variant binding states are noted, for which no priority has been established. The publisher's imprint on the spine of one state reads: "The Macmillan | Company"; the second reads: "Macmillan & Co." The cloth colour varies slightly in shading.

A47   THE OTHER HOUSE   1896

a. First edition:

THE OTHER HOUSE | BY | HENRY JAMES | IN TWO VOLUMES | VOL. i [ii] | LONDON | WILLIAM HEINE-MANN | 1896

$(7\frac{1}{4} \times 4\frac{3}{4})$: Volume i, [a]² A–N⁸, pp. iv, 208, followed by 32-page catalogue of advertisements. Volume ii, [a]² A–M⁸ N⁶, pp. iv, 204, followed by 32-page catalogue of advertisements. Crown 8vo.

Contents: Volume i: [i–ii], half-title, on verso list of books "By the Same Author"; [iii–iv], title, on verso reservation of rights; [1–2], divisional fly-title, verso blank; [3]–206, text; at bottom of p. 206 imprint, "Printed by Ballantyne, Hanson & Co. | London and Edinburgh"; [207–208], blank leaf; catalogue dated August 1896.

Volume ii: [i–iv], uniform with Vol. i; [1]–202, text; at bottom of p. 202 imprint, "Printed by Ballantyne, Hanson & Co. | London and Edinburgh"; [203–204], blank leaf; catalogue dated August 1896.

Issued in light blue diagonal-fine-ribbed cloth, lettered in gilt on front cover and spine, circular ornament in blind on front cover, publisher's device in blind on back cover; white end-papers; all edges trimmed.

Published 1 October 1896, at 10/-, the first printing consisting of 600 copies. A second impression of 400 copies was ordered simultaneously with the first; sheets were bound simultaneously, and issued as received. Copies of the second impression bear the imprint, "Second Edition," on the title-page; the publisher, however, appears to have ignored this distinction when issuing the one-volume edition in 1897. It bears an imprint on the verso of the title-leaf, "First edition, 2 vols., October 1896." There is no reference to a second two-volume "edition."

Some copies lack the circular ornament in blind on front cover. Advertisements vary; in some copies examined, the advertisements carry later dates and consist of numbered pages; in others there are 32 pages of unnumbered, undated advertisements, the recto of the first leaf advertising Hall Caine's *The Manxman*.

First appeared in the *Illustrated London News*, 4 July–26 September 1896. Considerable variance between serial and book text, and between English and American editions.

b. *First American edition:*

THE OTHER HOUSE | BY | HENRY JAMES | AUTHOR OF "DAISY MILLER," "THE EUROPEANS" | ETC., ETC. | NEW YORK | THE MACMILLAN COMPANY | LONDON: MACMILLAN & CO., LTD. | 1896 | ALL RIGHTS RESERVED

$(7\frac{1}{2} \times 5)$: [B]⁸ C–2B⁸ 2C⁶, pp. iv, 392. 12 mo.

Contents: [i–ii], half-title, on verso publisher's device; [iii–iv], title, on verso copyright notice and imprint, "Norwood Press | J. S. Cushing & Co.—Berwick & Smith | Norwood Mass. U.S.A."; [1–2], divisional fly-title, verso blank; 3–388, text; [389–391], advertisements; [392], blank.

Issued in claret linen-grain cloth, single-rule border in blind on front and back covers, lettering and single-rules underscoring the title in gilt on spine; white end-papers; top edge trimmed and gilt, other edges untrimmed.

Published October 1896, at $1.50, the first (and only) printing consisting of 2150 copies. Brussel gives this edition priority over the English, stating that the publisher reported publication date as 23

September 1896. The Library of Congress deposit, however, was not made until 7 October; the first advertisements appeared in both the *New York Times* and the *New York Tribune* on 17 October (probable date of publication), while the *New York Journal* on 18 October carried a lurid Sunday Supplement spread captioned "Henry James's New Novel of Immorality and Crime: The Surprising Plunge of the Great Novelist into the Field of Sensational Fiction." It referred to the work as a "forthcoming novel . . . which the Macmillan Company will publish immediately."

For copyright purposes type was set up during serialization and eight pamphlets were deposited in the Library of Congress, issued in light blue-grey paper wrappers, front cover duplicating title-page, $7\frac{1}{8} \times 5$. Title-leaf uniform with that in first edition, which was printed from these original plates, with revision of pagination. Only three copyright copies are known to exist, of which one is in the Library of Congress (part 3 missing) and one in the Colby College Library. The third is in the collection of Robert H. Taylor.

c. *Second English edition* (1897):

THE OTHER HOUSE [in red] | BY HENRY JAMES | [acorn device] | LONDON: WILLIAM HEINEMANN [in red] | MDCCCXCVII

($7\frac{1}{2} \times 5$): [a]² A–T⁸ U⁶, pp. iv, 316, followed by 16 pages of advertisements. Crown 8vo.

Contents: [i–ii], half-title, advertisement on verso; [iii–iv], title, on verso imprint, "First Edition, 2 vols., October 1896"; [1–2], divisional fly-title, verso blank; [3]–316, text; at bottom of p. 316 imprint, "Printed by Ballantyne, Hanson & Co. | London & Edinburgh"; 16 (or 32) unnumbered and undated pages of advertisements on lighter stock.

Issued in light blue diagonal-fine-ribbed cloth, lettered in gilt on front cover and spine, four irises in blind on front cover, publisher's device in blind on back cover; white end-papers; all edges untrimmed. Published 17 July 1897, at 6/-, the first (and only) printing consisting of 1500 copies.

Some copies are noted in the second standard binding (see SPECIAL NOTE, p. 101), lacking catalogue of advertisements at back.

Of the colonial issue 150 copies were transferred to the domestic market in the third standard binding.

A48   THE SPOILS OF POYNTON   1897

a. *First edition:*

THE | SPOILS OF POYNTON [in red-brown] | BY HENRY
JAMES | AUTHOR OF | "TERMINATIONS," "EMBAR-
RASSMENTS" | [acorn device] | LONDON: WILLIAM
HEINEMANN [in red-brown] | MDCCCXCVII

($7\frac{1}{2} \times 5$): [A]² B–T⁸, pp. iv, 288, followed by 32 pages of advertisements. Crown 8vo.

Contents: [i–ii], half-title, on verso advertisement of titles "By the
Same Author"; [iii–iv], title, on verso reservation of rights; [1]–286,
text; at bottom of p. 286 imprint, "Richard Clay & Sons, Limited,
London & Bungay."; [287–288], advertisement, verso blank; 32 unnumbered and undated pages of advertisements on lighter stock.

Issued in light blue diagonal-fine-ribbed cloth, lettered in gilt on front
cover and spine, four irises in blind on front cover, publisher's device
in blind on back cover; white end-papers; all edges untrimmed.

Published February 1897, at 6/-, the first (and only) printing consisting
of 2000 copies. The publisher's stock-book lists 9 February 1897 as
date of publication, but the usually accurate file copy is dated 6
February. Deposit was made in the British Museum on the latter date.
Some copies of the primary issue contain a blank leaf, pp. [287–288], in
place of advertisements.

Copies have been noted in the second standard binding (see SPECIAL
NOTE, p. 101), the title-brass on the spine appearing in two variant
states, the "of" in the first being in small capitals, the "of" in the
second being in large capitals (see Plate VII).

Of the colonial issue 300 copies were transferred to the domestic
market in the third standard binding. A few of these have been noted
with mixed domestic and colonial sheets.

First appeared, under the title *The Old Things*, in the *Atlantic Monthly*,
April–October 1896. Numerous revisions between serial and book
publication, and variations in text between the English and American
editions.

b. *First American edition:*

THE SPOILS OF POYNTON | BY | HENRY JAMES | [pub-
lisher's device] | BOSTON AND NEW YORK | HOUGHTON,
MIFFLIN AND COMPANY | THE RIVERSIDE PRESS,
CAMBRIDGE | 1897

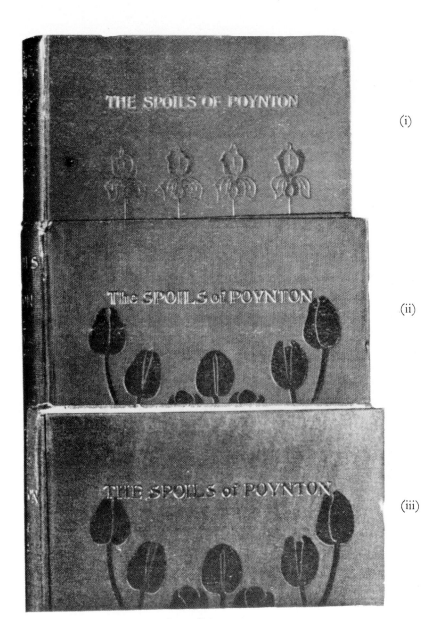

First edition 1897
(i) Domestic sheets in iris binding
(ii) Domestic sheets in tulip binding
(iii) Colonial sheets in tulip binding

PLATE VI

(i) (ii*a*) (ii*b*) (iii)

First edition 1897

(i) Domestic sheets in iris binding
(ii*a*) and (ii*b*) Domestic sheets in two variants of tulip bindings
(iii) Colonial sheets in tulip binding

PLATE VII

($7\frac{3}{8} \times 5$): [unsigned: 1–20^8 21^4], pp. iv, 324. 12 mo.

Contents: binder's fly-leaf at front; [i–ii], recto blank, advertisement on verso; [iii–iv], title, on verso copyright notice, reservation of rights, and imprint, "The Riverside Press, Cambridge, Mass., U.S.A. | Electrotyped and Printed by H. O. Houghton & Company."; [1]–323, text; [324], blank; binder's fly-leaf at back.

Issued in (*a*) dark green and (*b*) brown vertical-ribbed cloth, lettering and ornament within decorative panel in gilt on front cover, single-rule border in gilt on front cover and in blind on back cover, lettering and ornament in gilt on spine; white end-papers; top edge trimmed, other edges untrimmed.

Published 13 February 1897, at $1.50, the first printing consisting of 1500 copies. A second impression, in March 1897, consisted of 500 copies; these lack any imprint to distinguish them from the first issue.

A49   WHAT MAISIE KNEW   1897

a. *First edition:*

WHAT MAISIE KNEW [in red] | BY HENRY JAMES | [acorn device] | LONDON: WILLIAM HEINEMANN [in red] | MDCCCXCVIII [1897]

($7\frac{1}{2} \times 5$): [a]² A–T⁸, pp. iv, 304, followed by 32 pages of advertisements. Crown 8vo.

Contents: [i–ii], half-title, on verso advertisement of titles "By the Same Author"; [iii–iv], title, on verso reservation of rights; [1]–304, text; at bottom of p. 304 imprint, "Printed by Ballantyne, Hanson & Co. | London & Edinburgh"; 32 unnumbered and undated pages of advertisements on lighter stock.

Issued in light blue diagonal-fine-ribbed cloth, lettered in gilt on front cover and spine, four irises in blind on front cover, publisher's device in blind on back cover; white end-papers; all edges untrimmed.

Published September 1897, at 6/-, the first printing consisting of 2000 copies. The publisher's stock-book lists 1 October 1897 as date of publication, but the usually accurate file copy is dated 17 September. Deposit was made in the British Museum on the latter date. The book was advertised as "available" in the *Athenaeum*, 18 September.

The second impression was issued in the first standard binding (see SPECIAL NOTE, p. 101), but may be identified by imprint on verso of title-leaf, "First Edition, September 1897 | Reprinted, October 1897".

The catalogue of advertisements is dated Autumn 1897. The third impression was issued in the second standard binding.

Of the colonial issue 125 sets of sheets were transferred to the domestic market in the third standard binding.

Brussel records the colonial issue sheets in the third standard binding (the title-page of which he reproduces in a special plate) as advance review copies, citing the publisher as source of information. The Heinemann records, however, show that there was only one title-leaf printed for the first impression, and that the title-page Brussel cites is of the colonial issue. Despite an 1897 imprint (printed August 1897), the colonial issue was not published until March 1898.

BAL suggests, "It is entirely possible that the publishers distributed copies of the colonial issue for review, rather than copies of the printing dated MDCCCXCVIII", but offers no evidence. This bizarre suggestion contravenes all Heinemann practice.

First appeared in the *Chap Book*, 15 January–1 August 1897, and in the *New Review* (revised and abridged), February–September 1897. There were revisions between serial and book publication, and variations in text between English and American editions of the book, which presumably were revised independently.

b. *First American edition* (1897):

WHAT MAISIE KNEW | BY | HENRY JAMES | [heraldic design in red, within blind impression] | HERBERT S. STONE & CO. | CHICAGO & NEW YORK | MDCCCXCVII [Entire title enclosed within double-rule border]

$(7\frac{1}{2} \times 4\frac{3}{4})$: [i]² [1]⁸ 2–29⁸ 30⁴, pp. iv, 472. 12mo.

Contents: binder's double-fly-leaf at front; [i–ii], half-title, verso blank; [iii–iv], title, on verso copyright notice; [1]–470, text; [471–472], printer's device (John Wilson & Son, University Press), verso blank; binder's double-fly-leaf at back.

Issued in dark grey-green linen-grain cloth, lettering and three leaf devices in gilt and single-rule border in blind on front and back covers, lettering and two strapwork ornaments within single-rule panels in gilt on spine, dated "1897" in gilt at foot of spine; white end-papers; top edge trimmed and gilt, other edges untrimmed. Reference is made to a variant binding in *Gazette of the Grolier Club*, II (February 1947).

Published October 1897, at $1.50. No copyright entry made or copies deposited of either serial text or published book. Advertised under "Books of the Week," by Macy's Department Store, in the *New York*

Times, 16 October 1897 ("$1.08 . . . all new books as soon as issued at prices lower than elsewhere.")

Page size varies in copies examined, from $7\frac{3}{8} \times 4\frac{5}{8}$ to $7\frac{1}{2} \times 4\frac{3}{4}$.

Kramer states that first impression sheets bear a watermark "Stone & Kimball | New York" and that "Second Impression" sheets are watermarked "H. S. Stone & Company | Chicago | The Chap Book". However, we have noted both watermarks in first impression copies.

A50   JOHN DELAVOY   1897

Pre-publication copyright edition:

JOHN DELAVOY | BY | HENRY JAMES | AUTHOR OF "DAISY MILLER," "THE EUROPEANS" | ETC., ETC. | NEW YORK | THE MACMILLAN COMPANY | LONDON: MACMILLAN & CO., LTD. | 1897 | ALL RIGHTS RESERVED

$(7\frac{1}{4} \times 4\frac{7}{8})$: gathered in 4's, $[1-10]^4$; signed $[a]^2 [b]^8$ c–e^8 f^6, pp. iv, 76. [8vo]

Contents: [i–ii], half-title, on verso publisher's device; [iii–iv], title, on verso copyright notice and imprint, "Norwood Press | J. S. Cushing & Co.—Berwick & Smith | Norwood, Mass. U.S.A."; [1–2], fly-title, verso blank; 3–74, text; [75–76], blank leaf.

Issued in pale olive-grey fabric wrappers, cut flush, lettered in black on front cover; inner sides of wrappers blank; all edges trimmed.

Printed November 1897, for American copyright deposit on 4 December, anticipating publication of the tale in England, in *Cosmopolis Magazine*, January–February 1898. The tale was first published in America in *The Soft Side*, 1900.

Two copies are known to exist. One is in the Library of Congress. The second, rebound, is in the collection of Robert H. Taylor.

A51   IN THE CAGE   1898

a. First edition:

IN THE CAGE | BY | HENRY JAMES | [publisher's device] | LONDON | DUCKWORTH AND CO. | 3 HENRIETTA STREET, W.C. | 1898

$(7\frac{5}{16} \times 4\frac{7}{8})$: $[a]^2$ A–M^8 N^6, pp. iv, 204. Sm. Crown 8vo.

Contents: [i–ii], half-title, on verso reservation of rights and copyright notice; [iii–iv], title, on verso imprint, "Edinburgh: T. and A. Constable, Printers to Her Majesty"; [1]–187, text; at bottom of p. 187 imprint, as on p. [iv], plus "at the Edinburgh University Press"; [188], blank; [189–204], advertisements.

Issued in light buff buckram, lettered in black on front cover and spine, telephone pole and wire ornament in black on front cover, publisher's device in black on back cover; white end-papers; all edges untrimmed.

Published August 1898, at 3/6, the first (and only) printing consisting of 1500 copies. British Museum deposit made 8 August 1898. Noted under "This Week's Books" in the *Saturday Review*, 13 August.

Some copies lack publisher's device on back cover.

For Times Book Club remainder binding, see F26.

First appeared in this edition; no prior serialization.

b. *First American edition:*

IN THE CAGE | BY | HENRY JAMES | [heraldic design in red, within blind impression] | HERBERT S. STONE & COMPANY | CHICAGO & NEW YORK | MDCCCXCVIII [Entire title enclosed within double-rule border]

$(7\frac{3}{8} \times 4\frac{3}{4})$: [unsigned: 1^4 2–15^8 16^4 17^2], viii, 236. 12mo.

Contents: [i–iv], two blank leaves; [v–vi], half-title, verso blank; [vii–viii], title, on verso copyright notice; 1–229, text; [230], blank; [231–232], imprint, "Printed by R. R. Donnelley | and Sons Company at the | Lakeside Press, Chicago, Ill.," verso blank; [233–236], two blank leaves.

Issued in dark grey-green linen-grain cloth, lettering and three leaf devices in gilt and single-rule border in blind on front and back covers, lettering between single-rules and two strapwork ornaments in gilt on spine, dated "1898" in gilt at foot of spine; white end-papers; top edge trimmed and gilt, other edges untrimmed.

Published the week of 26 September 1898, at $1.25. Noted in "List of books to be published in September" in *Publishers' Weekly*, 24 September 1898; noted as received in the *New York Tribune*, 1 October 1898.

Page size varies in copies examined, from $7\frac{3}{8} \times 4\frac{3}{4}$ to $7\frac{1}{2} \times 4\frac{5}{8}$.

Reprinted from original plates by Fox Duffield & Company in 1906.

a. *First edition:*

THE TWO MAGICS [in red] | THE TURN OF THE SCREW |
COVERING END | BY HENRY JAMES | [acorn device] |
LONDON: WILLIAM HEINEMANN [in red] | MDCCCXCVIII

$(7\frac{1}{2} \times 5)$: [a]^2 A–T^8 U^4, pp. iv, 312, followed by 32 pages of advertisements. Crown 8vo.

Contents: [i–ii], half-title, on verso advertisement of titles "By the
Same Author"; [iii–iv], title, on verso copyright notice; [1–2],
divisional fly-title, verso blank; [3]–310, text; at bottom of p. 310
imprint, "Printed by Ballantyne, Hanson & Co. | London & Edin-
burgh"; [311–312], blank leaf; 32 unnumbered and undated pages of
advertisements on lighter stock.

Issued in light blue diagonal-fine-ribbed cloth, lettered in gilt on front
cover and spine, four irises in blind on front cover, publisher's device
in blind on back cover; white end-papers; all edges untrimmed.

Published October 1898, at 6/-, the first printing consisting of 1500
copies. The publisher's stock-book lists 13 October 1898 as date of
publication, but the usually accurate file copy is dated 5 October, which
coincides with the advertised "Wed. next" in the *Athenaeum*, 1 October.

Some copies of the second impression were issued in the first standard
binding (see SPECIAL NOTE, p. 101), but may be identified by imprint on
verso of title-leaf, "First Edition · January 1898. | New Impression ·
November 1898." Remaining copies of the second impression were
issued in the second standard binding, frequently with mixed domestic
and colonial sheets, and lacking the 32 pp. of advertisements at the back.

Of the colonial issue 300 copies were transferred to the domestic
market, some of them appearing in the third standard binding; the
balance replaced quire shortages in the domestic second impression.

For copyright purposes, a few copies of *The Turn of the Screw* were
made up, from the original typeset, bound in pale grey-green blank
wrappers, $7\frac{1}{8} \times 4\frac{5}{8}$, pp. ii, 176, all edges trimmed. These presumably
were uncorrected page proofs; deposits were made 27 January 1898 at
the British Museum and 15 February 1898 at the Cambridge University
Library. The title-page reads: THE TURN OF | THE SCREW | BY HENRY
JAMES | [acorn device] | LONDON: WILLIAM HEINEMANN | ALL RIGHTS
RESERVED MDCCCXCVIII

CONTENTS

The Turn of the Screw
>First appeared in *Collier's Weekly*, 27 January–16 April 1898. Minor revisions between serial and book publication.

Covering End
>First appeared here; no prior serialization.

b. *First American edition:*

THE TWO MAGICS | THE TURN OF THE SCREW | COVER-ING END | BY | HENRY JAMES | AUTHOR OF "DAISY MILLER," "THE EUROPEANS" | ETC., ETC. | NEW YORK | THE MACMILLAN COMPANY | LONDON: MAC-MILLAN & CO., LTD. | 1898 | ALL RIGHTS RESERVED

$(7\frac{1}{2} \times 5)$: [*]^8 C–2C^8 [2D]^2, pp. iv, 400. 12mo.

Contents: [i–ii], half-title, on verso publisher's device; [iii–iv], title, on verso copyright notice and imprint, "Norwood Press | J. S. Cushing & Co.—Berwick & Smith | Norwood Mass. U.S.A."; [1–2], divisional fly-title, verso blank; 3–393, text; [394], blank; [395–400], advertisements.

Issued in claret linen-grain cloth, single-rule border in blind on front and back covers, lettering and single-rules underscoring the title in gilt on spine; white end-papers; top edge trimmed and gilt, other edges untrimmed.

Published October 1898, at $1.50, the first printing consisting of 2250 copies. Brussel gives this edition priority over the English edition, stating that the publisher reported publication date as 30 September 1898. This, however, was date of copyright deposit. The first advertisement did not appear in the *New York Times* until 8 October; the book was first noted under "Weekly Record of New Publications" in *Publishers' Weekly*, 22 October. The date of the *New York Times* advertisement suggests publication may have been simultaneous with that of the English edition.

Some copies lack either the two leaves of advertisements, pp. [397–400], or final leaf, with p. [398] blank.

c. *Illustrated editions of "The Turn of the Screw":*

In December 1940 a limited edition of 200 copies of *The Turn of the Screw*, illustrated by Mariette Lydis, was published in England by the Hand and Flower Press at £2. The first issue (125 copies) was bound in pink half linen, tan and green mottled boards, lettered in brown on front cover and spine, and dated "1940" on spine. The second issue (75 copies) was bound in yellow-white half vellum, pale tan flecked paper boards, lettered in gilt on spine. The latter issue, remaindered by John & Edward Bumpus, Ltd., was sold at £3. 10s.

In September 1949 a limited edition of 1500 copies of *The Turn of the Screw*, with a new set of illustrations by Miss Lydis, was published in the United States by the Limited Editions Club at $12.50, bound in buff buckram, lettered in gilt and blocked in red-brown on front cover and spine.

A53   THE AWKWARD AGE   1899

a. *First edition:*

THE AWKWARD AGE [in red] | BY HENRY JAMES | AUTHOR OF | "THE TWO MAGICS," "WHAT MAISIE KNEW," | "THE SPOILS OF POYNTON," ETC. ETC. | [acorn device] | LONDON: WILLIAM HEINEMANN [in red] | MDCCCXCIX

(7½ × 5): *⁴ A–2C⁸, pp. [2], vi, 416, followed by 32 pages of advertisements. Crown 8vo.

Contents: [1–2], blank leaf, except for signature mark on recto, not reckoned in pagination; [i–ii], half-title, on verso list of "Novels for 1899"; [iii–iv], title, on verso copyright notice; v–vi, contents; [1]–414, text; at bottom of p. 414 imprint, "Printed by Ballantyne, Hanson & Co. | Edinburgh & London"; [415–416], advertisements; 32 pages of unnumbered and undated advertisements on lighter stock.

Issued in light blue diagonal-fine-ribbed cloth, lettered in gilt on front cover and spine, four irises in blind on front cover, publisher's device in blind on back cover; white end-papers; all edges untrimmed.

Published 25 April 1899, at 6/-, the first (and only) printing consisting of 2000 copies.

Some copies lack publisher's device in blind on back cover. Sadleir records two variants of the inserted advertisements at the back. In the earlier state, the last page lists "The Latest Fiction."

Of the colonial issue 475 copies were transferred to the domestic market in the third standard binding (see SPECIAL NOTE, p. 101), one copy being noted with the colonial half-title retained, and two copies containing the final leaf of advertisements ($2C_8$ in the first edition). This leaf was originally printed as part of the last gathering of the colonial issue, but was eliminated when copies of the issue were bound for export.

First appeared in *Harper's Weekly*, 1 October 1898–7 January 1899. Minor revisions between serial and book publication.

b. *First American edition:*

[double-rule] | THE AWKWARD AGE | [double-rule] | A NOVEL. BY HENRY JAMES | AUTHOR OF "WASHINGTON SQUARE" | "DAISY MILLER" "PICTURE AND TEXT" | "TERMINATIONS" "THE PRIVATE LIFE" | [double-rule] | [publisher's device] | [double-rule] | HARPER & BROTHERS PUBLISHERS | NEW YORK AND LONDON | 1899 | [double-rule]

($7\frac{3}{16} \times 4\frac{3}{4}$): [a]² [A]⁸ B–2E⁸ 2F⁶, pp. iv, 460. 12mo.

Contents: [i–ii], title, on verso list of titles "By the Same Author.", copyright notice and reservation of rights; [iii–iv], contents, verso blank; [1–2], divisional fly-title, verso blank; 3–[457], text; [458], blank; [459–460], advertisements.

Issued in red-brown vertical-ribbed cloth, lettered in gilt on front and back covers and spine; white end-papers; all edges trimmed. Volume is $1\frac{5}{8}''$ thick; publisher's imprint on spine has sans-serif "p" in "Harper."

Published 12 May 1899, at $1.50, the first printing consisting of 1000 copies.

A secondary issue has been noted, printed on a thinner stock, measuring $1\frac{3}{8}''$ thick. It is bound in lighter brown cloth than the first issue; the publisher's imprint on the spine has seriffed lettering, the capital "H" has pronounced feet and the "s" is slanted.

A54   THE SOFT SIDE   1900

a. *First edition:*

THE SOFT SIDE | BY | HENRY JAMES | METHUEN & CO. | 36 ESSEX STREET W.C. | LONDON | 1900

($7\frac{1}{2} \times 5$): [a]⁴ A–2A⁸ 2B⁴, pp. viii, 392. Crown 8vo.

Contents: [i–ii], blank leaf; [iii–iv], half-title, on verso list of titles "By the Same Author"; [v–vi], title, verso blank; [vii–viii], contents, verso blank; [1]–391, text; [392], imprint, "Printed by T. and A. Constable, Printers to Her Majesty | at the Edinburgh University Press".

Issued in deep red vertical-ribbed cloth, lettered within single-rule panels in gilt on front cover and spine; white end-papers; top edge trimmed, other edges untrimmed.

Published 30 August 1900, at 6/-, the first printing consisting of 3000 copies, divided between domestic and colonial issues.

Several copies examined, including James's presentation copies and the British Museum deposit copy, have no catalogue of advertisements at end. The earliest date of a catalogue, where found, is August 1900; some copies contain catalogue dated November 1900.

CONTENTS

The Great Good Place
> First appeared in *Scribner's Magazine*, January 1900.

'Europe'
> First appeared in *Scribner's Magazine*, June 1899.

Paste
> First appeared in *Frank Leslie's Popular Monthly*, December 1899.

The Real Right Thing
> First appeared in *Collier's Weekly*, 16 December 1899.

The Great Condition
> First appeared in the *Anglo-Saxon Review*, June 1899.

The Tree of Knowledge
> No serial publication recorded.

The Abasement of the Northmores
> No serial publication recorded.

The Given Case
> First appeared in *Collier's Weekly*, 31 December 1898–7 January 1899.

John Delavoy
> First appeared in *Cosmopolis*, January–February 1898.

The Third Person
> No serial publication recorded.

Maud-Evelyn
> First appeared in the *Atlantic Monthly*, April 1900.

Miss Gunton of Poughkeepsie
> First appeared in the *Cornhill Magazine*, May 1900, and in *Truth* (New York), May–June 1900.

b. *First American edition:*

THE SOFT SIDE | BY | HENRY JAMES | AUTHOR OF "THE OTHER HOUSE," "THE | TWO MAGICS," ETC. | NEW YORK | THE MACMILLAN COMPANY | LONDON: MACMILLAN & CO., LTD. | 1900 | ALL RIGHTS RESERVED

$(7\frac{1}{2} \times 5\frac{1}{8})$: B–Y⁸, pp. vi, 330. 12mo.

Contents: [i–ii], half-title, on verso publisher's device; [iii–iv], title, on verso copyright notice and imprint, "Norwood Press | J. S. Cushing & Co.—Berwick & Smith | Norwood Mass. U.S.A."; v–[vi], contents; 1–326, text; [327–328], advertisements; [329–330], advertisement, verso blank.

Issued in claret linen-grain cloth, single-rule border in blind on front and back covers, lettering and single-rules underscoring the title in gilt and single-rule at top and bottom in blind on spine; white endpapers; top edge trimmed and gilt, other edges untrimmed.

Published September 1900, at $1.50, the first (and only) printing consisting of 2800 copies. Brussel gives this edition priority over the English edition, stating that the publisher reported publication date as 23 August 1900. This, however, was date of copyright deposit. The book was first advertised in the *New York Times*, 22 September 1900, following an earlier announcement, in the same publication on 15 September, that the book "will be published toward the end of the present month."

A55　　　THE SACRED FOUNT　　　1901

a. *First edition:*

THE SACRED FOUNT | BY | HENRY JAMES | NEW YORK | CHARLES SCRIBNER'S SONS | 1901

$(7\frac{1}{2} \times 5\frac{1}{8})$: [unsigned: 1² 2–21⁸], pp. iv, 320. 12mo.

Contents: [i–ii], half-title, verso blank; [iii–iv], title, on verso copyright notice and imprint, "Trow Directory | Printing and Bookbinding Company | New York"; 1–319, text; [320], blank.

Issued in smooth silky biscuit cloth, lettering and single-rule panel in gilt on front cover, lettering and flame device plus single-rules at top and bottom in gilt on spine; white end-papers; top edge trimmed and gilt, other edges untrimmed.

Published 6 February 1901, at $1.50, the first printing consisting of 3000 copies.

Some copies, presumably of later issue, contain a first gathering of four leaves: [i–ii], blank leaf; [iii–iv], half-title, verso blank; [v–vi], title, verso uniform with first issue; [vii–viii], fly-title, verso blank. This issue sometimes contains a binder's fly-leaf at back. The additional leaves are lacking in Library of Congress deposit copy and in copies at Houghton and the library at Berkeley, University of California.

A variant binding is noted similar to the variant of A56a but with lettering and leaf device on spine and single-rule-border in blind on front and back covers. Size: $7\frac{3}{8} \times 5$.

A secondary binding is noted, consisting of dark blue cloth, lettered in white inside single-rule frame in black on front cover, lettering and flame device in gilt on spine; top edge trimmed but not gilt. Page size: $7\frac{3}{8} \times 5\frac{1}{8}$.

First appeared in this edition; no prior serialization.

b. *First English edition:*

THE SACRED FOUNT | BY | HENRY JAMES | METHUEN & CO. | 36 ESSEX STREET W.C. | LONDON | 1901

($7\frac{7}{16} \times 5$): [A]² B–U⁸ X⁶, pp. iv, 316, followed by 48-page catalogue of advertisements. Crown 8vo.

Contents: [i–ii], half-title, on verso list of titles "By the Same Author"; [iii–iv], title, on verso imprint, "Plymouth | William Brendon and Son | Printers"; [1]–316, text; at bottom of p. 316 imprint, as on p. [iv], in one line, with punctuation; catalogue dated November 1900.

Issued in lacquered crimson cloth, lettered in gilt within single-rule panel in blind and double-rule border and all-over flower and leaf ornaments in blind on front cover, lettered in gilt with author and title within single-rule panel in blind and single-rule border and all-over flower and leaf ornaments in blind on spine; white end-papers; top edge trimmed, other edges untrimmed.

Published 15 February 1901, at 6/-, the first (and only) printing consisting of 3500 copies, divided between domestic and colonial issues.

The Sacred Fount sold poorly—the poorest sale of all of the James titles published by Methuen. In 1911, apparently encouraged by the success of *The Outcry*, which went into four printings, the firm bound a quantity of remaining sheets of the earlier novel. This would explain inclusion in certain copies of a catalogue dated as late as March or August 1911.

A56   THE WINGS OF THE DOVE   1902

a. *First edition:*

THE WINGS OF | THE DOVE | BY | HENRY JAMES | VOLUME I [II] | NEW YORK | CHARLES SCRIBNER'S SONS | 1902

($7\frac{1}{2} \times 4\frac{7}{8}$): Volume I, [i]² [1]⁸ 2–20⁸ 21⁶, pp. iv, 332. Volume II, [i]² [1]⁸ 2–27⁸ 28⁶, pp. iv, 444. 8vo.

Contents: Volume I: [i–ii], half-title, on verso advertisement of work "By the Same Author"; [iii–iv], title, on verso copyright notice, publication date, and imprint, "Trow Directory | Printing and Bookbinding Company | New York"; [1–2], divisional fly-title, verso blank; 3–329, text; [330], blank; [331–332], blank leaf.

Volume II: [i–iv; 1–2], uniform with Vol. I; 3–439, text; [440], blank; [441–444], two blank leaves.

Issued in smooth sateen biscuit cloth, lettering and flame device in gilt on spine; white end-papers; top edge trimmed and gilt, other edges untrimmed.

Published 21 August 1902, at $2.50, the first printing consisting of 3000 copies. Copies actually were not issued until eight days after formal publication date.

Some copies contain a binder's fly-leaf at front of each volume and at back of Vol. II.

A variant binding state is noted, in russet vertical-ribbed cloth, lettered in gilt on front cover and spine, single-rule in gilt at top and bottom of spine and double-rule in gilt underscoring the title on front cover, double-rule in blind at top and bottom of front and back covers; all edges trimmed. Concerning this issue, David Randall reported that "a number of sets of sheets were sold to a New York jobbing house who put them out in the [variant] binding . . . As far as our records here indicate they were issued simultaneously."

First appeared in this edition; no prior serialization.

b. *First English edition:*

THE | WINGS OF THE DOVE | BY | HENRY JAMES | [leaf device] | WESTMINSTER | ARCHIBALD CONSTABLE AND CO., LTD. | 2 WHITEHALL GARDENS, S.W. | 1902

($7\frac{5}{16} \times 4\frac{7}{8}$): [a]² A–2N⁸, pp. iv, 576, followed by 16 pages of advertisements. Crown 8vo.

Contents: [i–ii], half-title, verso blank; [iii–iv], title, on verso imprint, "Edinburgh: T. and A. Constable, (late) Printers to Her Majesty"; [1–2], divisional fly-title, verso blank; 3–576, text; at bottom of p. 576 imprint, "Printed by T. and A. Constable, (late) Printers to Her Majesty | at the Edinburgh University Press"; 16 numbered pages of advertisements on lighter stock, undated.

Issued in dull blue vertical-ribbed cloth, lettered in gilt within single-rule panel in blind on front cover, all-over chain design in blind on front cover, lettered in gilt on spine; white end-papers; all edges trimmed.

Published 30 August 1902, at 6/-, the first (and only) printing consisting of 4000 copies.

A57   THE BETTER SORT   1903

a. *First edition (English):*

THE BETTER SORT | BY | HENRY JAMES | METHUEN & CO. | 36 ESSEX STREET W.C. | LONDON | 1903

$(7\frac{1}{2} \times 5)$: [A]⁴ B–U⁸ X⁴, pp. viii, 312, followed by 40-page catalogue of advertisements. Crown 8vo.

Contents: [i–ii], blank leaf; [iii–iv], half-title, on verso list of titles "By the Same Author"; [v–vi], title, verso blank; [vii–viii], contents, verso blank; [1]–312, text; at bottom of p. 312 imprint, "Plymouth: W. Brendon and Son, Printers."; catalogue dated February 1903.

Issued in (*a*) scarlet and (*b*) claret vertical-ribbed cloth, lettered within single-rule panels in gilt on front cover and spine; white end-papers; top edge trimmed, other edges untrimmed.

Published 26 February 1903, simultaneously with American edition, at 6/-, the first (and only) printing consisting of 3500 copies, divided between domestic and colonial issues.

A variant binding (believed to be a remainder) is noted in bright blue cloth, triple-rule border in blind on front and back covers and across top and bottom of spine, lettered with a single-rule panel enclosing author and title in gilt on spine; catalogue of advertisements omitted. Page size: $7\frac{3}{8} \times 4\frac{15}{16}$.

CONTENTS

Broken Wings
    First appeared in the *Century Magazine*, December 1900.

A. ORIGINAL WORKS

The Beldonald Holbein

> First appeared in *Harper's New Monthly Magazine*, October 1901.

The Two Faces

> First appeared, under the title "The Faces," in *Harper's Bazar*, 15 December 1900.

The Tone of Time

> First appeared in *Scribner's Magazine*, November 1900.

The Special Type

> First appeared in *Collier's Magazine*, 16 June 1900.

Mrs. Medwin

> First appeared in *Punch*, 28 August–18 September 1901.

Flickerbridge

> First appeared in *Scribner's Magazine*, February 1902.

The Story in It

> First appeared in the *Anglo-American Magazine*, January 1902.

The Beast in the Jungle

> First appeared here; no prior serialization.

The Birthplace

> No serial publication recorded.

The Papers

> No serial publication recorded.

b. *First edition (American):*

THE BETTER SORT | BY | HENRY JAMES | NEW YORK | CHARLES SCRIBNER'S SONS | 1903

$(7\frac{1}{2} \times 4\frac{7}{8})$: [unsigned: 1^4 2–28^8], pp. viii, 432. 12mo.

Contents: [i–ii], recto blank, on verso list of titles "By the Same Author"; [iii–iv], half-title, verso blank; [v–vi], title, on verso copyright notice, printer's device, and publication date; [vii–viii], contents, verso blank; 1–[429], text; [430], blank; [431–432], blank leaf.

Issued in faded rose-sateen smooth cloth, lettering and single-rule frame in gilt on front cover, lettering and flame device in gilt on spine; cream-white end-papers; top edge trimmed and gilt, other edges untrimmed.

Published 26 February 1903, simultaneously with English edition, at $1.50.

Publisher's imprint on spine has been noted in two variant brasses. Length and height of imprint vary by only $\frac{1}{32}''$, but the type is radically different. One is the standard condensed type, seriffed, noted on all Scribner issues of James's works. The other is also a condensed type, but of a finer lettering, only slightly seriffed. No priority has been established.

Merle Johnson's *American First Editions* (4th edition, 1942) reports copies in varying colours of cloth. It is possible that cloth variation is due to natural fading, the rose-sateen tending to turn to dull brown when exposed to strong light.

A58 THE AMBASSADORS 1903

a. *First edition:*

THE AMBASSADORS | BY | HENRY JAMES | METHUEN & CO. | 36 ESSEX STREET W.C. | LONDON | 1903

$(7\frac{3}{8} \times 4\frac{7}{8})$: [A]² B–2F⁸ 2G⁶, pp. iv, 460, followed by 40-page catalogue of advertisements. Crown 8vo.

Contents: [i–ii], half-title, on verso list of titles "By the Same Author"; [iii–iv], title, verso blank; [1–2], divisional fly-title, verso blank; [3]–458, text; [459–460], imprint, "Plymouth | William Brendon and Son | Printers", verso blank; catalogue dated July 1903.

Issued in crimson vertical-ribbed cloth, lettered within single-rule panels in gilt on front cover and spine; white end-papers; top edge trimmed, other edges untrimmed.

Published 24 September 1903, at 6/-, the first printing consisting of 3500 copies, divided between domestic and colonial issues.

The book was set up largely from revised proof of the *North American Review* serialization. Chapters 28 and 35, eliminated from the serial text, were reinserted in proper sequence under James's personal supervision.

The second impression was bound in blue vertical-ribbed cloth, triple-rule border in blind on front and back covers and across top and bottom of spine, lettered in gilt within single-rule panel on spine only, the panel enclosing publisher's imprint being eliminated.

First appeared in the *North American Review*, January–December 1903.

A. ORIGINAL WORKS

b. *First American edition:*

THE AMBASSADORS [in red-brown] | A NOVEL | BY | HENRY JAMES | AUTHOR OF "THE AWKWARD AGE" "DAISY MILLER" | "AN INTERNATIONAL EPISODE" ETC. | [publisher's device] | NEW YORK AND LONDON | HARPER & BROTHERS PUBLISHERS | MCMIII

$(8 \times 5\frac{1}{4})$: [i]^1 [1]^8 2–27^8, pp. ii, 432. 8vo.

Contents: [i–ii], title, on verso copyright notice, reservation of rights, and publication date; [1–2], divisional fly-title, verso blank; 3–[432], text.

Issued in light blue paper boards, lettering enclosed within horizontal rules in gilt on spine; white end-papers; top edge trimmed and gilt, other edges untrimmed. Issued with dark blue diagonal-fine-ribbed stiff fabric-paper dust jacket, lettered and ruled in gilt as on spine of book.

Published 6 November 1903, at $2, the first printing consisting of 4000 copies.

Remainder copies were issued (circa 1906) in dust jacket bound over boards, but otherwise uniform with primary issue.

The American publishing history of *The Ambassadors*, a work James considered "quite the best, 'all round,' of my productions," was marked by a curious error which remained unobserved until attention to it was drawn by Robert E. Young in the November 1950 issue of *American Literature*—that is, almost half a century after the book's appearance. Young showed that Chapters XXVIII and XXIX are in reverse order. He failed, however, to note that the error was confined to the American edition. The English edition, which James saw through the press, has the chapters in correct order. This edition acquires thus a certain uniqueness in comparison with the much-reprinted American edition. The error was perpetuated in the New York Edition, Scribner having set type from the American edition.

Sufficient correspondence has been preserved to show that the American edition was set up from a separate set of proofs of the serialized *Ambassadors* in the *North American Review*. James gave warning to the publisher, Harper & Brothers, through J. B. Pinker, his literary agent, that he had withheld certain chapters and that these would be re-inserted in the book. In July and September of 1901 he reminded his agent of this, saying he wanted "to put it on witnessed record that I formally ask for duplicate *Proofs* of the serial, and that I as formally give warning that the volume is to contain a small quantity

of additional material." (Unpublished letter, Yale University Library.)
The "additional material" came to about three and a half chapters.

His feeling that precautions were needed was well-founded.
Harper's were so dilatory in furnishing proof that James—who had
hoped to have the English edition set from American galleys—finally
furnished his English publisher, Methuen, with a separate manuscript,
consisting partly of carbon copies and tear-sheets from the *North
American Review*. As a result there are many differences between the
Methuen and Harper texts.

On 13 August 1903 the novelist wrote Pinker that he had received
the last third of the book from Harper, and told him that he had
supplied "some passages omitted in the serial form" (Yale). Actually
Chapters XVIII and XIX were conflated as XVIII with a new XIX
inserted, and V contains an insertion of more than four pages. One of
the inserted chapters was XXVIII of the correct version, which became XXIX of the American edition. The book was published
6 November with the chapters in reverse order. The error seems to
have resulted from the fact that in the author's version chapter
XXVIII takes place in the evening and XXIX returns briefly to the
preceding afternoon. A Harper editor apparently decided to restore
chronological sequence. An attempt to correct this in a later edition
was frustrated by the printer, who again restored the chronological
sequence.

See Brian Birch, "Henry James: Some Bibliographical and Textual
Matters" (London, The Bibliographical Society, 1965), 108–123. Mr
Birch, by collation of the British copyright deposits, the serial, and the
Harper and Methuen texts, demonstrates that the first English edition
is a patchwork of proof and carbon copy and thus an earlier text. It
must be considered as having less authority than the texts of the
Harper and New York Editions even if these have reversed chapters.
The ultimate text is that of the New York Edition. See also Leon
Edel, "The Text of *The Ambassadors*," *Harvard Library Bulletin*,
XIV (1960), 453–460.

The error seems to have been perpetuated in the New York Edition
because Scribner used the American edition and James did not subject
his late works to the close revision of his earlier writings. The reversal
of chapters was further concealed by the fact that all the chapters
were renumbered by James for this edition. Accordingly, Chapters I
and II of Book Eleventh are in the wrong order. Although James, in
the preface to *The Golden Bowl* (New York Edition, XXIII, xxi) says
revision was "reduced to nothing . . . in the presence of the altogether
better literary manners of *The Ambassadors*," he made further changes

in the proofs. For purposes of copyright, proof-sheets of nine instalments of the serial were deposited in England at the library of Cambridge University and in the Bodleian while the serialization proceeded. The earliest deposit was made on 3 March 1903; the latest, covering Chapter XXIV, on 12 October 1903. All nine parts at Cambridge, which vary slightly in size from $9\frac{7}{8}'' \times 6\frac{7}{8}''$ to $10\frac{1}{16}'' \times 6\frac{7}{8}''$, are bound in blue-grey wrappers, lettered in black on front COVER: THE AMBASSADORS | [rule] | HENRY JAMES The leaves are printed on the obverse side only; all edges trimmed.

A59   WILLIAM WETMORE STORY   1903
AND HIS FRIENDS

a. *First edition:*

WILLIAM WETMORE STORY | AND | HIS FRIENDS | FROM LETTERS, DIARIES, AND RECOLLECTIONS | BY | HENRY JAMES | IN TWO VOLUMES | VOL. I. [II.] | WILLIAM BLACKWOOD AND SONS | EDINBURGH AND LONDON | MCMIII | ALL RIGHTS RESERVED

$(8 \times 5\frac{1}{4})$: Volume I, [a]⁴ [A]⁸ B–Z⁸ 2A², pp. viii, 372. Volume II, [a]⁴ [A]⁸ B–X⁸ Y⁶, pp. viii, 348. 8vo.

Contents: Volume I: [i–ii], blank leaf; [iii–iv], half-title, verso blank; [v–vi], title, verso blank; [vii–viii], contents of Vol. I, verso blank; [1–2], divisional fly-title, verso blank; [3]–371, text; at bottom of p. 371 imprint, "Printed by William Blackwood and Sons."; [372], blank. Frontispiece photogravure portrait of Story, with tissue guard, tipped in, not reckoned in pagination.

Volume II: [i–vi], uniform with Vol. I; [vii–viii], contents of Vol. II, verso blank; [1–2], divisional fly-title, verso blank; [3]–338, text; [339]–345, Index; at bottom of p. 345 imprint, "Printed by William Blackwood and Sons."; [346], blank; [347–348], blank leaf. Frontispiece photogravure portrait of Story, with tissue guard, tipped in, not reckoned in pagination.

Issued in grey-blue linen-grain cloth, lettering and decorative rules at top and bottom in gilt on spine; white end-papers; all edges untrimmed (top edge trimmed in some copies).

Published September or October 1903, at 24/-, the first printing consisting of 1250 copies, with four subsequent impressions totalling another 1000 copies, of which a total of 1800 sets of sheets were exported for the American issue. Of the small remainder, only 416 copies of the English edition were offered for sale, the balance being distributed as gifts by the author. Publication date is uncertain; the publisher reports September, but can offer no specific date. Brussel reports 14 September, but offers no source. The *English Catalogue* reported publication as October, and the *New York Times,* in a note on 26 September, reported simultaneous publication with American issue on 7 October.

Some copies contain binder's fly-leaves at front and back of each volume. Page size of a few copies noted measures $7\frac{13}{16} \times 5$.

First appeared in this edition; no prior serialization.

b. *First edition, American issue:*

($7\frac{15}{16} \times 5\frac{1}{4}$): Consisted of imported sheets, uniform with collation and contents of English edition except for altered imprint on title-page: HOUGHTON, MIFFLIN & CO. | BOSTON | 1903 | ALL RIGHTS RESERVED Binder's fly-leaf at back of Vol. I.

Issued in dark green linen-grain cloth, one wide- and one narrow-rule in gilt across top of front cover and spine, lettered in gilt on spine; white end-papers; top edge trimmed and gilt, other edges untrimmed.

Published 7 October 1903, at $5, the first issue consisting of 520 copies, with five subsequent issues, up to September 1905, totalling an additional 1125 copies, lacking any imprint to distinguish them from first issue. Brussel reports 3 October as publication date, but cites no source. The *New York Times,* 26 September, reported simultaneous publication with the English edition on 7 October; this date is confirmed by the American publisher. The first American issue apparently consisted of sheets of the first English edition; the subsequent issues seem to have been on inferior paper. Copies have been seen with the imprint date altered to 1904.

A60   THE GOLDEN BOWL   1904

a. *First edition:*

THE GOLDEN BOWL | BY | HENRY JAMES | VOLUME I [II] | NEW YORK | CHARLES SCRIBNER'S SONS | 1904

($7\frac{1}{2} \times 4\frac{7}{8}$): Volume I, [i]² [1]⁸ 2–25⁸ 26⁶, pp. iv, 412. Volume II, [1]⁸ 2–24⁸, pp. iv, 380. 12mo.

A. ORIGINAL WORKS

Contents: Volume I: [i–ii], half-title, on verso list of "Books by Henry James"; [iii–iv], title, on verso copyright notice, publication date, and imprint, "Trow Directory | Printing and Bookbinding Company | New York"; [1–2], fly-title, verso blank; 3–412, text.

Volume II: [i–iv; 1–2], uniform with Vol. I; 3–377, text; [378], blank; [379–380], blank leaf.

Issued in faded rose-sateen smooth cloth, lettering and flame device in gilt on spine; cream-white end-papers; top edge trimmed and gilt, other edges untrimmed.

Published 10 November 1904, at $2.50, the first printing consisting of 2000 copies. A later printing, uniform with first edition but dated 1905 on title, retains the imprint "Published November 1904" on verso of title.

First appeared in this edition; no prior serialization.

b. *First English edition* (1905):

THE GOLDEN BOWL | BY | HENRY JAMES | METHUEN & CO. | 36 ESSEX STREET W.C. | LONDON [1905]

($7\frac{1}{2} \times 4\frac{15}{16}$): [i]^4 1–34^8 35^2, pp. viii, 548, followed by 40-page catalogue of advertisements. Crown 8vo.

Contents: [i–ii], blank leaf; [iii–iv], half-title, on verso list of titles "By the Same Author"; [v–vi], title, on verso imprint, "First Published in 1905"; [vii–viii], divisional fly-title, verso blank; [1]–548, text; at bottom of p. 548 imprint, "Printed by Morrison & Gibb Limited, Edinburgh"; catalogue dated February 1905.

Issued in drab blue linen-grain cloth, lettering and two ornamental corner brackets in gilt on front cover, lettering and entwined-leaf ornament plus double-rule at top and bottom in gilt on spine; white end-papers; top edge trimmed, other edges untrimmed.

Published 10 February 1905, at 6/-, the first printing consisting of 3000 copies, divided between domestic and colonial issues. HJ wrote to Edith Wharton (Lubbock, *Letters*, II), 19 November 1911, that "the Outcry is on its way to a fifth edition (in these few weeks), whereas it has taken the poor old G[olden] B[owl] eight or nine years to get even into a third." Nevertheless, the three impressions of *The Golden Bowl* exceeded the four impressions (a fifth never eventuated) of *The Outcry* by 1000 copies; it was exceeded in turn only by *Hawthorne* as the largest seller of any of James's English editions.

Catalogue of advertisements in some copies is dated March 1905.

a. *First edition, ordinary issue:*

THE QUESTION OF OUR | SPEECH | THE LESSON OF
BALZAC | TWO LECTURES | BY HENRY JAMES | [pub-
lisher's device, in olive-brown] | BOSTON AND NEW YORK |
HOUGHTON, MIFFLIN AND COMPANY | THE RIVER-
SIDE PRESS, CAMBRIDGE | 1905

$(7\frac{7}{16} \times 4\frac{1}{2})$: [unsigned: 1^{10} ($1_{2,3}$ are conjugate and inserted) $2-7^8$ 8^4],
pp. vi, 118. Narrow 12mo.

Contents: binder's fly-leaf at front; [i–ii], recto blank, on verso list of
titles "By Henry James"; [iii–iv], half-title, verso blank; [v–vi], title,
on verso copyright notice, reservation of rights, and publication date;
[1–2], divisional fly-title, verso blank; 3–[116], text; [117–118], recto
blank, on verso imprint, "The Riverside Press | Electrotyped and
printed by H. O. Houghton & Co. | Cambridge, Mass., U.S.A."

Issued in (*a*) dark blue, (*b*) black, and (*c*) maroon linen-grain cloth,
lettered in gilt on front cover and spine; white end-papers; top edge
gilt, other edges untrimmed.

Published 7 October 1905, at $1, the first printing consisting of 2000
copies. The volume was designed by Bruce Rogers.

CONTENTS

I. *The Question of Our Speech*
    First appeared in *Appleton's Booklovers Magazine*, August 1905.
II. *The Lesson of Balzac*
    First appeared in the *Atlantic Monthly*, August 1905.

b. *First edition, limited issue:*

Collation and contents uniform with ordinary issue except for
addition, on p. [vi], of limitation notice: "Of the First Edition Three
Hundred | Copies Have Been Printed and Bound | Entirely Uncut
With Paper Label."

Issued in yellow-tan half cloth, dark grey-green paper boards,
lettered and ruled in black on white paper label on spine: [two rules] |
THE | QUESTION | OF | OUR | SPEECH | [rule] | HENRY | JAMES | [TWO
rules] | FIRST | EDITION; white end-papers; all edges untrimmed.

Published simultaneously with ordinary issue, at $1.25.

a. *First edition:*

ENGLISH HOURS | BY | HENRY JAMES | [illustration] |
WITH NINETY-TWO ILLUSTRATIONS BY | JOSEPH
PENNELL | LONDON | WILLIAM HEINEMANN | 1905

($7\frac{13}{16} \times 5\frac{3}{4}$): [a]⁴ b² A–T⁸ U⁴ X², pp. xii, 316. Pott. 4to.

Contents: [i–ii], half-title and illustration, on verso list of books
"Uniform with this Volume"; [iii–iv], title, on verso acknowledgments, copyright notice, reservation of rights, and publication date;
v–vi, Note, signed "H.J."; vii–viii, contents; ix–xii, list of illustrations; 1–[315], text; at bottom of p. [315] imprint, "Printed by
Ballantyne & Co. Limited | Tavistock Street, London"; [316], blank.
Frontispiece and seven illustrations, with tissue guard fly-titles, tipped
in, not reckoned in pagination. 84 illustrations in the text.

Issued in grey linen-grain cloth, words separated by colon devices and
fleuron in black on front and back covers, publisher's device in gilt and
black on front cover, words separated by three fleurons in black and
publisher's imprint in gilt on spine; white end-papers; top edge gilt,
other edges untrimmed.

Published 18 October 1905, at 10/-, the first (and only) printing
consisting of 2000 copies.

Six copies were bound, in October 1905, in a trial "gift binding" in
red half calf, red linen-grain cloth boards, bogus raised bands on spine,
lettering and decorative devices in gilt on spine; pink and blue
marbled end-papers; top edge gilt, other edges untrimmed, with an
inserted ribbon marker. Distributed as gifts by the publisher.

Some copies of the primary issue measure $7\frac{3}{4} \times 5\frac{7}{8}$.

Of the original edition, 1000 copies were remaindered during 1914–16
in sheets to Chaundy of Oxford, and issued bound in dark green
half buckram, green linen boards, lettering and double-rule at top and
bottom in gilt on spine, otherwise uniform with primary issue. Copies
also noted in half vellum, rust-red or green mottled paper boards,
lettering, ornament and decorative rules in gilt on spine, or in limp
rust-coloured suede with yapp edges; these too are later bind-ups, as
the Heinemann records clearly show a single uniform bind-up for
copies issued by that firm.

CONTENTS

In a prefatory note James says: "I have nowhere scrupled to rewrite a
sentence or a passage on judging it susceptible of a better turn."

A. ORIGINAL WORKS

The following essays appear in book form for the first time:

Winchelsea, Rye, and 'Denis Duval'
> First appeared in *Scribner's Magazine*, January 1901.

Old Suffolk
> First appeared in *Harper's Weekly*, 25 September 1897. A misprint in the Contents (p. viii) erroneously credits original appearance as "1879."

The following essays had previously appeared in book form:

London; Browning in Westminster Abbey; Chester; Lichfield and Warwick; North Devon; Wells and Salisbury; An English Easter; London at Midsummer; Two Excursions; In Warwickshire; Abbeys and Castles; English Vignettes; An English New Year; An English Winter Watering-Place.

b. *First American edition, ordinary issue:*

ENGLISH HOURS [in red] | BY HENRY JAMES | WITH ILLUSTRATIONS | BY JOSEPH PENNELL | [illustration] | BOSTON AND NEW YORK | HOUGHTON, MIFFLIN AND COMPANY | THE RIVERSIDE PRESS, CAMBRIDGE [in red] | MDCCCCV

($7\frac{3}{4} \times 5$): [unsigned: 1^4 2^1 $3-29^8$], pp. xiv, 338, plus an unpaginated text leaf inserted between pp. vi and [vii], and 44 unpaginated leaves of illustrations in text. Crown 8vo.

Contents: binder's fly-leaf at front; [i–ii], half-title and illustration, verso blank; [iii–iv], title, on verso copyright notice, reservation of rights, and publication date; [v]–vi, Note, signed "H.J.," dated 1905; *Insert:* Publisher's Note, verso blank, not reckoned in pagination; [vii]–viii, contents; [ix]–xii, list of illustrations; [xiii–xiv], fly-title, verso blank; [1]–330, text; [331–332], divisional fly-title, verso blank; [333]–336, Index; [337–338], recto blank, on verso imprint, "The Riverside Press | Electrotyped and Printed by H. O. Houghton & Co. | Cambridge, Mass., U.S.A." Frontispiece, with tipped in tissue guard, not reckoned in pagination. 78 additional illustrations on text leaves.

Issued in dark blue-green cloth, lettered in yellow-green on front cover and in gilt on spine, decorative rule borders in yellow-green on front cover and spine, illustration of sailboat on the Thames in gilt and grey on front cover; off-white end-papers; top edge trimmed and gilt, other edges untrimmed.

Published 28 October 1905, at $3 in cloth, and at $5 in half polished Morocco, the first printing consisting of 2000 copies, advertised by the publisher as a "Holiday Edition." A Pocket Edition, printed from the original plates, was published 26 September 1914, at $1.75, bound in leather, the first (and only) printing consisting of 1000 copies.

The volume was designed by Bruce Rogers.

c. *First American edition, limited issue:*

ENGLISH HOURS [in red] | BY HENRY JAMES | WITH ILLUSTRATIONS BY | JOSEPH PENNELL | [illustration printed on white smooth stock, inserted] | CAMBRIDGE [in red] | PRINTED AT THE RIVERSIDE PRESS | MDCCCCV

($8\frac{3}{4} \times 5\frac{7}{8}$): [unsigned 1^{10} ($1_{2,6}$ inserted) 2–27^8 28^4], pp. [4], xiv, 338, and 44 unpaginated blank leaves on which illustrations are tipped. Crown 8vo.

Contents: uniform with ordinary issue, except for blank leaf [1_1], not reckoned in pagination, and the following insertions and eliminations: half-title printed in red and black, with imprint, "Large-Paper Edition"; limitation notice on verso of title-leaf, "Four Hundred Copies Printed"; printer's imprint on p. [338] eliminated.

Issued in white linen-finish half buckram, green paper boards, lettering in black and decorative bands and single-rules in red on white paper label on spine; white end-papers; all edges untrimmed.

Published 28 October 1905, simultaneously with ordinary issue, at $5, limited to 400 copies.

The illustrations appear in the same positions as those in the ordinary issue, but are printed on white smooth paper and are tipped in, either in the text or on blank leaves which form part of the signature gatherings but are unpaginated.

A63   THE AMERICAN SCENE   1907

a. *First edition:*

THE AMERICAN SCENE | BY | HENRY JAMES | LONDON | CHAPMAN AND HALL, LTD | 1907

($8\frac{9}{16} \times 5\frac{9}{16}$): [i]^4 1–29^8 30^4, pp. viii, 472. Demy 8vo.

Contents: [i–ii], half-title, verso blank; [iii–iv], title, on verso imprint,

A. ORIGINAL WORKS

"Richard Clay & Sons, Limited, | Bread Street Hill, E.C., and | Bungay, Suffolk."; [v]–vi, preface, signed "H.J."; [vii–viii], contents, verso blank; [1]–465, text; [466], imprint, as on p. [iv]; [467–472], advertisements, numbered pp. [1]–6.

Issued in burgundy red buckram, lettered in gilt on front cover and spine, double-rule border in blind on front cover, double-rule in gilt at top and bottom of spine; white end-papers; top edge gilt, other edges untrimmed (trimmed in some copies).

Published 30 January 1907, at 12/6, the first (and only) printing consisting of 1500 copies. Publication in England was delayed to coincide with the book's appearance in America; nevertheless it anticipated American publication by a week.

A secondary binding is noted, consisting of lighter red cross-grain cloth, lettered and blocked uniform with primary binding except for substitution of a single-rule border in blind on front cover, top edge trimmed but not gilt, other edges untrimmed. This is a remainder binding for 700 copies reported by the publisher as disposed of in 1913.

CONTENTS

I. *New England: An Autumn Impression*
   First appeared in the *North American Review*, April–June 1905.
II. *New York Revisited*
   First appeared in *Harper's Magazine*, February, March and May 1906.
III. *New York and the Hudson: A Spring Impression*
   First appeared in the *North American Review*, December 1905.
IV. *New York: Social Notes* [I and II]
   First appeared in the *North American Review*, January–February 1906.
   Part I only appeared also in the *Fortnightly Review*, February 1906.
V. *The Bowery and Thereabouts*
   First appeared here; no prior serialization.
VI. *The Sense of Newport*
   First appeared in *Harper's Magazine*, August 1906.
VII. *Boston*
   First appeared in the *North American Review* and the *Fortnightly Review*, March 1906.
VIII. *Concord and Salem*
   First appeared here; no prior serialization.

IX. *Philadelphia*
> First appeared in the *North American Review* and the *Fortnightly Review*, April 1906

X. *Baltimore*
> First appeared in the *North American Review*, August 1906.

XI. *Washington*
> First appeared in the *North American Review*, May–June 1906.

XII. *Richmond*
> First appeared, under the title "Richmond, Virginia," in the *Fortnightly Review*, November 1906.

XIII. *Charleston*
> First appeared here; no prior serialization.

XIV. *Florida*
> First appeared here; no prior serialization.

b. *First American edition:*

THE | AMERICAN SCENE | BY | HENRY JAMES | [publisher's device] | HARPER & BROTHERS PUBLISHERS | NEW YORK AND LONDON | MCMVII

$(8\frac{1}{8} \times 5\frac{3}{8})$: [i]⁴ [1]⁸ 2–28⁸, pp. [2], viii, 446. 12mo.

Contents: [1–2], blank leaf, not reckoned in pagination; [i–ii], title, on verso copyright notice, reservation of rights, and publication date; [iii–iv], contents, verso blank; v–vi, preface, dated 28 Sept., 1906, signed "H.J."; [vii–viii], fly-title, verso blank; 1–[443], text; [444], blank; [445–446], blank leaf.

Issued in cobalt blue vertical-ribbed cloth, lettered in gilt on front cover and spine (publisher's imprint in italics), decorative mirror panel in gilt on spine; white end-papers; top edge trimmed and gilt, other edges untrimmed.

Published 7 February 1907, at $3, the first printing consisting of 2500 copies.

A secondary binding is noted, issued in light blue cloth, lettered in black on front cover and spine (publisher's imprint in capitals), decorative mirror panel in black on spine; all edges trimmed, lacking gilt on top edge. Page size: $7\frac{13}{16} \times 5\frac{3}{16}$.

Section VII of the last essay, "Florida," which appears in the English edition, is eliminated in the American edition.

A64   THE NOVELS AND TALES 1907–09
OF HENRY JAMES
"NEW YORK EDITION"

a. *First edition, ordinary issue:*

Vol. I. *Roderick Hudson:*

RODERICK [in red] | HUDSON [in red] | BY | HENRY
JAMES | [ship and bridge device, in orange-tan and dull
brown, within blind impression] | NEW YORK | CHARLES
SCRIBNER'S SONS [in red] | 1907 [Entire title enclosed
within double-rule border]

($8\frac{5}{16} \times 5\frac{1}{2}$): [unsigned: 1^4 $2-35^8$], pp. [2], xxii, 528. 8vo.

Contents: binder's fly-leaf at front; [1–2], blank leaf, not reckoned in
pagination; [i–ii], series half-title, verso blank; [iii–iv], title, on verso
copyright notice and acknowledgment; v–[xx], preface, signed "Henry
James"; [xxi–xxii], fly-title, verso blank; 1–[527], text; [528], imprint,
"The Riverside Press | Cambridge . Massachusetts | U.S.A"; binder's
fly-leaf at back. Frontispiece portrait of James, with facsimile autograph on tissue-guard fly-leaf, tipped in, not reckoned in pagination.

Issued in smooth silky plum cloth, single-rule border and circled
monogram device in gilt on front cover, lettering and volume number
in gilt on spine; white end-papers; top edge trimmed and gilt, other
edges untrimmed.

A watermark monogram "H.J." appears on each text leaf, as well as on
any inserted binder's fly-leaves.

The remaining twenty-three volumes of the original issue are uniform
with Vol. I. All volumes excepting Vol. XVIII have a binder's fly-leaf
tipped in at the front. There are terminal binder's leaves only as noted
in collations.

II. *The American*: [unsigned: $1-2^2$ $3-37^8$], pp. xxiv, 544.

III. *The Portrait of A Lady* (Vol. 1): [unsigned: 1^2 $2-29^8$], pp.
xxii, 430.

IV. *The Portrait of A Lady* (Vol. 2): [unsigned: 1^2 $2-28^8$ 29^4], pp.
iv, 440.

V. *The Princess Casamassima* (Vol. 1): [unsigned: 1^2 $2-25^8$], pp.
xxiv, 364; binder's leaf at back.

VI. *The Princess Casamassima* (Vol. 2): [unsigned: 1^2 $2-28^8$], pp.
iv, 432; binder's leaf at back.

VII. *The Tragic Muse* (Vol. 1): [unsigned: 1^2 $2-25^8$ 26^6], pp. xxii, 378.

VIII. *The Tragic Muse* (Vol. 2): [unsigned: 1^2 $2-28^8$ 29^4 30^2], pp. iv, 444.

IX. *The Awkward Age*: [unsigned: 1^2 $2-36^8$ 37^4], pp. xxiv, 548.

X. *The Spoils of Poynton. A London Life. The Chaperon*: [unsigned: 1^2 $2-33^8$ 34^6], pp. xxvi, 502.

XI. *What Maisie Knew. In the Cage. The Pupil*: [unsigned: 1^2 $2-38^8$ 39^4], pp. xxiv, 580.

XII. *The Aspern Papers. The Turn of the Screw. The Liar. The Two Faces*: [unsigned: 1^2 $2-28^8$ 29^2], pp. xxvi, 414; binder's leaf at back.

XIII. *The Reverberator. Madame de Mauves. A Passionate Pilgrim. The Madonna of the Future. Louisa Pallant*: [unsigned: 1^2 $2-36^8$ 37^6], pp. xxiv, 552.

XIV. *Lady Barbarina. The Siege of London. An International Episode. The Pension Beaurepas. A Bundle of Letters. The Point of View*: [unsigned: 1^2 $2-40^8$ 41^2], pp. xxiv, 608; binder's leaf at back. James altered the original spelling of "Barberina" for this edition.

XV. *The Lesson of the Master. The Death of the Lion. The Next Time. The Figure in the Carpet. The Coxon Fund*: [unsigned: 1^2 2^8 (-2_1) $3-25^8$ 26^2], pp. xx, 370.

XVI. *The Author of Beltraffio. The Middle Years. Greville Fane. Broken Wings. The Tree of Knowledge. The Abasement of the Northmores. The Great Good Place. Four Meetings. Paste. Europe. Miss Gunton of Poughkeepsie. Fordham Castle*: [unsigned: 1^2 $2-28^8$ 29^4], pp. xiv, 430.

Fordham Castle first appeared in *Harper's Magazine*, December 1904. This was its first book appearance. Minor revisions between serial and book publication.

XVII. *The Altar of the Dead. The Beast in the Jungle. The Birthplace. The Private Life. Owen Wingrave. The Friends of the Friends. Sir Edmund Orme. The Real Right Thing. The Jolly Corner. Julia Bride*: [unsigned: 1^2 $2-36^8$ 37^6], pp. xxxii, 544.

The Friends of the Friends previously appeared under the title *The Way It Came*. *The Jolly Corner* and *Julia Bride* made their first book appearances here, slightly revised from serial publication. *The Jolly Corner* first appeared in the *English Review*, December 1908. *Julia Bride* first appeared in *Harper's Magazine*, March–April 1908.

XVIII. *Daisy Miller. Pandora. The Patagonia. The Marriages. The Real Thing. Brooksmith. The Beldonald Holbein. The Story in It. Flickerbridge. Mrs. Medwin*: [unsigned: 1^4 2^2 (inserted between $1_{3,4}$) $3-34^8$ 35^6], pp. [2], xxvi, 508.

XIX. *The Wings of the Dove* (Vol. 1): [unsigned: 1^2 2^2 $3-22^8$], pp. xxiv, 304.

XX. *The Wings of the Dove* (Vol. 2): [unsigned: 1^2 $2-26^8$ 27^4], pp. iv, 408.

XXI. *The Ambassadors* (Vol. 1): [unsigned: $1-2^2$ $3-21^8$], pp. xxiv, 288.

XXII. *The Ambassadors* (Vol. 2): [unsigned: 1^2 $2-21^8$ 22^4], pp. iv, 328; binder's leaf at back.

XXIII. *The Golden Bowl* (Vol. 1): [unsigned: 1^2 $2-27^8$ 28^6], pp. xxvi, 406.

XXIV. *The Golden Bowl* (Vol. 2): [unsigned: 1^2 $2-24^8$ 25^2], pp. iv, 372.

Published two volumes at a time between 14 December 1907 and 31 July 1909. Sold by subscription only, at $2 per volume in cloth. Also issued in half levant, at $4 per volume. The first printing of Vols. I–X consisted of 1500 copies each; the initial printing of the remaining volumes consisted of 1000 copies each.

As demand required it, additional quantities were reprinted from the original plates. In some impressions, all the preliminary leaves (including the text leaves immediately following, completing a signature) were printed on water-marked paper. The balance of the volume was printed on uniform Etherington laid paper lacking the watermark; in other impressions, only the first two leaves were printed on watermarked paper. Because of the smaller quantity of sheets printed for the first issue of Vols. XI–XXIV, it is not unusual to find sets in uniform first binding containing the watermark on all leaves in Vols. I–X and on preliminary leaves only in the remaining volumes. Several sets in later binding states have been noted with some volumes containing first impression watermarked sheets and other volumes containing later impression unwatermarked sheets.

Two secondary binding states are noted: (*a*) dull purple smooth fine-woven cloth; (*b*) uniform with (*a*) except for lacquered finish to cloth. The inclusion of binder's fly-leaves at the front of volumes in secondary issues is erratic.

Henry James wrote eighteen prefaces especially for the New York Edition, one to each of the novels, and one to each volume of tales.

Each volume contained a frontispiece from a photograph by Alvin Langdon Coburn. Revisions throughout are extensive.

In April 1918 two posthumous volumes were issued uniform with the original edition dated 1917 on title-page.

 XXV. *The Ivory Tower*: [unsigned: 1–23^8], pp. viii, 360.

XXVI. *The Sense of the Past*: [unsigned: 1–23^8], pp. viii, 360.

These were printed from plates of the first American edition (see A77 and A78). The publisher designed them as part of the edition and advertised it henceforth as being in 26 volumes. The frontispieces in these volumes are not, however, from the camera of Mr. Coburn.

A small quantity of sheets of *The Letters of Henry James* (see C4b) was issued in a binding uniform with the first issue binding of the New York Edition in 1920, but the volume was slightly larger in size, the sheets measuring $8\frac{3}{4}'' \times 5\frac{3}{4}''$ and the covers measuring $9'' \times 5\frac{7}{8}''$. A set of these volumes was acquired from Gordon Hollis in 1979 by the Rare Books Department of the Library of Congress.

b. *First edition, limited issue:*

This issue was printed from the same plates as the ordinary issue, on Ruisdael handmade paper, with a re-set half-title and title leaf. The half-title lacks the "New York Edition" imprint, and contains on the verso a limitation notice, "This edition is limited to one hundred and fifty-six copies. . . ." The title is lettered in red and black and the device is printed in white and two shades of brown. Page size: $9\frac{1}{4} \times 6$. Issued in cream half buckram, Italian handmade paper sides, lettered on spine in gilt on brown simulated-leather paper label.

Published simultaneously with ordinary issue, at $8 per volume. Vols. XXV and XXVI, as in the ordinary issue, were added in 1918.

Vols. III–VI carry a 1907 date on both title-page and copyright notice on verso, although the same volumes in the ordinary issue are dated 1908.

c. *First edition, English issue* (1908–1909):

This issue consisted of sheets of the ordinary issue of the American edition, with a new title-page bearing imprint: "Macmillan and Co."; bound in green buckram, ornamental devices in gilt on front cover and spine, lettered in gilt on spine.

Advertised as "Edition de Luxe." Vol. I was published 29 September 1908, the remaining volumes being issued 1908–1909, at 8/6 per volume. One hundred sets of sheets of each of the original 24 volumes were imported. The publisher reports that only a fraction of these was bound, the balance being used as package wrapping during the Second World War. Vols. IX and XI have been found, however,

dated 1913 on the title page, and a bookseller in South Africa has reported selling an entire set (with the watermark monogram) all
volumes dated 1913. This suggests that additional sheets were ordered
from Scribner at a later date, and that it was possibly these, rather than
the original issue, which served as wrapping.

Title-page dates are in several instances at variance with those in the
American edition, and have also been noted with variations within the
British issue itself. Vol. I appears with either (*a*) 1907 title, the prelims
being printed on stock heavier than the text leaves, and with copyright
notices and imprint "Published under special arrangement with
Houghton, Mifflin & Co." on verso, or (*b*) 1908 title, on stock uniform
with text leaves, lacking both copyright notices and imprint on verso.
Vols. VII and IX–XII have also been noted with 1908 titles and with
blank versos. A full set of 24 volumes was deposited for copyright in
the British Museum on 23 March 1910, of which Vol. 1 is dated 1907,
Vols. III, IV, XIII, and XIV are dated 1908, and the remaining volumes
dated 1909; all 24 volumes here contain copyright notices and imprint
on versos of title-leaves.

Volumes XXV and XXVI were not included later in this issue.

A65   VIEWS AND REVIEWS   1908

a. First edition, ordinary issue:

VIEWS | AND REVIEWS | BY | HENRY JAMES | NOW
FIRST COLLECTED | INTRODUCTION BY | LE ROY
PHILLIPS | COMPILER OF | ''A BIBLIOGRAPHY OF THE
WRITINGS | OF HENRY JAMES'' | BOSTON | THE BALL
PUBLISHING COMPANY | 1908

($7\frac{1}{2} \times 5\frac{1}{8}$): [unsigned: 1–16⁸], pp. xiv, 242. 12mo.

Contents: [i–ii], half-title, verso blank; [iii–iv], title, on verso copyright notice; v–ix, Introduction by Le Roy Phillips, dated Boston,
April 10, 1908; [x], blank; [xi–xii], contents, verso blank; [xiii–xiv],
divisional fly-title, on verso notes on first essay; 1–241, text; [242],
blank.

Issued in green vertical-ribbed cloth, single-rule border in gilt on front
cover, lettering and three rules in gilt on spine; white end-papers; top
edge gilt, other edges untrimmed.

Published May 1908, at $1.50. The *New York Times* announced, 9
May 1908, the publisher "will begin to issue in a few days." Reviewed
in the *Boston Transcript*, 27 May.

A. ORIGINAL WORKS

The size of the edition cannot be definitely ascertained, but Mr Phillips believes it to have been 1000 copies.

CONTENTS

The Novels of George Eliot
> First appeared in the *Atlantic Monthly*, October 1866.

On a Drama of Robert Browning
> First appeared, as a review of Browning's *The Inn Album*, in the *Nation*, 20 January 1876.

Swinburne's Essays
> First appeared, as a review of Swinburne's *Essays and Studies*, in the *Nation*, 29 July 1875.

The Poetry of William Morris
> First appeared, as reviews of Morris's *The Life and Death of Jason*, in the *North American Review*, October 1867, and of *The Earthly Paradise*, in the *Nation*, 9 July 1868.

Matthew Arnold's Essays
> First appeared, as a review of Arnold's *Essays in Criticism*, in the *North American Review*, July 1865.

Mr. Walt Whitman
> First appeared, as a review of Whitman's *Drum - Taps*, in the *Nation*, 16 November 1865.

The Poetry of George Eliot
> First appeared, as reviews of George Eliot's *The Spanish Gypsy*, in the *North American Review*, October 1868, and of *The Legend of Jubal, and Other Poems*, in the *North American Review*, October 1874.

The Limitations of Dickens
> First appeared, as a review of Dickens's *Our Mutual Friend*, in the *Nation*, 21 December 1865.

Tennyson's Drama
> First appeared, as reviews of Tennyson's *Queen Mary*, in the *Galaxy*, September 1875, and of *Harold*, in the *Nation*, 18 January 1877.

Contemporary Notes on Whistler vs. Ruskin
> First appeared, as untitled notes, in the *Nation*, 19 December 1878 and 13 February 1879.

A Note on John Burroughs
> First appeared, as a review of Burroughs's *Winter Sunshine*, in the *Nation*, 27 January 1876.

Mr. Kipling's Early Stories
> First appeared as a critical introduction to Kipling's *Mine Own People* (see B8).

b. *First edition, limited issue:*

Collation and contents uniform with ordinary issue except for
limitation notice on verso of title-leaf: "This edition is limited to one
hundred and sixty copies . . ."

Issued in white parchment wrapper over flexible boards, single-rule
border in gilt on front cover, lettered and ruled in gilt on dark red-
brown paper label on spine; white end-papers; all edges untrimmed.

Published simultaneously with ordinary issue, at $2.50.

A66   JULIA BRIDE   1909

First separate edition:

JULIA BRIDE [in red] | BY | HENRY JAMES | ILLUSTRATED
BY | W. T. SMEDLEY | [publisher's device] | NEW YORK
AND LONDON | HARPER & BROTHERS PUBLISHERS [in
red] | MCMIX [Entire title enclosed within a triple-rule
border, the inner rule black, the two outer rules red]

$(7\frac{7}{8} \times 5\frac{1}{16})$: $[1]^8$ 2–6^8, pp. viii, 88. Post 8vo.

Contents: [i–ii], blank leaf; [iii–iv], title, on verso copyright notice,
reservation of rights, and publication date; [v–vi], list of illustrations,
verso blank; [vii–viii], fly-title, verso blank; 1–[84], text; [85–88], two
blank leaves. Frontispiece, with tissue guard, and three illustrations
tipped in, not reckoned in pagination.

Issued in claret fine-wave-grain cloth, lettered in gilt on front cover
and spine, heart device in gilt on spine, heart-and-ribbon decorative
border within heavy-rule border panel in blind on front cover;
publisher's imprint, sans serif, $\frac{1}{10}''$ high on spine; white end-papers;
top edge gilt, other edges untrimmed.

Published 23 September 1909, at $1.25, the first printing consisting of
4000 copies. No separate English edition.

A variant binding state noted, issued in maroon diagonal-fine-ribbed
cloth, with serif-lettered publisher's imprint. No priority established.

Three secondary binding states also noted: (*a*) tan linen-grain cloth,
lettering and flower device in brown on front cover, lettering and
heart-and-flower devices in brown on spine; lacking gilt top, all edges
trimmed; page size, $7\frac{3}{4} \times 4\frac{7}{8}$; (*b*) greenish-tan paper boards, lettered
in dark brown on front cover, lettering and heart-and-flower devices
in brown on spine, publisher's imprint on spine $\frac{5}{64}''$ high; lacking

gilt top, all edges trimmed; page size: $7\frac{5}{16}''\times 4\frac{13}{16}''$; (c) red half cloth, buff paper boards, lettered in black on front cover and spine, heart device in black on spine, publisher's imprint on spine $\frac{5}{64}''$ high, initial letter "H" of imprint being $\frac{3}{32}''$ high; lacking gilt top, all edges trimmed; page size: $7\frac{13}{32}''\times 4\frac{15}{16}''$. Another secondary binding has been reported, in plum cloth, lettered in black on front cover and spine, lacking gilt top.

British Museum copy, deposited 24 September 1909, is presumably a copyright pre-publication state, bound identically with first issue but with blank front cover, off-white end-papers, and lacking gilt top edge. This copy, as well as all copies designed for export (including the author's, now in the Houghton Library), has a hand-stamped imprint, "Printed in U.S. of America", immediately below date of publication on verso of title-leaf.

First appeared in *Harper's Magazine*, March–April 1908. First book appearance in *The Novels and Tales of Henry James* ("New York Edition"), Vol. XVII (see A64a). Minor revisions between first and second book appearances.

A67   ITALIAN HOURS   1909

a. *First edition:*

ITALIAN HOURS [in red-brown] | BY | HENRY JAMES | AUTHOR OF "ENGLISH HOURS," "A LITTLE TOUR IN FRANCE," ETC. | ILLUSTRATED BY JOSEPH PENNELL | [publisher's device] | LONDON | WILLIAM HEINEMANN [in red-brown] | 1909

$(10\frac{3}{8}\times 8)$: [a]^4 b^2 A–Z^8 2A^4, pp. xii, 376. Demy 4to.

Contents: [i–ii], half-title, on verso list of "Other Works Illustrated by Joseph Pennell"; [iii–iv], title, on verso copyright notice; v–[vi], Preface, dated 1909, signed "H.J.", verso blank; vii–viii, contents; ix–xi, list of illustrations; [xii], "Errata"; [1]–364, text; [365–366], divisional fly-title, verso blank; 367–376, Index; at bottom of p. 376 imprint, "Printed by Ballantyne, Hanson & Co. | Edinburgh & London". 32 colour plates, with fly-title tissue guards, and 32 sepia plates tipped in, not reckoned in pagination. The colour plates are mounted on leaves, framed within single-rules against panels in pale grey-green.

Issued in olive-green buckram, lettered in gilt on front cover and

A. ORIGINAL WORKS

spine, medallion in gilt on front cover, single-rule border in blind on front and back covers, publisher's device in blind on back cover, three fleur-de-lys devices and single wide-rule at top and bottom in gilt on spine; white end-papers; top edge gilt, other edges untrimmed.

Published 28 October 1909, at 25/-, the first (and only) printing consisting of 1000 copies.

300 sets of sheets were remaindered to Heffer of Cambridge, on 31 August 1916, and were bound by this firm. These copies were issued in dull green linen-grain cloth, lettered and blocked in imitation of the primary binding, but with medallion in blind on back cover in place of publisher's device, sans-serif publisher's imprint on spine in place of original serif imprint, and blue-grey-stained top edges.

CONTENTS

In the Preface James states, "I have introduced a few passages that speak for a later and in some cases a frequently repeated vision of the places and scenes in question. I have not hesitated to amend my text, expressively, wherever it seemed urgently to ask for this."

The following essays appear in book form for the first time:

Casa Alvisi
> First appeared, as a Prefatory Note to Mrs Katharine de Kay Bronson's "Browning in Venice," in the *Cornhill Magazine*, and as a separate essay, under the title "The Late Mrs. Arthur Bronson," in the *Critic*, both in February 1902.

Two Old Houses and Three Young Women
> First appeared in the *Independent*, 7 September 1899.

Written expressly for this edition:
A Few Other Roman Neighbourhoods
Siena Early and Late: Part II
Other Tuscan Cities
The Saint's Afternoon and Others: Parts VI and VII

The following essays had previously appeared in book form:

In *Transatlantic Sketches:*
> *Venice: An Early Impression* (under the title "From Venice to Strasburg"); *From Chambéry to Milan; The Old Saint-Gothard* (under the title "The St. Gothard"); *A Roman Holiday; Roman Rides; Roman Neighbourhoods; The After-Season in Rome; From A Roman Note-Book; A Chain of Cities;* the first part of *Siena Early and Late* (under the title "Siena"); *The Autumn in Florence; Florentine Notes; Tuscan Cities; Ravenna;*

In *Portraits of Places*:
   Venice; Italy Revisited.
In *Great Streets of the World*:
   The Grand Canal.
In *The May Book*:
   The Saint's Afternoon and Others: Parts I to V (under the title
   "The Saint's Afternoon").

b. *First American edition:*

ITALIAN HOURS | BY HENRY JAMES | WITH ILLUSTRA-
TIONS IN COLOR | BY JOSEPH PENNELL | [publisher's
device, in red] | BOSTON AND NEW YORK | HOUGHTON
MIFFLIN COMPANY | MDCCCCIX

$(10\frac{9}{16} \times 8)$: [unsigned: 1^5 (1_3 inserted) 2^1 $3–33^8$ 34^4 35^1], pp. [2], x,
506. 4to.

Contents: [1–2], blank leaf, not reckoned in pagination; [i–ii], half-
title, verso blank; [iii–iv], title, on verso copyright notice and publication date; [v–vi], Preface, signed "H.J.", undated; verso blank; vii–
[viii], contents; ix–[x], list of illustrations; [1–2], fly-title, verso blank;
3–[505], text; [506], imprint, "The Riverside Press | Cambridge .
Massachusetts | U.S.A"; binder's fly-leaf at back. Thirty-two colour
plates, tipped in, not reckoned in pagination.

Issued in orange-brown cloth, lettering in cloth colour surrounded by
mosaic pattern and multi-ruled panels in gilt and varying shades of
green on front cover, lettering in gilt and mosaic pattern in gilt and
pale and dark green on spine; off-white end-papers; top edge trimmed
and gilt, other edges untrimmed.

Published 20 November 1909, at $7.50, boxed, the first printing con-
sisting of 1500 copies. The 32 colour plates were purchased from
Heinemann. This edition lacks the 32 additional sepia plates, as well
as the index, included in the English edition.

A68   THE FINER GRAIN   1910

a. *First edition:*

THE FINER GRAIN | BY | HENRY JAMES | NEW YORK |
CHARLES SCRIBNER'S SONS | 1910

$(7\frac{7}{16} \times 4\frac{13}{16})$: [unsigned: $1–20^8$], pp. viii, 312. 8vo.

Contents: [i–ii], recto blank, on verso list of "Books by Henry James"; [iii–iv], half-title, verso blank; [v–vi], title, on verso copyright notice, publication date, and printer's device; [vii–viii], contents, verso blank; [1–2], divisional fly-title, verso blank; 3–312, text.

Issued in dull olive-brown smooth sateen cloth, lettered within single-rule frame in gilt on front cover, lettering and flame device in gilt on spine; white end-papers; top edge trimmed and gilt, other edges untrimmed.

Published 6 October 1910, at $1.25.

CONTENTS

Minor revisions between serial and book publication.

The Velvet Glove
> First appeared in the *English Review*, March 1909.

Mora Montravers
> First appeared in the *English Review*, August–September 1909.

A Round of Visits
> First appeared in the *English Review*, April–May 1910.

Crapy Cornelia
> First appeared in *Harper's Magazine*, October 1909.

The Bench of Desolation
> First appeared in *Putnam's Magazine*, October 1909–January 1910.

b. *First English edition:*

THE | FINER GRAIN | BY | HENRY JAMES | METHUEN & CO. LTD. | 36 ESSEX STREET W.C. | LONDON [1910]

$(7\frac{3}{8} \times 5)$: a⁴ 1–19⁸ 20², pp. viii, 308, followed by 32-page catalogue of advertisements. Crown 8vo.

Contents: [i–ii], signature on recto, verso blank; [iii–iv], half-title, on verso list of titles "By the Same Author"; [v–vi], title, on verso, "First Published in 1910"; vii–[viii], contents, verso blank; 1–307, text; [308], imprint, "Edinburgh | Colstons Limited | Printers"; catalogue dated August 1910 (see note below).

Issued in rust-brown linen-grain cloth, lettered in gilt on front cover and spine, single-rule border in blind on front cover, entwined-leaf ornament and double-rule at top and bottom in gilt on spine; white end-papers; top edge trimmed, other edges untrimmed.

Published 13 October 1910, at 6/-, the first printing consisting of 1500 copies, divided between domestic and colonial issues.

To enthusiasts of states and issues, the advertisements in this volume offer considerable interest. No less than three distinct datings of catalogues are to be found in copies of the first edition: August 1910, September 1910, and October 1910. No priority has been established; it is doubtful if any ever can be. James's personal copy, for example, contains September dating, while an advance review copy has been noted with October dating. It is likely that the latest date (as both Muir and Carter, among others, have pointed out) will be found in the earliest issue. It is also possible that the binder may have inserted three datings simultaneously.

The text of the dust-jacket was taken from James's outline of the book to the publisher (quoted in full in E. V. Lucas, *Reading, Writing, and Remembering*; see B38): " 'The Finer Grain' consists of a series of five stories, the central figure in each is involved, as Mr. James loves his characters to be, in one of the tangles of highly civilized existence. By the 'finer grain' the author means, in his own phrase, 'a peculiar accessibility to surprise, to curiosity, to mystification or attraction—in other words, to moving experience.' It is needless to add that the book exhibits the most delicate comedy throughout."

A69   THE HENRY JAMES YEAR   1911
BOOK

a. *First edition:*

THE | HENRY JAMES | YEAR BOOK | [rule] | SELECTED AND ARRANGED BY | EVELYN GARNAUT SMALLEY | WITH AN INTRODUCTION BY | HENRY JAMES AND WILLIAM DEAN HOWELLS. | RICHARD G. BADGER: BOSTON [Entire title enclosed within single-rule border, in red-brown] [1911]

$(7\frac{3}{8} \times 5)$: [unsigned: 1–15^8 16^2], pp. 244 (unpaginated), on India tint paper. 12mo.

Contents: [1–2], half-title, verso blank; [3–4], title, on verso copyright notice, reservation of rights, acknowledgments, and imprint, "The Gorham Press, Boston, U.S.A."; [5–6], Dedication, verso blank; [7–8], Preface by Evelyn Garnaut Smalley, verso blank; [9],

Introduction: I, "The Author to the Public", a letter from Henry James, dated London, June 16, 1910; [10–11], Introduction: II, "One of the Public to the Author", a letter from W. D. Howells; [12], blank; [13–14], divisional fly-title, verso blank; [15–243], text; [244], blank. Text leaves ruled and bordered in red-brown. Photogravure frontispiece, with tissue guard, tipped in, not reckoned in pagination.

Issued (*a*) in dark rose sand-grain flexible cloth, lettering and leaf devices in gilt on front cover and spine, facsimile autographs of James and Howells in gilt on front cover, single-rule border in blind on front cover, publisher's device in blind on back cover; white end-papers; top edge gilt, other edges trimmed. Red ribbon marker inserted.

Issued (*b*) in binding uniform with (*a*); title-page varies, however, there being no full-stop after HOWELLS, and balance of the title reading "[rule, in red-brown] | [publisher's device] | [rule, in red-brown] | RICHARD G. BADGER | THE GORHAM PRESS | BOSTON"

Issued (*c*) in limp leather. No copy available for examination.

Published September 1911, at $1.50 in flexible cloth and $2 in limp leather. Noted in the "Weekly Record of New Books," *Publishers' Weekly*, 16 September 1911. Gibson & Arms erroneously assigned a 1912 publication date.

b. *First edition, English issue* (1912):

Issued from sheets of the first edition, bound in burgundy fine-woven cloth, lettered and blocked uniform with the American edition except for addition of divisional single-rules in blind on front cover and single-rule border and divisional rules in blind on spine, with substitution of British publisher's imprint on spine. The title-leaf is a cancel, uniform with issue (*b*) of the American edition, substituting British publisher's imprint: "LONDON | J. M. DENT & SONS, LTD. | COVENT GARDEN", verso blank. Page size: $7\frac{7}{16} \times 5$, Crown 8vo.

Published 24 October 1912, at 3/6, the issue consisting of 850 copies.

A70   THE OUTCRY   1911

a. *First edition* (*English*):

THE OUTCRY | BY | HENRY JAMES | METHUEN & CO. LTD. | 36 ESSEX STREET W.C. | LONDON [1911]

($7\frac{1}{2} \times 4\frac{15}{16}$): a² 1–19⁸ 20⁴, pp. iv, 312, followed by 32 page catalogue of advertisements. Crown 8vo.

Contents: [i–ii], half-title, on verso list of titles "By the Same Author"; [iii–iv], title, on verso imprint, "First Published in 1911"; [1–2], divisional fly-title, verso blank; 3–311, text; [312], imprint, "Edinburgh | Colstons Limited | Printers"; catalogue dated August 1911. Issued in green rough-linen-grain cloth, lettered in gilt on front cover and spine, single-rule border in blind on front cover, entwined-leaf ornament and double-rule at top and bottom in gilt on spine; white end-papers; top edge trimmed, other edges untrimmed.

Published 5 October 1911, simultaneously with American edition, at 6/-, the first printing consisting of 2000 copies.

As in the English edition of *The Finer Grain* (A68b), the text of the dust-jacket was derived from James's own prospectus for the book written for the publisher. Whereas the earlier text was revised, quoting James only briefly, the statement on the jacket of *The Outcry* appears to be entirely his. It reads: "'The Outcry' deals with a question sharply brought home of late to the conscience of English Society— that of the degree in which the fortunate owners of precious and hitherto transmitted works of art hold them in trust, as it were, for the nation, and may themselves, as lax guardians, be held to account by public opinion. Mr. Henry James's study of the larger morality of the matter, if we may so call it, and which is the case of a lax rather than a jealous guardian, becomes conspicuous and acute. Hence springs the drama, almost a national as well as a personal crisis—a rapid, precipitated action, moving through difficulties and dangers to a happy issue."

First appeared in this edition; no prior serialization.

b. *First edition (American)*:

THE OUTCRY | BY | HENRY JAMES | NEW YORK | CHARLES SCRIBNER'S SONS | 1911

$(7\frac{1}{2} \times 4\frac{7}{8})$: [unsigned: 1–16⁸ 17⁶], pp. vi, 262. 8vo.

Contents: [i–ii], recto blank, on verso list of "Books by Henry James"; [iii–iv], half-title, verso blank; [v–vi], title, on verso copyright notice, publication date, and printer's device; [1–2], divisional fly-title, verso blank; 3–261, text; [262], blank.

Issued in dull olive-brown smooth sateen cloth, lettered within single-rule frame in gilt on front cover, lettering and flame device in gilt on spine; white end-papers; top edge trimmed and gilt, other edges untrimmed.

Published 5 October 1911, simultaneously with English edition, at $1.25.

Although verso of title-leaf carries imprint, "Published September, 1911", publication was delayed at the request of J. B. Pinker, HJ's agent, who was attempting through Paul R. Reynolds, New York literary agent, to arrange for serialization. Scribner's agreed to hold back publication; there was, however, no serial appearance of the novel.

A71   A SMALL BOY AND OTHERS   1913

a. *First edition:*

A SMALL BOY | AND OTHERS | BY | HENRY JAMES | NEW YORK | CHARLES SCRIBNER'S SONS | 1913

$(8\frac{3}{16} \times 5\frac{1}{2})$: [unsigned: 1–26^8 27^6], pp. viii, 420. 8vo.

Contents: [i–ii], recto blank, on verso list of "Books by Henry James"; [iii–iv], half-title, verso blank; [v–vi], title, on verso copyright notice, publication date, and printer's device; [vii–viii], fly-title, verso blank; 1–419, text; [420], blank. Frontispiece portrait of HJ Sr. and Jr., from a daguerreotype by Mathew Brady (1854), with tissue guard, tipped in, not reckoned in pagination.

Issued in dull olive-brown smooth sateen cloth, lettered within single-rule panel in gilt on front cover, lettered in gilt on spine; white endpapers; top edge gilt, other edges untrimmed.

Published 29 March 1913, at $2.50.

In the first issue, seven James titles and the New York Edition are listed on p. [ii]. On 19 April 1913 James wrote to Scribner's regretting their failure to insert an "In Preparation" notice for *Notes of a Son and Brother*: "This indication would have been in a considerable degree explanatory of the First Instalment character of the Book, accounting for certain omissions, postponements and other provisional matters." (Unpublished letter, Scribner archives.) The publisher immediately inserted into all remaining copies of the first impression a cancel leaf, [1_1], reading: "By Henry James | [rule] | A Small Boy and Others | In preparation | Notes of A Son and Brother".

b. *First English edition:*

A SMALL BOY | AND OTHERS | BY | HENRY JAMES | MAC-MILLAN AND CO., LIMITED | ST. MARTIN'S STREET, LONDON | 1913

$(8\frac{13}{16} \times 5\frac{5}{8})$: [A]^2 B–2E^8 2F^4, pp. iv, 440. 8vo.

Contents: [i–ii], half-title, on verso publisher's device and addresses; [iii–iv], title, on verso copyright notice; 1–436, text; at bottom of p. 436 imprint, "Printed by R. & R. Clark, Limited, Edinburgh."; [437–438], advertisements; [439–440], blank. Frontispiece, uniform with American edition.

Issued in dark blue smooth cloth, double-rule in blind at top and bottom of front and back covers, lettering and double-rule at top and bottom in gilt on spine; white end-papers; all edges untrimmed.

Published 1 April 1913, at 12/-, the first printing consisting of 1000 copies.

A second issue of the first impression is noted, containing an inserted leaf between 2F$_{2,3}$: imprint on recto, "In Preparation | By the Same Author | Notes of | A Son and Brother" (enclosed within a single-rule panel), verso blank. As in the American edition, this was done at the special request of the author.

A72　　　NOTES OF A SON AND　　1914
　　　　　　　　BROTHER

a. *First edition:*

NOTES OF A SON AND BROTHER | BY | HENRY JAMES | ILLUSTRATED | NEW YORK | CHARLES SCRIBNER'S SONS | 1914

$(8\frac{3}{16} \times 5\frac{1}{2})$: [unsigned: 1–33^8], pp. x, 518. 8vo.

Contents: [i–ii], recto blank, on verso list of titles "By Henry James"; [iii–iv], half-title, verso blank; [v–vi], title, on verso copyright notice, publication date, and printer's device; [vii–viii], list of illustrations, verso blank; [ix–x], fly-title, verso blank; 1–515, text; [516], blank; [517–518], blank leaf. Frontispiece, with tissue guard, and five illustrations tipped in, not reckoned in pagination.

Issued in dull olive-brown smooth sateen cloth, lettered within single-rule panel in gilt on front cover, lettered in gilt on spine; white end-papers; top edge trimmed and gilt, other edges trimmed.

Published 7 March 1914, at $2.50, the first printing consisting of 3000 copies. Brussel gives the British edition priority over the American, stating that the publishers report publication date as October 1914. The Scribner copyright records and library copy of the book, however, both record 7 March as formal date of publication.

b. *First English edition:*

NOTES | OF | A SON & BROTHER | BY | HENRY JAMES | MACMILLAN AND CO., LIMITED | ST. MARTIN'S STREET, LONDON | 1914

$(8\frac{13}{16} \times 5\frac{5}{8})$: [A]⁴ B–2H⁸ [2I]¹, pp. viii, 482. 8vo.

Contents: [i–ii], half-title, on verso title of work "By the Same Author"; [iii–iv], recto blank, on verso publisher's device; [v–vi], title, on verso copyright notice; vii–[viii], list of illustrations, verso blank; 1–479, text; at bottom of p. 479 imprint, "Printed by R. & R. Clark, Limited, Edinburgh."; [480], blank; [481–482], advertisements. Frontispiece and five illustrations, uniform with American edition.

Issued in dark blue smooth cloth, double-rule in blind at top and bottom of front and back covers, lettering and double-rule at top and bottom in gilt on spine; white end-papers; all edges untrimmed.

Published 13 March 1914, at 12/-, the first (and only) printing consisting of 1250 copies.

The illustrations, printed for the American edition and imported for the British edition, are smaller than text page size, measuring $8\frac{3}{16} \times 5\frac{1}{2}$.

A73   NOTES ON NOVELISTS   1914

a. *First edition:*

NOTES ON NOVELISTS [in red] | WITH | SOME OTHER NOTES | BY | HENRY JAMES | [publisher's device] | MCMXIV | J. M. DENT & SONS LTD. [in red] | ALDINE HOUSE, BEDFORD ST., W.C.

$(8\frac{3}{16} \times 5\frac{7}{8})$: [A]⁸ B–Z⁸, pp. viii, 360. Small demy 8vo.

Contents: [i–ii], half-title, verso blank; [iii–iv], title, verso blank; v–vi, Preface, signed "H.J."; vii–[viii], contents, verso blank; [1]–360, text; at bottom of p. 360 imprint, "The Temple Press, Printers, Letchworth".

Issued in dull green rough-linen-grain cloth, publisher's device and double-rule border in blind on front cover, lettering and flower device in gilt on spine; white end-papers; top edge trimmed and (*a*) green- or (*b*) brown-stained other edges untrimmed (trimmed in some copies).

Published 13 October 1914, at 6/-, the first (and only) printing consisting of 1100 copies. Price increased to 7/6 early in 1915, and later (1919 or 1920) to 9/6.

CONTENTS

The dates affixed to several of the essays are at variance with dates of serialization and, in some instances, with the subject-matter. For example, the essay on Serao is so dated as to appear to have been written after date of publication.

Robert Louis Stevenson, 1894

First appeared in the *North American Review*, January 1900.

Emile Zola, 1902

First appeared in the *Atlantic Monthly*, August 1903.

Gustave Flaubert, 1902

First appeared, 1902, as an Introduction to a translation of *Madame Bovary* (see B22).

Honoré de Balzac, 1902

First appeared, 1902, as an Introduction to a translation of *Deux Jeunes Mariées* (*The Two Young Brides*) (see B21).

Honoré de Balzac, 1913

First appeared, under the title "Balzac," in *The Times Literary Supplement*, 19 June 1913.

George Sand, 1897

First appeared, under the title "She and He: Recent Documents," in the *Yellow Book*, January 1897.

George Sand, 1899

First appeared, under the title "George Sand: the New Life," in the *North American Review*, April 1902.

George Sand, 1914

First appeared, as a review of Vol. III of Karénine's *George Sand, Sa Vie et Ses Oeuvres*, in the *Quarterly Review*, April 1914.

Gabriele D'Annunzio, 1902

First appeared in the *Quarterly Review*, April 1904.

Matilde Serao, 1902

First appeared in the *North American Review*, March 1901.

The New Novel, 1914

First appeared, under the title "The Younger Generation," in *The Times Literary Supplement*, 19 March and 2 April 1914. Extended and revised for book publication.

Dumas the Younger, 1895

First appeared in the *New York Herald* and the *Boston Herald*, 23 February 1896; also appeared, under the title "On the Death of Dumas the Younger," in the *New Review*, March 1896.

A. ORIGINAL WORKS

The Novel in "The Ring and the Book," 1912

> First appeared in the *Transactions of the Royal Society of Literature*, Second Series, XXXI, Part IV, 1912. For first book appearance, in *Browning's Centenary*, 1912, see B31. A revised text appeared in the *Quarterly Review*, July 1912, reprinted in *Living Age*, 24 August 1912. The later text is reproduced here (see D564).

An American Art-Scholar: Charles Eliot Norton, 1908

> First appeared in the *Burlington Magazine*, January 1909.

London Notes, January, 1897

> Portion of a larger article which first appeared, under the heading "London," in *Harper's Weekly*, 6 February 1897.

London Notes, June, 1897

> Portion of a larger article which first appeared, under the heading "London," in *Harper's Weekly*, 26 June 1897.

London Notes, July, 1897

> First appeared, under the heading "London," in *Harper's Weekly*, 31 July 1897.

London Notes, August, 1897

> First appeared, under the heading "London," in *Harper's Weekly*, 21 August 1897.

b. *First American edition:*

NOTES ON NOVELISTS | WITH SOME OTHER NOTES | BY | HENRY JAMES | NEW YORK | CHARLES SCRIBNER'S SONS | 1914

($8\frac{1}{8} \times 5\frac{1}{2}$): [unsigned: 1–29^8], pp. viii, 456. 8vo.

Contents: [i–ii], half-title, on verso list of titles "By Henry James"; [iii–iv], title, on verso copyright notice, publication date, and printer's device; v–vi, contents; [vii–viii], fly-title, verso blank; 1–455, text; [456], blank.

Issued in dull olive-brown smooth sateen cloth, lettered in gilt on front cover and spine; egg-shell end-papers; top edge trimmed and gilt, other edges untrimmed.

Published 14 October 1914, at $2.50, the first printing consisting of 2000 copies.

The American edition lacks the brief preface by James included in the English edition. In the table of contents no date is affixed to the essays on Stevenson, Zola, Flaubert and Serao. The other essays are dated as in the English edition.

a. *First uniform edition:*

The Uniform Tales of Henry James were issued by Martin Secker in
fourteen volumes over a period of six years. In all instances but one
the text used was that of the New York Edition (1907–09). The sole
exception was *Glasses*, the text of which had been revised by James
especially for the Secker edition. As this volume constitutes a first
revised edition, it is here collated as the representative volume of the
Uniform Tales, although it was issued more than a year after the
edition was first undertaken.

GLASSES | BY HENRY JAMES | [leaf device] | LONDON:
MARTIN SECKER | NUMBER FIVE JOHN STREET ADELPHI
[1916]

($6\frac{5}{8} \times 4\frac{1}{4}$): [A]⁸ B–F⁸, pp. 96. F'cap 8vo.

Contents: [1–2], half-title, on verso list of titles "Uniform With This
Volume"; [3–4], title, on verso publication date and revision note;
5–[93], text; [94], blank; [95–96], imprint, "Printed by | Knight's West
Norwood", verso blank.

Issued in dull chocolate-brown linen-grain cloth, lettering and leaf
device in gilt on front cover and spine, two single-rules in gilt at top
and bottom of spine, double-rule border and two vertical divider rules
in blind on front and back covers; white end-papers; top edge trimmed
and gilt, other edges untrimmed.

Published September 1916, at 2/6, the first printing consisting of 1000
copies.

The revision note, p. [4], reads: " 'Glasses' is not included in the
Definitive Edition: it first appeared in the volume 'Embarrassments,'
published by Mr William Heinemann in 1897. The text was revised
by the author for this edition very shortly before his death."

The remaining volumes in the edition were issued as follows:

April 1915:   *The Turn of the Screw*. [A]⁸ B–N⁸, pp. 208.
1500 copies printed.
The Lesson of the Master. [A]⁸ B–G⁸ H⁴, pp. 120.
1500 copies printed.
The Aspern Papers. [A]⁸ B–L⁸, pp. 176.
1500 copies printed.

Daisy Miller. [A]^8 B–G^8 H^4, pp. 120.
1500 copies printed.

November 1915: *The Death of the Lion.* [A]^8 B–E^8, pp. iv, 76. [A$_1$]
and E$_8$ serve as paste-down end-papers.
1500 copies printed.
The Coxon Fund. [A]^8 B–G^8, pp. 112.
1500 copies printed.
The Reverberator. [A]^8 B–Q^8 R^2, pp. 260.
1500 copies printed.
The Beast in the Jungle. [A]^8 B–E^8 F^4, pp. 88.
1500 copies printed.

September 1916: *The Altar of the Dead.* [A]^8 B–D^8 E^4 F^2, pp. 76.
1500 copies printed.
The Figure in the Carpet. [A]^8 B–E^8, pp. 80.
1000 copies printed.
The Pupil. [A]^8 B–E^8 F^4, pp. 88.
1000 copies printed.

February 1919: *The Jolly Corner.* [A]^8 B–D^8 E^4, pp. 72.
1000 copies printed, at 3/6. Verso of title-leaf
erroneously records 1918 publication date.

February 1920: *In the Cage.* [A]^8 B–L^8, pp. 176.
1000 copies printed, at 3/6. Verso of title-leaf
erroneously records 1919 publication date.

Colour of binding cloth of individual volumes issued varies considerably, ranging from orange-brown to dark violet-brown.

The edition was published with James's sanction "on [Secker's] distinct understanding, please, that he conform literatim and punctuatim to [the New York Edition] text. It is vital that he adhere to that authentic punctuation—to the last comma or rather, more essentially, no-comma." (Unpublished letter, HJ to J. B. Pinker, 11 September 1914, in the Yale University Library.)

b. *First American issue* (1917–18):

Bound copies of six titles (200 copies each) were made up with the imprint of Le Roy Phillips, in May 1917, but the shipment was lost at sea owing to enemy action. Replacement copies were issued as follows:

September 1917: *The Turn of the Screw.* 400 copies.
This volume had not been included in the earlier shipment owing to shortage of stock. Sheets were supplied from a second impression.

December 1917: *The Lesson of the Master*. 200 copies.
　　　　　　The Aspern Papers. 200 copies.
　　　　　　The Figure in the Carpet. 200 copies.
　　　　　　Glasses. 200 copies.
　　　　　　The Pupil. 200 copies.
January 1918:　*The Reverberator*. 200 copies.

All copies contain a re-set title-leaf, the publisher's imprint on the recto reading: "Le Roy Phillips | Boston", the verso being uniform with the English edition except for addition of an imprint, "Printed in Great Britain". The Phillips imprint was also substituted at foot of spine. Top edge violet-stained. Copies sold at 75 cents.

c. *Second American issue* (1924):

Sheets of *The Turn of the Screw* and *The Aspern Papers* were imported by Albert & Charles Boni in 1924, to be issued in The American Library series, at $1.50, with cancel title-leaves, bound in olive-drab polished buckram, series device in blind on front cover, lettered in gilt on spine; top edge grey-green-stained. The Macmillan Company of New York claimed infringement of copyright of *The Turn of the Screw* and this tale, as a result, was not "officially" published; it was never advertised in the series, 100 bound copies were remaindered and 100 sets of unbound sheets were destroyed. *The Aspern Papers*, No. 8 in the series, was issued as scheduled.

A75　THE QUESTION OF THE MIND　1915
First edition:

ENGLAND | [rule] | AT WAR: | [rule] | AN ESSAY | THE QUESTION OF THE MIND | BY | HENRY JAMES | ISSUED BY | THE CENTRAL COMMITTEE | FOR NATIONAL PATRIOTIC ORGANISATIONS | C. P. BUILDING, 62 CHARING CROSS, LONDON, W.C. | [rule] | PRICE ONE PENNY. [1915]

($8\frac{1}{2} \times 5\frac{1}{2}$): a single unsigned quire of ten leaves, pp. 20, stapled. 8vo. Contents: [1–2], title, copyright notice on verso; 3–[20], text; at bottom of p. [20] imprint, "Printed by the Press Printers, Ltd., Long Acre, London."

Issued without wrappers; all edges trimmed.

Published July 1915, at one penny. British Museum copy deposited 14 July; noted under "New Books and Reprints," *The Times Literary Supplement*, 5 August. Brussel erroneously calls for "22 pp., including the outside wrappers."

This essay, coupled with A. Clutton-Brock's "England," pp. 13–19, and several brief quotations by German and Viennese writers, was originally designed to be the preface to a larger volume. HJ to W. Robinson of the Central Committee, 4 June 1915: "It alarms me a little, just a little, that the thing isn't to play the merely prefatory part ... which I more or less took for granted in attempting it." (Unpublished letter, courtesy of the late Sir Ronald Storrs.)

James's essay first appeared in this edition, occupying pp. 3–12. It was reprinted, under the title "The Mind of England At War," in the *New York Sun* and the *Philadelphia Ledger*, 1 August 1915. HJ to Henry Cust, 18 June 1915: "If any scrap of lucre does accrue to it from America, please consider that it must have nothing whatever to do with *me*, and that I devote every penny of the sum to the expenses of the Central Committee." (Unpublished letter, courtesy of the late Sir Ronald Storrs.)

A76   PICTURES AND OTHER   1916
PASSAGES FROM HENRY JAMES

a. *First edition:*

PICTURES | AND OTHER PASSAGES FROM | HENRY JAMES | [eagle device within panel] | SELECTED BY | RUTH HEAD | LONDON | CHATTO & WINDUS | MCMXVI

$(7\frac{1}{16} \times 4\frac{7}{8})$: [A]^6 B–I^8 K^4, pp. xii, 136. Sq. Crown 8vo.

Contents: [i–ii], half-title, verso blank; [iii–iv], title, on verso reservation of rights and imprint, "Printed by | William Clowes and Sons, Limited, | London and Beccles."; v–ix, Preface by Ruth Head, dated 28 May 1916; [x], acknowledgments; [xi–xii], contents, verso blank; 1–[134], text; [135–136], publisher's device, on verso imprint, uniform with p. [iv].

Issued in grey half cloth, black and white mottled paper boards, lettering and rules in black on white paper label on spine; white end-papers; top edge trimmed and grey-stained, other edges untrimmed.

Published 14 September 1916, at 3/6, the first (and only) printing consisting of 1000 copies, of which 300 were exported for American issue.

The extracts were authorized by HJ (letter to Miss Head on p. viii).

b. *First edition, American issue* (1917)*:*

PICTURES | AND OTHER PASSAGES FROM | HENRY JAMES | [eagle device within panel] | SELECTED BY | RUTH HEAD | NEW YORK | FREDERICK A. STOKES COMPANY | PUBLISHERS [1917]

($7\frac{1}{8} \times 5$): [A]⁷ ([A₆] is inserted) B–I⁸ K³, pp. xiv, 134. 16mo.

Contents: [i–x], uniform with English edition; [xi–xii], list of sources of quotations, verso blank; [xiii–xiv], contents; 1–[134], text.

Issued in binding uniform with English edition.

Published October 1917, at $1, the issue being limited to 300 copies, consisting of imported sheets and binding materials. Noted in the "Weekly Record of New Publications," *Publishers' Weekly*, 6 October.

Title-leaf is a cancel. Lacks final leaf (K₄) included in the English edition.

A77   THE IVORY TOWER   1917

a. *First edition:*

THE IVORY TOWER | BY | HENRY JAMES | LONDON: 48 PALL MALL | W. COLLINS SONS & CO. LTD. | GLASGOW MELBOURNE AUCKLAND [1917]

($7\frac{11}{16} \times 5\frac{1}{8}$): [a]⁴ A–X⁸ Y⁶, pp. viii, 348. Ex. Crown 8vo.

Contents: [i–ii], half-title, verso blank; [iii–iv], title, on verso copyright notice; v–vi, Preface by Percy Lubbock; [vii–viii], contents, verso blank; 1–[348], text; at bottom of p. [348] imprint, "Glasgow: Printed at the University Press by Robert Maclehose and Co. Ltd." Frontispiece portrait by E. O. Hoppé, with tissue guard, tipped in, not reckoned in pagination.

Issued in blue-black smooth cloth, lettered in gilt on front cover and spine; white end-papers; top edge trimmed, other edges untrimmed.

Published 6 September 1917, as a two-volume set, with *The Sense of the Past* (A78a), at 12/-. Sold separately also, at 6/-. The first printing consisted of 2000 copies.

First appeared in this edition; no prior serialization. This is one of two novels unfinished by James at the time of his death; it was published with the author's notes.

b. *First American edition:*

THE IVORY TOWER | BY | HENRY JAMES | NEW YORK | CHARLES SCRIBNER'S SONS | 1917

($7\frac{7}{16} \times 4\frac{13}{16}$): [unsigned: 1–23⁸], pp. [2], viii, 358. 8vo.

Contents: [1–2], recto blank, on verso list of "Books by Henry James", not reckoned in pagination; [i–ii], half-title, verso blank; [iii–iv], title, on verso copyright notice, publication date, and printer's device; v–vi, Preface by Percy Lubbock; [vii–viii], contents, verso blank; 1–357, text; [358], blank.

Issued in dull olive-brown smooth sateen cloth, lettering and flame device in gilt on spine; white end-papers; top edge trimmed and gilt, other edges untrimmed. Also noted without gilt top.

Published 26 October 1917, at $1.50, the first printing consisting of 1500 copies. A small number of copies of this impression was bound uniformly with the New York Edition (1907–09), becoming Volume XXV of an enlarged edition, available only to subscribers to the earlier volumes.

A78   THE SENSE OF THE PAST   1917

a. *First edition:*

THE SENSE OF | THE PAST | BY | HENRY JAMES | LONDON: 48 PALL MALL | W. COLLINS SONS & CO. LTD. | GLAS-GOW MELBOURNE AUCKLAND [1917]

($7\frac{9}{16} \times 5\frac{1}{8}$): [a]⁴ A–Y⁸, pp. viii, 352. Ex. Crown 8vo.

Contents: [i–ii], half-title, verso blank; [iii–iv], title, on verso copyright notice; v–vi, Preface by Percy Lubbock; [vii–viii], contents, verso blank; 1–[351], text; at bottom of p. [351] imprint, "Glasgow: Printed at the University Press by Robert Maclehose and Co. Ltd."; [352], blank. Frontispiece portrait by Alvin Langdon Coburn, with tissue guard, tipped in, not reckoned in pagination.

Issued in blue-black smooth cloth, lettered in gilt on front cover and spine; white end-papers; top edge trimmed, other edges untrimmed.

Published 6 September 1917, as a two-volume set, with *The Ivory Tower* (A77a), at 12/-. Sold separately also, at 6/-. The first printing consisted of 2000 copies.

Some copies of the second impression appear in primary binding; others are noted in a secondary binding of black cloth, lettered in brick-red on front cover and spine; all edges trimmed. Lacking frontispiece. Page size: $7\frac{3}{8} \times 5$.

First appeared in this edition; no prior serialization. This is one of two novels unfinished by James at the time of his death; it was published with the author's notes.

b. *First American edition:*

THE | SENSE OF THE PAST | BY | HENRY JAMES | NEW YORK | CHARLES SCRIBNER'S SONS | 1917

$(7\frac{7}{16} \times 4\frac{7}{8})$: [unsigned: 1–23^8], pp. x, 358. 8vo.

Contents: [i–ii], recto blank, on verso list of "Books by Henry James"; [iii–iv], half-title, verso blank; [v–vi], title, on verso copyright notice, publication date, and printer's device; [vii–viii], Preface by Percy Lubbock; [ix–x], contents, verso blank; 1–358, text.

Issued in dull olive-brown smooth sateen cloth, lettering and flame device in gilt on spine; white end-papers; top edge trimmed and gilt, other edges untrimmed.

Published 26 October 1917, at $1.50, the first printing consisting of 1500 copies. A small number of copies of this impression was bound uniformly with the New York Edition (1907–09), becoming Volume XXVI of an enlarged edition, available only to subscribers to the earlier volumes.

A secondary binding is noted, issued in dark tan linen-grain cloth, lettering and flame device in gilt on spine; top edge trimmed but not gilt, fore-edge untrimmed, bottom edge trimmed. Page size: $7\frac{3}{8} \times 4\frac{15}{16}$.

A79   THE MIDDLE YEARS   1917

a. *First edition:*

THE | MIDDLE YEARS | BY | HENRY JAMES | LONDON: 48 PALL MALL | W. COLLINS SONS & CO. LTD. | GLASGOW MELBOURNE AUCKLAND [1917]

$(7\frac{9}{16} \times 5\frac{3}{16})$: [a]^4 A–G^8 H^4, pp. viii, 120. Ex. Crown 8vo.

Contents: [i–ii], blank leaf; [iii–iv], half-title, on verso copyright notice; [v–vi], title, verso blank; [vii–viii], Editor's Note by Percy Lubbock, verso blank; 1–[118], text; at bottom of p. [118] imprint, "Glasgow: Printed at the University Press by Robert Maclehose and Co. Ltd."; [119–120], blank. Frontispiece photogravure of portrait drawing by W. Rothenstein, with tissue guard, tipped in, not reckoned in pagination.

Issued in blue-black smooth cloth, lettered in gilt on front cover and spine; off-white end-papers; top edge trimmed, other edges untrimmed.

Published 18 October 1917, at 5/-, the first printing consisting of 2000 copies.

First appeared in *Scribner's Magazine*, October–November 1917. The text is a seven-chapter fragment of what was to have been the third volume of James's autobiography. It was dictated during the autumn of 1914, and was unrevised at the time of James's death.

b. *First American edition:*

THE | MIDDLE YEARS | BY | HENRY JAMES | NEW YORK | CHARLES SCRIBNER'S SONS | 1917

($8\frac{1}{8} \times 5\frac{1}{2}$): [unsigned: 1–8⁸], pp. viii, 120. 8vo.

Contents: [i–ii], recto blank, on verso list of titles "By Henry James"; [iii–iv], half-title, verso blank; [v–vi], title, on verso copyright notice, publication date, and printer's device; [vii–viii], Editor's Note by Percy Lubbock, verso blank; 1–119, text; [120], blank. Frontispiece portrait, from a photograph by Elliott and Fry, with tissue guard, stitched in by stub, not reckoned in pagination.

Issued in dull olive-brown smooth sateen cloth, lettered within single-rule panel in gilt on front cover, lettered in gilt on spine; white end-papers; top edge trimmed, other edges untrimmed.

Published 23 November 1917, at $1.25, the first printing consisting of 1300 copies.

A80   GABRIELLE DE BERGERAC   1918

First edition:

GABRIELLE DE BERGERAC | BY HENRY JAMES | [publisher's device] | NEW YORK | BONI AND LIVERIGHT | 1918

($7\frac{5}{16} \times 4\frac{1}{2}$): [unsigned: 1–9⁸ 10⁶], pp. 156. 12mo.

Contents: [1–2], half-title, verso blank; [3–4], title, on verso copy-right notice; [5–6], fly-title, verso blank; 7–153, text; [154], blank; [155–156], blank leaf.

Issued in white half linen, green paper boards, lettering and double-rule border with decorative corner devices in black on front cover, lettered in black on spine; white end-papers; all edges trimmed.

Published 23 November 1918, at $1.25, No. 1 in The Penguin Series (though not identified as such in first impression copies). Albert Boni, the publisher, recalls the first printing as "probably" consisting of 2000 copies. Albert Mordell, editor of the volume, reports receiving royalties on 1300 copies, inclusive of first and second impressions, suggesting a smaller printing.

Second impression, December 1918 (so noted on verso of title-leaf), is uniform with first impression except for substitution of a "Penguin Series" title and device for the publisher's monogram device on title-page; the penguin device is added in black on spine.

A81   WITHIN THE RIM   1919

First edition:

WITHIN THE RIM | AND OTHER ESSAYS | 1914–15 | HENRY JAMES | [publisher's device] | LONDON: 48 PALL MALL | W. COLLINS SONS & CO. LTD. | GLASGOW MELBOURNE AUCKLAND [1919]

(7½ × 5¼): [A]⁸ B–G⁸ H⁴ pp. 120. Ex. Crown 8vo.

Contents: [1–2], half-title, verso blank; [3–4], title, on verso copyright notice; [5–6], acknowledgments, verso blank; [7–8], contents, verso blank; [9–10], divisional fly-title, verso blank; 11–[119], text; at bottom of p. [119] imprint, "Glasgow: W. Collins Sons and Co. Ltd."; [120], blank.

Issued in blue-black smooth cloth, lettered in gilt on front cover and spine; white end-papers; top edge trimmed, other edges untrimmed.

Published March 1919, at 6/-. Announced for publication "next month" in *The Times Literary Supplement*, 27 February 1919, and advertised as "ready," in the same paper, 13 March.

There was no American edition of this book.

CONTENTS

Within the Rim

     First appeared in the *Fortnightly Review*, August 1917, and in

Living Age, 8 September 1917. First American book publication in *Harper Essays*, 1927.

Refugees in Chelsea

First appeared, under the title "Refugees in England," in the *New York Times* and the *Boston Sunday Herald*, 17 October 1915. Reprinted, under the title "Refugees in Chelsea," with some textual variation, in *The Times Literary Supplement*, 23 March 1916 (see D576).

The American Volunteer Motor-Ambulance Corps in France

First appeared as a separate pamphlet, 1914 (see C2); reprinted, in abbreviated form, under the title "Famous Novelist Describes Deeds of U.S. Motor Corps," in the *New York World*, 4 January 1915.

France

First appeared in *The Book of France*, 1915.

The Long Wards

First appeared in *The Book of the Homeless*, 1916.

A82   TRAVELLING COMPANIONS   1919

First edition:

TRAVELLING | COMPANIONS | BY | HENRY JAMES | [publisher's device] | BONI AND LIVERIGHT | NEW YORK | 1919

($7\frac{5}{16} \times 4\frac{7}{8}$): [unsigned: 1–20^8], pp. x, 310. 12mo.

Contents: [i–ii], half-title, verso blank; [iii–iv], title, on verso copyright notice; [v–vi], contents, verso blank; vii–ix, Foreword by Albert Mordell, dated Philadelphia, 6 February 1919; [x], blank; 1–309, text; [310], blank.

Issued in pine-green linen-grain cloth, lettered within single-rule panels in gilt on front cover, lettered in gilt on spine, publisher's device on spine in seriffed lettering, the "Liveright" being $\frac{3}{4}''$ long; white end-papers; all edges trimmed.

Published April 1919, at $1.75, the first (and only) printing consisting of approximately 2000 copies. Reviewed in the *New York Times*, 20 April.

A secondary binding state is noted, issued in dull green cloth, publisher's imprint on spine being in wider spaced sans-serif lettering, the "Liveright" measuring one inch in length. The gilt is of an obviously cheaper quality than in the primary state. Some copies are lettered in green.

CONTENTS

Travelling Companions
> First appeared in the *Atlantic Monthly*, November–December 1870.

The Sweetheart of M. Briseux
> First appeared in the *Galaxy*, June 1873.

Professor Fargo
> First appeared in the *Galaxy*, August 1874.

At Isella
> First appeared in the *Galaxy*, August 1871.

Guest's Confession
> First appeared in the *Atlantic Monthly*, October–November 1872.

Adina
> First appeared in *Scribner's Monthly*, May–June 1874.

De Grey: A Romance
> First appeared in the *Atlantic Monthly*, July 1868.

None of these stories had previously appeared in book form either in an American or an English edition.

A83   A LANDSCAPE PAINTER   1920

a. *First edition, ordinary issue:*

A LANDSCAPE | PAINTER | BY | HENRY JAMES | [publisher's device] | NEW YORK | SCOTT AND SELTZER | 1919 [1920]

$(7\frac{1}{4} \times 4\frac{7}{8})$: [unsigned: 1–17^8 18^4 19^8], pp. vi, 290. 12mo.

Contents: [i–ii], half-title, verso blank; [iii–iv], title, on verso copyright notice and reservation of rights; [v–vi], contents, verso blank; 1–4, Preface by Albert Mordell, dated Philadelphia, 10 July 1919; [5–6], divisional fly-title, verso blank; 7–287, text; [288], blank; [289–290], blank leaf.

Issued in dark green vertical-ribbed cloth, single-rule border and crossed single-rules forming four panels in blind on front cover, lettered in gilt on spine; white end-papers; all edges trimmed.

Published 2 January 1920, at $1.75, the first printing consisting of approximately 2000 copies. Price of the second impression copies, issued in February 1920, was increased to $2.

CONTENTS

A Landscape Painter
    First appeared in the *Atlantic Monthly*, February 1866.
Poor Richard
    First appeared in the *Atlantic Monthly*, June–August 1867.
A Day of Days
    First appeared in the *Galaxy*, 15 June 1866.
A Most Extraordinary Case
    First appeared in the *Atlantic Monthly*, April 1868.

Although all four tales had been collected and revised in *Stories Revived* (London, 1885), none had previously appeared in book form in an American edition; they were published here in their unrevised state.

b. *First edition, limited issue:*

($7\frac{5}{8} \times 5\frac{1}{8}$): collation and contents uniform with ordinary issue.

Issued in indigo-blue linen-grain cloth, lettered within double-rule panel in black on white paper label on spine; white end-papers; all edges untrimmed. On the label is imprinted limitation notice: "Special issue of the | First Edition | Limited to 250 copies". Sold at $5, published simultaneously with ordinary issue.

A84   REFUGEES IN CHELSEA   1920

First separate edition:

REFUGEES IN CHELSEA | BY HENRY JAMES | CHELSEA, AT THE ASHENDENE PRESS [1920]

($11\frac{1}{4} \times 8\frac{1}{8}$): [unsigned 1–2^4], pp. iv, 12. 4to.
Contents: [i–ii] title, verso blank; [iii–iv], foreword, verso blank; 1–11, text; [12], colophon. Rubricated initial letter on p. 1, six lines high.

Issued in Holland half canvas, grey-blue paper boards, lettered in black on front cover; double end-papers of same paper as text; all edges untrimmed.

Colophon, p. [12], reads: "Printed by the kind permission of the Proprietors and Editor from 'The Times Literary Supplement' of March 23, 1916 by C. H. St J. Hornby at the Ashendene Press, Shelley House, Chelsea, in the month of April of the year 1920." 50 copies were printed on hand-made paper, watermarked with Hornby's initials, and 6 copies on vellum, for private circulation only. The vellum copies were bound in morocco. This was the 31st publication of the Ashendene Press.

First appeared in the *New York Times* and the *Boston Sunday Herald*, 17 October 1915. Reprinted, with some textual variation, in *The Times Literary Supplement*, 23 March 1916, with an unsigned prefatory note by Logan Pearsall Smith, used as the Foreword to the present edition. First book appearance in *Within the Rim*, 1919.

A85   MASTER EUSTACE   1920

a. First edition, ordinary issue:

MASTER EUSTACE | BY | HENRY JAMES | [publisher's device] | NEW YORK | THOMAS SELTZER | 1920

$(7\frac{5}{16} \times 4\frac{15}{16})$: [unsigned: $1-18^8$], pp. vi, 282. 12mo.

Contents: [i–ii], half-title, verso blank; [iii–iv], title, on verso copyright notice and reservation of rights; [v–vi], contents, verso blank; 1–4, Preface by Albert Mordell, dated Philadelphia, August 1920; [5–6], divisional fly-title, verso blank; 7–280, text; [281–282], blank. Issued in dark green vertical-ribbed cloth, single-rule border and crossed single-rules forming four panels in blind on front cover, lettered in gilt on spine; white end-papers; all edges trimmed.

Published November 1920, at $2, the first (and only) printing consisting of approximately 1500 copies. Noted in the "Weekly Record of New Publications," *Publishers' Weekly*, 20 November, a literary note in the same issue reporting that the book had "just been published."

CONTENTS

Master Eustace
     First appeared in the *Galaxy*, November 1871.
Longstaff's Marriage
     First appeared in *Scribner's Monthly*, August 1878.

A. ORIGINAL WORKS

Théodolinde

> First appeared in *Lippincott's Magazine*, May 1878. A revised version, under the title "Rose-Agathe," appeared in *Stories Revived*, 1885.

A Light Man

> First appeared in the *Galaxy*, July 1869.

Benvolio

> First appeared in the *Galaxy*, August 1875.

"A Light Man" (completely rewritten) had previously appeared in book form in an American edition (see B2). This was, however, the first American book appearance of the four other tales. All five were reprinted from their original, unrevised serial texts.

b. *First edition, limited issue:*

($7\frac{11}{16} \times 5\frac{1}{8}$): collation and contents uniform with ordinary issue.

Issued in dark blue cloth, title and author lettered in black on white paper label on spine, lacking publisher's imprint on spine, published simultaneously with ordinary issue at $5, limited to 300 copies.

THE NOVELS AND STORIES OF
A86   HENRY JAMES   1921–1923

The Novels and Stories of Henry James, announced as a "New and Complete Edition" in 35 volumes, were edited, with prefatory notes, by Percy Lubbock. The advertisement of the edition announced: "The text used in this issue is that of the 'New York' edition, and the critical prefaces written for that series are retained in the volumes to which they refer. While, however, many stories were omitted from the 'New York' edition, either because they did not satisfy their author's later taste, or because he could not find room for them in the limited space at his disposal, the present edition contains all the fiction that he published in book-form during his life. The only writings which have been excluded are a small number of very early pieces, contributed to magazines and never reprinted, and the plays." This statement fails to take into account the particular design of the New York Edition and the fact that James himself decided upon the number of volumes it would contain. The "limited space" was of his own choosing and the exclusions were not merely matters of "taste" but related distinctly to the "architecture" of the Edition. Three pieces of fiction derived from original play versions, *The Other House*, "Covering End" and *The Outcry*, are also not included, as well as the two unfinished novels which had been added to the New York Edition after James's death—without regard to the novelist's view of that edition as "definitive."

Although the edition consisted almost entirely of reprinted materials, publication of *Watch and Ward* (Vol. 24) constituted the first English appearance of the short novel. For this reason it has been selected for sample collation.

WATCH AND WARD | LONGSTAFF'S MARRIAGE | EUGENE PICKERING | AND OTHER TALES | BY | HENRY JAMES | MACMILLAN AND CO., LIMITED | ST. MARTIN'S STREET, LONDON | 1923

$(7\frac{1}{2} \times 5)$: [A]^4 B–2F^8 2G^6, pp. viii, 460. Crown 8vo. Issued also in a pocket edition, F'cap 8vo $(6\frac{3}{4} \times 4\frac{3}{8})$.

Contents: [i–ii], half-title, on verso publisher's device and addresses; [iii–iv], title, on verso copyright notice and imprint, "Printed in Great Britain"; v–[vi], Note, signed P[ercy] L[ubbock], verso blank; vii–[viii], contents, verso blank; 1–[2], divisional fly-title, verso blank; 3–[457], text; at bottom of p. [457] imprint, "Printed in Great Britain by R. & R. Clark, Limited, Edinburgh."; [458], blank; [459–460], advertisement of "The Novels and Stories of Henry James".

Issued in two styles: (*a*) Crown 8vo: dark blue cloth, decorative initials "HJ" in gilt on front cover, lettering and decorative border at top and bottom in gilt on spine; white end-papers; all edges untrimmed; (*b*) F'cap 8vo (Pocket Edition): dark blue cloth, lettered within decorative panel in gilt on front cover, lettering and decorative rules and flower-and-leaf ornament in gilt on spine; white end-papers; all edges trimmed.

A. ORIGINAL WORKS

Published 9 January 1923, at 7/6, the first printing of this volume consisting of 2000 copies.

———

Volume 1 was published 11 January 1921. The remaining volumes were issued at intervals up to 30 November 1923, most of them being issued bi-monthly in pairs despite the nominal announcement of "monthly issuance." The initial printing of the first four volumes consisted of 3000 copies each; the initial printing of each of the later volumes was 2000 copies.

Later impressions were issued in the Pocket Edition only. Copies issued in recent years (including first-impression sheets of slow-selling volumes) have been cheaply bound in blue-green linen-grain cloth, lettered in gilt on spine.

CONTENTS

Edmund Orme. The Real Right Thing. The Jolly Corner. Julia Bride.

23. *Daisy Miller. Pandora. The Patagonia. The Marriages. The Real Thing. Brooksmith. The Beldonald Holbein. The Story in It. Flickerbridge. Mrs. Medwin.*

24. *Watch and Ward. Longstaff's Marriage. Eugene Pickering. Benvolio. The Impressions of A Cousin.*

25. *The Diary of A Man of Fifty. A New England Winter. The Path of Duty. A Day of Days. A Light Man. Georgina's Reasons. A Landscape Painter. Rose-Agathe. Poor Richard.*

26. *The Last of the Valerii. Master Eustace. The Romance of Certain Old Clothes. A Most Extraordinary Case. The Modern Warning. Mrs. Temperly. The Solution. Sir Dominick Ferrand. Nona Vincent.*

27. *Lord Beaupré. The Visits. The Wheel of Time. Collaboration. Glasses. The Great Condition. The Given Case. John Delavoy. The Third Person. The Tone of Time.*

28. *Maud Evelyn. The Special Type. The Papers. The Velvet Glove. Mora Montravers. Crapy Cornelia. A Round of Visits. The Bench of Desolation.*

29. *The Sacred Fount.*

30–31. *The Wings of the Dove.*

32–33. *The Ambassadors.*

34–35. *The Golden Bowl.*

A87   NOTES AND REVIEWS   1921

First edition:

NOTES AND REVIEWS | BY | HENRY JAMES [in red] | WITH A PREFACE BY PIERRE DE CHAIGNON LA ROSE | [rule] | A SERIES OF TWENTY-FIVE PAPERS HITH- | ERTO UNPUBLISHED IN BOOK FORM | [rule] | [oval wood-cut illustration] | [rule] | DUNSTER HOUSE [in red] | CAM-BRIDGE, MASSACHUSETTS | MDCCCCXXI

($8\frac{3}{4} \times 5\frac{3}{4}$): [unsigned: $1-14^8$ 15^4 16^8], pp. xx, 228. 8vo.

Contents: [i–ii], half-title, verso blank; [iii–iv], title, on verso copyright notice and imprint, "The University Press, Cambridge, U.S.A."; v–xvi, Preface by Pierre de Chaignon La Rose, dated 18 February 1921; xvii–xx, contents; 1–227, text; [228], blank.

A. ORIGINAL WORKS

Issued in dark blue half cloth, light blue paper boards, lettered in gilt on front cover and spine; pale buff end-papers; all edges untrimmed.

Published 25 April 1921, at $5, the edition consisting of 1000 copies on India tint Albion Text paper; in addition 30 copies were issued, of which 24 were for sale at $10, on Normandy Vellum, bound in écru half linen, grey paper boards, with binder's fly-leaf inserted at front and back.

This was the sixth publication of the Dunster House Press. No separate English edition; bound copies of the American edition were imported by William Jackson, London distributor, in November 1921, and sold at 30/-.

CONTENTS

A. ORIGINAL WORKS

X. *"The Gayworthys"*

First appeared, as a review of Mrs A. D. Whitney's *The Gayworthys*, in the *North American Review*, October 1865.

XI. *A French Critic*

See note, D14a.

XII. *Miss Braddon*

First appeared, as a critical note on M. E. Braddon's *Aurora Floyd* and other novels, in the *Nation*, 9 November 1865.

XIII. *Eugénie de Guérin's Journal*

First appeared, as a review of G. S. Trébutien's *The Journal of Eugénie de Guerin*, in the *Nation*, 14 December 1865.

XIV. *"The Belton Estate"*

First appeared, as a review of Anthony Trollope's *The Belton Estate*, in the *Nation*, 4 January 1866.

XV. *Swinburne's "Chastelard"*

First appeared, as a review of A. C. Swinburne's *Chastelard: a Tragedy*, in the *Nation*, 18 January 1866.

XVI. *Kingsley's "Hereward"*

First appeared, as a review of Charles Kingsley's *Hereward, the Last of the English*, in the *Nation*, 25 January 1866.

XVII. *"Winifred Bertram"*

First appeared, as a review of Mrs E. R. Charles's *Winifred Bertram and the World She Lived In*, in the *Nation*, 1 February 1866.

XVIII. *Mrs. Gaskell*

First appeared, as a review of Mrs Gaskell's *Wives and Daughters*, in the *Nation*, 22 February 1866.

XIX. *"Marian Rooke"*

First appeared, as a review of Henry D. Sedley's *Marian Rooke*, in the *Nation*, 22 February 1866.

XX. *"A Noble Life"*

First appeared, as a review of Mrs D. M. M. Craik's *A Noble Life*, in the *Nation*, 1 March 1866.

XXI. *Epictetus*

First appeared, as a review of T. W. Higginson's *The Works of Epictetus*, in the *North American Review*, April 1866.

XXII. *Victor Hugo's Last Novel*

First appeared, as a review of Hugo's *Les Travailleurs de la Mer*, in the *Nation*, 12 April 1866.

XXIII. *Felix Holt, the Radical*

First appeared, as a review of George Eliot's *Felix Holt*, in the *Nation*, 16 August 1866.

XXIV. *Eugénie de Guérin's Letters*
> First appeared, as a review of *Lettres d'Eugénie de Guérin*, in the
> *Nation*, 13 September 1866.

XXV. *The Last French Novel*
> First appeared, as a review of Dumas's *Affaire Clémenceau*:
> *Mémoire de l'Accusé*, in the *Nation*, 11 October 1866.

A88 LITTLE BLUE BOOKS 1931

First separate edition:

LITTLE BLUE BOOK NO. 1671 [volume number occupies
two lines] | EDITED BY E. HALDEMAN-JULIUS | QUEER
PEOPLE AND A | DAMNING PASSION | (DE GREY: A
ROMANCE) | HENRY JAMES | HALDEMAN-JULIUS
PUBLICATIONS | GIRARD, KANSAS [1931]

($5\frac{1}{8} \times 3\frac{3}{8}$): a single unsigned quire of 32 leaves, pp. 64, stapled. 32mo.

Contents: [1–2], title, on verso copyright notice and imprint, "Printed
in the United States of America"; [3–4], fly-title, verso blank; [5]–64,
text.

Issued in pale blue stiff paper wrappers, cut flush, lettered in black on
front cover; inner sides of wrappers blank; all edges trimmed.

Published 17 August 1931, at 10 cents. 10,000 copies were printed.

Issued uniform with this volume were four additional titles, all but one
of which were re-titled.

No. 1672. *The Sweetheart of M. Briseux* (19 August 1931). 10,000
copies were printed.

No. 1673. *The Runaway Wife* (originally *At Isella*) (5 October
1931). 20,000 copies were printed.

No. 1674. *Spiritual Magnetism* (originally *Professor Fargo*) (27
August 1931). 5000 copies were printed.

No. 1675. *The Mad Lovers and the Emperor's Topaz* (originally *Adina*)
(5 October 1931). 13,000 copies were printed.

Later issues of the above titles contain the copyright inscription on
verso of title-leaf, but lack the date of copyright. These issues are
frequently noted in a binding of cheap brown flexible paper, with a
series device and printer's union label in black on back cover.

A reprint of *Daisy Miller* was published by Haldeman-Julius on 18
September 1922 in the Ten Cent Pocket Series (No. 182). 60,000
copies.

A89   THE ART OF THE NOVEL   1934

a. *First separate edition:*

THE ART OF THE NOVEL | CRITICAL PREFACES | BY | HENRY JAMES | WITH AN INTRODUCTION | BY | RICHARD P. BLACKMUR | [leaf device] | CHARLES SCRIBNER'S SONS | NEW YORK · LONDON | MCMXXXIV

($7\frac{7}{8} \times 5\frac{7}{16}$): [unsigned: 1–12^{16} 13^4], pp. xlii, 350. 8vo.

Contents: [i–ii], half-title, verso blank; [iii–iv], title, on verso copyright notice, reservation of rights, printer's device, and imprint, "Printed in the United States of America"; [v–vi], divisional fly-title, verso blank; vii–xxxix, Introduction by Richard P. Blackmur; [xl], blank; xli–[xlii], contents, verso blank; [1–2], fly-title, verso blank; 3–348, text; [349–350], blank leaf.

Issued in black smooth cloth, lettering and leaf device in gilt on front cover and spine; white end-papers; all edges trimmed.

Published 2 November 1934, at $3, the first printing consisting of 1900 copies.

First issue may be identified by code letter "A" on verso of title-leaf. This edition contains the 18 prefaces included in the 24 original volumes of the New York Edition (see A64), collected here for the first time.

b. *First separate edition, English issue* (1935)*:*

Uniform with American edition except for cancel title-leaf, the publisher's imprint reading: "London | Charles Scribner's Sons | MCMXXXV". Top and bottom edges are trimmed, fore-edge untrimmed.

Published April 1935, at 10/6.

A90   THE AMERICAN NOVELS AND   1947
STORIES OF HENRY JAMES

First edition:

THE AMERICAN NOVELS | AND STORIES | OF | HENRY JAMES | EDITED, WITH AN INTRODUCTION, BY | F. O. MATTHIESSEN | 1947 | [publisher's device] | NEW YORK: ALFRED A. KNOPF.

($8\frac{5}{16} \times 5\frac{5}{8}$): [unsigned: 1–32^{16}], pp. [2], xxviii, 994. 8vo.

Contents: [1–2], blank leaf, not reckoned in pagination; [i–ii], half-title, verso blank; [iii–iv], title, on verso copyright notice, reservation of rights, and imprint, "First Edition | This is a Borzoi Book, published by Alfred A. Knopf, Inc."; [v–vi], contents, verso blank; vii–[xxvii], Introduction by F. O. Matthiessen; [xxviii], blank; [1–2], fly-title, verso blank; 3–993, text; [994], "A Note on the Type."; binder's fly-leaf at back.

Issued in dark green linen-grain cloth, decorative initials of the author in gilt on front cover, publisher's device in blind on back cover, lettering with two filler devices and decorative gold rules and band in gilt on spine; white end-papers; top edge trimmed and purple-stained, other edges untrimmed.

Published 20 February 1947, at $5, the first printing consisting of 6200 copies. The second impression, issued in August 1951, consisting of 1500 copies, contained the *Notes for The Ivory Tower* omitted from the first impression (see A91).

CONTENTS

The following tale is collected in book form for the first time:

The Story of A Year

First appeared in the *Atlantic Monthly*, March 1865.

The remaining novels and tales had previously appeared in book form:

The Europeans; Washington Square; The Point of View; A New England Winter; Pandora; The Bostonians; "Europe"; Julia Bride; The Jolly Corner; Crapy Cornelia; A Round of Visits; The Ivory Tower.

A91   NOTES FOR THE IVORY   1947
                    TOWER

First separate issue:

EDITOR'S AND PUBLISHER'S NOTE | FOR | THE AMERICAN NOVELS AND STORIES | OF HENRY JAMES | [decorative band] | [Note signed by F. O. Matthiessen and Alfred A. Knopf, Inc.] | [publisher's device] [1947]

($8\frac{1}{4} \times 5\frac{7}{16}$): a single unsigned quire of 24 leaves, pp. [993–1040], stapled. 8vo.

Contents: [993], explanatory title-leaf (described above); 994–1036, text, "Notes for The Ivory Tower"; [1037–1040], two blank leaves. Issued on text paper uniform with that of *The American Novels and Stories of Henry James*, without wrappers, all edges trimmed.

Published May 1947, after issuance of the first edition of *The American Novels and Stories of Henry James* (A90) for inclusion in all unsold copies of the edition, the note on p. [993] reading: "Henry James' *Notes for The Ivory Tower*, here reprinted, were unintentionally omitted from our first edition . . . and will be included in any future printings."

4000 copies of the booklet were issued. The plates were later used for inclusion of the material in the second impression of the book, August 1951, the publisher's and compiler's note being eliminated.

A92   THE NOTEBOOKS OF   1947
                  HENRY JAMES

a. *First edition:*

THE NOTEBOOKS OF HENRY JAMES | [rule] | EDITED BY
F. O. MATTHIESSEN AND KENNETH B. MURDOCK |
[publisher's device] | NEW YORK | OXFORD UNIVERSITY
PRESS | 1947

($9\frac{1}{4} \times 6\frac{1}{8}$): [unsigned: $1-13^{16}$ 14^4 15^{16}], pp. xxviii, 428. Med. 8vo.
Contents: [i–ii], half-title, on verso facsimile of "A Page from Henry James' Notebooks"; [iii–iv], title, on verso copyright notice and imprint, "Printed in the United States of America"; [v–vi], contents, verso blank; [vii–viii], acknowledgments, verso blank; ix–xx, Introduction, signed "F.O.M." and "K.B.M."; xxi–xxiii, "A Note on the Text"; [xxiv], blank; xxv–xxviii, "Chronological List of Henry James' Chief Publications in Book Form"; [1–2], fly-title, verso blank; 3–415, text; [416], blank; 417–418, Appendix; 419–425, Index; [426], blank; [427–428], blank leaf.

Issued in royal blue linen-grain cloth, on front cover panel blocked in gilt with cloth showing through in facsimile of HJ's initials; lettering and decorative panel enclosing title in gilt on spine; white end-papers; all edges trimmed.

Published 30 October 1947, at $6, the first printing consisting of 7500 copies.

Nine scribblers containing notes by Henry James were found among his posthumous papers. Some were the working notebooks in which he outlined themes for his fiction; others were journal records of personal happenings which James recorded, largely retrospectively. These were published together as "notebooks" in this volume, but with a few omissions in the text, some of which are noted by the editors.

In addition, the editors added certain detached sheets of notes, including the preliminary sketch for "The 'K.B.' Case" and "Mrs. Max," an abandoned project, and a preliminary sketch for *The Sense of the Past* (which James dictated before the detailed "scenario" published in 1917; see A78). The editors also included a document not written by James for his own use, as was the case with the notebooks, but prepared as an outline for Harper & Brothers, of *The Ambassadors*, a portion of which had originally appeared in the Henry James issue of *Hound and Horn*, 1934 (see D580).

b. *First edition, English issue* (1948):

Consisted of sheets of the American edition, with unchanged title-leaf, issued in dark blue linen-grain cloth, lettering and decorative panel enclosing title in gilt on spine; white end-papers; all edges trimmed.

Published 26 August 1948, at 30/-. The issue consisted of 1250 copies.

A93   THE SCENIC ART   1948

a. *First edition:*

HENRY JAMES | THE SCENIC ART | NOTES ON ACTING & THE DRAMA: | 1872–1901 | EDITED, WITH AN INTRO-DUCTION | AND NOTES, BY | ALLAN WADE | NEW BRUNSWICK | RUTGERS UNIVERSITY PRESS | 1948 [Entire title enclosed within double-rule border]

$(8\frac{3}{16} \times 5\frac{5}{16})$: [unsigned: 1–13^{16}], pp. [2], xxvi, 388. [8vo]

Contents: [1–2], half-title, verso blank, not reckoned in pagination; [i–ii], title, on verso copyright notice, reservation of rights, publisher acknowledgments, and imprint, "Manufactured in the United States of America | A.B."; iii–[iv], acknowledgments, verso blank; v–viii,

A. ORIGINAL WORKS

Foreword by Leon Edel, dated New York, 1948; [ix–x], contents; xi–xxv, Editor's introduction; [xxvi], blank; [1–2], fly-title, verso blank; 3–328, text; 329–376, Appendix; 377–384, Index; [385–388], two blank leaves. Four double-sided plates of illustrations tipped in, not reckoned in pagination.

Issued in dull green linen-grain cloth, lettering in gilt (title and author against red-brown panels) and alternating bands of multiple rules and triangles in gilt on spine; white end-papers; top edge green, other edges trimmed.

Published 3 May 1948, at $4.50, the first printing consisting of 3500 copies.

CONTENTS

The following materials appear in book form for the first time:

"The School for Scandal" at Boston
>First appeared, under the heading "The Drama," in the *Atlantic Monthly*, December 1874.

Madame Ristori
>First appeared, under the heading "Fine Arts," in the *Nation*, 18 March 1875.

Mr. George Rignold
>First appeared, under the heading "Notes," in the *Nation*, 27 May 1875.

Mr. Henry Irving's Macbeth
>First appeared, as an unheaded note, in the *Nation*, 25 November 1875.

Paris Revisited
>First appeared, as a portion of the first of a series of letters in the *New York Tribune*, 11 December 1875.

The Parisian Stage (1875–76)
>First appeared as the fifth of a series of letters in the *New York Tribune*, 29 January 1876.

Notes from Paris
>Part 1 first appeared, under the heading "Parisian Life," as a portion of the sixth of a series of letters in the *New York Tribune*, 5 February 1876.
>Part 2 first appeared, under the heading "Paris in Election Time," as a portion of the eighth of a series of letters in the *New York Tribune*, 4 March 1876.
>Part 3 first appeared, under the heading "Parisian Affairs," as a

portion of the ninth of a series of letters in the *New York Tribune*, 25 March 1876.

Part 4 first appeared, under the heading "Parisian Topics," as a portion of the tenth of a series of letters in the *New York Tribune*, 1 April 1876.

Part 5 first appeared, under the heading "Parisian Topics," as a portion of the sixteenth of a series of letters in the *New York Tribune*, 17 June 1876.

Part 6 first appeared, under the heading "Notes," in the *Nation*, 16 November 1876.

Part 7 first appeared, as a note on MM. Erckmann-Chatrian's "Ami Fritz," in the *Nation*, 4 January 1877.

The London Theatres (1877)

First appeared in the *Galaxy*, May 1877.

Henry Irving as Louis XI; Olivia *at the Court Theatre*

First appeared, under the heading "Notes," in the *Nation*, 13 June 1878.

M. Émile Augier

First appeared, under the heading "Notes," in the *Nation*, 27 June 1878.

The London Theatres (1879)

First appeared in the *Nation*, 12 June 1879.

The Comédie Française in London

First appeared in the *Nation*, 31 July 1879.

The London Theatres (1880)

First appeared in *Scribner's Monthly*, January 1881.

London Plays

First appeared, as the second part of an essay titled "London Pictures and London Plays," in the *Atlantic Monthly*, August 1882.

Tommaso Salvini: I: In Boston, II: In London

Part I first appeared in the *Atlantic Monthly*, March 1883, and was reprinted in abridged form in *The American Theatre as Seen by Its Critics*, 1934.

Part II first appeared, under the title "A Study of Salvini," in the *Pall Mall Gazette*, 27 March 1884.

A Poor Play Well Acted

First appeared in the *Pall Mall Gazette*, 24 October 1883.

The Acting in Mr. Irving's "Faust"

First appeared in the *Century Magazine*, December 1887.

Mr. Henry Irving's Production of "Cymbeline"
> First appeared in *Harper's Weekly,* 21 November 1896.

Irving's "Richard III."; "Little Eyolf"
> First appeared, under the heading "London," as a portion of the first of a series of letters in *Harper's Weekly,* 23 January 1897.

The Blight of the Drama
> First appeared, under the heading "London," as the fifth of a series of letters in *Harper's Weekly,* 24 April 1897.

Edmond Rostand
> First appeared in the *Cornhill Magazine* and the *Critic,* November 1901.

The following materials had previously appeared in book form:

The Parisian Stage (see A2)
The Théâtre Français (see A5)
Notes on the Theatres: New York (see B39)
Coquelin (revised text, 1915; see B34)
After the Play (see A38)
Henrik Ibsen: I. On the Occasion of Hedda Gabler (see A40)
          II. On the Occasion of The Master Builder (originally titled "Ibsen's New Play") (see A40)
Dumas the Younger (see A73)
John Gabriel Borkman (originally part of the second "London" letter in *Harper's Weekly,* 6 February 1897; later reprinted as part of "London Notes," in *Notes on Novelists,* 1914; see A73)

b. *First edition, English issue* (1949) :

HENRY JAMES | THE SCENIC ART | NOTES ON ACTING AND THE DRAMA | 1872–1901 | EDITED | WITH AN INTRODUCTION AND NOTES | BY | ALLAN WADE | AND A FOREWORD BY LEON EDEL | [device] | LONDON | RUPERT HART-DAVIS | 1949

(8 × 5): [A]⁸ B–2C⁸, pp. [2], xxvi, 388. Large Crown 8vo.

Reproduced from American edition by offset. Contents uniform except for a few changes in the preliminaries, including correction of misprints, elimination of some acknowledgments, and addition of list of books "uniform with this volume" on verso of half-title; new title-leaf; illustrations omitted.

Issued in rust-red cloth, lettered in gilt on spine; white end-papers; top edge rust-red, other edges trimmed.

Published 23 September 1949, at 21/-, the first printing consisting of 1500 copies.

A94   THE GHOSTLY TALES OF   1949
HENRY JAMES

First edition:

THE | GHOSTLY TALES | OF | HENRY JAMES | EDITED WITH AN INTRODUCTION | BY | LEON EDEL | NEW BRUNSWICK | RUTGERS UNIVERSITY PRESS | 1948 [1949]

($8\frac{1}{4} \times 5\frac{5}{8}$): [unsigned: 1–25^{16}], pp. xxxiv, 766. 8vo.

Contents: [i–ii], half-title, verso blank; [iii–iv], title, on verso copyright notice, reservation of rights, publisher's acknowledgments, and imprint, "Manufactured in the United States of America"; [v]–xxxii, Introduction by Leon Edel, dated New York, April, 1948; [xxxiii]–xxxiv, contents; [1–2], fly-title, verso blank; [3]–762, text; [763]–765, Chronological Table; [766], "A Note on Sources and An Acknowledgment," signed "L.E."

Issued in dull green linen-grain cloth, lettering in gilt (title and author against red-brown panels) and two decorative bands of multiple rules and triangles in gilt on spine; grey end-papers; top edge violet-brown, fore-edge untrimmed, bottom edge trimmed.

Published 28 February 1949, at $5, the first printing consisting of 5000 copies.

CONTENTS

The following tale appears in book form for the first time:

The Ghostly Rental
    First appeared in *Scribner's Monthly,* September 1876.

The remaining tales had previously appeared in book form:
The Romance of Certain Old Clothes; De Grey: A Romance; The Last of the Valerii; Sir Edmund Orme; Nona Vincent; The Private Life;

Sir Dominick Ferrand; Owen Wingrave; The Altar of the Dead; The Friends of the Friends; The Turn of the Screw; The Real Right Thing; The Great Good Place; Maud-Evelyn; The Third Person; The Beast in the Jungle; The Jolly Corner.

A95   THE COMPLETE PLAYS OF   1949
HENRY JAMES

a. *First edition:*

THE | COMPLETE PLAYS | OF | HENRY JAMES | EDITED BY | LEON EDEL | [publisher's device] | J. B. LIPPINCOTT COMPANY | PHILADELPHIA AND NEW YORK [1949]

$(9\frac{3}{16} \times 6\frac{3}{16})$: [unsigned: $1–2^{16}$ 3^{8} $4–27^{16}$], pp. 848. Med. 8vo.

Contents: [1–2], half-title, verso blank; [3–4], title, on verso copyright notices, reservation of rights, and imprint, "Printed in the United States of America | First Edition"; 5–6, contents; 7–[8], list of illustrations, verso blank; 9–11, Foreword, signed "L.E."; [12], blank; 13–15, Acknowledgment, signed "L.E."; [16], blank; [17–18], divisional fly-title, on verso quotation from Henry James; 19–69, "Henry James: The Dramatic Years," an introductory essay, signed Leon Edel; [70], blank; [71–72], divisional fly-title, verso blank; 73–74, Editor's Foreword to "Pyramus and Thisbe," on verso cast of characters; 75–816, text; [817–818], divisional fly-title, verso blank; 819–823, A Note on the Texts; [824], blank; 825–839, Notes; [840], blank; 841–846, Index; [847–848], blank leaf.

Issued in light tan half buckram, red-brown linen-grain cloth, lettering and two decorative bands in gilt against red-brown panel and publisher's imprint in red-brown on spine; white end-papers; all edges trimmed, top edge brown-stained.

Published 12 October 1949, at $10, the first printing consisting of 6600 copies, of which 2500 were bound, 3000 were exported in sheets for the English issue, and the balance remains unbound.

All copies of the first edition contain a cancel title-leaf. As complete copy for the wording of the copyright page was not ready at the time of going to press, a cancel title-leaf had to be printed and inserted at the bindery.

A. ORIGINAL WORKS

CONTENTS

Pyramus and Thisbe
>First appeared in the *Galaxy*, April 1869.

Still Waters
>First appeared in *Balloon Post*, 12 April 1871.

A Change of Heart
>First appeared in the *Atlantic Monthly*, January 1872.

Daisy Miller
>First appeared in the *Atlantic Monthly*, April–June 1883. The play had been privately printed in July 1882 (see A18).

The American
>Privately printed in September 1891 (see A35). This was the first published appearance of the play. A fragment of a variant fourth act, the manuscript of which is in the Houghton Library, first appeared here.

Tenants
Disengaged
The Album
The Reprobate
>These four plays had been published previously (see A42 and A44).

Note for The Chaperon
>First published here.

Guy Domville
>Privately printed in October 1894 (see A43). This was the first published appearance of the play.

Summersoft
>First published here.

The High Bid
>First published here.

Rough Statement for Three Acts Founded on The Chaperon
>First published here.

The Saloon
>First published here.

The Other House
>First published here.

The Outcry
>First published here.

Monologue Written for Ruth Draper
>First appeared, as a portion of an article titled "Three Unpublished Letters and A Monologue by Henry James," in the *London Mercury*, September 1922.

b. *First edition, English issue:*

This issue consisted of sheets of the American edition, with a new title-page printed by Lippincott for the English publisher, Rupert Hart-Davis Ltd. The volume was issued in rust-red linen-grain cloth, lettered in gilt on spine.

Published 5 December 1949, at 35/-. The issue consisted of 3000 sets of sheets, of which 1100 were bound as above. The remaining 1900 copies were later bound up in geranium fabroleen, lettered in silver.

A96   EIGHT UNCOLLECTED TALES   1950

First edition:

EIGHT | UNCOLLECTED TALES | OF | HENRY JAMES | EDITED WITH AN INTRODUCTION BY | EDNA KENTON | RUTGERS UNIVERSITY PRESS | NEW BRUNSWICK, N.J. | 1950

$(8\frac{5}{16} \times 5\frac{3}{8})$: [unsigned: $1-10^{16}$], pp. vi, 314. 8vo.

Contents: [i–ii], half-title, verso blank; [iii–iv], title, on verso copyright notice and reservation of rights; [v–vi], contents, verso blank; [1–2], divisional fly-title, verso blank; 3–20, Introduction by Edna Kenton, dated November 15, 1949; [21–22], divisional fly-title, verso blank; 23–312, text; 313–314, "Chronological List of the First Twenty-Eight Tales" of Henry James.

Issued in dull green linen-grain cloth, lettered in gilt on spine; white end-papers; all edges trimmed.

Published 11 September 1950, at $4.25, the first printing consisting of 2500 copies.

By "uncollected" Miss Kenton sought to designate those tales of Henry James's which were never published in book form during his lifetime and which had not been "collected" since his death. There were fifteen uncollected tales in all. Seven were assembled by Albert Mordell in *Travelling Companions*, 1919 (A82). The remaining eight were here reprinted. Three of the tales in Miss Kenton's collection did, however, have book appearances before the publication of her volume, but were included by her, she explained, to make her volume complementary to Mordell's.

CONTENTS

The following tales appear in book form for the first time:

My Friend Bingham
> First appeared in the *Atlantic Monthly*, March 1867.

The Story of A Masterpiece
> First appeared in the *Galaxy*, January–February 1868.

A Problem
> First appeared in the *Galaxy*, June 1868.

Osborne's Revenge
> First appeared in the *Galaxy*, July 1868.

Crawford's Consistency
> First appeared in *Scribner's Monthly*, August 1876.

The following tales had previously appeared in book form:

The Story of A Year
Gabrielle de Bergerac
The Ghostly Rental

A97   DAUMIER, CARICATURIST   1954

First separate edition:

DAUMIER [in red] | CARICATURIST | [device] | HENRY JAMES | [initials "HJ" in red] | MINIATURE BOOKS | [single rule] | RODALE PRESS [1954] [Entire title against chartreuse panel within double-rule frame in black]

($7\frac{13}{16} \times 6\frac{5}{16}$): [unsigned: $1-2^8\ 3^4$], pp. iv, 36. Crown 6mo.
Contents: [i–ii], half-title, verso blank; [iii–iv], title, on verso publication date, publisher's imprint, and imprint "Printed in England"; 1–[36], text. Sixteen illustrations by Daumier on text pages, of which thirteen are printed against pastel-coloured panels.

Issued in black half cloth, cream paper boards ruled in red on front and back covers, lettered in gilt on front cover and spine, star device and oval panel in gilt on spine; white end-papers; all edges trimmed.

Published 9 April 1954, at 5/-, the first printing consisting of 10,000 copies, of which 6000 constitute the American issue, at $1.25.

First appeared in the *Century Magazine*, January 1890; reprinted with numerous revisions, under the title "Honoré Daumier," in *Picture and Text*, 1893. The present text follows that of the serial publication.

First edition:

HENRY JAMES | THE AMERICAN ESSAYS | EDITED WITH
AN INTRODUCTION | BY LEON EDEL | [star device] | VIN-
TAGE BOOKS | NEW YORK | 1956

($7\frac{7}{32} \times 4\frac{1}{4}$): consisting entirely of singleton leaves, glued together at
the backstrip, lacking stitching or stapling, by a process termed "per-
fect binding" by the publisher. Pp. [2], xx, 288, x. [16mo]

Contents: [1–2], blank leaf; [i–ii], half-title, verso blank; [iii–iv], title,
on verso copyright notice, reservation of rights, and imprint, "Manu-
factured in the United States of America. | Published simultaneously
in Canada by McClelland and Stewart | Limited. | FIRST EDITION";
[v]–xvii, Introduction by Leon Edel; [xviii], blank; [xix]–xx,
contents; [1–2], divisional fly-title, verso blank; [3]–288, text; [i]–viii,
Index; [ix–x], biographical notes and colophon, on verso list of titles in
series.

Issued in white stiff paper wrappers, cut flush, printed in red, blue, and
black on front and back covers and on spine; inner sides of wrappers
blank; all edges trimmed.

Published 10 September 1956, at 95 cents, Vol. K40 in the Vintage
Books series published by Alfred A. Knopf, Inc., the first printing
consisting of 20,000 copies.

CONTENTS

The following essays appear in book form for the first time:

Hawthorne's French and Italian Journals
> First appeared, as a review of *Passages from the French and Italian
> Note-Books of Nathaniel Hawthorne*, in the *Nation*, 14 March
> 1872.

The Correspondence of Carlyle and Emerson
> First appeared, as a review of *The Correspondence of Thomas
> Carlyle and Ralph Waldo Emerson*, *1834–1872*, in the *Century
> Magazine*, June 1883.

Francis Parkman: The Old Régime in Canada
> First appeared, as a review of Parkman's book, in the *Nation*, 15
> October 1874.

The Story-Teller at Large: Mr. Henry Harland
> First appeared in the *Fortnightly Review*, April 1898.

A. ORIGINAL WORKS

The American Novel
> First appeared, under the heading "American Letter," in *Literature*, 9 April 1898.

Grant's Letters; Whitman's Calamus
> First appeared, under the heading "American Letter," in *Literature*, 16 April 1898. The passage on Whitman was reprinted in F. O. Matthiessen, *The James Family*, 1947.

Democracy and Theodore Roosevelt
> First appeared, under the heading "American Letter," in *Literature*, 23 April 1898.

Winston Churchill; Bret Harte
> First appeared, under the heading "American Letter," in *Literature*, 30 April 1898.

Whitman's The Wound Dresser
> First appeared, under the heading "American Letter," in *Literature*, 7 May 1898.

Local History; American Criticism
> First appeared, under the heading "American Letter," in *Literature*, 21 May 1898.

Military Novels
> First appeared, under the heading "American Letter," in *Literature*, 28 May 1898.

American Magazines; John Jay Chapman
> First appeared, under the heading "American Letter," in *Literature*, 11 June 1898.

American Democracy and American Education
> First appeared, under the heading "American Letter," in *Literature*, 25 June 1898.

The Novel of Dialect; W. D. Howells
> First appeared, under the heading "American Letter," in *Literature*, 9 July 1898.

Mr. and Mrs. Fields
> First appeared in *Cornhill Magazine* and the *Atlantic Monthly*, July 1915.

Notes for an Essay on Mr. and Mrs. Fields
> Previously unpublished passages from the draft typescript of the essay "Mr. and Mrs. Fields."

The Founding of the Nation: Recollections of the "Fairies" that Attended its Birth
> First appeared in the *Nation*, 8 July 1915.

The remaining essays had previously appeared in book form:

In *The Library of the World's Best Literature:*
    Nathaniel Hawthorne
    James Russell Lowell (1819–1891)
In *The Proceedings in Commemoration of the One Hundredth Anniversary of the Birth of Nathaniel Hawthorne:*
    Letter from Henry James to the Hon. Robert S. Rantoul
In *Partial Portraits:*
    Emerson (a review of Cabot's *A Memoir of Ralph Waldo Emerson*)
    Miss Woolson
In *Essays in London and Elsewhere:*
    James Russell Lowell
In *Notes on Novelists:*
    An American Art-Scholar: Charles Eliot Norton
In *Views and Reviews:*
    Mr Walt Whitman (a review of Whitman's *Drum-Taps*)
In *The Shock of Recognition:*
    William Dean Howells
In *The Letters of Henry James,* ed. Percy Lubbock:
    Letter to William Dean Howells on His Seventy-Fifth Birthday
In *The Average Woman:*
    Wolcott Balestier
In *Literary Opinion in America:*
    American Letter: The Question of the Opportunities

A99   THE FUTURE OF THE NOVEL   1956

First edition:

HENRY JAMES | THE FUTURE OF THE NOVEL | ESSAYS ON THE ART OF FICTION | EDITED WITH AN INTRODUCTION | BY LEON EDEL | [star device] | VINTAGE BOOKS | NEW YORK | 1956

$(7\frac{5}{32} \times 4\frac{5}{16})$: consisting entirely of singleton leaves, glued together at the backstrip, lacking stitching or stapling, by a process termed "perfect binding" by the publisher. Pp. [2], xviii, 288, xii. [16mo]

Contents: [1–2], blank leaf; [i–ii], half-title, verso blank; [iii–iv], title, on verso copyright notice, reservation of rights, text sources, and imprint, "Manufactured in the United States of America. | Published simultaneously in Canada by McClelland and Stewart | Limited. | FIRST EDITION"; [v]–xvi, Introduction by Leon Edel; [xvii]–xviii, contents; [1–2], divisional fly-title, verso blank; [3]–286, text; [287–288], "Bibliographical Note", verso blank; [i–v], Index; [vi], blank; [vii–viii], biographical notes and colophon, verso blank; [ix–xi], blank; [xii], list of titles in series.

Issued in white stiff paper wrappers, cut flush, printed in purple, blue, and black on front cover, in purple and black on back cover, and in black on spine; inner sides of wrappers blank; all edges trimmed.

Published 10 September 1956, at 95 cents, Vol. K41 in the Vintage Books series published by Alfred A. Knopf, Inc., the first printing consisting of 20,000 copies.

CONTENTS

The following essays appear in book form for the first time:
Middlemarch
> First appeared, as a review of George Eliot's *Middlemarch*, in the *Galaxy*, March 1873.

Nana
> First appeared, as "A Review of Zola's Novel *Nana*," in the *Parisian*, 26 February 1880. Reprinted in the *Colby Library Quarterly*, June 1943.

The remaining essays had previously appeared in book form:
In *Partial Portraits:*
> The Art of Fiction
> Guy de Maupassant
> Anthony Trollope

In *Literary Opinion in America:*
> The Great Form (originally titled "The Summer School at Deerfield")

In *The International Library of Famous Literature:*
> The Future of the Novel

In *The Novels and Tales of Henry James* (New York Edition):
> Extracts from nine of the prefaces

In *Views and Reviews:*
> Our Mutual Friend (under the title "The Limitations of Dickens")

In *The Question of Our Speech:*
> The Lesson of Balzac

In *Madame Bovary* (Century of French Romance series, 1902):
> Gustave Flaubert

A. ORIGINAL WORKS

In *Notes on Novelists:*
   Émile Zola
   The New Novel (originally titled "The Younger Generation")
In *Library of the World's Best Literature:*
   Turgenev and Tolstoy (under the title "Ivan Turgenieff")

A100   THE PAINTER'S EYE   1956

a. *First edition:*

THE PAINTER'S EYE | NOTES AND ESSAYS ON THE
PICTORIAL ARTS BY | HENRY JAMES | SELECTED AND
EDITED | WITH AN INTRODUCTION BY | JOHN L.
SWEENEY | [publisher's device] | LONDON | RUPERT
HART-DAVIS | 1956

(8 × 5⅛): [A]⁸ B–Q⁸ R¹⁰, pp. 276. Large Crown 8vo.

Contents: [1–2], half-title, verso blank; [3–4], title, on verso imprint,
"Printed in Great Britain by Robert MacLehose and Co. Ltd | The
University Press, Glasgow"; [5–8], contents; 9–31, Introduction by
John L. Sweeney; 32, acknowledgments and "Note on the Text";
33–261, text; 262–266, three appendices; 267–271, "General Index";
272–274, "Index of Pictures"; [275–276], blank leaf. Frontispiece
portrait tipped in, not reckoned in pagination.

Issued in rust-red linen-grain cloth, lettered in gilt on spine; white
end-papers; top edge rust-red, other edges trimmed.

Published 11 October 1956, at 20/-, the first printing consisting of
4000 copies, of which 1500 constituted the American issue.

CONTENTS

An English Critic of French Painting, 1868
   First appeared, as a review of P. G. Hamerton's *Contemporary
   French Painters: An Essay*, in the *North American Review*, April
   1868.
French Pictures in Boston, 1872
   First appeared, as critical notes under the heading "Art," in the
   Atlantic Monthly, January 1872.
Pictures by William Morris Hunt, Gérôme and Others, 1872
   First appeared, as a portion of a series of critical notes under the
   heading "Art," in the *Atlantic Monthly*, February 1872.

A. ORIGINAL WORKS

The Metropolitan Museum's '1871 Purchase,' 1872
First appeared, under the title "Art: The Dutch and Flemish Pictures in New York," in the *Atlantic Monthly*, June 1872.

The Wallace Collection in Bethnal Green, 1873
First appeared, under the title "The Bethnal Green Museum," in the *Atlantic Monthly*, January 1873.

The Duke of Montpensier's Pictures in Boston, 1874
First appeared, as critical notes under the heading "Art," in the *Atlantic Monthly*, November 1874.

On Some Pictures Lately Exhibited
First appeared in the *Galaxy*, July 1875.

Duveneck and Copley, 1875
First appeared, as untitled notes, in the *Nation*, 9 September 1875.

The American Purchase of Meissonier's 'Friedland,' 1876
First appeared, under the heading "Parisian Sketches," as a portion of the fourth of a series of letters in the *New York Tribune*, 22 January 1876.

Two Pictures by Delacroix
First appeared, under the heading "Parisian Topics," as a portion of the seventh of a series of letters in the *New York Tribune*, 19 February 1876.

The Impressionists, 1876
First appeared, under the heading " Parisian Festivity," as a portion of the thirteenth of a series of letters in the *New York Tribune*, 13 May 1876.

Les Maîtres d'Autrefois, 1876
First appeared, as a review of Fromentin's *Les Maîtres d'Autrefois: Belgique-Hollande* under the title "A Study of Rubens and Rembrandt," in the *Nation*, 13 July 1876.

The National Gallery, 1877
First appeared, as an untitled note, in the *Nation* 25 January 1877.

The Old Masters at Burlington House, 1877
First appeared in the *Nation*, 1 February 1877.

The Picture Season in London, 1877
First appeared in the *Galaxy*, August 1877.

The Norwich School
First appeared, under the title "The Old Masters at Burlington House," in the *Nation*, 31 January 1878.

Ruskin's Collection of Drawings by Turner
First appeared, as an untitled note, in the *Nation*, 18 April 1878.

A. ORIGINAL WORKS

The Grosvenor Gallery, 1878

First appeared, as an untitled note, in the *Nation*, 23 May 1878.

The Royal Academy, 1878

First appeared, as an untitled note, in the *Nation*, 6 June 1878.

On Whistler and Ruskin, 1878

First appeared, as an untitled note, in the *Nation*, 19 December 1878. Reprinted, as Part I of "Contemporary Notes on Whistler vs. Ruskin," in *Views and Reviews*, 1908.

On Art-Criticism and Whistler, 1879

First appeared, as an untitled note, in the *Nation*, 13 February 1879. Reprinted, as Part II of "Contemporary Notes on Whistler vs. Ruskin," in *Views and Reviews*, 1908.

The Royal Academy and the Grosvenor Gallery, 1879

First appeared in the *Nation*, 29 May 1879.

The Letters of Eugène Delacroix

First appeared, as a review of *Lettres d'Eugène Delacroix (1815 à 1863)*, ed. Philippe Burty, in the *International Review*, April 1880.

London Pictures, 1882

First appeared, as part of an essay under the title "London Pictures and London Plays," in the *Atlantic Monthly*, August 1882. The remaining portion of the essay was reprinted, under the title "London Plays," in *The Scenic Art*, 1948.

John S. Sargent

First appeared in *Harper's New Monthly Magazine*, October 1887. Reprinted, with minor revisions, in *Picture and Text*, 1893. The revised text is reprinted here.

Honoré Daumier

First appeared, under the title "Daumier, Caricaturist," in the *Century Magazine*, January 1890. Reprinted, with minor revisions, in *Picture and Text*, 1893. The revised text is reprinted here. The original serial text was reprinted as a separate work in 1954 (see A97).

The New Gallery, 1897

First appeared, as a portion of a series of notes under the heading "London," in *Harper's Weekly*, 23 January 1897.

Lord Leighton and Ford Madox Brown, 1897

First appeared, as a portion of a series of notes under the heading "London," in *Harper's Weekly*, 20 February 1897.

The Guildhall and the Royal Academy, 1897

First appeared, as a portion of a series of notes under the heading "London," in *Harper's Weekly*, 5 June 1897.

The Grafton Galleries, 1897

First appeared, as a portion of a series of notes under the heading "London," in *Harper's Weekly*, 26 June 1897. The balance of the material was reprinted in *Notes on Novelists*, 1914.

b. *First edition, American issue:*

The issue consisted of imported sheets with a re-set title-leaf, lacking the Reynard device, the publisher's imprint on the recto reading: HARVARD UNIVERSITY PRESS | CAMBRIDGE, MASSACHUSETTS | 1956 On the verso is imprinted, "Copyright 1956 by the President and Fellows Harvard College". Binding uniform with English edition.

Published 21 November 1956, at $4, the issue consisting of 1500 copies.

A101   PARISIAN SKETCHES   1957

a. *First edition:*

HENRY JAMES | PARISIAN SKETCHES | LETTERS TO THE NEW YORK TRIBUNE | 1875–1876 | [decorative rule] | EDITED WITH AN INTRODUCTION BY | LEON EDEL AND ILSE DUSOIR LIND | [publisher's device] | NEW YORK UNIVERSITY PRESS | WASHINGTON SQUARE | 1957

$(8 \times 5\frac{3}{8})$: [unsigned: $1–8^{16}$ 9^8 10^{16}], pp. xxxviii, 266.

Contents: [i–ii], half-title, verso blank; [iii–iv], title, on verso copyright notice, Library of Congress catalogue number, and imprint, "Manufactured in the United States of America"; v–vi, Preface, signed "L.E." and "I.D.L."; [vii–viii], contents, verso blank; ix–xxxvii, Introduction, signed Leon Edel and Ilse Dusoir Lind; [xxxviii], blank; [1–2], fly-title, verso blank; 3–207, text; [208], blank; 209–227, "Appendix: Documents relating to Henry James's Association with the New York 'Tribune' including his correspondence with Whitelaw Reid"; [228], blank; 229–256, Notes; 257–262, Index; [263–266], two blank leaves.

Issued in light blue linen-grain cloth, lettering, five decorative devices, and publisher's Washington Square device in gilt on spine; white endpapers; all edges trimmed.

Published 7 October 1957, at $5, the first printing consisting of 3000 copies.

CONTENTS

First appeared as a series of letters in the *New York Tribune*. Date of original appearance follows each title:

Paris Revisited (11 December 1875)
Paris As It Is (25 December 1875)
Versailles As It Is (8 January 1876)
Parisian Sketches (22 January 1876)
The Parisian Stage (29 January 1876)
Parisian Life (5 February 1876)
Parisian Topics (19 February 1876)
Paris in Election Time (4 March 1876)
Parisian Affairs (25 March 1876)
Parisian Topics (1 April 1876)
Art and Letters in Paris (22 April 1876)
Chartres Portrayed (29 April 1876)
Parisian Festivity (13 May 1876)
Art in France (27 May 1876)
Art in Paris (5 June 1876)
Parisian Topics (17 June 1876)
Parisian Topics (1 July 1876)
George Sand (22 July 1876)
Summer in France (12 August 1876)
A French Watering Place (26 August 1876)

Of these essays, "Chartres Portrayed," under the title "Chartres," "Summer in France," under the title "Rouen," and "A French Watering Place," under the title "Etretat," had previously appeared in *Portraits of Places*, 1883; "The Parisian Stage" and extracts from six additional letters had appeared in *The Scenic Art*, 1948; extracts from three letters had appeared in *The Painter's Eye*, 1956.

b. *First edition, English issue:*

This issue, published by Rupert Hart-Davis Ltd., consisted of sheets of the American edition, with revised title-page and copyright page. The volume was issued in rust-red linen-grain cloth, lettered in gilt on spine.

Published 6 June 1958, at 25/-, the issue consisting of 1500 copies.

A102   THE HOUSE OF FICTION   1957

THE HOUSE OF | FICTION | ESSAYS ON THE NOVEL BY | HENRY JAMES | EDITED WITH AN INTRODUCTION BY | LEON EDEL | [publisher's device] | LONDON | RUPERT HART-DAVIS | 1957

$(8\frac{1}{16} \times 5\frac{1}{8})$: [A]^8 B–S^8, pp. 288. Large Crown 8vo.

Contents: [1–2], half-title, verso blank; [3–4], title, on verso imprint, "Printed in Great Britain by Robert MacLehose and Co. Ltd | The University Press, Glasgow"; [5–6], dedication, verso blank; [7–8], contents, verso blank; 9–19, Introduction, signed Leon Edel; [20], blank; [21–22], divisional fly-title, verso blank; 23–280, text; 281–[282], Bibliographical Note, verso blank; 283–286, Index; [287–288], blank.

Issued in rust-red rough linen-grain cloth, lettered in gilt on spine; white end-papers; top edge rust-red, other edges trimmed.

Published 18 October 1957, at 25/-, the first printing consisting of 4000 copies.

CONTENTS

The following essay appears in book form for the first time:

Far from the Madding Crowd
> First appeared, as a review of Thomas Hardy's novel, in the *Nation*, 24 December 1874.

The volume also includes all of the selections previously published in *The Future of the Novel* (A99), with the exception of the essay "The New Novel" and the extracts from nine of the prefaces to the New York Edition, and contains two additional essays: "Robert Louis Stevenson" (reprinted from *Partial Portraits*, 1888) and "Nathaniel Hawthorne" (reprinted from *The Library of the World's Best Literature*, 1897).

A103   LITERARY REVIEWS AND   [1957]
ESSAYS

LITERARY | REVIEWS | AND ESSAYS | BY HENRY JAMES | ON AMERICAN, ENGLISH, AND | FRENCH LITERATURE | EDITED BY | ALBERT MORDELL | TWAYNE PUBLISHERS | NEW YORK [1957]

$(8\frac{15}{16} \times 6\frac{1}{16})$: [unsigned: 1–13^{16}], pp. 416.

Contents: [1–2], half-title, verso blank; [3–4], title, on verso copyright notice and imprint, "Manufactured in the United States of America by | United Printing Services, Inc. | New Haven, Conn."; [5–8], Table of Contents; 9–27, Introduction, signed Albert Mordell, dated August 1957; [28], blank; [29], divisional fly-title; 30–353, text; 354–361,

A. ORIGINAL WORKS

"Notes to Introduction"; 362–402, "Notes to Articles"; 403–406, Postscript; 407–409, Appendix; [410–416], blank.

Issued in blue simulated buckram, lettered in gilt, the title being stamped upon a panel of black, on spine; white end-papers; all edges trimmed.

Published 16 December 1957, at $10, the first printing consisting of 1000 copies.

A second impression carries the imprint of Vista House. A subsequent paperback edition was issued by Grove Press on 8 September 1958, at $2.45.

CONTENTS

ESSAYS ON FRENCH LITERATURE

The Reminiscences of Ernest Renan
>First appeared in the *Atlantic Monthly*, August 1883.

Renan's Dialogues and Philosophic Fragments
>First appeared, as a part of "Parisian Topics," in the *New York Tribune*, 17 June 1876.

Taine's Italy
>First appeared in the *Nation*, 7 May 1868.

Taine's Notes on England
>First appeared in the *Nation*, 25 January 1872.

Taine's English Literature
>First appeared, under the title "English Literature," in the *Atlantic Monthly*, April 1872.

Taine's Notes on Paris
>First appeared in the *Nation*, 6 May 1875.

Taine's Ancient Regime
>First appeared, as a part of "Versailles As It Is," in the *New York Tribune*, 8 January 1876.

Sainte-Beuve's Portraits
>First appeared in the *Nation*, 4 June 1868.

Sainte-Beuve's First Articles
>First appeared in the *Nation*, 18 February 1875.

Sainte-Beuve's English Portraits
>First appeared in the *Nation*, 15 April 1875.

Gautier's Winter in Russia
>First appeared in the *Nation*, 12 November 1874.

Constantinople by Gautier
>First appeared, under the title "Constantinople," in the *Nation*, 15 July 1875.

A. ORIGINAL WORKS

Gautier's Posthumous Works
> First appeared, under the title "Theophile Gautier, Souvenirs Intimes. Histoire du Romantisme . . .," in the *North American Review*, October 1874.

Maurice de Guérin
> First appeared in the *Nation*, 7 March 1867.

Dumas Fils and Goethe
> First appeared, under the title "Dumas and Goethe," in the *Nation*, 30 October 1873.

Schérer's Literary Studies
> First appeared in the *Nation*, 6 April 1876.

George Sand's Mademoiselle Merquem
> First appeared, under the title "Mademoiselle Merquem," in the *Nation*, 16 July 1868.

Last Gleanings from George Sand's Writings
> First appeared, under the title "Dernières Pages," in the *Nation*, 25 October 1877.

George Sand
> First appeared in the *New York Tribune*, 22 July 1876.

Hugo's Légende des Siècles
> First appeared, as an untitled note, in the *Nation*, 3 May 1877.

Victor Hugo's Ninety-Three
> First appeared, under the title "Ninety-Three," in the *Nation*, 9 April 1874.

Flaubert's Temptation of St. Anthony
> First appeared in the *Nation*, 4 June 1874.

Henry Beyle
> First appeared in the *Nation*, 17 September 1874.

Minor French Novelists: The Goncourts, etc.
> First appeared, as a part of "The Minor French Novelists," in the *Galaxy*, February 1876. The remaining portion was reprinted in *French Poets and Novelists*, 1878.

Edmond de Goncourt's La Fille Elisa
> First appeared, as an untitled note, in the *Nation*, 10 May 1877.

Mérimée's Letters to Another Unknown
> First appeared, under the title "Lettres à Une Autre Inconnue," in the *Nation*, 27 January 1876.

Mérimée's Last Tales
> First appeared, under the title "Dernières Nouvelles," in the *Nation*, 12 February 1874.

A. ORIGINAL WORKS

Octave Feuillet's Camors
> First appeared in the *Nation*, 30 July 1868.

Octave Feuillet's Les Amours de Philippe
> First appeared, under the title "Les Amours de Philippe," in the *Nation*, 15 November 1877.

Alphonse Daudet
> First appeared in the *Atlantic Monthly*, June 1882.

Ivan Turgenev's Virgin Soil
> First appeared, under the title "Terres Vierges," in the *Nation*, 26 April 1877.

ESSAYS ON AMERICAN AND ENGLISH LITERATURE

Howells's Italian Journeys
> First appeared, under the title "Italian Journeys," in the *North American Review*, January 1868.

Howells's A Foregone Conclusion
> First appeared, under the title "A Foregone Conclusion," in the *North American Review*, January 1875.

Howells's A Foregone Conclusion (Second Article)
> First appeared, under the title "A Foregone Conclusion," in the *Nation*, 7 January 1875.

Howells's Poems
> First appeared in the *Independent*, 8 January 1874.

Francis Parkman: The Jesuits in North America
> First appeared, under the title "The Jesuits in North America," in the *Nation*, 6 June 1867.

Later Lyrics by Julia Ward Howe; Poems by Elizabeth Akers (Florence Percy); Poems by Amanda T. Jones; Women of the Gospels: The Three Wakings and Other Poems by the Author of The Schonberg-Cotta Family
> First appeared, under the title "Recent Volumes of Poems," in the *North American Review*, April 1867.

The Prophet. A Tragedy. By Bayard Taylor
> First appeared in the *North American Review*, January 1875.

Nero: An Historical Play—By W. W. Story
> First appeared in the *Nation*, 25 November 1875.

Honest John Vane: A Story by J. W. De Forest
> First appeared in the *Nation*, 31 December 1874.

We and Our Neighbors: Records of An Unfashionable Street By Harriet Beecher Stowe
> First appeared in the *Nation*, 22 July 1875.
> Mordell erroneously dates this 22 June.

A. ORIGINAL WORKS

Eight Cousins: Or the Aunt-Hill By Louisa M. Alcott
First appeared in the *Nation*, 14 October 1875.

Idolatry By Julian Hawthorne
First appeared, under the title "Idolatry: A Romance," in the *Atlantic Monthly*, December 1874.

Garth By Julian Hawthorne
First appeared in the *Nation*, 21 June 1877.

Saxon Studies By Julian Hawthorne
First appeared in the *Nation*, 30 March 1876.

Charles Nordhoff's Communistic Societies
First appeared, under the title "Nordhoff's Communistic Societies," in the *Nation*, 14 January 1875.

Carlyle's Translation of Goethe's Wilhelm Meister
First appeared, under the title "Wilhelm Meister's Apprenticeship and Travels," in the *North American Review*, July 1865.

Mr. Froude's Short Studies
First appeared in the *Nation*, 31 October 1867.

Historical Novels: The Household of Sir Thomas More; Jacques Bonneval, or The Days of the Dragonnades by the Author of Mary Powell (Anne Manning)
First appeared, under the title "Historical Novels," in the *Nation*, 15 August 1867.

The Spanish Gypsy By George Eliot
First appeared in the *Nation*, 2 July 1868.

George Eliot's Lifted Veil; and Brother Jacob
First appeared, as an untitled note, in the *Nation*, 25 April 1878.

Hardy's Far from the Madding Crowd
First appeared, under the title "Far from the Madding Crowd," in the *Nation*, 24 December 1874.

Charles Kingsley's Life and Letters
First appeared, under the title "Life and Letters," in the *Nation*, 25 January 1877.

Lothair By Lord Beaconsfield
First appeared in the *Atlantic Monthly*, August 1870.

Tyndall's Hours of Exercise in the Alps
First appeared, under the title "Hours of Exercise in the Alps," in the *Atlantic Monthly*, November 1871.

Stopford Brooke's Theology in the English Poets
First appeared, under the title "Theology in the English Poets," in the *Nation*, 21 January 1875.

Professor David Masson's "Three Devils: Luther's, Milton's, and Goethe's With Other Essays"
> First appeared, under the title "Professor Masson's Essays," in the *Nation*, 18 February 1875.

Mrs. Browning's Letters to R. H. Horne
> First appeared, under the title "Mrs. Browning's Letters," in the *Nation*, 15 February 1877.

George Barnett Smith's Poets and Novelists
> First appeared, under the title "Poets and Novelists: A Series of Literary Studies," in the *Nation*, 30 December 1875.

Thackerayana
> First appeared in the *Nation*, 9 December 1875.

Rev. Francis Hodgson, A Friend of Lord Byron
> First appeared, under the title "A Friend of Lord Byron," in the *North American Review*, April 1879.

Matthew Arnold
> First appeared in the *English Illustrated Magazine*, January 1884.

A104 FRENCH WRITERS AND 1960
AMERICAN WOMEN

FRENCH WRITERS AND AMERICAN WOMEN | ESSAYS | BY HENRY JAMES | EDITED WITH AN INTRODUCTION BY PETER BUITENHUIS | THE COMPASS PUBLISHING COMPANY, BRANFORD, CONNECTICUT | 1960

($9\frac{3}{4} \times 6\frac{15}{16}$): [unsigned: $1-24^2$], pp. [4], x, 82. 4to.

Contents: [1–2], title, on verso copyright notice; [3–4], Preface, signed Peter Buitenhuis, on verso Table of Contents; i–viii, Introduction; ix–x, "A Note on the Development of James's Style"; 1–80, text; 81, Notes; [82], blank.

Issued in white stiff coated paper wrappers, lettering in red and drawing of James with facsimile signature in black on front cover; inner sides of wrappers blank; all edges trimmed. Text is typewritten and reproduced by an offset process.

Published December 1960, at $2, the first printing consisting of 500 copies.

A. ORIGINAL WORKS

CONTENTS

The following essays appear in book form for the first time:

Alphonse Daudet
> First appeared in *Literature*, 25 December 1897.

Prosper Mérimée
> First appeared in *Literature*, 23 July 1898.

The Present Literary Situation in France
> First appeared in the *North American Review*, October 1899.

The Speech of American Women
> First appeared in *Harper's Baȝar*, November 1906–February 1907.

The Manners of American Women
> First appeared in *Harper's Baȝar*, April–July 1907.

The lecture *The Question of Our Speech* had previously been collected in book form with *The Lesson of Balȝac*, 1905 (see A61).

A105   THE COMPLETE TALES   1962–64

a. *First edition:*

THE COMPLETE TALES OF | HENRY | JAMES | EDITED WITH AN | INTRODUCTION BY | LEON EDEL | I | 1864–1868 | RUPERT HART-DAVIS | SOHO SQUARE LONDON | 1962

($7\frac{7}{8} \times 5\frac{1}{2}$): [unsigned: 1–12^{16} 13^{24}], pp. 432.

Contents: [1–2], half-title, verso blank; [3–4], title, on verso copyright notice; [5–6], contents, verso blank; 7–16, General Introduction; 17–22, Introduction: 1864–1868; 23–428, text; 429–430, note on the text; [431–432], blank.

Issued in grey cloth, with purple label on spine, lettered in gold; white end-papers; all edges trimmed; top purple-stained. Volumes I and II published 16 April 1962; Vols III and IV 29 October 1962; V and VI 22 April 1963; VII and VIII 26 August 1963; IX and X 25 May 1964; XI and XII 23 November 1964. 2000 copies printed of Vols I and II, 3000 of Vols III–XII.

First six vols priced 35/-, second six 42/-.

The following tale appears in book form for the first time:
A Tragedy of Error
> First appeared, unsigned, in the *Continental Monthly*, Feb. 1864.

b. *First American edition:*

Photographed from English edition with imprint of J.B. Lippincott
Company on title and spine with revised copyright page. Issued in
beige linen-grain cloth, with "HJ" decoration in blind in silver circle
on front cover; lettered and banded in silver (on black panels) and in
black on spine; off-white end-papers; top and bottom edges trimmed,
top green- or orange-brown stained.

Vols I and II published 23 May 1962 at $5.95. The other volumes
followed in pairs, soon after their English counterparts.

FRENCH POETS AND NOVELISTS (see p. 36)

d. *First American edition* (1964)*:*

HENRY JAMES | FRENCH POETS AND | NOVELISTS |
WITH AN INTRODUCTION BY | LEON EDEL | [decorative
device] | THE UNIVERSAL LIBRARY | GROSSET AND
DUNLAP | NEW YORK [1964]

(8 × 5⅜): [unsigned: 1–7^{16} 8^{20} 9–10^{16} 11^{20}], pp. xiv, 354.

Contents: [i–ii], blank; [iii–iv], half-title, verso blank; [v–vi], title, on
verso copyright notice; vii–xi, Introduction; xii, Bibliographical Note;
[xiii–xiv], contents, verso blank; 1–341, text; [342], blank; [two unnumbered pages], fly-title, verso blank; 343–344, biographical notes;
345–350, index; [351–352], blank.

Issued in illustrated paper wrappers, printed in black and burnt orange;
inner sides of wrappers have patterned design; all edges trimmed.

Published 29 February 1964, at $1.95 paperback and $4 hardback.
Reproduced photographically from the Tauchnitz setting (A5b).

Leon Edel indicates, in his Bibliographical Note, "In the original
edition . . . James appended an essay on the French theatre. This
essay has been dropped from the present publication and James's paper
on Sainte-Beuve [D374] has been substituted as being more relevant."

A106   1976

THE AMERICAN
(Manuscript Facsimile)

First edition:

HENRY JAMES THE AMERICAN | THE VERSION OF 1877 |
REVISED IN AUTOGRAPH AND TYPESCRIPT FOR |

A. ORIGINAL WORKS

THE NEW YORK EDITION OF 1907 | REPRODUCED IN
FACSIMILE FROM THE ORIGINAL IN | THE HOUGHTON
LIBRARY, HARVARD UNIVERSITY, | WITH AN INTRO-
DUCTION BY RODNEY G. DENNIS | THE SCOLAR PRESS
1976

(11 × 8⅞): [unsigned: 1⁴ 2–31⁸], pp. viii, 480.

Contents: [i–ii], blank leaf; [iii–iv], title, on verso copyright notice
and acknowledgment; [v–vi], Introduction, by Rodney G. Dennis;
[vii–viii], holograph half-title in facsimile, on verso accession date of
manuscript in Harvard College Library; 1–478, text; [479–480], blank
leaf.

Issued in brown linen-grain cloth, lettered in gilt on spine; light
brown end-papers; all edges trimmed. Although the editor describes
James as using the version of 1883—*i.e.*, the Macmillan Collective
Edition (A20), which was extensively revised—he calls this, in his
title, the version of 1877 (A4).

Published 1976 at £25 in the United Kingdom and at $48 in the
United States, the first printing consisting of 250 copies. A further
printing of 300 copies was issued in 1978.

A107   1979
THE EUROPEANS
(Manuscript Facsimile)

First edition:

HENRY JAMES | THE EUROPEANS | A FACSIMILE OF THE
MANUSCRIPT | WITH AN INTRODUCTION BY | LEON
EDEL | [publisher's device] | HOWARD FERTIG | NEW
YORK 1979

(10½ × 7¼): [unsigned: 1–16⁸ 17¹⁰ 18–19⁸], pp. xvi, [unpaginated, 292].
Contents: [i–ii], half-title, verso blank; [iii–iv], title, on verso copyright notice, Library of Congress catalogue number, and record of
manuscript possession by "four owners: W. Jones, Wayzata, Minn.
(p. 1–13), Beinecke Rare Book and Manuscript Library, Yale University (p. 14–95), Robert H. Taylor Collection, Princeton University
Library (p. 96–197), and Henry James Collection, Clifton Waller
Barrett Library, University of Virginia Library (p. 197–294)"; [v–vi],
contents, verso blank; vii–xiii, Introduction, signed by Leon Edel;
[xiv], blank; xv, Acknowledgments; [xvi], blank; [1–2], fly-title, verso

A. ORIGINAL WORKS

blank; [3–290], text, with erroneous manuscript pagination; [291–292], blank.

Issued in orange-brown linen-grain cloth, black label on spine which is lettered in gilt; white end-papers; all edges trimmed.

Published 28 November 1979 at $35, the first printing consisting of 750 copies. The facsimile comprises the first nine chapters of the novel. Manuscript of the remaining three chapters has never been found. After some hundred copies had been circulated, a cancel-leaf for pp. vii and viii was inserted in the remaining copies to make certain corrections and clarifications on p. viii.

a. *First edition, illustrated:*

NANA: | A REALISTIC NOVEL. | BY | ÉMILE ZOLA. |
TRANSLATED WITHOUT ABRIDGMENT FROM THE
127TH FRENCH EDITION. | ILLUSTRATED WITH SIX-
TEEN PAGE ENGRAVINGS, | FROM DESIGNS BY BEL-
LENGER, CLAIRIN, AND ANDRÉ GILL. | LONDON: |
VIZETELLY & CO., 42 CATHERINE STREET, STRAND. |
1884.

($7\frac{7}{16} \times 5$): [a]⁶ A–2B⁸, pp. xvi, [5]–400. Frontispiece, engraved title-
page, and 14 illustrations inserted. Crown 8vo.

Issued in (*a*) peacock-blue diagonal-fine-ribbed cloth, lettered in gilt on
front cover and spine, illustrated in gilt, red, and blue within decorative
frame in black on front cover, triple-rule border in blind on back cover,
four rules in red at top and bottom of spine; (*b*) brown diagonal fine-
ribbed cloth, lettering and rules in black on white paper label on spine;
green-on-white floral-patterned end-papers; all edges untrimmed.

Published March 1884, at 6/-. Noted under "New Books" in the
Athenaeum, 29 March 1884; advertised in the same publication, 5 April,
with a quotation from Henry James's review.

Contains:
Prefatory note, *Mr. Henry James on "Nana."* Pp. [xiv]–xv.

This is an excerpt from James's review of *Nana*, which originally
appeared in the *Parisian*, 26 February 1880. Republication was
probably unauthorized.

b. *Later editions:*

The popularity of Zola's novel in England led to numerous reprintings within a few months of original publication. Vizetelly
rapidly issued new "editions" with an increase in the number of
illustrations from the original 16 to 24, and later to 32. A cheaper

issue, without the illustrations, appeared in June 1884 and a yellowback issue in 1887.

A portion of the material quoted in these editions of *Nana* was reprinted by Vizetelly in a pamphlet, issued as a protest against the legal suppression of Zola's work which was being attempted in England. It was described by Arthur Waugh, in his "London Letter," the *Critic*, 14 October 1893, as "a curiosity of bibliography, and one which, I fancy, is catalogued in very few libraries." According to Thomas Seccombe in the *Dictionary of National Biography*, only twelve copies were printed.

EXTRACTS │ PRINCIPALLY FROM │ ENGLISH CLASSICS: │ SHOWING │ THAT THE LEGAL SUPPRESSION OF M. ZOLA'S NOVELS │ WOULD LOGICALLY INVOLVE │ THE BOWDLERIZING OF SOME OF THE GREATEST WORKS │ IN ENGLISH LITERATURE. │ LONDON: 1888.

($9\frac{1}{2} \times 7\frac{1}{8}$): B–F⁸ G⁴, pp. 88. 8vo.

A separate four-page leaflet, dated 18 September 1888, is inserted at front or back of all copies known.

Issued in brown or black cloth spine, grey paper boards; white endpapers; all edges trimmed.

Published April or May 1888, distributed gratis.

Contains:

Mr. Henry James On the Modern Novel. Pp. 6–7.
    Brief quotation of one and a half paragraphs from the *Nana* review.

B2   STORIES BY AMERICAN   1884
                   AUTHORS

STORIES BY │ AMERICAN AUTHORS │ V. │ [Titles and authors are listed within a single-rule panel] A LIGHT MAN. │ BY HENRY JAMES. │ YATIL. │ BY F. D. MILLET. │ THE END OF NEW YORK. │ BY PARK BENJAMIN. │ WHY

THOMAS WAS DISCHARGED. | BY GEORGE ARNOLD. |
THE TACHYPOMP. | BY E. P. MITCHELL. | NEW YORK |
CHARLES SCRIBNER'S SONS | 1884

($6\frac{7}{16} \times 4\frac{3}{8}$): [unsigned: 13 signatures gathered in alternate 6's and 10's: 1^6 2^{10}, etc.], pp. ii, 202. 16 mo.

Issued in bright yellow cloth, lettered in black on front cover and spine, publisher's device and panel enclosing story titles and authors (with single-rules underscoring general title) in black on front cover, single-rule at top and bottom and five dots signifying volume number in black on spine; white paste-down end-papers, lacking free end-papers; all edges trimmed.

Published 23 July 1884, at 50 cents.

Reissued 4 June 1891, each volume containing sheets of two volumes of the first impression, complete with individual title-leaves, in deep russet diaper cloth, lettered within single-rule panels in gilt against russet solid-background panels on spine. Vol. V–VI contains frontispiece portrait of James, with tissue guard, tipped in, not reckoned in pagination. This portrait, lacking in primary issue, is also noted in single volumes issued with an 1894 imprint.

Reissued November 1904, under the title "The Library of American Fiction," with imprint of The Success Company, New York.

James contributed:

A Light Man. Pp. [5]–53.

> First appeared in the *Galaxy*, July 1869.
>
> James used the original magazine pages as his "copy" for the publisher but incorporated into them so many revisions as to amount almost to a rewriting of the story.

B3   A CATALOGUE OF DRAW-   1886
INGS BY ABBEY

A CATALOGUE OF THE | DRAWINGS BY MR. ED- | WIN
A. ABBEY FOR "SHE | STOOPS TO CONQUER." A |
COMEDY BY DR. OLIVER | GOLDSMITH [eight dots] |
GROLIER CLUB | DECEMBER FIFTEENTH TO | TWENTY-
SECOND, EIGHTEEN | HUNDRED AND EIGHTY-SIX |
NEW YORK

($8 \times 5\frac{7}{16}$): a single unsigned quire of six leaves, pp. 12, sewn. [8vo]

Issued, without wrappers, on stiff white laid paper; all edges untrimmed. Decorative initial letter within panel, p. 3.

Published 15 December 1886, simultaneously with opening of the exhibition, copies being sent gratis to all 184 members of the club. It is probable that copies were sold to non-members. George L. McKay, curator of the Grolier Club, reports the exhibit was attended by 2500 visitors in the one week.

James contributed:

Edwin A. Abbey. Pp. 3–7.

> First appeared in *Harper's Weekly*, 4 December 1886. This edited text eliminates about a quarter of the original material. The full text (with minor revisions) was first published in book form in *Picture and Text*, 1893 (See A38).

B4   THE ODD NUMBER   1889

a. *First edition:*

THE ODD NUMBER | [rule] | THIRTEEN TALES | BY | GUY DE MAUPASSANT [in red] | THE TRANSLATION | BY JONATHAN STURGES | AN INTRODUCTION | BY HENRY JAMES | NEW YORK | HARPER & BROTHERS, FRANKLIN SQUARE | 1889

($6\frac{13}{16} \times 4\frac{5}{16}$): [i]⁹ ([i₂] is an insert) [1–2]⁸ 3–14⁸ 15², pp. xviii, 228. 16mo.

Issued in dark blue linen-grain cloth, lettered in gilt on front cover and spine, single-rule border and decorative frame enclosing two decorative-banded panels and publisher's device in silver on front cover, decorative bands in silver on spine; off-white end-papers; top edge trimmed, other edges untrimmed.

Published 29 October 1889, at $1.

Reissued in Harper's Master-Tales series about 1894, in various cloths and colours. Contents uniform with first edition except for addition of frontispiece portrait, with tissue guard, tipped in.

James contributed:

Introduction, "Guy de Maupassant", dated August 6, 1889. Pp. [vii]–xvii. First appeared in *Harper's Weekly*, 19 October 1889.

b. *First English issue* (1891):

In October 1891 James R. Osgood, McIlvaine & Co. published an English issue, from the American plates, in the Red Letter Stories series at 2/6 in paper wrappers and 3/6 in cloth. The title-leaf is a cancel. A facsimile signature at the end of the introduction in the American edition is replaced by a printed signature.

B5   THE ART OF AUTHORSHIP   1890

a. *First edition:*

THE | ART OF AUTHORSHIP | LITERARY REMINIS-CENCES, | METHODS OF WORK, AND ADVICE TO YOUNG BEGINNERS, | PERSONALLY CONTRIBUTED BY | LEADING AUTHORS OF THE DAY. | COMPILED AND EDITED BY | GEORGE BAINTON. | LONDON: | JAMES CLARKE & CO., 13 & 14, FLEET STREET. | [rule] | 1890.

$(7\frac{1}{2} \times 4\frac{7}{8})$: [i]^6 1–22^8 [23]^2, pp. xii, 356, followed by 8 pp. of advertisements on lighter stock. Post 8vo.

Issued in brown-olive smooth cloth, lettering and flower ornaments in gilt and decorative circle and basket-weave ornaments in red-brown on front cover and spine, double-rule border in red-brown on front cover, triple-rule in red-brown at top and bottom of spine; (*a*) brown-coated or (*b*) white end-papers; all edges untrimmed.

Published April 1890, at 5/-. Announced as a May publication in the *English Catalogue*, but noted under April publications in the *Bookseller*, May 1890. Editor's inscribed copies all contain April dating.

A variant binding is noted, issued in blue smooth cloth, uniform with binding described above except for substitution of black blocking for red-brown.

Contains:

Note on literary form. P. 208.

> James's statement, like most of the others in the book, was elicited for use in connection with a school course in composition. Publication was unauthorized, and created a controversy, the details of which are recounted in "The Art of Authorship," the *Author*, I (16 June 1890), 44–46.

b. *First edition, American issue:*

THE ART | OF AUTHORSHIP | LITERARY REMINIS-

CENCES, METHODS OF WORK, | AND ADVICE TO YOUNG
BEGINNERS | PERSONALLY CONTRIBUTED | BY LEAD-
ING AUTHORS OF THE DAY | COMPILED AND EDITED
BY | GEORGE BAINTON | NEW YORK | D. APPLETON
AND COMPANY | 1890

$(7\frac{1}{4} \times 4\frac{3}{4})$: [1]^8 2–23^8, pp. x, 358. 12mo.

Issued in olive-green cloth, lettering in gilt and decorative ornament
in gilt and green on front cover, lettering and decorative ornament in
gilt on spine; lime green-coated end-papers; top edge trimmed and
yellow-ochre-stained, other edges untrimmed.

Published 5 June 1890, at $1.25, the issue consisting of imported sheets
of the English edition, with a new title-leaf and minor alterations in
arrangement of contents. Phillips erroneously reported date of publication as 1891.

B6   PORT TARASCON   1890

a. *First edition:*

ALPHONSE DAUDET | [rule] | PORT TARASCON [in red] |
THE LAST ADVENTURES | OF THE | ILLUSTRIOUS
TARTARIN | TRANSLATED | BY HENRY JAMES | ILLUS-
TRATED | BY ROSSI, MYRBACH, MONTÉGUT, BIELER |
AND MONTENARD | [publisher's device] | NEW YORK |
HARPER & BROTHERS, FRANKLIN SQUARE | 1891 [1890]

$(8\frac{7}{8} \times 6\frac{1}{8})$: [i]^2 [ii]^1 1–22^8 [23]^6, pp. vi, 364, on coated paper. 8vo.

Issued in dark blue diagonal-fine-ribbed cloth, lettered in gilt on front
cover and spine, decorative border and panel in silver on front cover,
decorative bands at top and bottom and three fleur-de-lys devices in
silver on spine; off-white end-papers; top edge trimmed and gilt,
other edges untrimmed.

Published 30 October 1890, at $2.50. The English translation was
published before the original French edition.

A secondary binding is noted, issued in (*a*) cream-white or (*b*) orange
smooth-bead-grain cloth, lettered and blocked uniform with primary
binding in black on front cover and spine, except for shifting of fleur-
de-lys devices on spine from bottom to top; top edge is trimmed but
not gilt.

Frontispiece varies in the two binding states. The primary state contains either a portrait facing left and signed J. W. A[lexander]., or one facing right and signed T. A. Butler; only the latter portrait is found in the secondary state.

First appeared in *Harper's New Monthly Magazine*, June–November 1890. There are several variations between serial and book publication, including minor revisions, an enlarged preface, and the inclusion in the book of a full chapter (Chapter V) eliminated from the serial text. Concerning this elimination, Henry Mills Alden, editor of *Harper's*, wrote: "There were passages in the chapter which would give offence to a large number of our Christian readers. . . . I found by actual test that there was a chance of its being misunderstood. We followed our usual rule in such a case, and left it out." (J. Henry Harper, *The House of Harper*, New York, 1912, pp. 620–621.)

The undertaking by an author of Henry James's creative capacities of a translating chore was explained by him to Frederick Macmillan, 24 March 1890: "I was bribed with gold—more gold than the translator (as I suppose) is accustomed to receive. The book is charming." (HJ, *Letters*, III, 1980, p. 274.) The only other translations made by James, invariably from the French, were a brief prose poem of Ivan Turgenev's (see D272), Daudet's article on the Russian novelist written shortly after Turgenev's death for publication in the *Century Magazine* (see D395), and an essay by Maurice Barrès, "The Saints of France," as a contribution to *The Book of France*, 1915 (see B33).

b. *First English edition:*

ALPHONSE DAUDET | [rule] | PORT TARASCON | THE LAST ADVENTURES | OF THE | ILLUSTRIOUS TAR-TARIN | TRANSLATED | BY HENRY JAMES | ILLUS-TRATED | BY ROSSI, MYRBACH, MONTÉGUT, BIELER | AND MONTENARD | LONDON | SAMPSON LOW, MAR-STON, SEARLE & RIVINGTON | LIMITED | ST DUN-STAN'S HOUSE, FETTER LANE. | 1891 [1890] | ALL RIGHTS RESERVED. [Final line is bracketed]

($8\frac{3}{4} \times 5\frac{13}{16}$): [i]² 1–22⁸ 23⁴, pp. iv, 360, followed by 32-page catalogue of advertisements. Square 8vo.

Issued in blue-grey smooth cloth, bevelled edges, lettered in gilt on front cover and spine, illustrations blocked in black and silver on front cover and in black on back cover, publisher's device in black on back cover, triangular dotted device in gilt on spine; dark-green-coated end-papers; top edge gilt, other edges untrimmed.

Published November 1890, at 7/6. Advertised as "Now Ready" in the *Athenaeum*, 22 November 1890. Phillips erroneously gave date of publication as 1892.

Several variants have been noted, issued in blue sand-grain, blue-green smooth, and cherry-red sand-grain cloths, with green-coated or white end-papers, lacking bevelled edges, and generally lacking catalogue of advertisements. These variants range widely in page size, from $7\frac{5}{16} \times 5\frac{7}{16}$ to $8\frac{3}{4} \times 5\frac{7}{8}$. All edges trimmed.

For Times Book Club remainder binding, see F35.

Phillips recorded that the English edition was printed from American plates, a fact which has frequently been disputed by bibliographers. The evidence, however, tends to support this statement. The text and illustrations are uniform, except for alterations in the preliminaries and inclusion of British printer's imprint, and the printing records of Messrs William Clowes & Sons reveal no composition charges, the total cost to the publisher for printing and binding being £75.18.0. It is therefore reasonable to assume that stereotypes were imported by the English publisher to avoid the heavy cost of reproducing the substantial number of engraved illustrations. Unfortunately the records of both the American and English publishers are no longer extant.

B7   CATALOGUE OF A COLLECTION 1891
OF DRAWINGS BY ALFRED
PARSONS

CATALOGUE | OF A | COLLECTION OF DRAWINGS | BY | ALFRED PARSONS, R.I. | WITH A PREFATORY NOTE | BY | HENRY JAMES. | EXHIBITED AT | THE FINE ART SOCIETY'S. | 148, NEW BOND STREET, W., | LONDON. | 1891.

($8\frac{3}{8} \times 5\frac{7}{16}$): a single unsigned quire of eight leaves, pp. 16, stapled and sewn. [8vo]

Issued in grey-blue paper wrappers, cut flush, stapled to the single gathering of stitched sheets, front cover uniform with title-page except for addition of underscored, italicized *Exhibition No. 84.* in black; advertisement for the Fine Art Society in black on back cover; advertisements on inner sides of wrappers; all edges trimmed.

Published at sixpence, simultaneously with opening of the exhibit on 9 March 1891, but copies were available for the Private View on 7 March.

James contributed:

Preface. Pp. [3]–11.

This was the first appearance of the essay, later collected, under the title "Alfred Parsons," in *Picture and Text*, 1893, with very slight textual alterations.

B8   MINE OWN PEOPLE   1891

MINE OWN PEOPLE | BY | RUDYARD KIPLING | AUTHOR OF | "PLAIN TALES FROM THE HILLS," "SOLDIERS THREE," "THE PHANTOM | 'RICKSHAW'," "THE LIGHT THAT FAILED," ETC. | WITH A CRITICAL INTRO-DUCTION BY | HENRY JAMES | AUTHORIZED EDITION | NEW YORK | UNITED STATES BOOK COMPANY | SUC-CESSORS TO | JOHN W. LOVELL COMPANY | 150 WORTH ST., COR. MISSION PLACE [1891]

$(7\frac{5}{16} \times 4\frac{7}{8})$: b–c^8 2–17^8, pp. [2], xxvi, 9–268. Frontispiece and tissue guard inserted. 12mo.

Issued in burgundy smooth cloth, bevelled edges, lettering and decorative bands with filler devices in gilt on front cover and spine; white end-papers; top edge trimmed and gilt, other edges trimmed. Lacks publisher's imprint on spine.

Published May 1891, at $1.25. Reviewed in the *New York Tribune*, 10 May 1891, but first noted in *Publishers' Weekly*, 23 May.

There are numerous cheaper editions and reissues of the work, some of which are frequently mistaken for the first edition. One of these is the tan paper-wrappered edition containing the same title-page as the first edition, with the imprint "Lovell's International Series, No. 153" and a single-rule above the title. A second is issued from plates or sheets of the first edition, in uniform binding, but lacking frontispiece, and with imprint on title-page reading: "New York | Lovell, Coryell & Company | 310–318 Sixth Avenue." Publisher's imprint appears on spine.

James contributed:

Introduction. Pp. [vii]–xxvi.

> First appeared here. Reprinted, 1891, as introduction to *Soldiers Three* in the English Library (see B9). Reprinted in *Views and Reviews*, 1908 (see A65).

B9   SOLDIERS THREE   1891

SOLDIERS THREE | SETTING FORTH CERTAIN PAS-SAGES IN THE LIVES | AND ADVENTURES OF PRIVATES TERENCE MULVANEY, | STANLEY ORTHERIS, AND JOHN LEAROYD | WITH OTHER STORIES | BY | RUDYARD KIPLING | WITH A CRITICAL INTRODUCTION BY | HENRY JAMES | "WE BE SOLDIERS THREE— | PARDONNEZ-MOI, JE VOUS EN PRIE" [*in italics*] | LEIPZIG | HEINEMANN AND BALESTIER | LIMITED, LONDON | 1891

$(6\frac{5}{16} \times 4\frac{9}{16})$: [a]³ [b]⁴ [A]⁸ B–S⁸ [T]¹, pp. [6], xxiv, 274. Sm. 8vo.

Issued in light buff paper wrappers, cut flush, uniform with series (see F1), lettered and ruled in dark brown on front cover and spine; advertisements in brown on back cover and inner sides of wrappers; all edges untrimmed.

Published 1891, at M. 1.60 or 2 francs, No. 59 in the English Library.

James contributed:

Introduction. Pp. [i]–xxi.

> This is the first Continental appearance of the introduction written for the first Authorized American edition of Kipling's *Mine Own People* (see B8).

a. *First edition:*

THE | AVERAGE | WOMAN | [parallel with the three lines of
the main title are the five lines of the titles of the three
stories included in the volume] A COMMON | STORY
[device] RE | FFEY [device] CAP | TAIN MY CAP | TAIN! |
BY | WOLCOTT BALESTIER | WITH A BIOGRAPHICAL |
SKETCH BY HENRY JAMES | LONDON WILLIAM HEINE-
MANN | MDCCCXCII BEDFORD STREET W.C.

$(7\frac{3}{16} \times 4\frac{13}{16})$: [a]^8 [b]^6 A–L^8 M^4 N^2 [O]^1, pp. xxviii, 190, followed by
8 pp. of advertisements. Sm. Crown 8vo.

Issued in light blue cloth, lettered in dark green on front cover and in
gilt on spine, peacock feather ornament in dark green on front cover
and spine; publisher's device in dark green on back cover; white end-
papers; all edges untrimmed.

Published 17 June 1892, at 3/6, the first (and only) printing consisting
of 2000 copies, of which 620 were later pulped.

James contributed:

Wolcott Balestier. Pp. vii–xxviii.

> First appeared in *Cosmopolitan Magazine*, May 1892. Reprinted
> in *The American Essays of Henry James*, 1956.

b. *First American edition:*

THE AVERAGE WOMAN | BY | WOLCOTT BALESTIER |
WITH A PREFACE BY HENRY JAMES | NEW YORK |
UNITED STATES BOOK COMPANY | 5 AND 7 EAST
SIXTEENTH STREET | [rule] | CHICAGO: 266 & 268
WABASH AVE. [1892]

$(7\frac{1}{4} \times 4\frac{3}{4})$: [unsigned: 1–16^8 17^4], pp. ii, 262. 12mo.

Issued in tan linen-grain cloth, lettered within single-rule oval panel in
brown against glazed grey background on front cover and spine; white
end-papers; all edges trimmed. Lacks publisher's imprint on spine.

Published June 1892, at $1.25. Noted under "Books Received" in the
New York Times, 26 June 1892.

This edition omits the tribute by William Heinemann included in the English edition, p. [189].

James contributed:

Wolcott Balestier. Pp. [11]–34.

B11   THE GREAT STREETS OF   1892
                THE WORLD

a. *First edition:*

THE GREAT STREETS | OF THE WORLD | BY | RICHARD HARDING DAVIS W. W. STORY | ANDREW LANG HENRY JAMES | FRANCISQUE SARCEY PAUL LINDAU | ISABEL F. HAPGOOD | ILLUSTRATED BY | A. B. FROST ETTORE TITO | W. DOUGLAS ALMOND ALEXANDER ZEZZOS | G. JEANNIOT F. STAHL | ILYA EFIMOVITCH RÉPIN | NEW YORK | CHARLES SCRIBNER'S SONS | 1892

($9\frac{3}{4} \times 6\frac{7}{8}$): [unsigned: 1–17⁸], pp. [2], xiv, 256. Large 8vo.

Issued in dark blue smooth cloth, lettering and armorial ornaments in gilt and wreath ornament and decorative border in dull yellow on front cover, title in cloth colour against decorative panel in gilt and dull yellow and ornaments in gilt and lettering in dull yellow on spine; cocoa-brown-coated end-papers; top edge trimmed and gilt, other edges trimmed.

Published December 1892, at $4. Advertised in the *New York Tribune*, 17 December 1892.

James contributed:

The Grand Canal. Pp. [143]–172.

> First appeared in *Scribner's Magazine*, November 1892. The essay is illustrated with 13 drawings by Alexander Zezzos in both serial and book publication. Reprinted in *Italian Hours*, 1909.

b. *First edition, English issue:*

($9\frac{7}{8} \times 7$): collation and contents uniform with American edition except for altered imprint on title-page: LONDON: 45, ALBEMARLE STREET | JAMES R. OSGOOD, MCILVAINE, & CO. | 1892 Described by publisher as Royal 8vo.

Issued in dark blue fine-woven cloth, London street scene illustration in gilt on front cover, lettered in gilt on spine; green-coated end-papers; top edge trimmed and gilt, other edges untrimmed.

Published December 1892, or January 1893, at 18/-. British Museum deposit not made until 30 January 1893, but the work is listed as a December 1892 issue in the *English Catalogue*.

A secondary binding is noted, sheets of the first English issue being bound in indigo vertical-ribbed cloth, lettered in gilt on spine, bearing publisher's imprint "Harpers" on spine; white end-papers; all edges untrimmed.

B12   FAME'S TRIBUTE TO   1892
                   CHILDREN

FAME'S | TRIBUTE TO CHILDREN | BEING A COLLEC-
TION OF AUTOGRAPH SENTIMENTS CON- | TRIBUTED
BY FAMOUS MEN AND WOMEN FOR THIS | VOLUME.
DONE IN FAC-SIMILE AND PUB- | LISHED FOR THE
BENEFIT OF THE | CHILDREN'S HOME, OF THE |
WORLD'S COLUMBIAN EXPOSITION | [illustration] |
CHICAGO | A. C. MCCLURG AND COMPANY | 1892

$(9\frac{7}{8} \times 7\frac{5}{8})$: [unsigned: 1–18⁴ 19⁴ (—19₄)], pp. 150. 4to.

Issued in white linen, lettering and wreath device in gilt on front cover; white end-papers; all edges trimmed.

Published 1892. Copyright deposit made 16 December 1892. Date of publication and price not ascertained.

The second edition, issued in 1893, contains an added group of contributions, separately paginated, printed on both sides of the leaf, with seven illustrations tipped in. Bound in green, white, or steel-blue half linen, floral-patterned paper boards in varying colours, lettered in gilt on front cover. Many of these copies were distributed, presumably gratis, with the imprint, "Presented by the Chicago Great Western Railway, 'The Maple Leaf Route,'" on front cover and map of the route within a maple leaf ornament on back cover, in gilt.

James contributed:

Facsimile holograph transcript of a brief passage from "The Pupil." P. 39.

In the second edition, James's contribution appears in Part I, p. 29.

The only other holograph facsimile noted during the period of James's lifetime is a brief extract of "Impressions of A Cousin," reproduced in Part III of Caroline Ticknor's "Characteristic Manuscripts," *Truth* (New York), XIX (May 1900), 122–123.

B13   THE QUEST OF THE   1895–1901
                      HOLY GRAIL

a. *First text* (1895):

"THE QUEST OF | THE HOLY GRAIL." | THE FIRST PORTION OF A SERIES OF | PAINTINGS TO BE DONE FOR THE | DECORATION OF THE | PUBLIC LIBRARY OF BOSTON, U.S.A. | BY EDWIN A. ABBEY. | [rule] | NOW SHOWN FOR A LIMITED PERIOD | AT THE GALLERIES 9, CONDUIT ST., W. | DAILY FROM 10 A.M. TO 6 P.M. | JANUARY 1895.

($7\frac{1}{2} \times 4\frac{7}{8}$): a single unsigned quire of four leaves, pp. 8 (unpaginated), sewn. [8vo]

Issued without wrappers, on white laid paper; all edges untrimmed.

Published 19 January 1895.

The only copy we have seen is owned by Mr C. Waller Barrett.

b. *First revised text* (1895):

THE QUEST OF THE HOLY GRAIL | A SERIES OF PAINT-INGS DONE FOR | THE DECORATION OF THE DELIVERY | ROOM IN THE PUBLIC LIBRARY OF THE | CITY OF BOSTON BY . . . . . . | EDWIN A. ABBEY | [publisher's device, incorporating imprint R. H. RUSSELL | AND SON | PUBLISHERS | N.Y.] | MDCCCXCV

($11\frac{7}{8} \times 9\frac{1}{8}$): [unsigned: $1–4^2$], pp. 16 (unpaginated), on glossed paper, sewn. Large 4to.

Issued in white half Japan, off-white paper boards, ornate lettering and decoration in red and black on front cover; white end-papers; all edges trimmed.

Published June 1895, at $1.25. Advertised in *Publishers' Weekly*,

1 June 1895. Announced as "to be published at once," in the "Literary Notes" of the *New York Tribune*, 16 June, and noted under "Books Received," in the *New York Times*, 22 June.

c. *Second revised text* (1901):

THE CORPORATION OF LONDON. | [decorative device] | EXHIBITION | AT THE | GUILDHALL ART GALLERY | OF THE | SERIES OF PAINTINGS | PRESENTING | ''THE QUEST OF THE HOLY GRAIL.'' | EXECUTED FOR THE DECORATION OF | THE PUBLIC LIBRARY OF BOSTON, U.S.A. | BY | EDWIN A. ABBEY, R.A. | [three leaf devices] | OPEN DAILY 10 A.M. TO 4 P.M., FROM MONDAY, 28TH OCTOBER, TO | TUESDAY, 19TH NOVEMBER, 1901, INCLUSIVE. | ADMISSION FREE.

$(7\frac{9}{16} \times 4\frac{1}{2})$: a single unsigned quire of eight leaves, pp. 16, sewn. [8vo] Issued in blue-grey paper wrappers, cut flush, lettering and Guildhall coat-of-arms device in black on front cover; inner sides of wrappers blank; all edges trimmed.

Published 28 October 1901, at sixpence.

The only copy we have located is in the library of the Guildhall, London. This second revised text was reprinted in a catalogue issued for the exhibition of the Grail paintings at the American Art Galleries, New York, 9–21 December 1901. The text was later reprinted by the Boston Public Library, on two double-columned folio sheets, $11\frac{1}{2} \times 7\frac{3}{4}$, versos blank, the first column of the first sheet being headed: BOSTON PUBLIC LIBRARY. | [decorative rule] | THE QUEST AND ACHIEVEMENT | OF THE HOLY GRAIL. | WALL PAINTINGS IN THE BOSTON PUBLIC LIBRARY | INSTALLED IN 1895 | BY | EDWIN AUSTIN ABBEY, R.A. | [rule] | AN OUTLINE | OF THIS VERSION OF THE LEGEND | BY HENRY JAMES. The catalogue of the American Art Association, 6–7 December 1933, records a copy uniform with the above description but worded WALL PAINTINGS IN THE DELIVERY ROOM for the fifth line of the heading, and with "laid in original wrappers, with cloth back and paper label." The Boston Public Library has been unable to locate a record of such a wrappered issue.

―――――

There seems to be sufficient evidence to warrant inclusion of these three texts in a bibliography of Henry James's works, although his would have been largely the revising, rather than the author's, hand. A devoted friend of the American artist and illustrator, Edwin A. Abbey,

The Quest Of The Holy Grail

By

Edwin A. Abbey

With Explanatory Notes

By

Henry James

New York

R. H. Russell & Son

1895

and of his wife, James was interested from the first in the series of Arthurian paintings commissioned from the artist by the Boston Public Library and executed by him during the 1890's. According to Abbey's biographer, E. V. Lucas, James assisted Mrs Abbey in preparing a text for the catalogue of the exhibition of the first five panels of the Grail Series held at the Conduit Galleries in January 1895. In an undated letter of the autumn of 1895, quoted by Lucas, the novelist wrote to Mrs Abbey: "My 'help' last winter wasn't worth any kind of recognition—it was help most lame and inadequate."

The Conduit Gallery text was the basis for the textual material included in *The Quest of the Holy Grail*, published later in 1895 in New York. An important piece of circumstantial evidence, in the Collamore Collection at Colby College, links James's name with this book. It consists of a printer's dummy of the volume, on the title-page of which is pencilled "With Explanatory Notes | By | Henry James". Moreover, in announcing the book—which was brought out in America shortly after the exhibition in New York of the first five panels—*Publishers' Weekly* noted (27 April 1895): "The pictures are to be reproduced in a small volume of popular character . . . to be written by Mr. and Mrs. Abbey, with the valuable assistance of Henry James."

James's name, however, does not appear on the published title-page, and it is to be presumed from his remark to Mrs Abbey that he did not want it used.

Two later catalogues of the Guildhall Exhibition, London, and the American Art Association, New York, both in 1901, and the leaflet of the Boston Public Library (which to this day is distributed to viewers of the panels), have texts which are uniform, being slightly revised reprints of the Conduit Galleries text with added descriptions of the later panels.

Lucas specifically attributes to James the entire description of the fifth panel, "Galahad's First Coming to the Castle of the Grail." In quoting this passage in full he uses the Guildhall text of 1901. A collation of all the texts leaves the distinct impression that the two versions subsequent to the Conduit Galleries text must be considered as emended and elaborated reprintings of that text. There are some differences between the text relating to the fifth panel as given in the Conduit booklet and that of 1901. The possibility must not be dismissed that Lucas was attributing to James a text originally by the novelist and later modified either by him or by other hands.

The Boston Public Library issue, clearly based on the Guildhall text of 1901, has frequently been assigned to 1895. Brussel records the issue as limited to 30 copies, without citing any source of information, and quotes H. W. Mathews of the Library as saying the item was "presumably issued" in January 1895, in conjunction with the Conduit Galleries exhibition. The Library, however, is now unable to turn up any record of the date of first printing or the number of copies printed. Copies are still issued as needed, from the original plates. At an unspecified date a decorative border was added. In the current issues the copies are dated at the bottom with the number of copies printed, i.e. "3,16,51, 100." The 30-copy figure might, presumably, have come from a similar source, but in that case the date should also have been available.

A search conducted during the past decade has failed to turn up the James letters to the Abbeys to which Lucas had access, and which might disclose the exact extent of the novelist's participation in the writing of the Grail notes.

B14   THE DRAMA BIRTHDAY BOOK   1895

THE [decorative device] | DRAMA | BIRTHDAY | BOOK | [illustration, in brown and black] | 1895 COMPILED | BY | PERCY S. PHILLIPS | LONDON: JOHN MACQUEEN

($6\frac{5}{8} \times 4\frac{1}{4}$): [a]² [b]⁴ [A]² B–Q⁸ R², pp. 260 (unpaginated). F'cap 8vo. Issued in russet fine-bead-grain cloth, lettered in gilt and black on front cover and in gilt on spine, decorative ornaments in gilt and black on front cover and in black on spine; pale lemon end-papers; top edge trimmed and gilt, other edges untrimmed.

Published November 1895, at 3/6. Noted in "List of New Books," in the *Athenaeum*, 23 November 1895, and advertised as "Now Ready" on the same date.

James contributed :

Quotation from *The American* (under date of June 29)

Quotation from *Guy Domville* (under date of May 20)

> These authorized quotations, plus those of *Guy Domville* in *The George Alexander Birthday Book*, 1903 (see B23), were the only portions of the two plays published during James's lifetime.

B15   LIBRARY OF THE WORLD'S   1896
BEST LITERATURE

LIBRARY | OF THE | WORLD'S BEST LITERATURE | ANCIENT AND MODERN | CHARLES DUDLEY WARNER |

B. CONTRIBUTIONS TO BOOKS

EDITOR | HAMILTON WRIGHT MABIE, LUCIA GILBERT RUNKLE, | GEORGE H. WARNER | ASSOCIATE EDITORS | THIRTY VOLUMES | VOL. I [II–XXX] | NEW YORK | R. S. PEALE AND J. A. HILL | PUBLISHERS [1896–1897]

(9¾ × 6⅞): Royal 8vo.

Issued in maroon fine-cross-ribbed cloth, double-rule border in blind on front and back covers, lettering within blind impression and single-rule at top and bottom in gilt on spine; white end-papers; all edges trimmed.

Published, by subscription only, from October 1896 to Spring 1897, at $3 per volume in cloth. Also issued at $3.50 in quarter Russia, $4 in half Morocco, and $5.50 in full Morocco. Advertised as "now in course of publication . . . the first two volumes are ready," in *Harper's Weekly*, 17 October 1896.

The earliest volumes bear imprint, "Copyright 1896 | By R. S. Peale and J. A. Hill", on verso of title-leaf. Later volumes have 1897 imprint. In 1897 a University Edition was issued, in 45 volumes, bound in tan buckram, limited to 1000 copies, under the imprint of The International Society. Later issues include a Teacher's Edition in 31 volumes, under the imprint of J. A. Hill (circa 1902), and a Memorial Edition De Luxe in 46 volumes, under the imprint of J. A. Hill (circa 1902).

James contributed:

Nathaniel Hawthorne. Vol. XII, 7053–7061.

James Russell Lowell. Vol. XVI, 9229–9237.

Ivan Turgenieff. Vol. XXV, 15057–15062.

> All three essays were written especially for this edition. "Hawthorne" was reprinted in *The Warner Classics*, Vol. II, 1899, "Turgenieff" in *The Art of Fiction and Other Essays*, 1948, and "Lowell" in *The American Essays of Henry James*, 1956.

B16   LAST STUDIES   1897

LAST STUDIES | BY | HUBERT CRACKANTHORPE | AUTHOR OF | "SENTIMENTAL STUDIES," "WRECK-AGE," | "VIGNETTES," & C. | WITH A POEM BY STOP-FORD A. BROOKE, AND | AN APPRECIATION BY HENRY JAMES | LONDON | WILLIAM HEINEMANN | 1897

(7½ × 4¹⁵⁄₁₆): [a]⁸ b⁶ B–P⁸, pp. [2], xxvi, 224, followed by 16-page catalogue of advertisements. Frontispiece and tissue guard inserted. Crown 8vo.

Issued in light green smooth cloth, lettering and acorn device in black on front cover, publisher's device in blind on back cover, lettering and acorn device in gilt on spine; white end-papers; all edges untrimmed.

Published 1 November 1897, at 6/-, the first (and only) printing consisting of 1000 copies, of which 300 were later pulped.

James contributed:

Hubert Crackanthorpe, an appreciation. Pp. xi–xxiii.
    First appeared here; never reprinted.

B17   IMPRESSIONS   1898

a. *First edition:*

IMPRESSIONS | BY [underscored by leaf device] PIERRE LOTI | WITH AN INTRODUCTION BY HENRY JAMES | ARCHIBALD CONSTABLE AND CO. | WESTMINSTER [leaf device] MDCCCXCVIII. [Entire title surrounded by rubricated full-page poppy design and double-rule frame]

($8\frac{9}{16} \times 6\frac{3}{4}$): [unsigned: 1^2 2–13^8], pp. iv, 192. Tissue guard inserted between [1_{1-2}]. Imperial 16mo.

Issued in white half parchment, light green linen-grain cloth, lettering and tree ornament within double-rule vertical panel in black against background in gilt on front cover, lettering and leaf device in gilt on spine; white end-papers; all edges untrimmed. Tissue guard inserted before title.

Published November 1898, at 10/6. Noted in "List of New Books," in the *Athenaeum*, 12 November 1898, and advertised in the same publication, 19 November.

Two secondary bindings are noted: (*a*) uniform with primary binding except for elimination of gilt blocking on front cover and substitution of green lettering on front cover and spine; (*b*) dark green linen-grain full cloth, lettered in green on front cover and spine, blocking in green on front cover, lacking tissue guard.

For Times Book Club remainder binding, see F36.

James contributed:

Pierre Loti. Pp. [1]–21.
    First appeared here; never reprinted.

b. *First edition, American issue* (1900)*:*

IMPRESSIONS | BY [underscored by leaf device] PIERRE
LOTI | WITH AN INTRODUCTION BY HENRY JAMES |
NEW YORK: BRENTANO'S: MDCCCC. [Rubricated title-
page panel and ornamentation uniform with English edition]

$(8\frac{9}{16} \times 6\frac{3}{4})$: [unsigned: 1^3 (1_2 is an insert) 2^8 (-2_1) $3-13^8$], pp. iv, 192.
Small 4to.

Issued uniform with primary binding state of English edition.

Published in the autumn of 1900, at $2. Noted in the "Index to Fall
Announcements," *Publishers' Weekly*, 29 September 1900. No later
listing or advertisement discovered.

B18 [THE FUTURE OF THE NOVEL] 1899

a. *First edition:*

THE INTERNATIONAL | LIBRARY OF | FAMOUS LITERA-
TURE [in orange-brown] | SELECTIONS FROM THE
WORLD'S GREAT WRITERS | ANCIENT, MEDIAEVAL,
AND MODERN, WITH BIO- | GRAPHICAL AND EX-
PLANATORY NOTES | AND | CRITICAL ESSAYS | BY |
MANY EMINENT WRITERS. | EDITED BY | DR. RICHARD
GARNETT, C.B. [in orange-brown] | OF THE BRITISH
MUSEUM | (1851–1899) | IN ASSOCIATION WITH | [eight
lines listing associate editors] | WITH NEARLY FIVE
HUNDRED FULL-PAGE ILLUSTRATIONS AND COLORED
PLATES | IN TWENTY VOLUMES [in orange-brown] |
VOLUME XIV | LONDON | ISSUED BY | THE STANDARD
[in orange-brown] | 1899.

$(9\frac{1}{4} \times 6\frac{1}{2})$: [unsigned: 1^{12} $2-31^8$ 32^4], pp. [2], xxii, 488 (numbered
6337–6824). Frontispiece, tissue guard and 29 illustrations inserted.
8vo.

Issued in deep red simulated half leather ("half Persian calf"), dull
maroon cloth sides, lettering and decorative ornaments within four
single-rule panels in gilt and bogus raised bands on spine; white and
gold mottled end-papers; top edge trimmed and gilt, other edges
trimmed.

Issued also in cloth, three-quarter red levant, and full Morocco (no copies available for examination).

Published November 1899. The full set of twenty volumes was advertised in the *Standard*, 26 September 1899, at £6/16/6 in cloth, £8/18/6 in half Persian calf, £11/0/6 in three-quarter red levant, and £15/4/6 in full Morocco.

James contributed:

The Future of the Novel. Pp. [xi]–xxii.

> Note on divisional fly-title, p. [ix], reads: "Written for 'The International Library of Famous Literature' by Henry James..." The essay was reprinted in *The Future of the Novel*, 1956.

b. *First American edition* (1901):

WESTMINSTER EDITION [in red] | [rule, in red] | THE | UNIVERSAL ANTHOLOGY | A COLLECTION OF THE BEST LITERATURE, ANCIENT, MEDIAEVAL AND MODERN, [in red] | WITH BIOGRAPHICAL AND EX-PLANATORY NOTES [in red] | EDITED BY | RICHARD GARNETT | [five lines listing associate editors] | [rule] | VOLUME TWENTY-EIGHT [in red] | [rule] | PUBLISHED BY | THE CLARKE COMPANY, LIMITED, LONDON | MER-RILL & BAKER, NEW YORK | EMILE TERQUEM, PARIS | BIBLIOTHEK VERLAG, BERLIN [1901]

($9\frac{13}{16} \times 7$): [1–2]^8 3–25^8, pp. xxiv, 25–400. Frontispiece and four illustrations inserted. 4to.

Issued in light blue-green linen-grain cloth, lettered in black within pale grey-green panels on white paper label on spine; white endpapers; top edge trimmed and gilt, other edges untrimmed.

Issued also in half leather, marble paper boards, lettering and ornament in gilt on spine.

Published December 1901, at $3.50, the 33-volume edition being limited to 1000 sets "in English." Copyright entry for the full anthology was made 2 January 1900, but Vol. 28 was not deposited until 13 August 1901, and was first noted in the "Weekly Record of New Publications," *Publishers' Weekly*, 21 December 1901.

The anthology has also been noted in an "Academic Edition," bound in olive drab vertical-ribbed cloth, and in a "Mouseion Edition," bound in grey cloth, but otherwise uniform with the "Westminster

Edition." These variant editions are also limited to 1000 sets each "in English."

James contributed:

The Future of the Novel. Pp. xiii–xxiv. The essay also appeared in the *Saturday Review of Books and Art* (*New York Times*), 11 August 1900.

B19   THE VICAR OF WAKEFIELD   1900

THE CENTURY CLASSICS | [rule] | THE VICAR | OF WAKEFIELD | A TALE | BY OLIVER GOLDSMITH | SPERATE MISERI, CAVETE FELICES. [*in italics*] | WITH AN INTRODUCTION BY | HENRY JAMES | [publisher's device, in black and brown] | NEW YORK | THE CENTURY CO. | MCM [Entire title enclosed within single-rule border, in red-brown]

($7\frac{5}{8} \times 4\frac{13}{16}$): [1]⁴ 2–21⁸ 22⁶, pp. xxiv, 316. Frontispiece and tissue guard inserted. Tall 12mo.

Issued in uniform series binding, in bright green cloth, embossed all-over design in blind, single-rule border in gilt across front and back covers and spine, lettered in gilt on front and back covers, lettering and paired rules in gilt on spine; cover design in lime-green on white end-papers; top edge trimmed and gilt, other edges untrimmed.

Published 1 November 1900, at $1, in the Century Classics series, the first printing consisting of 3000 copies.

James contributed:

Introduction. Pp. xi–xx.

> Written specially for this edition. Reprinted in *A Book of Modern Essays*, edited by Bruce McCullough and Edwin Berry Burgum, New York, 1926.

B20   THE MAY BOOK   1901

a. *First edition, ordinary issue:*

THE | MAY BOOK | COMPILED BY MRS. [Eliza] ARIA | IN AID OF | CHARING CROSS HOSPITAL | [quotation, three lines] | LONDON | MACMILLAN & CO. LIMITED | 1901

($11\frac{1}{4} \times 9\frac{3}{8}$): [a]⁴ b² A–U⁴ X² [Y–Z]⁴, pp. xii, 180. Frontispiece, with holograph facsimile on tissue guard, and eight illustrations inserted. 4to.

Issued in pale azure blue linen-grain cloth, lettering in cream-white on front cover and spine, ornamental branches of apple blossom and varied rules in cream-white and London scenic illustration in cream-white, grey, lavender, and black on front cover, double-rule in cream-white at top and bottom of spine; white end-papers; all edges trimmed.

Published May 1901, at 10/-. Noted under "New Books" in the *Athenaeum*, 18 May.

A variant binding is noted, issued in blue-grey cloth, lettering and decorative band at top and bottom in light and dark green on front cover and spine, illustration of woman against poppy-and-leaf background in rose and dark green and pansy ornament in light and dark green on front cover. Both variant bindings have also been noted in variant colour cloths and blocking.

Some copies contain a blank leaf inserted between b_2 and A_1. In all copies page 22 is erroneously numbered 23.

James contributed:

The Saint's Afternoon. Pp. 1–10.

> First appeared here; reprinted in *Italian Hours*, 1909.

b. *First edition, limited issue:*

An Edition De Luxe, limited to 100 copies, was issued simultaneously with ordinary issue, in full white vellum over limp boards, lettered in gilt on front cover and spine, ornamental branches of apple blossoms in gilt on front cover; gold-grained end-papers; all edges untrimmed. Two pink ribbon ties are attached to the covers.

The text and illustrations for this impression have been rearranged, and the pages number xii, 222. No new text or illustrations added. On p. [222] is imprinted: "Printed by Ballantyne, Hanson & Co. | London & Edinburgh". The second and fifth lines of the title-page are printed in brown. Lacks advertisements at back. Page-size: $11\frac{3}{4} \times 8\frac{1}{2}$.

B21   THE TWO YOUNG BRIDES   1902

a. *First edition, English issue:*

THE TWO YOUNG [decorative initial "T" in blue-green and black, five lines high] | BRIDES [two devices] | TRANS-LATED FROM THE | FRENCH OF HONORE | DE BALZAC [two devices] | WITH A CRITICAL INTRODUCTION BY | HENRY JAMES [four devices] | [device] | LONDON: WILLIAM HEINEMANN: MCMII

$(8\frac{1}{2} \times 5\frac{3}{4})$: [a]^8 b–c^8 [d]^2 1–22^8 23^2 24^6 (on coated stock), pp. lii, 368. Frontispiece and three colour plates inserted. Demy 8vo.

Issued in light blue cloth, lettered within ornamental-mirror panel in gilt on front cover, publisher's device in blind on back cover, lettering and ornamental devices in gilt on spine; white end-papers; top edge gilt, other edges untrimmed.

Published 30 September 1902, Vol. 7 of "A Century of French Romance" series, edited by Edmund Gosse, the first printing consisting of 2000 copies, of which 1000 were issued as part of a 12-volume "Library Edition" at four guineas the set, and the balance issued singly at 7/6.

Although published nearly three months earlier than the American edition, this issue was printed from the American plates. The colour illustrations, however, were printed in England and exported for the American edition.

Publication of the British edition approximately three months before the American has led to the assumption that the latter was printed from the British plates. The reverse, however, appears to have been the case. The Heinemann cost-book records "U.S. plates," the edition was copyrighted by Appleton in Washington and James had to receive authorization from the American publisher in 1914 to include the Balzac and Flaubert prefaces (see also B22) in *Notes on Novelists*. The colour illustrations for the volume were provided by Heinemann.

Reissued, in July 1905, under the imprint of the London Book Company, in a Subscription Edition, consisting of 450 sets of sheets of the initial impression, with a new title-leaf.

James contributed:

Honoré de Balzac. Pp. v–xliii.

> Written specially for this edition. Reprinted, under the title "Honoré de Balzac, 1902," in *Notes on Novelists*, 1914.

b. *First edition, American issue (limited):*

THE TWO | YOUNG BRIDES | TRANSLATED FROM THE FRENCH OF | HONORE DE BALZAC | BY | THE LADY MARY LOYD | WITH A CRITICAL INTRODUCTION BY | HENRY JAMES | [rule] | ILLUSTRATED | NEW YORK | D. APPLETON & CO. [Entire title in red-brown, enclosed within ornately decorated panels in green] [1902]

$(8\frac{1}{4} \times 5\frac{1}{2})$: [a]^1 [A]^8 B–C^8 D^2 (inserted between C$_{4, 5}$) 1–22^8 23^2 [24]^6

(on coated stock), pp. liv, 368. Frontispiece and three colour plates inserted. 12mo.

Issued in four bindings, the "popular" limited issue (Parisian Edition) being bound in brown half leather, tan, green and violet mottled paper boards, ruled in gilt at jointures of leather and boards on front and back covers, lettering and decorative flower devices and dotted-rules over raised bands in gilt on spine; multicolour-patterned end-papers; top edge trimmed and gilt, other edges untrimmed. The remaining three issues were bound in more expensive leathers, with elaborate half-title, and with title in gilt and black within ornate frame in gilt, black and yellow, entwined with blue-ribboned garlands of flowers in pink and blue. End-papers consisted of tooled leather and velvet linings.

Published December 1902, Vol. 2 of "A Century of French Romance" series, edited by Edmund Gosse, the Parisian Edition consisting of 1000 sets, at $5 per volume. The Versailles Edition (limited to 250 sets) sold at $10 per volume, the Grand Format Edition (limited to 50 sets) at $25, and the Grand Prix Edition at $50. Noted in the "Weekly Record of New Publications," *Publishers' Weekly*, 27 December 1902.

Reprinted in 1905 under the imprint of P. F. Collier & Son, New York, in the "French Classical Romance" series. This issue contains no date on title-page, and carries the 1902 copyright imprint of Appleton on verso of title-leaf. This has frequently led to the erroneous belief that this is the first American edition.

B22   MADAME BOVARY   1902

a. *First edition, English issue:*

MADAME BOVARY [Decorative initial "M" in blue-green and black, five lines high] | [two devices] TRANSLATED | FROM THE FRENCH OF | GUSTAVE FLAUBERT | WITH A CRITICAL INTRODUCTION | BY HENRY JAMES [three devices] | [device] | LONDON: WILLIAM HEINEMANN: MCMII

$(8\frac{1}{2} \times 5\frac{3}{4})$: [*]¹ [2*]⁴ [a]² b–c⁸ [d]² 1–26⁸ 27⁶ 28⁴ (on coated stock), pp. l, 436. Frontispiece and three colour plates inserted. Demy 8vo.

Issued in light blue cloth, lettered within ornamental-mirror panel in gilt on front cover, publisher's device in blind on back cover, lettering and ornamental devices in gilt on spine; white end-papers; top edge trimmed and gilt, other edges untrimmed.

Published 15 May 1902, Vol. 9 of "A Century of French Romance" series, the first printing consisting of 2000 copies, of which 1000 were issued as part of a 12-volume "Library Edition" at four guineas the set, and the balance issued singly at 7/6. A copy also noted with 1904 imprint on title-page.

Although issued seven months earlier than the American edition and containing textual variations, this issue was published from the American plates (see B22b). The colour illustrations, however, were printed in England and exported for the American edition. The "Biographical Note," pp. xlv–xlviii, and the Octave Uzanne essay, "The Portraits of Gustave Flaubert," pp. [429]–435, are newly set-up.

Reissued, in July 1905, under the imprint of the London Book Company, in a Subscription Edition, consisting of 450 sets of sheets of the initial impression, with a new title-leaf.

James contributed:

Gustave Flaubert. Pp. v–xliii.

> Written specially for this edition. Reprinted in *Notes on Novelists*, 1914.

b. *First edition, American issue (limited):*

MADAME | BOVARY | TRANSLATED FROM THE FRENCH OF | GUSTAVE FLAUBERT | BY | W. G. BLAYDES | WITH A CRITICAL INTRODUCTION BY | HENRY JAMES | [rule] | ILLUSTRATED | NEW YORK | D. APPLETON & CO. [Entire title in red-brown, enclosed within ornately decorated panels in green] [1902]

$(8\frac{1}{4} \times 5\frac{1}{2})$: [a]² A–C⁸ [1]⁸ 2–26⁸ 27⁴ 28⁶ (—28₅, ₆) (on coated stock), pp. lii, 432. Frontispiece and three colour plates inserted. 12mo.

Issued in four bindings, uniform with *The Two Young Brides* (see B21b).

Published December 1902, Vol. 10 of "A Century of French Romance" series, edited by Edmund Gosse. Price and size of printings uniform with *The Two Young Brides* (B21b).

As with *The Two Young Brides*, English publication preceded the American, in this instance by seven months, although the English issue was published from American plates. Moreover, the texts of the two editions of *Madame Bovary* are at variance. A comparison reveals uniformity through p. 321, after which numerous excisions occur in the American edition. The matching sections of text, however, reveal identical broken type, suggesting that the American type was reset *after* stereotype moulds of the original plates were made for export. It is conceivable that a decision to excise this text (and possibly that of other volumes in the series) was the cause for delay in issuing the American edition. The publishers, unfortunately, have no extant records to substantiate this premise. It is perhaps ironic that so staunch a defender of the artist's right to freedom as Henry James should unknowingly have prefaced a bowdlerized *Madame Bovary*.

Reprinted in 1905 under the imprint of P. F. Collier & Son, New York, in the "French Classical Romance" series (see note, B21b).

B23   THE GEORGE ALEXANDER   1903
BIRTHDAY BOOK

THE GEORGE | ALEXANDER [in red] | BIRTHDAY BOOK | [decorative device] | PRINTED & PUBLISHED BY JOHN LANE | VIGO STREET, LONDON, & NEW YORK. 1903

($7\frac{1}{2} \times 4\frac{11}{16}$): [A]^8 B–Q^8, pp. 256. Frontispiece and tissue guard inserted. Crown 8vo.

Issued in smooth white linen, lettered in gilt on front cover and spine, four fleur-de-lys ornaments and illustration of mounted knight within single-rule border and panels in gilt on front cover, single-rule in gilt at top and bottom of spine; white end-papers; top edge trimmed and gilt, other edges untrimmed.

Published February 1903, the front cover being imprinted: "Souvenir of the 200th Performance of | 'If I Were King' | by Justin Huntly McCarthy | At the St. James's Theatre Feb. 26th 1903 | Presented by Mr. George Alexander". The publisher has been unable to locate any record of publication, and no contemporary advertisement or "Books Received" listing has been discovered. There are copies in the Harvard University library and in the William Andrews Clark Memorial Library of the University of California.

James contributed:

Nine quotations from *Guy Domville*. Pp. 10, 14, 58, 62, 68, 96, 110, 130, 148. These authorized quotations, plus one in *The Drama Birthday Book*, 1895 (see B14), were the only portions of the play published during James's lifetime.

B24 AMERICAN LITERARY 1904
CRITICISM

AMERICAN | LITERARY CRITICISM | SELECTED AND
EDITED, WITH AN | INTRODUCTORY ESSAY | BY |
WILLIAM MORTON PAYNE, LL.D. | ASSOCIATE EDITOR
OF "THE DIAL" | LONGMANS, GREEN, AND CO. | 91
AND 93 FIFTH AVENUE, NEW YORK | LONDON AND
BOMBAY | 1904

$(7\frac{7}{8} \times 5\frac{3}{8})$: $[1]^8$ 2–20^8 $[21]^8$, pp. xii, 324. 12mo.

Issued in dark carmine vertical-ribbed cloth, ornamental wampum
border and series title in blind on front cover, lettered in gilt on spine;
white end-papers; all edges trimmed.

Published October 1904, at $1.40, No. 2 in the Wampum Library
series, the first (and only) printing consisting of 1000 copies. Noted
under "Books Received," in the *New York Times*, 22 October 1904.

James contributed:

Sainte-Beuve. Pp. 299–318.

First appeared in the *North American Review*, January 1880.
Revised by James for the present edition.

B25 [THE HAWTHORNE 1905
CENTENNIAL]

THE | PROCEEDINGS [in red] | IN COMMEMORATION
OF | THE ONE HUNDREDTH ANNIVERSARY | OF THE
BIRTH OF | NATHANIEL HAWTHORNE [in red] | HELD
AT | SALEM, MASSACHUSETTS | JUNE 23, 1904 | [Etched
vignette of the Hawthorne Birthplace, within blind im-
pression] | SALEM, MASS. | THE ESSEX INSTITUTE [in
red] | 1904. [1905]

$(9\frac{1}{2} \times 6\frac{1}{8})$: [unsigned: 1^4 2–3^2 4–17^4 18^2 19^4; first and final signatures
serve as end-papers, leaves $1_{1,\,2}$ and $19_{3,\,4}$ being pasted to front and back
covers]; pp. [2], vi, 116. Frontispiece and three plates with tissue
guards and 18 additional illustrations inserted. 8vo.

Issued in blue half cloth, blue-grey paper boards, lettered in black on
white paper label on spine; white end-papers (double-unopened-leaf
free end-paper at front and back); all edges untrimmed.

Published late February or early March 1905, at $3.50, the limitation notice, p. [ii], reading: "Two Hundred and Fifty Copies Printed." Copyright deposit made on 24 February 1905; noted in the *Nation*, 16 March.

James contributed:

Letter to the Hon. Robert S. Rantoul, President of The Essex Institute, dated Rye, 10 June 1904. Pp. 55–62.

> Reprinted in F. O. Matthiessen, *The James Family* (New York, 1947).

B26   THE TEMPEST   1907

a. *First edition:*

THE COMPLETE WORKS | OF | WILLIAM SHAKESPEARE [in red] | WITH ANNOTATIONS AND A GENERAL | INTRODUCTION | BY SIDNEY LEE | VOLUME XVI | THE TEMPEST [in red] | WITH A SPECIAL INTRODUCTION BY | HENRY JAMES | AND AN ORIGINAL FRONTISPIECE BY | GERTRUDE DEMAIN HAMMOND | NEW YORK | GEORGE D. SPROUL [in red] | 1907

(11 × 8¼): [i]⁴ [ii]⁸ [iii]⁴ [1]² 2–7⁸ [8]⁴ [9]², pp. xxxii, 112. Frontispiece and tissue guard inserted. 4to.

Issued in dark green half cloth, blue-grey paper boards, lettered in black on white paper label on spine; white end-papers; all edges untrimmed.

Published March 1907, Vol. 16 of the Renaissance Edition, at $2 per volume, sold by subscription only. Noted in the "Weekly Record of New Publications," *Publishers' Weekly*, 2 March 1907. Copyright entry and deposit, however, were not made until 21 October 1907.

The Renaissance Edition was conceived and executed by William Dana Orcutt, at the University Press. A separate issue was published, late in 1907, by Mr Orcutt under the imprint of the Renaissance Press. This issue was bound in blue half cloth, grey paper boards, lettered within small decorative panel in blue at lower right-hand corner of front cover, lettered in red and black on white paper label on spine; all edges trimmed. Page size: $9\frac{5}{16} \times 7\frac{9}{16}$.

Reprinted, from original plates, in The Harper Edition of Shakespeare's Works, Vol. VIII, in 1909 or 1910.

James contributed:

Introduction. Pp. ix–xxxii.

 Written specially for this edition; never reprinted.

b. *First edition, English issue:*

This issue consisted of bound copies of the first edition with a cancel title-leaf, publisher's imprint on title-page reading: LONDON | GEORGE G. HARRAP & CO. | 15, YORK STREET, COVENT GARDEN | 1907

Published November 1907, at 7/6. British Museum deposit made on 7 November 1907.

Reprinted, from stereotypes, in the Imperial Edition, Vol. IV, under the imprint of The Standard Literature Co., Ltd., London & Calcutta, c1910, and in The Caxton Shakespeare, Vol. VIII, under the imprint of the Caxton Publishing Co., London, 1910, at 6/6.

B27   THE WHOLE FAMILY   1908

a. *First edition:*

THE WHOLE | FAMILY | A NOVEL BY | TWELVE AUTHORS | [bowknot device, in blue] | WILLIAM DEAN HOWELLS | MARY E. WILKINS FREEMAN | MARY HEATON VORSE | MARY STEWART CUTTING | ELIZABETH JORDAN | JOHN KENDRICK BANGS | HENRY JAMES | ELIZABETH STUART PHELPS | EDITH WYATT | MARY R. SHIPMAN ANDREWS | ALICE BROWN HENRY VAN DYKE | [bowknot device, in blue] | NEW YORK AND LONDON | HARPER & BROTHERS PUBLISHERS | MCMVIII [Entire page enclosed within double-rule frame containing decorative ribbon, in blue]

$(7\frac{3}{8} \times 5)$: [i]^1 (on coated stock) [1]^8 2–20^8, pp. vi, 316. Frontispiece with tissue guard and 11 illustrations inserted. 12mo.

Issued in royal blue vertical-ribbed cloth, lettered in gilt with names of authors outlined by circular gilt ribbon ornament on front cover, lettering and leaf device in gilt on spine; white end-papers; all edges trimmed.

Published October 1908, at $1.50. Library of Congress deposit made on 15 October 1908; advertised in the *New York Times*, 17 October.

A secondary binding is noted, issued in bright crimson cloth, lettering and blocking on front cover and spine uniform with primary state, in black.

James contributed:

Chapter VII. *The Married Son*. Pp. 144–[184].
    First appeared in *Harper's Bazar*, June 1908.

b. *First edition, English issue:*

Identical with American edition except for transposed imprint of place of publication on recto of title-leaf: LONDON AND NEW YORK

Published November 1908, at 6/-. Advertised under the heading, "New and Forthcoming Fiction," in the *Athenaeum*, 10 October; British Museum deposit, however, was not made until 6 November, and the volume was first noted in the "New Books" columns of *The Times Literary Supplement*, 19 November.

B28   REPORT ON STAGE PLAYS   1909
              (CENSORSHIP)

REPORT | FROM THE | JOINT SELECT COMMITTEE OF THE HOUSE OF LORDS | AND THE HOUSE OF COMMONS | ON THE | STAGE PLAYS (CENSORSHIP); | TOGETHER WITH THE | PROCEEDINGS OF THE COMMITTEE, MINUTES OF EVIDENCE, | AND APPENDICES. | [rule] | ORDERED, BY THE HOUSE OF COMMONS, TO BE PRINTED, | 2 NOVEMBER 1909. | [rule] | LONDON: | PRINTED FOR HIS MAJESTY'S STATIONERY OFFICE, | BY WYMAN AND SONS, LIMITED, 109, FETTER LANE, E.C. | [rule] | AND TO BE PURCHASED, EITHER DIRECTLY OR THROUGH ANY BOOKSELLER, FROM | WYMAN AND SONS, LIMITED, 109, FETTER LANE, FLEET STREET, E.C.; AND | 32, ABINGDON STREET, WESTMINSTER, S.W.; OR | OLIVER AND BOYD, TWEEDDALE COURT, EDINBURGH; OR | E. PONSONBY, 116, GRAFTON STREET, DUBLIN. | [rule] | 1909 | 303.

($12\frac{11}{16} \times 8\frac{3}{16}$): a–e⁴ A–3A⁴, pp. xl, 376. Folio.

Issued in blue paper wrappers, spine lettered in black, front and back covers lettered in black, uniform with title-page except for addition of price, weight of volume, and full-stop after date; inner sides of wrappers blank; all edges trimmed. Errata slip inserted between front wrapper and title-leaf.

Published November 1909, at 3/3. An Index, pp. 377–[414], was published separately in 1910.

Apparently the first impression sold so rapidly that a new impression was ordered less than a week later. The title-page was altered slightly, the lines "ORDERED, BY THE HOUSE OF COMMONS, TO BE PRINTED, | 2 NOVEMBER 1909." being replaced by the single line "ORDERED TO BE PRINTED 8 NOVEMBER 1909." The number "303" of the bottom line was altered to "(214)" and the Errata slip was eliminated.

Contains:

Letter from Henry James to John Galsworthy. P. 128.

> This statement was read at James's request by Galsworthy during the proceedings, 12 August 1909. A verbatim report of the proceedings was reprinted in *Censorship and Licensing*, London, 1909. A digest of the report was reprinted in John Palmer's *The Censor and the Theatres*, London 1912, and New York, 1913. James's letter is reproduced, with certain errors in transcription.

B29   IN AFTER DAYS   1910

IN AFTER DAYS | THOUGHTS ON THE FUTURE LIFE | BY | W. D. HOWELLS, HENRY JAMES, JOHN | BIGELOW, THOMAS WENTWORTH | HIGGINSON, HENRY M. ALDEN | WILLIAM HANNA THOMSON | GUGLIELMO FERRERO | JULIA WARD HOWE | ELIZABETH STUART | PHELPS | WITH PORTRAITS | [publisher's device] | HARPER & BROTHERS PUBLISHERS | NEW YORK AND LONDON | MCMX

($7\frac{5}{8} \times 5\frac{1}{16}$): [i]^1 [1]^8 2–15^8, pp. viii, 234. Frontispiece with tissue guard and 8 illustrations inserted. 8vo.

Issued in mauve cloth, decorative panel and single-rule border in blind on front cover, lettering and decorative ornament in gilt on front cover and spine; white end-papers; top edge trimmed and gilt, other edges untrimmed.

Published 10 February 1910, at $1.25.

Two secondary bindings are noted: (*a*) issued in faded blue linen-grain cloth, single-rule border and decorative panel in black on front cover, lettering in black on front cover and spine; all edges trimmed, gilt top lacking; page size: $7\frac{1}{8} \times 4\frac{13}{16}$; (*b*) issued in rust-brown half cloth, buff paper boards, lettering and decorative ornaments in black on front cover and spine, publisher's imprint on spine in a variant black-letter type; all edges trimmed, gilt top lacking; page size: $7\frac{7}{16} \times 5\frac{1}{16}$.

James contributed:

Is There A Life After Death? Pp. 199–[233].

First appeared in *Harper's Bazar*, January–February 1910.
Reprinted in F. O. Matthiessen, *The James Family* (New York, 1947).

B30   THE DAYS OF A YEAR   1912

THE DAYS | OF A YEAR | BY [Miss] M. D. ASHLEY DODD | WITH AN APPRECIATION | BY HENRY JAMES | ''BEAUTY IS TRUTH, TRUTH BEAUTY,—THAT IS ALL | YE KNOW ON EARTH, AND ALL YE NEED TO KNOW.'' | [publisher's device] | HERBERT JENKINS LIMITED | [leaf device] 12 ARUNDEL PLACE [leaf device] | HAYMARKET · LONDON · SW | MCMXIII [1912]

($6\frac{3}{8} \times 3\frac{7}{8}$): [*]⁴ a–l⁸ m⁴, pp. viii, 184. F'cap 8vo.

Issued in dull green smooth linen-grain cloth, lettering and leaf devices in gilt and pattern of falling leaves in green on front cover and spine, two double-rules forming border with boxed corners in gilt on front cover, publisher's device in blind on back cover, two double-rules in gilt at top and bottom of spine; green-tinted illustrated end-papers; all edges trimmed.

Also issued in velvet calf lined with flexible boards, gilt top.

Published 7 October 1912, at 2/6 in cloth, 5/- in calf. This was a new edition of a Nature Diary first issued a number of years earlier.

Some copies lack gilt ruling on front cover and spine; these, however, are not necessarily late bindings, as an inscribed author's copy, dated November 1912, has been noted in the variant binding state.

James contributed:

Foreword: a letter published with his permission. Pp. v–vii.

ROYAL SOCIETY OF LITERATURE | [rule] | THE ACA-
DEMIC COMMITTEE [heavy single-rule underscoring] |
BROWNING'S CENTENARY | [rule] | EDMUND GOSSE |
SIR ARTHUR PINERO | HENRY JAMES | [rule] | TUESDAY,
MAY 7TH, 1912 | (REPRINTED FROM 'TRANSACTIONS
R.S.L.,' VOL. XXXI, PART IV.) | LONDON | ASHER AND
CO. | 14, BEDFORD STREET, W.C. | [rule] | 1912.

$(8\frac{1}{2} \times 5\frac{1}{2})$: $[1]^8$ 2–3^8 4^1, pp. 50. Demy 8vo.

Issued in light blue-grey paper wrappers, cut flush, lettered on front
cover in black, uniform with title-page except for additional line at
bottom, reading "Price Three Shillings."; inner sides of wrappers
blank; all edges trimmed.

Published probably in November 1912, at 3/-, from the type of the
Transactions of the Royal Society of Literature (see below).

James contributed:

The Novel in 'The Ring and the Book.' Pp. 21–50.
> First appeared in *Transactions of the Royal Society of Literature,
> Second Series*, XXXI, Part IV (1912). Reprinted, with textual
> deletions and additions (see D564), in the *Quarterly Review*, July
> 1912, and in *Living Age*, 24 August 1912.

B32   SIXTY AMERICAN OPINIONS   1915
ON THE WAR

SIXTY AMERICAN | —OPINIONS— | ON THE WAR |
[publisher's device] | LONDON: | T. FISHER UNWIN,
LTD. | 1 ADELPHI TERRACE W.C. [Entire title enclosed
within double-rule border] [1915]

$(7\frac{1}{4} \times 4\frac{3}{4})$: $[a]^4$ A–K^8 L^4, pp. viii, 168. Crown 8vo.

Issued in pale grey-green linen-grain cloth, lettered in black on front
cover and spine, publisher's device in black on spine; white end-
papers; all edges trimmed.

Also issued in paper wrappers; no copy available for examination.

Published May 1915, at 1/-, the first (and only) printing consisting of 2000 copies in wrappers and 2000 copies in cloth. Advertised in *The Times Literary Supplement*, 20 May 1915, with quotation from a review in the *Pall Mall Gazette*; noted under "Books Published This Week," in the *Athenaeum*, 22 May.

We have identified the editors as Samuel Robertson Honey and James Fullarton Muirhead.

James contributed:

Extract from "a private letter . . . communicated with the writer's consent." P. 92.

B33   THE BOOK OF FRANCE   1915

THE | BOOK OF FRANCE | IN AID OF | THE FRENCH PARLIAMENTARY COMMITTEE'S FUND | FOR THE RELIEF OF THE INVADED DEPARTMENTS | EDITED BY | WINIFRED STEPHENS | PUBLISHED UNDER THE AUSPICES OF AN | HONORARY COMMITTEE PRESIDED OVER BY | HIS EXCELLENCY MONSIEUR PAUL CAMBON | MACMILLAN AND CO., LIMITED | ST. MARTIN'S STREET, LONDON | ÉDOUARD CHAMPION, PARIS | 1915

$(8\frac{5}{16} \times 6\frac{1}{2})$: [A]⁸ B–S⁸, pp. xvi, 272. Frontispiece with tissue guard and 8 illustrations inserted. F'cap 4to.

Issued in dark blue-violet linen-grain cloth, lettering and embossed insignia of the French Republic in gilt on front cover, lettering and ornamental device in gilt on spine; white end-papers; all edges trimmed.

Published 14 July 1915, at 5/-, the first printing consisting of 5000 copies.

James contributed:

France. Pp. 1–8.

"Remarks at the Meeting of the Committee held on June 9, 1915." Reprinted in *Within the Rim*, 1919.

The Saints of France. Pp. 176–182.

English translation by James of "Les Saints de la France," by Maurice Barrès, which appears on pp. 169–175.

B34   ART AND THE ACTOR   1915

PAPERS ON ACTING | II | ART AND THE ACTOR | BY |
CONSTANT COQUELIN | TRANSLATED BY ABBY LANG-
DON ALGER | WITH AN INTRODUCTION BY | HENRY
JAMES | [ornamental device encircled by quotation from
Molière] | PRINTED FOR THE | DRAMATIC MUSEUM OF
COLUMBIA UNIVERSITY | IN THE CITY OF NEW YORK |
MCMXV

($8\frac{7}{8} \times 5\frac{7}{8}$): [unsigned: 1–12⁴ 13⁶], pp. vi, 102. 12mo.

Issued in blue-grey paper boards, lettered in black on white paper label across spine and overlapping front and back covers; white end-papers; all edges untrimmed.

Published October or November 1915, one of a series of four volumes, sold as a unit, at $5, by subscription only. The limitation notice, p. [100], reads: "Of this book three hundred and thirty-three copies were printed from type by Corlies, Macy and Company . . ." Reported in *Publishers' Weekly*, 9 October 1915, as due to appear "this month," but not recorded in the periodical's "Weekly Record of New Publications" until 4 December.

James contributed:

Introduction. Pp. 1–36.

> First appeared, under the title "Coquelin," in the *Century Maga-
> zine*, January 1887. Extensively revised for this publication. An
> abridgment of the serial text was reprinted in *The American
> Theatre as Seen by Its Critics*, 1934. Allan Wade reprinted the
> revised text in *The Scenic Art*, 1948.

B35   THE BOOK OF THE HOMELESS   1916

a. *First edition, ordinary issue:*

THE | BOOK OF THE HOMELESS | (LE LIVRE DES SANS-
FOYER) | EDITED BY EDITH WHARTON | [three dots
forming triangle] | ORIGINAL ARTICLES IN VERSE AND
PROSE | ILLUSTRATIONS REPRODUCED FROM ORI-
GINAL PAINTINGS & DRAWINGS | [device] | THE BOOK
IS SOLD | FOR THE BENEFIT OF THE AMERICAN HOSTELS
FOR REFUGEES | (WITH THE FOYER FRANCO-BELGE) |

B. CONTRIBUTIONS TO BOOKS

AND OF THE CHILDREN OF FLANDERS RESCUE COM-
MITTEE | NEW YORK | CHARLES SCRIBNER'S SONS |
MDCCCCXVI

($10\frac{13}{16} \times 8\frac{1}{8}$): [unsigned: 1^4 $2-15^8$], pp. [2], xxvi, 160, plus 22 fly-title leaves not reckoned in pagination. 22 illustrations inserted. Large 8vo.

Issued in red-brown half buckram, muddy grey laid paper boards, lettering in black and decorative leaf frame and illustration within circular panel in dull blue-grey on front cover, lettering and leaf device in gilt on spine; white end-papers; all edges trimmed.

Published 22 January 1916 at $5, the only printing consisting of 3300 copies. The French edition, dated 1915, may have preceded this.

Limitation notice, p. [157], reads: "Of this book, in addition to the regular edition, there have been printed and numbered one hundred and seventy-five copies de luxe, of larger format. Numbers 1–50 on French hand-made paper, containing four facsimiles of manuscripts and a second set of illustrations in portfolio. Numbers 51–175 on Van Gelder paper."

James contributed:
The Long Wards. Pp. 115–125.

> First appeared here. James wrote this article for the *New York Tribune*; when it exceeded the prescribed length he offered it instead for *The Book of the Homeless.* Reprinted in *Within the Rim*, 1919.

b. *First edition, limited issue:*

($12\frac{3}{4} \times 9\frac{5}{8}$): [unsigned: $1-31^4$], pp. [4], xxvi, 160, plus 22 fly-title leaves and 7 blank leaves with tipped-in illustrations not reckoned in pagination. 4to.

Supplementary title and divisional fly-title printed in green and black. Fifteen illustrations inserted, the balance being affixed to text leaves.

Issued in tan half canvas, grey-blue laid paper boards, lettering and leaf device in gilt on front cover and spine; buff end-papers; all edges untrimmed.

Colophon (see B35a) numbered and signed by D. B. Updike. Published simultaneously with ordinary issue, at $25 for the Edition de Luxe (Nos. 26–125), and at $50 for the Edition de Grande Luxe (Nos. 1–25).

c. *First edition, English issue:*

($10\frac{13}{16} \times 8\frac{1}{8}$): collation uniform with American edition except for publisher's imprint on title-page: LONDON | MACMILLAN & CO., LIMITED | MDCCCCXVI The issue consists of imported sheets.

Bound uniform with American edition except for publisher's imprint on spine.

Published the week of 28 February 1916, at 21/-. Advertised under the heading "New Books," in *The Times Literary Supplement*, 2 March.

B36   LETTERS FROM AMERICA   1916

a. *First edition:*

LETTERS FROM AMERICA | BY RUPERT BROOKE. | WITH A PREFACE BY HENRY JAMES | NEW YORK: CHARLES SCRIBNER'S SONS | 597–599 FIFTH AVENUE. 1916

($7\frac{7}{16} \times 5\frac{1}{8}$): [unsigned: 1–14^8], pp. xlii, 182. Frontispiece with tissue guard inserted. 12mo.

Issued in dark blue-green vertical-ribbed cloth, lettered in gilt on front cover and spine; white end-papers; top edge trimmed, other edges untrimmed.

Published 28 January 1916, at $1.25, the first printing consisting of 2750 copies.

James contributed:

Rupert Brooke. Pp. ix–xlii.

    First appeared here; never reprinted.

    This piece of work, the last to be written by the novelist, became the subject of a dispute as he lay dying in 1916. Certain remarks in the introduction about the *Westminster Gazette* (in which Brooke's essays originally appeared) were deemed libellous by that journal, and revisions were called for. With the approval of Mrs William James, these were made by Theodora Bosanquet, James's amanuensis. A few minor variations exist between the English and American texts.

b. *First English edition:*

LETTERS FROM AMERICA | BY RUPERT BROOKE. | WITH A PREFACE BY HENRY JAMES | LONDON: SIDGWICK & JACKSON, LTD. | 3 ADAM STREET, ADELPHI, W.C. 1916

($7\frac{7}{8} \times 5\frac{5}{16}$): [a]^6 b–c^8 A–L^8 M^2, pp. [2], xlii, 180. Frontispiece with tissue guard inserted. Ex. Crown 8vo.

Issued in black buckram, lettered in black within single-rule panel in red on white paper label on spine; white end-papers; top edge gilt, other edges untrimmed.

Published 8 March 1916, at 7/6, the first printing consisting of 2800 copies.

The label on spine is noted in two states, leading to such statements as the following, seen recently in a dealer's catalogue: "First edition, first issue, with label in first state. Very rare." There is, however, nothing rare about the "first state" label, which was printed in 1915, before publication had been delayed by James's illness. For purposes of economy, the "1915" labels were altered to "1916" by hand. These labels were affixed by the binder *simultaneously* with "second state" labels bearing the correct date. Copies are frequently found with one state affixed to the spine and the alternate state tipped into the back of the book, all copies containing a spare label. The first label measures $2\frac{1}{16} \times 1\frac{5}{16}$, the publisher's imprint being in roman type; the second measures $1\frac{7}{8} \times 1\frac{5}{16}$, the publisher's imprint being in italic type.

A variant binding is noted, issued in navy-blue linen-grain cloth. This issue is printed on lighter-weight stock, and has been noted only with "1916" label, suggesting it is a secondary issue. One copy has been noted with an inscription date, 25 December 1915, but this appears to be an error since the publisher reports no copies were bound by that date.

A few copies of both variant issues have been noted with binder's fly-leaves tipped in at front and back.

James contributed:

Rupert Brooke. Pp. ix–xlii.

> There are a few minor variations between the American and English texts.

B37   HARPER ESSAYS   1927

First edition:

HARPER ESSAYS | [rule] | EDITED BY | HENRY SEIDEL CANBY, PH.D., LITT.D | EDITOR OF "THE SATURDAY REVIEW OF LITERATURE" | MEMBER OF THE ENGLISH

DEPARTMENT | OF YALE UNIVERSITY | [rule] | [pub-
lisher's device] | NEW YORK AND LONDON | HARPER &
BROTHERS PUBLISHERS | MCMXXVII

$(8\frac{9}{16} \times 5\frac{3}{4})$: [unsigned: 1–20⁸ 21⁴], pp. xiv, 314. 8vo.

Issued in olive-brown half cloth, multicoloured horizontal-striped
paper boards, lettering and decorative border at top and bottom in
black on gold paper label on front cover, uniform blocking and lettering in gilt and publisher's imprint in gilt on spine; white end-papers;
top edge trimmed, other edges untrimmed.

Published 6 October 1927, at $2.50, the first printing consisting of
2100 copies.

Contains:

Within the Rim. Pp. 221–234.

> First appeared in the *Fortnightly Review*, August 1917, and in
> *Living Age*, 8 September 1917. Although the essay was published
> in *Within the Rim*, 1919, this was its first American book
> publication.

B38   READING, WRITING AND   1932
REMEMBERING

a. *First edition:*

READING, WRITING | AND REMEMBERING | A LITERARY
RECORD | BY | E. V. LUCAS | [five lines of quotations] |
WITH 31 PLATES AND 50 ILLUSTRATIONS IN THE
TEXT | [publisher's device] | METHUEN & CO. LTD. | 36
ESSEX STREET W.C. | LONDON [1932]

$(8\frac{11}{16} \times 5\frac{9}{16})$: [i]¹⁰ ([i₁] serves as free end-paper) 1–20⁸ 21¹⁰, pp. xviii,
340, followed by eight page catalogue of advertisements. Frontispiece
and 15 leaves of illustrations inserted. Demy 8vo.

Issued in crimson linen-grain cloth, lettering and double-rule at top
and bottom in gilt on spine; white end-papers; top edge trimmed,
other edges untrimmed.

Published 22 September 1932, at 18/-, the first printing consisting of
2500 copies.

Contains:

James's outline of scope and character of tales collected in *The Finer Grain*. Pp. 184–185.

> Lucas prints the full original text submitted to Methuen, of which a fragment was used on the dust-jacket (see A68b).

b. *First American edition:*

READING, WRITING | AND REMEMBERING | A LITERARY RECORD | BY | E. V. LUCAS | [four lines of quotations] | [publisher's device] | HARPER & BROTHERS PUBLISHERS | NEW YORK AND LONDON | 1932

($9\frac{3}{8} \times 6\frac{3}{16}$): [unsigned: $1–22^8\ 23^4$], pp. xviii, 342. Frontispiece and 15 leaves of illustrations inserted. Royal 8vo.

Issued in dark green buckram, lettering and ornamental crisscross-rule pattern and ten pairs of horizontal rules in gilt on spine; white endpapers; top edge trimmed, other edges untrimmed.

Published 6 October 1932, at $4, the first printing consisting of 1800 copies.

Contains:

Same material as English edition. P. 184.

B39   THE AMERICAN THEATRE AS   1934
         SEEN BY ITS CRITICS

THE | AMERICAN | THEATRE | AS SEEN BY ITS CRITICS | 1752–1934 | [two rules] | EDITED BY | MONTROSE J. MOSES | AND | JOHN MASON BROWN | W. W. NORTON & COMPANY, INC. | NEW YORK [1934] [Entire title enclosed within proscenium-arch-and-stage design]

($9\frac{3}{8} \times 6\frac{1}{4}$): [unsigned: $1–24^8\ 25^4$], pp. 392. 8vo.

Issued in red linen-grain cloth, lettering in gilt with title printed against black scroll panels with gilt edges over gilt design; white endpapers; top edge trimmed, other edges untrimmed.

Published 24 October 1934, at $3.75, the first printing consisting of 2000 copies.

Contains:

Some Notes on the Theatre. Pp. 122–126.

First appeared, under the heading "Fine Arts," in the *Nation*, 11 March 1875.

Salvini's Othello. Pp. 126–128.

An abridgment of an article which first appeared, under the title "Tommaso Salvini," in the *Atlantic Monthly*, March 1883.

Coquelin. Pp. 128–132.

An abridgment of an article which first appeared in the *Century*, January 1887. Although the essay was reprinted, with revisions, as an introduction to Constant Coquelin's *Art and the Actor*, 1915, the present text follows that of the serial publication.

B40   THE SHOCK OF RECOGNITION 1943

a. *First edition:*

THE SHOCK | OF | RECOGNITION | [decorative rule] | THE DEVELOPMENT OF LITERATURE | IN THE UNITED STATES | RECORDED BY THE MEN | WHO MADE IT | EDITED BY | EDMUND WILSON | [Illustration] | DOUBLE-DAY, DORAN AND COMPANY, INC. | GARDEN CITY NEW YORK | 1943

($7\frac{1}{2} \times 4\frac{3}{8}$): [unsigned: 1–41^{16}], pp. [2], xviii, 1292. 8vo.

Issued in dark blue linen-grain cloth, initial "W" within decorative panel in blind on front cover, lettered in gilt on spine; white end-papers; top edge blue-stained, all edges trimmed.

Published 4 June 1943, at $5, the first printing consisting of 3500 copies.

Contains:

William Dean Howells. Pp. 570–579.

First appeared in *Harper's Weekly*, 19 June 1886. Reprinted in *The American Essays of Henry James*, 1956.

Also contains a reprint of *Hawthorne*, 1879, pp. 427–565.

b. *First English issue (1955):*

In 1955 the work was reissued in New York by Farrar, Straus and Cudahy. Sheets of this second issue comprised the first English issue, which was published by W. H. Allen in the same year.

B41   HENRY JAMES AND ROBERT   1948
               LOUIS STEVENSON

a. *First edition:*

HENRY JAMES | AND | ROBERT LOUIS STEVENSON | A
RECORD OF FRIENDSHIP | AND CRITICISM | EDITED
WITH AN INTRODUCTION BY | JANET ADAM SMITH |
[publisher's device] | RUPERT HART-DAVIS: LONDON |
1948 [Entire title enclosed within triple-rule border]

(8 × 5⅛): [A]⁸ B–G⁸ [H]⁸ I–R⁸ S⁸ (S₈ serves as paste-down end-paper),
pp. 284. Two illustrations inserted. Large Crown 8vo.

Issued in grey buckram, lettered in gilt on spine; white end-papers;
top edge pale-blue, other edges trimmed.

Published 29 October 1948, at 12/6, the first printing consisting of 5000
copies, of which 2000 sheets were remaindered to Heffer's of Cambridge to be bound by the latter firm.

Contains:

Letter from James to Stevenson (four-page fragment), two pages of
which are reproduced in facsimile. Pp. 228–231. Also 15 previously
published letters from James to Stevenson and reprints of three James
essays, *The Art of Fiction*, *Robert Louis Stevenson*, and *The Letters of
Robert Louis Stevenson* (see A25, A30, and A73).

b. *First edition, American issue* (1949):
Published by the Macmillan Company, at $2.50. Not seen.

B42   LITERARY OPINION IN   1951
                     AMERICA

LITERARY OPINION | IN AMERICA | [decorative rule] |
ESSAYS ILLUSTRATING THE STATUS, METHODS, | AND
PROBLEMS OF CRITICISM IN THE | UNITED STATES IN
THE TWENTIETH CENTURY | [decorative rule] | EDITED
BY | MORTON DAUWEN ZABEL | REVISED EDITION |
[publisher's device] | HARPER & BROTHERS | NEW YORK
[1951]

(9¼ × 6⅛): [unsigned: 1–26¹⁶ 27¹² 28–29¹⁶], pp. xxviii, 892. 8vo.

Issued in maroon linen-grain cloth, lettering and ornamental device in
gilt on front cover and spine, double-rule panel in blind on front
cover, two double-rules in blind on spine; white end-papers; all edges
trimmed.

Published 14 March 1951, the first printing consisting of 2500 copies, of which 2000 were issued in a college edition at $6 and 500 in a trade edition at $8.

Contains:

The Question of the Opportunities. Pp. 51–55.

First appeared as "American Letter: The Question of the Opportunities," in *Literature*, 26 March 1898.

The Great Form. Pp. 56–57.

First appeared as "The Summer School at Deerfield" in the New York *Tribune*, 4 August 1889.

Mr Zabel also includes a reprint, *Criticism*, originally titled "The Science of Criticism" (see D444).

B43   HENRY JAMES AND   1958
H. G. WELLS

a. *First edition:*

HENRY JAMES │ AND │ H. G. WELLS │ A RECORD OF THEIR FRIENDSHIP, │ THEIR DEBATE ON THE ART OF FICTION, │ AND THEIR QUARREL │ EDITED WITH AN INTRODUCTION BY │ LEON EDEL & GORDON N. RAY │ [publisher's device] │ LONDON │ RUPERT HART-DAVIS │ 1958

$(8 \times 5\frac{1}{8})$: [A]⁸ B–R⁸, pp. 272. Large Crown 8vo.

Issued in rust-red linen-grain cloth, lettered in gilt on spine; white end-papers; top edge red, other edges trimmed.

Published 28 February 1958, at 21/-, the first printing consisting of 3000 copies.

Contains:

Fifty-five letters from James to H. G. Wells and/or Mrs Wells (including one letter written jointly by James and Edith Wharton). Thirteen of the letters to Wells had appeared previously in Lubbock (1920).

Also contains a reprint of "The Younger Generation" (see A73 and D566).

b. *First edition, American issue:*

This issue consisted of sheets of the English edition, with a revised title-page, published by the University of Illinois Press, and copyright page. The volume was issued in rust-red linen-grain cloth, lettered in gilt on spine.

Published 21 April 1958, at –3.50, the issue consisting of 1500 copies.

B. CONTRIBUTIONS TO BOOKS

ADDENDA

B. CONTRIBUTIONS TO BOOKS

ADDENDA

C. PUBLISHED LETTERS

Part I: SEPARATELY PUBLISHED

C1   70TH BIRTHDAY LETTER   1913

($10\frac{13}{16} \times 8\frac{1}{2}$): one double-leaf, unpaginated, on handmade paper, watermarked. [Large Post 4to]

To honour Henry James on his seventieth birthday, his friends in England presented him with a "really splendid 'golden bowl,' of the highest interest and most perfect taste" (HJ to Mrs William James, 15 April 1913, in Lubbock, *Letters*, II) and a request that he sit for his portrait to Sargent. A committee which included Lubbock, Sargent, Edmund Gosse, J. M. Barrie, and Hugh Walpole, issued a series of six printed letters: (*a*) February 1913, the committee inviting subscriptions and expressing the hope that the proposal will not reach James prematurely; (*b*) April 1913, the committee to the subscribers, covering the enclosure of the letter designed to reach James on his birthday; (*c*) 15 April 1913, the subscribers to James, offering their congratulations and announcing their gift; (*d*) 21 April 1913, James to the subscribers, acknowledging "with boundless pleasure" the letter and gift; (*e*) July 1913, Gosse and Lubbock to the subscribers, reporting completion of the portrait and an account of the total subscription; (*f*) December 1913, Gosse and Walpole to the subscribers, inviting them to a showing of the portrait in Sargent's studio.

The letter of 21 April from James to the subscribers, headed "Dear Friends All," is addressed from 21, Carlyle Mansions, Cheyne Walk, S.W., and occupies the recto of the first leaf only; the remaining three pages contain a list of 270 donors of the gift. At the bottom of p. [4] is imprinted: "London: Chiswick Press."

300 copies were printed, 29 April 1913, under the supervision of Percy Lubbock. The Houghton and Colby Libraries have copies of this letter; neither possesses a full set of six letters.

The full text of James's letter was reprinted in Lubbock, *Letters*, II.

C2 THE AMERICAN VOLUNTEER 1914 MOTOR-AMBULANCE CORPS IN FRANCE

THE AMERICAN VOLUNTEER | MOTOR-AMBULANCE CORPS | IN FRANCE | A LETTER TO THE EDITOR OF AN AMERICAN JOURNAL | BY | HENRY JAMES | MACMILLAN AND CO., LIMITED | ST. MARTIN'S STREET, LONDON | 1914 | PRICE ONE PENNY

($8\frac{1}{2} \times 5\frac{1}{2}$): a single unsigned quire of six leaves, pp. 12, stapled or sewn. 8vo.

Contents: 1–12, text; at bottom of p. 12 imprint, "Printed in Great Britain by R. Clay and Sons, Ltd., | Brunswick Street, Stamford Street, S.E., and Bungay, Suffolk."

Issued in blue-grey paper wrappers, cut flush, lettered (as above) in black on front cover, which serves as title-page; inner side of front and both sides of back wrappers blank; all edges trimmed. Issued in white paper envelope, $8\frac{15}{16} \times 6\frac{1}{16}$, with imprint, "A Motor Ambulance in France | By Henry James", in upper left-hand corner.

Published 15 December 1914, at one penny, the first (and only) printing consisting of 2000 copies.

First appeared in this edition, the letter being dated (on p. 12): "London, November 25th, 1914." An abbreviated, extensively edited version, under the caption, "Famous Novelist Describes Deeds of U.S. Motor Corps," printed as a news dispatch with the by-line of Henry James, appeared in the *New York World*, 4 January 1915. Reprinted in full in *Within the Rim*, 1919.

C3 LETTERS TO AN EDITOR 1916

LETTERS | TO | AN EDITOR | BY | HENRY JAMES [Entire title enclosed within single-rule border] [1916]

($9 \times 7\frac{1}{4}$): a single unsigned quire of ten leaves, pp. ii, 18, sewn. Small 4to.

Contents: [i–ii], blank; [1–2], title, on verso limitation notice; 3–4, "A Foreword" by Clement Shorter, dated April 1, 1916; 5–12, text; 10–16, Bibliography of Henry James; [17–18], blank leaf.

Issued in plum stiff paper wrappers, cut flush, lettered and ruled in black on front cover uniform with title page; the inner covers lined with white; all edges trimmed.

Limitation notice, p. [2], reads: "Of this little book, containing hitherto unpublished letters by Henry James, twenty-five copies only have been privately printed by Clement Shorter for distribution among his friends. London, April 1st, 1916." The third and fourth letters (dated 14 March and 6 May 1896) had, however, been published two weeks earlier by Shorter in "A Literary Letter," the *Sphere*, LXIV (18 March 1916), 304. The text of the letters is corrupt, containing errors in transcription, misreadings and the omission of a portion of one of the letters.

There have been frequent conjectures by dealers and bibliographers (most recently by Richard Purdy in his *Thomas Hardy: A Bibliographical Study*, 1954) as to the reliability of the 25-copy limitation of the various Shorter editions. Certainly copies of the James *Letters to An Editor* turning up in dealers' catalogues (considering the number firmly anchored in libraries) have seemed more numerous than would normally be expected in an edition of so limited a quantity. Further, although some of the copies contain a number, and Shorter's autograph, on p. 4, several have been noted without numbering or autograph, leading to suspicion of an overprint. In extenuation, Thomas J. Wise wrote to the American Art Association, on 28 February 1931, concerning Shorter's edition of Bernard Shaw's *A Discarded Defence of Roger Casement*, "Mr Shorter never made a practice of numbering and signing the many books and pamphlets he printed. He had a little black-covered book in which he kept a record of them all. He would head a page with the title of a book, and then run the numbers down from 1 to 25. Whenever he gave away or sold a copy he entered the name of the recipient against the number whose turn it was. If the person to whom any particular copy went requested him to do so, he wrote against the printed Certificate of Issue the number, and initialled it. In some cases [he] signed his name in full. If such a request was not made, then the book was left untouched ... This question has been raised before. Some while after Mr Shorter's death, Mr Richard Curle spoke to me upon the subject. I saw that misunderstanding might easily arise in the future, and went to Messrs Eyre & Spottiswoode, the printers; these gentlemen were slightly annoyed at such a suggestion being made, and regarded it as a reflection upon their business honour. They gave me a written certificate definitely stating that in no single instance was *one* copy printed by them of *any* book or pamphlet beyond the number stated. I *think* I gave this letter to Mr Curle—if not I have it still."

Since Wise's testimony might now be suspect and since Mr Curle has written us that he does not possess the letter and cannot recall ever having had it; since, moreover, the records of the printer were blitzed during World War II, and since the copy of Wise's letter we have examined is only a typescript (kindly lent to us by Mr Maxwell Steinhardt), the problem can hardly be considered as resolved. There is, however, the testimony of the pamphlets themselves. We have been able to record the existence of only sixteen copies of *Letters to An Editor* (seven of them numbered), plus a single proof copy consisting of uncut leaves loosely inserted into a specimen wrapper. One copy has been noted lacking the limitation notice on p. 2.

NUMBERED: Library of Congress (No. 4); University of Cincinnati (No. 5); Princeton University (No. 10); University of Virginia (No. 11); McMaster University, Hamilton, Ontario (No. 13); University of Michigan (No. 16); the late P. S. O'Hegarty (No. 19, formerly Thomas Hardy's copy). No. 18 appeared in the catalogue of the Paul Lemperly sale, but has not been located.

UNNUMBERED: Leon Edel (2 copies, one with original letters inserted and containing the Shorter bookplate), Richard Foley, British Museum, Huntington Library, University of Pennsylvania, Harvard University, Rosenbach Foundation. In addition, the University of Virginia owns the proof copy described above.

C4   THE LETTERS OF   1920
                    HENRY JAMES

a. *First edition:*

THE LETTERS | OF | HENRY JAMES | SELECTED AND EDITED BY | PERCY LUBBOCK | VOLUME I [II] | MAC-MILLAN AND CO., LIMITED | ST. MARTIN'S STREET, LONDON | 1920

($8\frac{3}{4} \times 5\frac{11}{16}$): Volume I, [a]^8 b^8 A–2D^8 2E^6, pp. xxxii, 444. Volume II, [a]^6 A–2I^8 2K^{10}, pp. xii, 532. Demy 8vo.

Contents: Volume I: [i–ii], half-title, on verso publisher's device; [iii–iv], title, on verso copyright notice and imprint, "Glasgow: Printed at the University Press | By Robert Maclehose and Co. Ltd."; v–x, contents; [xi–xii], listing of single illustration, verso blank; xiii–xxxi, Introduction by Percy Lubbock; [xxxii], acknowledgment note; [1]–441, text; [442], imprint, "End of Vol. I." and printer's imprint, as on p. [iv]; [443–444], blank leaf. Frontispiece portrait, from a drawing by John S. Sargent, with tissue guard, tipped in, not reckoned in pagination.

Volume II: [i–iv], uniform with Vol. I; v–xi, contents; at bottom of p. xi, list of illustrations; [xii], blank; [1]–520, text; 521–529, Index; at bottom of p. 529 imprint, as on p. [iv] but in one line; [530], blank; [531–532], blank leaf. Frontispiece portrait, from a camera portrait by E. O. Hoppé, with tissue guard, and a triple-fold insert facsimile of a 1906 page of revisions for *The American* tipped in, not reckoned in pagination.

Issued in dark blue smooth cloth, double-rule at top and bottom in blind across front and back covers and in gilt across spine, lettered in gilt on spine; white end-papers; all edges untrimmed.

Published 8 April 1920, at 36/-, the first (and only) printing consisting of 1500 copies. Publication had originally been set for 9 April, simultaneously with that of the American edition, but Macmillan did not adhere to this arrangement and anticipated the transatlantic issue.

The letters, while highly representative, constitute but a small proportion of James's massive correspondence and are largely those of his middle and later years. Owing to their length and their often repetitious character, only portions of some of the letters are reproduced. There are occasional misreadings and errors in punctuation due to faulty transcription, so that the texts, while close to the original, are not always reliable in minute details. Later letters, many of which James dictated to a typist, are faithfully reproduced.

On pp. xx and xxi of Vol. I, Lubbock quotes briefly from James's rough notes for a contemplated, but abandoned, novel. There are a few misreadings in this passage; the full text was later published as "The 'K.B.' Case and 'Mrs. Max,' " in *The Notebooks of Henry James*, 1947.

Included in Vol. I, pp. 337–338, is "The Golden Dream: a Little Tale," written by James in Mary Anderson's autograph album, and published here for the first time.

b. *First American edition:*

THE LETTERS | OF | HENRY JAMES | SELECTED AND EDITED BY | PERCY LUBBOCK | VOLUME I [II] | NEW YORK | CHARLES SCRIBNER'S SONS | 1920

($8\frac{11}{16} \times 5\frac{3}{4}$): Volume I, [unsigned: 1–28⁸ 29¹⁰], pp. xxxiv, 434. Volume II, [unsigned: 1–33⁸], pp. xiv, 514. 8vo.

Contents: Volume I: [i–ii], half-title, verso blank; [iii–iv], title, on verso copyright notice and printer's device; v–x, contents; [xi–xii], listing of single illustration, verso blank; xiii–xxxi, Introduction by Percy Lubbock; [xxxii], blank; [xxxiii–xxxiv], acknowledgment note, verso blank; 1–434, text. Frontispiece portrait uniform with English edition.

Volume II: [i–iv], uniform with Vol. I; v–xi, contents; [xii], blank; [xiii–xiv], list of illustrations, verso blank; 1–502, text; 503–511, Index; [512], blank; [513–514], blank leaf. Frontispiece portrait and facsimile of revisions for *The American* uniform with English edition.

Issued in black-green linen-grain cloth, double-rule at top and bottom in blind across front and back covers and in gilt across spine, lettered in gilt on spine; white end-papers; top edge trimmed, other edges untrimmed (bottom edge trimmed in some copies). [See also p. 138.]

Published 9 April 1920, at $10, the first printing consisting of 3000 copies.

The separate settings of type for the English and American editions resulted in some textual variants and differences in pagination.

C5   A LETTER TO MRS. LINTON   1921

A LETTER | FROM HENRY JAMES | TO | MRS. LINTON | PRIVATELY PRINTED [1921]

(6 × 4$\frac{13}{16}$): a single unsigned quire of eight leaves, pp. 16, unpaginated. [16mo]

Contents: [1–2], blank leaf; [3–4], title, on verso quotation from unpublished letter from HJ to his nephew, William James; [5–6], dedication, verso blank; [7–9], compiler's note; [10], blank; [11–13], text of letter to Mrs Linton, dated July 23d [1882]; [14], blank; [15–16], colophon, verso blank.

Issued in pressed fibre multicoloured flower-patterned paper wrappers; no lettering on wrappers; top edge trimmed, other edges untrimmed.

Printed by George Parker Winship "At the Sign of the George," Shandygraft Farm, Charles River, Mass., the sixth publication of this private press. Dedicated to Franklin James, to whom it was presented as a Christmas gift, 1921. Copies in the first state were distributed with the initials "G.P.W." inscribed in ink beneath the text on p. [9], sometimes with the additional dating, "Christmas 1921." Remaining copies were distributed in off-white paper wrappers with varied all-over designs (i.e., horizontal zigzag rules and dots in green, vertical series of decoratively-designed panels in blue, etc.), bearing inscription, if any, on recto of second leaf.

Quotation, p. [4], reads: " 'Give him some handsome and pictorial name . . . Most of our names are rather colourless—collez-lui dessus, therefore, a little patch of brightness . . . a name quite to himself.' " This refers to HJ's unheeded request that his grand-nephew not be "saddled" with a "tiresome and graceless" William *Junior* (cf HJ to William James, Jr., Lubbock, *Letters*, II, letter dated 18 June 1913).

Colophon, p. [15], reads: "This letter has been put into type on the fifty-first anniversary of the inception of a great novelist's happiest romance At the Sign of The George [St George device]". The word "romance" is ambiguous. If *inception* refers to the writing of a novel of romance, *The Portrait of A Lady*, the dating is wrong, this having actually been the forty-first anniversary of the first appearance of the novel in *Macmillan's Magazine* and the *Atlantic Monthly*, 1880. If the writer was seeking to hint at a "romance" between James and his correspondent, he was speculating gratuitously.

C6   A MOST UNHOLY TRADE   1923

"A MOST UNHOLY TRADE" | BEING LETTERS ON THE | DRAMA BY HENRY JAMES | [scarab device] | THE SCARAB PRESS | PRIVATELY PRINTED | MCMXXIII

($6 \times 4\frac{1}{2}$): [unsigned: A–B⁴ C² D⁴], pp. ii, 26. [32mo]

Contents: [i–ii], blank leaf; [1–2], half-title, on verso engraved frontispiece portrait, from a drawing by John S. Sargent, printed on tissue and pasted onto leaf, with tipped-in tissue guard; [3–4], title, on verso imprint, "Copyright, 1923, by Dunster House | Bookshop, Cambridge, Massachusetts."; [5–6], acknowledgment note, verso blank; 7–[18], text; [19–20], colophon, verso blank; [21–26], blank.

Issued in brown half cloth, light cream paper over flexible boards, lettered within double-rule panel in black on front cover, against light tan background on which is superimposed a decorative scarab in silver-grey and yellow; white end-papers; top and bottom edges trimmed, fore-edge untrimmed.

Colophon, p. [19], reads: "Of this, the first book printed by The Scarab Press, one hundred copies are for sale at Dunster House . . . The cover was designed by Waldo Murray and also cut by him on linoleum."

Ransom reports The Scarab Press was "a name used to preserve

anonymity by one man who printed and bound the book alone."
This was the ninth publication of the Dunster House Press, sold at
$2.50. One hundred issued copies were numbered beneath the
colophon; an over-run is suggested by the large number of copies
examined which lack the "Copy Number" imprint on p. [19].

C7   LETTERS TO JOSEPH CONRAD   1926

THREE LETTERS | FROM | HENRY JAMES | TO | JOSEPH
CONRAD [Entire title enclosed within wide decorative
border] [1926]

$(8\frac{3}{8} \times 6\frac{3}{4})$: a single unsigned quire of six leaves, pp. 12, unpaginated.
Sewn.

Contents: [1–2], title, on verso limitation notice; [3–4], introductory
notes [by G. Jean-Aubry]; [5–10], text of the letters; [11–12], blank.

Issued without wrappers, lettered and blocked in black (as above) on
recto of first leaf; top edge trimmed, other edges untrimmed. Printed
on pale green laid paper.

Limitation notice reads: "220 copies of these letters from Henry James
to Joseph Conrad have been printed for the First Edition Club,
London, 1926, at the Curwen Press."

Published September 1926, as one of twelve booklets of varying sizes
under the collective title, *Twenty Letters to Joseph Conrad*, with an
introduction and notes by G. Jean-Aubry, designed by Oliver Simon.
Issued in an attractively designed portfolio, blue half buckram, blue
and white checker-patterned boards, lettered in gilt on spine. The
complete series was sold to members of the First Edition Club at 35/-.

C8   LETTERS TO WALTER BERRY   1928

LETTERS OF HENRY JAMES TO WALTER BERRY [Upper
and lower case italics, in red] | THE BLACK SUN PRESS |
ÉDITIONS NARCISSE [in red] | RUE CARDINALE | PARIS
[in red] | MCMXXVIII

$(10\frac{3}{4} \times 9\frac{1}{8})$: [unsigned: 1–9⁴ (1₁ and 9₄ inserted under fold-over flaps
of the wrappers, serving as end-papers)], pp. 72, unpaginated. 4to.

Contents: [1–4], two blank leaves; [5–6], half-title, verso blank; [7–8], title, verso blank; [9–65], text; [66], blank; [67–68], colophon, on verso imprint, "Tous droits de reproduction et de traduction | réservés pour tous pays y compris la Norvège."; [69–72], two blank leaves. Facsimile letter, consisting of a singleton leaf, between two protective tissue-guards, tipped in between [1₂, ₃].

Issued in white laid paper wrappers with fold-over flaps, covered by transparent jacket, lettered on front cover uniform with title-leaf; top edge trimmed, other edges untrimmed.

Published 15 October 1928, for distribution in New York by Harry F. Marks.

Colophon, p. [67], reads: "This first edition of the Letters of Henry James to Walter Berry printed at the Black Sun Press (Maître-Imprimeur Lescaret) Paris October 1928 for Harry and Caresse Crosby is strictly limited to 16 copies on Japan Paper each copy supplemented by one of the original letters, and 100 numbered copies on Hollande Van Gelder Zonen to be sold at the Bookshop of Harry Marks, New York." The 100 numbered copies sold at $10; the 16 copies numbered A–P, containing original letters, sold at $50. Mr Marks reports that four additional copies, numbered i–iv, were issued *hors commerce*. This was the ninth publication of the Black Sun Press.

Of the sixteen letters published in this edition, only one (dated 8 February 1912) had previously appeared in print, in Lubbock, *Letters*, II. A comparison of the facsimile letter with the published text shows several misreadings and creates a presumption that the texts of the other letters in this volume may be equally corrupt.

C9   LETTERS TO BENSON AND   1930
MONOD

HENRY JAMES: | LETTERS TO A. C. BENSON AND | AUGUSTE MONOD; NOW FIRST | PUBLISHED, AND EDITED | WITH AN INTRODUCTION BY | E. F. BENSON | [publisher's device, designed with date of publication, 1930, in individual numerals in the four corners] | LONDON: ELKIN MATHEWS & MARROT | NEW YORK: CHARLES SCRIBNER'S SONS

C. PUBLISHED LETTERS

$(8\frac{9}{16} \times 5\frac{11}{16})$: [a]^8 A–G^8 H^4, pp. [4], xii, 120. Demy 8vo.

Contents: [1–4], two blank leaves, not reckoned in pagination; [i–ii], half-title, on verso limitation notice; [iii–iv], title, on verso imprint, "Printed in Great Britain by Robert Maclehose and Co. Ltd. | The University Press, Glasgow"; v–[ix], Introduction by E. F. Benson; [x], blank; [xi–xii], divisional fly-title, verso blank; [1]–118, text; [119–120], blank leaf.

Issued in green woven cloth, ornamentally decorated with diagonal sawtooth points in varying shades of green, black and silver, lettered within single-rule panel in silver on dark green paper label on spine; cream-white end-papers; top edge green, other edges untrimmed.

Published September 1930, at 15/- in England and at $6 in America. Published late September in England, being reviewed in *The Times Literary Supplement*, 25 September. Presumably published simultaneously in America, being noted as already issued in *Publishers' Weekly*, 4 October.

Limitation notice, p. [ii], reads: "This Edition is limited to 1050 copies, of which numbers 1 to 1000 are for sale and numbers 1001 to 1050 for presentation." Scribner's imported 500 bound copies for the American market, the balance of the edition being marketed by Elkin Mathews in England.

When this volume appeared, E. F. Benson was asked whether there was any special reason for the juxtaposition of the two series of unrelated letters. He replied that the Monod letters were purchased in a London bookshop by his publisher "who thought they would be a suitable addition to the book." (Unpublished letter from E. F. Benson to Leon Edel, 12 October 1930.)

The copy at Harvard, presented by Henry James, nephew and literary executor of the novelist, contains the following note: "When E. F. Benson asked me for permission to use Uncle Henry's letters to his brother and to Monod, I thought he was proposing to incorporate them in something about his brother and consented. Behold what he's done! I don't think that Uncle Henry took A.C.B. very seriously—I suspect the elaborate verbal generosities of these notes as being the cover and manner that he, often enough—put on and exaggerated when there was really not much that he wanted to say—not much that he wanted to do except be kind and cordial and encouraging to admiration and an offer of friendship, which, as always, were almost pathetically welcome to him."

C10   THEATRE AND FRIENDSHIP   1932

a. *First edition:*

THEATRE | AND FRIENDSHIP | SOME | HENRY JAMES
LETTERS | WITH A COMMENTARY | BY | ELIZABETH
ROBINS | [publisher's device] | LONDON | JONATHAN
CAPE | BEDFORD SQUARE [1932]

($7\frac{7}{8} \times 5\frac{3}{8}$): [A]^8 B–T^8 U^4, pp. 312. Large Crown 8vo.

Contents: [1–2], half-title, on verso list of titles "By the Same Author";
[3–4], title, on verso publication date and imprint, "Printed in Great
Britain in the city of Oxford | At the Alden Press | Paper made by John
Dickinson & Co., Ltd. | Bound by A. W. Bain & Co., Ltd."; 5–6,
contents, on verso list of illustrations; [7–8], prefatory note and
quotation from James letter; [9–10], fly-title, verso blank; 11–23,
"Introductory"; [24], blank; 25–305, text; [306], blank; 307–311,
appendix; [312], blank. Frontispiece and three additional illustrations
tipped in, not reckoned in pagination.

Issued in green linen-grain cloth, publisher's device in blind on back
cover, lettered in gilt on spine; white end-papers; top edge green,
fore-edge trimmed, bottom edge untrimmed.

Published July 1932, at 10/6, the first printing consisting of 1500
copies. Reissued in Cape's "Life and Letters" series, October 1934,
at 4/6.

b. *First American edition:*

THEATRE | AND FRIENDSHIP | SOME | HENRY JAMES |
LETTERS | WITH A COMMENTARY BY | ELIZABETH
ROBINS | [publisher's device] | NEW YORK | G. P. PUT-
NAM'S SONS | 1932

($8\frac{1}{8} \times 5\frac{1}{2}$): [unsigned: 1–19^8], pp. 304. [8vo]

Contents: [1–2], half-title, on verso list of titles "By the Same Author";
[3–4], title, on verso copyright notice, reservation of rights, and im-
print, "Manufactured in the United States of America | At the Van
Rees Press"; [5–6], special acknowledgments, verso blank; [7–8],
quotation from James letter, verso blank; [9–10], contents, verso
blank; [11–12], list of illustrations, verso blank; [13–14], fly-title,
verso blank; 15–27, "Introductory"; [28], blank; 29–298, text;

299–303, Appendix; [304], blank. Frontispiece and five additional illustrations tipped in, not reckoned in pagination.

Issued in burgundy linen-grain cloth, four hinge devices in gilt on front and back covers, lettering, leaf device, and six bands of rules in gilt on spine, author's name in cloth colour against solid gilt panel on spine; off-white end-papers; top edge trimmed and red-purple-stained, other edges untrimmed.

Published 16 September 1932, at $3.50.

A secondary binding is noted, issued in lavender-brown cloth, lettered and blocked uniform with primary binding in orange-yellow.

CII   SELECTED LETTERS OF   1955
HENRY JAMES

a. *First edition:*

THE | SELECTED LETTERS OF | HENRY JAMES | [rule] | EDITED WITH AN INTRODUCTION BY | LEON EDEL | NEW YORK | FARRAR, STRAUS AND CUDAHY [1955]

$(8\frac{1}{4} \times 5\frac{1}{2})$: [unsigned: $1-7^{16}$ 8^8 9^{16}], pp. xxxiv, 238. 8vo.

Contents: [i–ii], half-title, on verso series advertisement; [iii–iv], title, on verso publication date, copyright notice and reservation of rights, printer's imprint, and acknowledgment; [v–vi], dedication, verso blank; vii–viii, "A Note on the Text," signed L.E.; ix–x, Acknowledgment, signed L.E.; [xi–xii], contents, verso blank; xiii–xxx, Introduction, signed Leon Edel; xxxi–xxxiv, "James Family and Other Correspondents" biographical list; [1–2], fly-title, verso blank; 3–228, text; [229–230], divisional fly-title, verso blank; 231–235, Index; [236–238], blank.

Issued in orange-brown linen-grain cloth, title and author lettered in gilt against dark brown panel with gilt single-rule at top and bottom and publisher's imprint in black on spine; white end-papers; all edges trimmed.

Published 30 November 1955, at $4, the first printing consisting of 4000 copies.

Contains one hundred and eleven letters and one telegram, of which approximately half are published for the first time.

b. *First English edition* (1956):

SELECTED LETTERS OF | HENRY JAMES | EDITED WITH
AN INTRODUCTION BY | LEON EDEL | [epigraph] | [pub-
lisher's device] | LONDON | RUPERT HART-DAVIS | 1956

$(7\frac{15}{16} \times 5\frac{1}{8})$: [A]^8 B–P^8 Q^6 R^8, pp. 268. Large Crown 8vo.

Contents: [1–2], half-title, verso blank; [3–4], title, on verso printer's imprint; [5–6], dedication, verso blank; [7–8], contents, verso blank; 9–10, "A Note on the Text," signed "L.E."; 11–26, Introduction, signed Leon Edel; 27–30, "James Family and other Correspondents" biographical list; [31–32], divisional fly-title, verso blank; 33–261, text; 262–263, acknowledgments, signed "L.E."; 264–268, Index.

Issued in rust-red linen-grain cloth, lettered in gilt on spine; white end-papers; top edge rust-red, other edges trimmed.

Published 20 January 1956, at 16/-, the first printing consisting of 3000 copies.

The English edition is more fully and precisely annotated than the American and certain textual inaccuracies have been eliminated. In some places the letters are given in different order.

→ *See also ADDENDA, p. 284.*

Part II: MISCELLANEOUS

Even before Henry James's death, examples of his epistolary art had begun to appear in the memoirs of his contemporaries. He was a constant letter-writer; correspondence was an elaborate ritual of friendship to be practised with the artistry he brought to bear whenever he sat down at his writing-table. Each letter—indeed each telegram, when he resorted to that medium—is stamped with his unmistakeable style. The result was that even when he enjoined his correspondents to burn his letters, these were treasured and preserved. Thousands are extant. Those which, through chance, have crept into memoirs and reminiscences are often less happy examples of the novelist's letter-writing art. They are casual letters, many dealing with the observances of social amenities, representing what James himself termed the "mere twaddle of graciousness." The letters to many more intimate friends (who did not write their memoirs) remain to be published; and large portions of the family correspondence preserved at Harvard—some letters filling as many as thirty or forty half-sheets—are represented only by excerpts in the admirable two volumes of correspondence published by Percy Lubbock in 1920.

The list here given comprises those volumes or articles which we have been able to trace containing first published appearances of one or more complete letters (L), extracts (E), or telegrams (T).

C11a Anderson, Mary, *A Few More Memories* (London, 1936).
  2L, 1E to Mary Anderson de Navarro.

C12 Archer, Charles, *William Archer: Life, Work and Friendships* (London 1931; New Haven, Conn., 1931).
  1L to Archer.

C13 Asquith, H. H. (first Earl of Oxford and Asquith), *Memories and Reflections, 1852–1921* (London, 1928; Boston, 1928), 2 vols.
  1L to Asquith.

C14 Asquith, Margot, *An Autobiography* (London, 1920; New York, 1920).
  1L to Mrs Asquith.

C15 Atherton, Gertrude, *Adventures of A Novelist* (New York, 1932; London, 1932).
  1L to Mrs Atherton.

C16 Bainton, George (ed.), *The Art of Authorship* (London, 1890; New York, 1890).
  See B5.

C17 Battersea, Baroness (Constance Flower), *Reminiscences of Constance Battersea* (London, 1922).
  1L to Lord Battersea (Cyril Flower).

C17a Bell, Millicent, "Edith Wharton and Henry James: The Literary Relation," *PMLA*, LXXIV (December 1959), 619–637.
  6E to Mrs Wharton.

C18 Benedict, Clare, *The Benedicts Abroad* (privately printed, London, 1930).
  32E to Clara W. and Clare Benedict.

C. PUBLISHED LETTERS

C19 Benson, E. F., *Our Family Affairs, 1867–1896* (London, 1920; New York, 1921).
2E to Benson.

C20 Betham-Edwards, Matilda, *Mid-Victorian Memories* (London, 1919; New York, 1919).
1L, 1E to Mrs Betham-Edwards; 1T to Hale White.

C21 Bishop, Ferman, "Henry James Criticizes *The Tory Lover*," *American Literature*, XXVII (May 1955), 262–264.
1L to Sarah Orne Jewett.

C22 Blanche, Jacques-Émile, *Mes Modèles* (Paris, 1928).
Translations of 2L to William James and 1L each to R. L. Stevenson and Walter Berry, all previously published.

C23 ———, *Portraits of A Lifetime* (London, 1937; New York, 1938).
6L, 1E to Blanche.

C24 Bode, Carl, "Henry James and Owen Wister," *American Literature*, XXVI (May 1954), 250–252.
1L to Wister.

C25 Boit, Louise, "Henry James as Landlord," *Atlantic Monthly*, CLXXVIII (August 1946), 118–121.
4L to Mrs Boit; 1L to Miss Horstmann.

C26 Burlingame, Roger, *Of Making Many Books* (New York, 1946).
3E to Charles Scribner.

C27 Burnett, Vivian, *The Romantick Lady (Frances Hodgson Burnett): The Life Story of An Imagination* (New York 1927; London, 1927).
8L to Mrs F. H. Burnett.

C28 Burr, Anna Robeson (ed.), *Alice James: Her Brothers—Her Journal* (New York, 1934; London, 1934).
1L, 1E to Robertson James; 1L to Edward Emerson; 1E to Caroline James; 1L to Mary James Vaux.

C29 ———, *Weir Mitchell: His Life and Letters* (New York, 1929).
2L to Dr Mitchell.

C30 Bynner, Witter, "On Henry James's Centennial: Lasting Impressions of A Great American Writer," *Saturday Review of Literature*, XXVI (22 May 1943), 23, 26, 28.
3E (plus several fragments) to Bynner.

C31 Callender, L. (ed.), *The Windmill* (London, 1923; New York, 1923).
1L to Guy [Millar], reproduced in facsimile.

C32 Carrington, C. E., *The Life of Rudyard Kipling* (London, 1955; Garden City, N.Y., 1955).

1E to Kipling; 1E to Caroline Kipling; 2E to William James; 1E to Gosse.

C33 Carter, Morris, *Isabella Stewart Gardner and Fenway Court* (Boston and New York, 1925; London, 1926).

1L (plus several fragments) to Mrs Gardner.

C34 Charnwood, Lady, *An Autograph Collection and the Making of It* (London, 1930; New York, 1930).

2E to Lady Charnwood.

C35 Clodd, Edward, *Memories* (London, 1916; New York, 1916).

1E to Mrs Lynn Linton.

C35a Cohen, B. Bernard, "Henry James and the Hawthorne Centennial," Essex Institute *Historical Collections*, XCII (July 1956), 279–283.

3L to Robert S. Rantoul; 1L to George F. Dow.

C36 Cortissoz, Royal, *The Life of Whitelaw Reid* (New York, 1921; London, 1921), 2 vols.

2L, 1E to Reid.

C37 Da Costa, Isaac, *Noble Families Among the Sephardic Jews* (London, 1936).

1L to Anton E. Capadose. Reprinted in *The Notebooks of Henry James*, 1947.

C38 Daly, Joseph Francis, *The Life of Augustin Daly* (New York, 1917).

2L, 1E to Daly.

C39 Dodd, M. D. Ashley, *The Days of A Year* (London, 1913).

See B30.

C40 Edel, Leon (ed.), *The Complete Plays of Henry James* (Philadelphia and New York, 1949; London, 1949).

Includes 2L to G. Bernard Shaw, and quotes from more than 100 unpublished letters to, among others, Sir George Alexander, William Archer, Theodora Bosanquet, Mrs W. K. Clifford, Augustin Daly, Sir Johnston and Lady Forbes-Robertson, Isabella Stewart Gardner, Harley Granville-Barker, William Dean Howells, R. U. Johnson, Gertrude Kingston, Urbain Mengin, Helena Modjeska, Grace Norton, J. R. Osgood, Jocelyn Persse, Sir Arthur Pinero, Henrietta Reubell, Elizabeth Robins, H. E. Scudder, G. W. Smalley, Julian R. Sturgis, Dame Ellen Terry, Dr C. E. Wheeler, as well as various members of the James family.

C41 —— (ed.), *The Ghostly Tales of Henry James* (New Brunswick, N.J., 1948).
1E each to Mrs John L. (Isabella) Gardner and Gertrude Kingston, and fragments of letters to Edmund Gosse, George du Maurier, and others.

C42 ——, *Henry James: les années dramatiques* (Paris, 1931).
6L to Miss Theodora Bosanquet; 1L each to Madame de Navarro (Mary Anderson) and Sir George Henschel.

C43 ——, *Henry James: The Untried Years* (New York, 1953; London, 1953).
Numerous extracts and fragments, principally to Mr & Mrs Henry James, Sr., William and Alice James, William Dean Howells, Grace Norton, and Charles Eliot Norton.

C44 ——, "Henry James and *The Outcry*," *University of Toronto Quarterly*, XVIII (July 1949), 340–346.
2E to Miss Theodora Bosanquet; 1E each to Harley Granville-Barker and J. B. Pinker.

C44a ——, Introduction to Henry James's *The Ambassadors* (Boston, 1960).
1E to [William James].

C45 ——, Introduction to Henry James's *The Other House* (London, 1948; New York, 1948).
1E to Mrs William James, and fragments to Paul Bourget and Miss Theodora Bosanquet.

C46 ——, Introduction to Henry James's *The Portrait of a Lady* (Boston, 1956).
1E to Mrs Henry James Sr., 3E to William James, 1E to William Dean Howells.

C47 ——, *The Prefaces of Henry James* (Paris, 1931).
1L to Mrs Lynn Linton.

C47a ——, Introduction to Henry James's *Roderick Hudson* (New York, 1960).
1E to [Mrs Wister].

C48 ——, Introduction to Henry James's *The Sacred Fount* (New York, 1953).
1E to Mrs Humphry Ward; 1E to the Duchess of Sutherland.

C48a ——, Introduction to Henry James's *The Sacred Fount* (London, 1959).
1E to Mrs Humphry Ward.

c48b ——, Introduction to Henry James's *The Tragic Muse* (New York, 1960).
1E to [Grace Norton].

c48c ——, Introduction to Henry James's *Watch and Ward* (London, 1959).
1E to [J. T. Fields].

c49 ——, "The Texts of Henry James's Unpublished Plays," *Harvard Library Bulletin*, III (Autumn 1949), 395–406.
1L to Martin Secker; 1E each to J. R. Osgood and William James; 1T to Miss Theodora Bosanquet.

c49a ——, "The Text of The Ambassadors," *Harvard Library Bulletin*, XIV (Autumn 1960), 453–460.
2E to William James; 1E to Mrs Humphry Ward.

c50 ——, *The American Essays of Henry James* (New York, 1956).
1E to Manton Marble.

c51 ——, and Dan H. Laurence, *A Bibliography of Henry James* (London, 1957).
4E each to Sir Frederick Macmillan and J. B. Pinker; 3E each to HJ Sr. and Mrs HJ Sr.; 1E each to Elizabeth Boott, Chatto & Windus, Henry Cust, W. D. Howells, W. Robinson, and Scribner's.

c51a ——, and Ilse Dusoir Lind, *Parisian Sketches* (New York, 1957; London, 1958).
12L to Whitelaw Reid. (See also A101, C36 and C105.)
2E to Alice James.

c51b ——, and Lyall H. Powers, "Henry James and the *Bazar* Letters," *Bulletin of the New York Public Library*, LXII (February 1958), 75–103. Offprinted, with W. D. Howells's "Novel-Writing and Novel-Reading," as a brochure, under the title *Howells and James: A Double Billing* (1958).
30L to Elizabeth Jordan. (See also C93.)

c51c ——, "Who *Was* Gilbert Osmond?" *Modern Fiction Studies*, VI (Summer 1960), 164.
1E to William James.

c52 ["Elizabeth," Countess von Arnim], *In the Mountains* (Garden City, N.Y., 1920; London, 1920).
1L to Elizabeth Mary, Countess von Arnim.

c53 Elliott, Maud Howe, *John Elliott: The Story of An Artist* (Boston and New York, 1930).
3L to John Elliott.

C54 ——, *This Was My Newport* (Cambridge, Mass., 1944).
1L to Julia Ward Howe; 1L to Mrs Elliott.

C55 ——, *Three Generations* (Boston, 1923; London, 1925).
2L to Mrs Elliott.

C56 Ellis, S. M., *The Solitary Horseman, or The Life and Adventures of G.P.R. James* (London, 1927).
1E to Ellis.

C57 *Favorite Fairy Tales*, illustrated by Peter Newell (New York, 1907).
1E to [Elizabeth Jordan].
Full letter first published in *The Selected Letters of Henry James*, 1955.

C58 Ferguson, Alfred R., "The Triple Quest of Henry James: Fame, Art, and Fortune," *American Literature*, XXVII (January 1956), 475–498.
12E to Mr and Mrs HJ Sr.; 15E to WJ; 2E to Alice James; 11E to W. D. Howells; 4E to J. B. Pinker; 2E to Grace Norton; 2E to C. E. Norton; 1E to Theodora Sedgwick.

C59 ——, "Some Bibliographical Notes on the Short Stories of Henry James," *American Literature*, XXI (November 1949), 292–297.
1E to J. B. Pinker.

C59a Gale, Robert L., "A Letter from Henry James to Francis Marion Crawford," *Studi Americani*, series 4 (Rome, 1958), 415–419.
1L to F. M. Crawford.

C60 Gardner, Burdett, "An Apology for Henry James's 'Tiger-Cat,'" *PMLA*, LXVIII (September 1953), 688–695.
5L to Vernon Lee (Violet Paget).

C61 Garnier, Marie-Reine, *Henry James et la France* (Paris, 1927).
1L to J. J. Jusserand.

C62 Godkin, E. L., *Life and Letters of Edwin Lawrence Godkin*, ed. by Rollo Ogden (New York, 1907; London, 1907), 2 vols.
1L to Godkin.

C63 Goldring, Douglas, *The Last Pre-Raphaelite: A Record of the Life and Writings of Ford Madox Ford* (London, 1948). American edition entitled *Trained for Genius* (New York, 1949).
10L to Ford Madox Hueffer; 7L to Mrs Hueffer (Elsie Martindale); 1L to Archibald Marshall.

C64 [Gosse, Edmund], *A Catalogue of the Gosse Correspondence in the Brotherton Collection* [of Leeds University] (Leeds, England, 1950).
Facsimile of p. 1 of undated letter to Gosse.

c65 ——, *The Library of Edmund Gosse*, compiled by E. H. M. Cox (London, 1924).
1L to Gosse.

c66 Gower, Sir George Leveson, *Years of Endeavour* (London, 1942).
1L to Gower.

c67 Hardy, Arthur Sherburne, *Things Remembered* (Boston and New York, 1923; London, 1924).
1L to Hardy.

c68 Harlow, Virginia, "Thomas Sergeant Perry and Henry James," *The Boston Public Library Quarterly*, I (July 1949), 43–60.
27L to Perry.

c69 ——, *Thomas Sergeant Perry: A Biography* (Durham, N.C., 1950; Cambridge, England, 1951).
81L to Perry, including those noted in C68.

c70 Harrier, Richard C. (ed.), "Letters of Henry James," *Colby Library Quarterly*, Series III, No. 10 (May 1953), 153–164.
9L to Edmund Gosse; 1L to Mrs Gosse; 1L to J. R. Osgood.

c71 Harris, Marie P., "Henry James, Lecturer," *American Literature*, XXIII (November 1951), 302–314.
1E to William Dean Howells.

c72 Hart-Davis, Rupert, *Hugh Walpole: A Biography* (London, 1952; New York, 1952).
32E to Walpole; 1E to Marie Belloc Lowndes.

c72a Hassall, Christopher, *Edward Marsh, Patron of the Arts* (London, 1959). American edition entitled *A Biography of Edward Marsh* (New York, 1959).
10E to Edward Marsh.

c73 Havens, Raymond D., "Henry James on One of His Early Stories," *American Literature*, XXIII (March 1951), 131–133.
1L to J. A. Hammerton.

c74 Head, Ruth (ed.), *Pictures and Other Passages from Henry James* (London, 1916; New York, 1917).
See A76.

c75 Herrick, Robert, "A Visit to Henry James," *Yale Review*, n.s. XII (July 1923), 724–741.
1L to Herrick.

c76 Horner, Frances, *Time Remembered* (London, 1933).
1L to Lady Horner.

c77 Howe, Mark DeWolfe, "The Letters of Henry James to Mr. Justice Holmes," *Yale Review*, XXXVIII (Spring 1949), 410–433.
2IL to Oliver Wendell Holmes.

c78 Howe, M. A. De Wolfe (ed.), *Memories of A Hostess: A Chronicle of Eminent Friendships* (Boston, 1922; London, 1923).
IE to Howe; IE (in facsimile) to Mrs James T. Fields.

c79 Howells, William Dean, *Life in Letters of William Dean Howells*, ed. by Winifred Howells (Garden City, New York, 1928; London, 1929), 2 vols.
2L to Howells.

c80 Hueffer, Ford Madox, *Thus to Revisit* (London, 1921; New York, 1921).
IT to Hueffer.
(See also c63.)

c81 Hunt, Violet, *The Flurried Years* (London, 1926). American edition entitled *I Have This to Say* (New York, 1926).
5L, 6E (plus several fragments) to Miss Hunt.

c82 Jacob, H. E., *The World of Emma Lazarus* (New York, 1949).
IE to Miss Lazarus.

c83 James, Henry, "Allen D. Loney—In Memoriam," *New York Times*, 12 September 1915.
See D575.

c84 ——, "The British Theatre Libre," the *Weekly Comedy*, 21 December 1889.
See D438.

c85 ——, "The Summer School at Deerfield . . .," *New York Tribune*, 4 August 1889.
See B42 and D435.

c85a ——, "Fourteen Letters," *Botteghe Oscure*, XIX (Spring 1957), 182–194. A supplement to Henry Brewster's "Henry James and the Gallo-American," pp. 170–181 of the same issue.
14L to Henry B. Brewster.

c86 ——, "A Henry James Centenary Exhibition," *Colby Library Quarterly*, Series I, No. 3 (June 1943), 33–44.
2L each to Lawrence Barrett and Louis E. Shipman; 2L, IE to Mrs F. H. Hill; IL to Edwin A. Abbey and Alfred Parsons jointly; IL each to Richard Watson Gilder, Sir George Henschel, Pierre de Chaignon la Rose, and Walter Wyckoff; IL each to three unidentified correspondents.

c87 ——, "International Copyright" (A Letter to the American Copyright League), the *Critic*, 10 December 1887.
See D417.

c88 ——, "A Letter to Mr Howells," *North American Review*, Apr 1912.
See D563.

c89 ——, "Mr Henry James on England," the *Observer*, 18 April 1915.
See D570.

c90 ——, "Three Unpublished Letters and A Monologue," *London Mercury*, September 1922.
See D579.

c91 ——, "Two Unpublished Letters," *Hound and Horn*, April–June 1934.
1L each to William Heinemann and Richard Watson Gilder.

c92 Johnson, Willis Fletcher, *George Harvey: 'A Passionate Patriot'* (Boston and New York, 1929; London, 1930).
1E to Col. Harvey.

c93 Jordan, Elizabeth, *Three Rousing Cheers* (New York, 1938; London, 1938).
4L to Miss Jordan. The letters printed by Miss Jordan were freely edited and certain portions were deleted, apparently in a misguided desire to clarify James's meaning. Certain words have been misread. (See also c51b.)

c94 Jusserand, Jules J., *What Me Befell* (London, 1933; Boston and New York, 1933).
2E to Jusserand.

c94a Keynes, Geoffrey, "Henry James in Cambridge," *London Magazine*, VI (March 1959), 50–61.
7L to Charles Sayle; 1L to Geoffrey Keynes; 3L jointly to Sayle, Keynes, and A. Theodore Bartholomew.
Reprinted, revised, as a book, *Henry James in Cambridge* (Cambridge, 1967).

c95 Kirk, Rudolf, "Five Letters of Henry James," the *Journal of the Rutgers University Library*, XII (June 1949), 54–58.
2L to Matilda Betham-Edwards; 1L each to Edmund Gosse and W. Barclay Squire. The first letter, to Sir Joseph Boehm, is not by the novelist but by Sir Henry James, the Victorian barrister.

c96 LaFarge, John, "Henry James's Letters to the LaFarges," *New England Quarterly*, XXII (June 1949), 173–192.
2L to John LaFarge, the painter; 9L to LaFarge's widow, son, and daughter; 1L to Edward Holton James.

C. PUBLISHED LETTERS

C97 Laski, Margharita, *Mrs. Ewing Mrs. Molesworth and Mrs. Hodgson Burnett* (London, 1950).
1E to Frances M. Peard.

C98 Layard, George Somes, *Mrs. Lynn Linton: Her Life, Letters, and Opinions* (London, 1901).
1L to Mrs Linton.

C99 LeClair, Robert C., "Henry James and Minny Temple," *American Literature*, XXI (March 1949), 35–48.
1L, 1E to Mrs HJ Sr.; 1L to William James.

C100 ——, *The Young Henry James* (New York, 1955).
Numerous extracts and fragments, principally to Mr and Mrs HJ Sr. and WJ.

C101 Lee, Elizabeth, *Ouida: A Memoir* (London, 1914).
2E to Miss Lee.

C102 Leigh, James W., *Other Days* (London, 1921).
1L to Dean Leigh.

C103 Leslie, Shane, "A Note on Henry James," *Horizon*, VII (June 1943), 405–413.
11E to an unidentified correspondent (Jocelyn Persse).

C104 Leslie, Mrs Shane (Marjorie Ide), *Girlhood in the Pacific* (London, 1943).
1L to Henry C. Ide.

C104a "Letters to the London Library," *ADAM International Review*, Nos. 397–400 (1976–1977), 26–29.
1L to Charles Hagberg Wright.

C105 Lind, Ilse Dusoir, "The Inadequate Vulgarity of Henry James," *PMLA*, LXVI (December 1951), 886–910.
6L to Whitelaw Reid (and summaries of 6 additional letters).

C106 Lowndes, Marie Belloc, *The Merry Wives of Westminster* (London, 1946).
1L to Mrs Lowndes.

C107 Lucas, E. V., *The Colvins and Their Friends* (London, 1928; New York, 1928).
6L, 14E to Sidney Colvin; 2L, 3E to Mrs Frances Sitwell (later Lady Colvin).

C108 ——, *Edwin Austin Abbey: Royal Academician: The Record of His Life and Work* (New York and London, 1921), 2 vols.
3L, 18E, 1T to Mr and Mrs E. A. Abbey.

C109 Mackenzie, Compton, *Gallipoli Memories* (London, 1929; Garden City, N.Y., 1930).
1L to Mackenzie.

C109a Markow-Totevy, Georges, *Henry James* (Paris, 1958).
5L to Paul and Minnie Bourget (one in the original French, the others translated from the English). A translation of the book (London, 1969; New York, 1969), by John Cummings, contains only the one letter, originally in French, now translated into English.

C110 Marsh, Sir Edward, *A Number of People* (London, 1939; New York, 1939).
1L to Marsh.

C111 Marshall, Archibald, *Out and About: Random Reminiscence* (London, 1933; New York, 1934).
1L to Marshall.

C112 Mason, A. E. W., *Sir George Alexander & the St. James's Theatre* (London, 1935).
3E to Alexander.

C113 Matthiessen, F. O., *The James Family* (New York, 1947).
14L to Mr and Mrs HJ Sr.; 19L to William James (some previously quoted in part); 4L to William Dean Howells; 1L to Grace Norton; several letters to younger members of the James family.

C114 ——, and Kenneth B. Murdock (eds.), *The Notebooks of Henry James* (New York, 1947; London, 1948).
3E to Horace Scudder; 1E to James R. Osgood.

C115 McElderry, B. R., Jr., "Hamlin Garland and Henry James," *American Literature*, XXIII (January 1952), 433–446.
10L to Garland.

C116 McLane, James, "A Henry James Letter," *Yale Review*, XIV (October 1924), 205–208.
1L to Lilla Cabot Perry. Reprinted in Morse, John T., *Thomas Sergeant Perry* (Boston and New York, 1929).

C116a Meredith, William M. [Four letters from HJ to Meredith.] *Desiderata* I (2 April 1948), 3–4.

C117 Meynell, Viola (ed.), *Friends of A Lifetime: Letters to Sydney Carlyle Cockerell* (London, 1940).
1L to Cockerell.

C118 Michaels, Herbert S., "An Unpublished Letter of Henry James,"

Colby Library Quarterly, Series III, No. 2 (May 1951), 23–26.
1L to Marion Terry.

C119 Millar, C. C. Hoyer, *George du Maurier and Others* (London, 1937).
2L, 1E to Mrs Millar; 1L to Guy Millar (HJ's godson).

C120 Mills, J. Saxon, *Sir Edward Cook, K.B.E.* (London, 1921; New York, 1921).
1L to Cook.

C121 Morgan, Charles, *The House of Macmillan (1843–1943)* (London, 1943; New York, 1944).
1E to Sir Frederick Macmillan.

C122 Nevins, Allan, *Henry White: Thirty Years of American Diplomacy* (New York, 1930; London, 1930).
1L to Mrs Henry White; 5E (plus several fragments) to White.

C123 Nowell-Smith, Simon (ed.), *The Legend of the Master: Henry James* (London, 1947; New York, 1948).
1E to Edmund Gosse (pp. 62–63); 1E to Lady Macmillan (pp. 101–102); 1E to *The Times* (see D574).

C123a ——, *The House of Cassell* (London, 1958).
1E to Wemyss Reid.

C124 O'Connor, Mrs T. P., *I Myself* (London, 1910).
1L to Mrs O'Connor.

C125 Orcutt, William Dana, *Celebrities Off Parade* (Chicago and New York, 1935).
1E to Orcutt.

C126 ——, *In Quest of the Perfect Book* (New York, 1926; London, 1926).
1L to William James; 1E (in facsimile) to Horace Fletcher.

C126a Pearson, Justus R., Jr., "Story of A Magazine: New York's *Galaxy* 1866–1878," *Bulletin of the New York Public Library*, LXI (May 1957), 217–237; (June 1957), 281–302.
7E to William and Francis Church.

C127 Perry, Bliss, *The Life and Letters of Henry Lee Higginson* (Boston, 1921).
2L to Higginson, plus a fragment from William James to HJ erroneously credited to HJ (p. 338n).

C127a Perrin, Noel, "The Henry James Papers," *New Yorker*, XXXVI (12 November 1960), 191–198.
1E to Fanny Lady Prothero.

C. PUBLISHED LETTERS

C128 Perry, Ralph Barton, "The James Collection," *Harvard University Library Notes*, No. 32, IV, No. 2 (March 1942), 77.
1L (earliest extant) to Master E. Van Winkle.

C129 ——, *The Thought and Character of William James* (Boston, 1935; London, 1935), 2 vols.
28L to William James; 4L to Mr and Mrs HJ Sr; 1L to E. L. Godkin. A chapter of the book, "Henry James in Italy," containing 2L to William James, first appeared in the *Harvard Graduates' Magazine*, XLI (June 1933), 189–200.

C130 Phelps, William Lyon, "Henry James, the Great Exile," *Literary Digest International Book Review*, III (July 1925), 521–522.
1E to G. W. Smalley (portion of same letter as extract in C131).

C131 ——, "A Hitherto Unpublished Letter and A Volume of Short Stories by Henry James," *New York Times Review of Books* (11 January 1920), 9: 2–4.
1E to G. W. Smalley (see also C130).

C132 ——, *Howells, James, Bryant, and Other Essays* (New York, 1924; London, 1924).
1L to Phelps (reprinted in Phelps's *Autobiography With Letters*, New York, 1939; London 1939).

C133 Phillips, Le Roy, *A Bibliography of the Writings of Henry James* (New York, 1930).
1L to Phillips (reproduced in facsimile).

C134 Pope-Hennessy, James, *Monckton Milnes: The Flight of Youth* (London, 1951; New York, 1955).
1L to Richard Monckton Milnes (Lord Houghton).

C135 *The Proceedings in Commemoration of the One Hundredth Anniversary of the Birth of Nathaniel Hawthorne* (Salem, Mass., 1904).
See B25.

C136 Ray, Gordon N., "The Bentley Papers," The *Library* (Transactions of the Bibliographical Society of England), Fifth Series, VII, 3 (September 1952), 178–200.
1E to George Bentley.

C137 Reid, Forrest, *Private Road* (London, 1940).
2L to Reid.

C138 *Report from the Joint Select Committee of the House of Lords and the House of Commons on the Stage Plays (Censorship)* . . . (London, 1909).
See B28.

C. PUBLISHED LETTERS

C139 Repplier, Agnes, *J. William White, M.D.* (Boston and New York, 1919).
19E to Dr White.

C140 Ridge, W. Pett, *A Story Teller: Forty Years in London* (London, 1923; New York, 1924).
1L to Ridge.

C141 Ritchie, Hester Thackeray, *Thackeray and His Daughter: The Letters and Journals of Anne Thackeray Ritchie* (New York, 1924; London, 1924).
1L to Mrs Ritchie (reprinted in *Thackeray's Daughter*, ed. by H. T. (Ritchie) Fuller and Violet Hammersley, Dublin, 1951).

C141a Rosenbaum, S. P., "Two Henry James Letters on *The American* and *Watch and Ward*," *American Literature*, XXX (January 1959), 533–537.
2L to J. R. Osgood.

C141b ——, "Letters to the Pell-Clarkes from Their 'Old Cousin and Friend' Henry James," *American Literature*, XXXI (March 1959), 46–58.
1L each to Leslie and Henrietta Pell-Clarke.

C142 Rothenstein, William, *Men and Memories: Recollections of William Rothenstein, 1872–1922* (London, 1931–32; New York, 1935), 2 vols.
2L to Rothenstein.

C143 Roughead, William, "To Meet Miss Madeleine Smith," *Mainly Murder* (London, 1938). American edition entitled *Enjoyment of Murder* (New York, 1938), dedicated "To the happy memory of Henry James."
1E to Roughead.

C144 ——, *Tales of the Criminous*, ed. W. N. Roughead (London, 1956).
14L to Roughead (five had been published previously).

C145 Russell, John, "Henry James and His Architect," *Architectural Review*, XCIII (March 1943), 69–72.
Copious extracts and fragments from 20 or more letters to Edward P. Warren.

C146 ——, "Henry James and the Leaning Tower," *New Statesman and Nation*, XXV (17 April 1943), 254–255.
16E to Edward P. Warren.

C147 —— (ed.), *A Portrait of Logan Pearsall Smith* (London, 1950).
1L to Smith.

C148 Sanchez, Nellie Van De Grift, *The Life of Mrs. Robert Louis Stevenson* (London, 1920; New York, 1920).

1E to Mrs Stevenson; 1L to Mrs Strong (Fanny Stevenson's daughter). The first letter is reprinted in Sidney Colvin's "Robert Louis Stevenson and Henry James," in *Scribner's Magazine* and in the *Empire Review*, March 1924.

C149 Sedgwick, Henry Dwight, *Francis Parkman* (Boston and New York, 1904; London, 1904).

1E to Parkman.

C150 Sergeant, Elizabeth S., *Willa Cather, A Memoir* (Philadelphia and New York, 1953; London, 1954).

1L to Witter Bynner.

C151 Seznec, Jean, "Lettres de Tourguéneff à Henry James," *Comparative Literature*, I (Summer 1949), 193–209.

1E to W. D. Howells.

C152 Sheridan, Clare, *Nuda Veritas* (London, 1927; New York, 1928, re-titled *Naked Truth*).

1E to Clare Frewen (later Mrs Wilfred Sheridan); 1E to Moreton Frewen.

C153 Shorter, Clement, "A Literary Letter," the *Sphere*, LXIV (18 March 1916), 304.

2L to Shorter. Reprinted in *Letters to An Editor*, 1916 (see C3).

C154 *Sixty American Opinions on the War* (London, 1915).

See B32.

C155 Smalley, Evelyn Garnaut (ed.), *The Henry James Year Book* (Boston, 1911; London, 1912).

See A69.

C156 Smith, Janet Adam, *Henry James and Robert Louis Stevenson: A Record of Friendship and Criticism* (London, 1948).

See B41.

C157 Smith, Logan Pearsall, "Robert Bridges, Recollections," *Society For Pure English Tract 35* (London, 1931).

1L to Smith and Bridges. Reprinted in the *Periodical*, house publicity magazine of the Oxford University Press, XVI (14 February 1931), 11–12.

C158 ——, "Slices of Cake," *New Statesman and Nation*, XXV (5 June 1943), 367–368. Also, under the title "Notes on Henry James," *Atlantic Monthly*, CLXXII (August 1943), 75–77.

1E to Smith.

C159 Stedman, Laura, and George M. Gould, *The Life and Letters of*

C. PUBLISHED LETTERS

E. C. Stedman (New York, 1910), 2 vols.
1E to Stedman.

c160 Swan, Michael, "Henry James and H. G. Wells: A Study of Their Friendship Based on Their Unpublished Correspondence," *Cornhill Magazine*, No. 997 (Autumn 1953), 43–65.
1L, 7E to Wells; 1L, 1E to Mrs Wells.

c161 ——, "Henry James and the Heroic Young Master," *London Magazine*, II (May 1955), 78–86; *Harper's Bazaar*, LXXXIX (September 1955), 226–227, 270, 272.
Contains substantial extracts from eight letters to Hendrik Christian Andersen and one almost in its entirety.

c162 Ticknor, Caroline, *Glimpses of Authors* (Boston, 1922; London, 1923).
1E, presumably to J. R. Osgood. The text corresponds largely to the outline of *The Bostonians* and *Lady Barberina* copied by HJ into his *Notebooks* and there described as incorporated into a letter to Osgood.

c163 Trevelyan, George M., *Sir George Otto Trevelyan: A Memoir* (London and New York, 1932).
1L to George O. Trevelyan.

c164 Trevelyan, Janet Penrose, *The Life of Mrs. Humphry Ward* (London, 1923; New York, 1923).
1E to Mrs Ward.

c165 Wade, Allan (ed.), *The Scenic Art* (New Brunswick, N.J., 1948; London, 1949).
3E to Sir Sidney Lee (one identified only as to editor of the *Cornhill*); 1L, 2E to Brander Matthews; 1E to Edmund Gosse; 1E unidentified, p. 197 (to Mr and Mrs HJ Sr.).

c166 Wagnière, Laura, *From Dawn to Dusk* (privately printed, Vevey, Switzerland, 1930).
4L to Mrs Laura Wagnière-Huntington.

c167 Ward, Mrs Humphry, Preface to Westmoreland [*sic*] Edition of *Robert Elsmere* (Boston and New York, 1911; London, 1911), Vol. I.
2L to Mrs Ward.

c168 ——, *A Writer's Recollections* (London, 1918; New York, 1918).
2E to Mrs Ward.

c169 Weber, Carl J., "Henry James and His 'Tiger-Cat,'" *PMLA*,

LXVIII (September 1953), 672–687.
7L to Vernon Lee (Violet Paget); 2E to William James.

C170 Welby-Gregory, Victoria, *Other Dimensions*, ed. by Mrs Henry
Cust (London, 1931).
1L to Lady Welby.

C171 Wells, H. G., *Experiment in Autobiography* (London, 1934), 2
vols.; (New York, 1934), 1 vol.
1L to Wells.

C172 Wise, Thomas J., *The Ashley Library: A Catalogue of Printed
Books, Manuscripts and Autograph Letters*, XI (London, 1936).
2E to Edmund Gosse.

C173 [Wister, Owen]. *Owen James Wister. October 5, 1825–February
24, 1896*. N.p., n.d. [?1896]. An anonymous memoir, containing
resolutions of organisations and letters of condolence.

1E to Mrs Wister.

C174 Zabel, Morton Dauwen, *The Art of Ruth Draper* (London and
New York, 1959).
3L to Ruth Draper.

ADDENDA TO C (PART I)

C175   LETTERS   1974–

Volume I:

a. First edition:

HENRY JAMES | LETTERS | EDITED BY | LEON EDEL |
VOLUME I | 1843–1875 | THE BELKNAP PRESS | OF |
HARVARD UNIVERSITY PRESS | CAMBRIDGE, MASSA-
CHUSETTS | 1974

($8\frac{3}{8} \times 5\frac{5}{8}$): [unsigned: 1–13^{16} 14^8 15^{12} 16^8 17–18^{16}], pp. xxxviii, 498.
Contents: [i–ii], half-title, on verso portrait; [iii–iv], title-page, on
verso copyright notice; [v–vi], epigraph, verso blank; vii–viii, acknowledgment; [ix–x], contents, verso blank; [xi–xii], list of illustrations,
verso blank; xiii–xxxvi, Introduction by Leon Edel; [xxxvii–xxxviii],
brief chronology, verso blank; [1]–487, text; [488], blank; 489–493,
Index; [494–498], blank.
Issued in black linen-grain cloth, lettered in gilt against lacquered
black panel on spine; red end-papers; all edges trimmed.

Published 16 December 1974, at $15, the first printing consisting of 5500 sheets, of which 3500 were bound and the balance shipped to Macmillan & Co., London, for the English issue.

b. First English edition (1975):

($8\frac{3}{8} \times 5\frac{3}{8}$): Consisted of imported sheets, uniform with collation and contents of American edition except for publisher's imprint (a large initial "M") on title, and revised information on verso.

Issued in orange-brown simulated-cloth paper boards, decorative rule in gilt above and below title on spine, lettered in gilt on spine; red end-papers; all edges trimmed.

Published 3 April 1975, at £10, the first issue consisting of 2000 copies.

Volume II:

a. First edition:

HENRY JAMES | LETTERS | EDITED BY | LEON EDEL | VOLUME II | 1875–1883 | THE BELKNAP PRESS | OF | HARVARD UNIVERSITY PRESS | CAMBRIDGE, MASSA- CHUSETTS | 1975

($8\frac{3}{8} \times 5\frac{3}{8}$): [unsigned: $1-12^{16}$ 13^{20} 14^{16}], pp. xvi, 440.

Contents: [i–ii], half-title, on verso portrait; [iii–iv], title-page, on verso copyright notice; v–vi, acknowledgments; [vii–viii], contents, verso blank; [ix–x], list of illustrations, verso blank; xi–xiv, Introduction by Leon Edel; xv–[xvi], brief chronology, verso blank; [1]–426, text; 427–438, Index; [439–440], blank leaf.

Issued in black linen-grain cloth, lettered in gilt against lacquered black panel on spine; blue end-papers; all edges trimmed.

Published 5 August 1975, at $15, the first printing consisting of 5900 sheets, of which 3900 were bound.

b. First English edition (1980):

Photographed from American edition after many corrections had been made. Title-page and binding uniform with Volume I.

Published 6 March 1980, at £15, the first issue consisting of 912 copies.

Volume III:

a. First edition:

HENRY JAMES | LETTERS | EDITED BY | LEON EDEL |

VOLUME III | 1883–1895 | THE BELKNAP PRESS | OF | HARVARD UNIVERSITY PRESS | CAMBRIDGE, MASSA-CHUSETTS | 1980

($8\frac{3}{8} \times 5\frac{5}{8}$): [unsigned: 1–19^{16}], pp. xxii, 586.

Contents: [i–ii], half-title, on verso photograph; [iii–iv], title-page, on verso copyright notice; v–vii, acknowledgments; [viii], blank; [ix–x], contents, verso blank; [xi–xii], list of illustrations, verso blank; xiii–xx, Introduction by Leon Edel; xxi–xxii, brief chronology; [1]–562, text; 563–579, Index; [580–586], blank.

Issued in black linen-grain simulated cloth, lettered in gilt against blind (unlacquered) black panel on spine; olive green end-papers; all edges trimmed.

Published 22 December 1980, at $20, the first printing consisting of 4000 bound copies, of which 3000 were for domestic sale, and 1000, shipped to Macmillan & Co., London, for English sale.

b. First English edition (1981):

Consisted of imported bound copies, uniform with American edition except for substitution of Macmillan's "M" device for American publisher's imprint on title and on spine, and revision of copyright page.

Issued in rust-red simulated cloth, lettered between decorative rules in gilt on spine; dark olive-green end-papers; all edges trimmed.

Published 5 March 1981, at £17.50, the first issue consisting of 1000 copies.

ADDENDA TO C (PART II)

c176 Allen, Gay W., *William James: A Biography* (New York, 1967; London, 1967).

55E to William James; 2E to Henry James, Sr.; 1E each to Jane Norton, Grace Norton, Mrs William James, and Mrs Henry James, Sr.

c177 Beerbohm, Max, *Letters to Reggie Turner*, ed. Rupert Hart-Davis (London, 1964), retitled *Max Beerbohm's Letters to Reggie Turner* (Philadelphia, 1965).

1L to Beerbohm.

c178 Bell, Millicent, *Edith Wharton and Henry James* (New York, 1965; London, 1966).

More than 50 extracts and fragments, principally to Mrs Wharton, William James, Mary Cadwalader Jones, and Howard Sturgis.

c179 Bowden, Edwin T., "Henry James and the Struggle for International Copyright," *American Literature*, XXIV (January 1953), 537–539.
1E to Robert U. Johnson.

c180 Bruneau, Jean, "Une lettre inédite de Henry James à Gustave Flaubert: Autour de Monckton Milnes, Lord Houghton," *Revue de littérature comparée*, XLII (October-December 1968), 520–533.
1L to Gustave Flaubert.

c181 Buitenhuis, Peter, *The Grasping Imagination* (Toronto, 1970).
6E to C. E. Norton; 1E each to Elizabeth Boott, Isabella Stewart Gardner, Francis Anne Kemble, John Hay, Mrs Francis Childs, J. B. Pinker, Col. George Harvey, Jocelyn Persse. Also contains a number of brief extracts from James's unpublished notes (at Harvard) for *The Ivory Tower*.

c182 Donovan, Alan B., "My Dear Pinker: The Correspondence of Henry James with His Literary Agent," *Yale University Library Gazette*, XXXVI (October 1961), 78–88.
1L, 39E or F to James B. Pinker.

c183 Edel, Leon, Introduction to *The Diary of Alice James* (New York, 1964).
6E to William James; 2E each to Alice James, Mrs Henry James, Sr., and Catherine Walsh; 1E each to Mary James Vaux and an unidentified correspondent.

c184 ——, *Henry James: The Conquest of London* (New York, 1962; London, 1962).
Numerous extracts and fragments, principally to Mr and Mrs Henry James, Sr., William James, Alice James, W. D. Howells, Charles Eliot Norton, Grace Norton, and Sarah Butler Wister.

c185 ——, *Henry James: The Middle Years* (New York, 1962; London, 1963).
Numerous extracts and fragments, principally to William James Alice James, Elizabeth Boott, W. D. Howells, Grace Norton, T. S. Perry, and C. F. Woolson.

c186 ——, *Henry James: The Treacherous Years* (New York, 1969; London, 1969).
Numerous extracts and fragments, principally to William James, Paul Bourget, Edmund Gosse, W. D. Howells, and Grace Norton.

c187 ——, *Henry James: The Master* (New York, 1972; London, 1972).
Numerous extracts and fragments, principally to Mr and Mrs William James, Lucy Clifford, Morton Fullerton, Edmund Gosse,

W. D. Howells, Grace Norton, Howard Sturgis, Hugh Walpole, and Edith Wharton.

C188 ——, "Henry James Letters", *Times Literary Supplement* (17 June 1965), 523.

1L to Edmund Gosse (first publication of full and correct text of letter of 7 January 1893).

C189 ——, "A Young Man from the Provinces: Rudyard Kipling and Wolcott Balestier," in John Gross (ed.), *Rudyard Kipling: The Man, His Work and His World* (London, 1972); retitled *The Age of Kipling* (New York, 1972).

1E to Edmund Gosse; 1E each to five unidentified correspondents.

C189a ——, "Henry James Criticizes a Sonnet," *Antaeus* 1970–1980 (New York, 1981), 531–532.

1L to Sir George Henschel.

C190 Gale, Robert L., "An Unpublished Letter from Henry James to F. Marion Crawford," *Revue des langues vivantes*, XLII (March-April 1976), 179–182.

1L to Crawford.

C191 Gernsheim, Helmut and Alison (eds.), *Alvin Langdon Coburn Photographer: An Autobiography* (London, 1966; New York, 1966).

5E to Coburn.

C192 Hasler, Jörg, *Switzerland in the Life and Work of Henry James* (Bern, 1966).

28L to Clara W. and Clare Benedict (some of which were quoted previously in Clare Benedict, *The Benedicts Abroad*, 1930).

C193 Hoffman, Daniel G., "An Unwritten Life of Stephen Crane," *Columbia Library Columns*, II (February 1953), 12–16.

1E to Cora Crane.

C194 Hyde, H. Montgomery, *Henry James at Home* (London, 1969; New York, 1969).

Numerous extracts and fragments, principally to William James, Alice James, Edmund Gosse, and Edward Warren.

C195 James, Henry, *The American Scene*, ed. Leon Edel (Bloomington, Indiana, 1968).

3E to J. B. Pinker; 2E each to Col. George Harvey, Edmund Gosse, Mary Cadwalader Jones, and Mrs William James; 1E each to Mrs George Hunter, William James, Howard Sturgis, Jessie Allen, W. E. Norris, and five unidentified correspondents.

C196 Lewis, R. W. B., *Edith Wharton: A Biography* (New York, 1975; London, 1975).

C. PUBLISHED LETTERS

Numerous extracts and fragments, principally to Edith Wharton and Morton Fullerton, many of which had earlier appeared in the Lubbock edition of the *Letters*, in Edel's biography, and in Millicent Bell's *Edith Wharton and Henry James*.

C197 McClary, Ben Harris, "'In Abject Terror of Rising': An Unpublished Henry James Letter," *English Language Notes*, III (March 1966), 208–211.
1L to Clement Shorter.

C198 Major, John C., "Henry James, Daudet, and Oxford," *Notes and Queries*, n.s. XIII (February 1966), 69–70.
7E to Margaret L. Woods.

C199 Monteiro, George, "The Manuscript of *The Tragic Muse*," *American Notes and Queries*, I (January 1963), 68.
1F to John Hay.

C200 ——, "An Unpublished Henry James Letter," *Notes and Queries*, n.s. X (April 1963), 143–144.
1L to Henry Adams.

C201 —— (ed.), "Letters of Henry James to John Hay," *Texas Studies in Literature and Language*, IV (Supplement, 1963), 639–695.
36L to John Hay; 2L to Clara Stone Hay.
These letters were reprinted by Monteiro in *Henry James and John Hay: The Record of a Friendship* (Providence, R.I., 1965), with six additional letters to the Hays, and one to Henry Adams reprinted from *Notes and Queries*, April 1963 (C200).

C202 Nowell-Smith, Simon (ed.), *Letters to Macmillan* (London, 1967; New York, 1967).
5L, 1E to Macmillan and Company.

C203 Palgrave, Gwenllian, *Francis Turner Palgrave* (London, 1899; New York, 1899).
2L to Palgrave.

C203a Pancost, David W., "Henry James and Julian Hawthorne," *American Literature*, L (November 1978), 461–465.
1L to Julian Hawthorne.

C204 Putt, S. Gorley, "Henry James haggles over terms for 'Guy Domville,'" *Times Literary Supplement* (11 January 1974), 35–36.
4L to Isaac Austen Henderson.

C205 "Rambler, The," *The Book Buyer*, XIII (May 1896), 222.
1E to unidentified correspondent, on R. L. Stevenson's *The Weir of Hermiston*.

C. PUBLISHED LETTERS

c206 Stallman, R. W., *Stephen Crane: A Biography* (New York, 1968).
11E to Cora Crane.

c207 Standley, Fred L., "Henry James to Stopford Brooke: An Unpublished Letter," *Victorian Newsletter*, No. 27 (Spring 1965), 29.
1L to Brooke.

c208 Tharp, Louise Hall, *Mrs. Jack* (Boston, 1965).
5E to Ariana Curtis; 12E to Isabella Stewart Gardner (several of which were published previously in Edel's *Henry James: The Middle Years*, 1962).

c209 White, William, "Unpublished Henry James on Whitman," *Review of English Studies*, n.s. XX (August 1969), 321–322.
1L to Dr John Johnston.

c210 Winner, Viola Hopkins, *Henry James and the Visual Arts* (Charlottesville, Va., 1970).
3E to Charles Eliot Norton: 1E to William James.

D. CONTRIBUTIONS TO PERIODICALS

1864

D1 A TRAGEDY OF ERROR (Unsigned)

The *Continental Monthly*, V (February), 204–216. Reprinted in the *New England Quarterly*, XXIX (September 1956), 291–317. This story was identified by Leon Edel in *Henry James: The Untried Years*, 1953. The story is explicitly named as by James in a letter written by Mrs George De Kay of Newport to her son Charles De Kay, 29 February 1864.

D2 [NASSAU W. SENIOR'S] ESSAYS ON FICTION (Unsigned review)

North American Review, XCIX (October), 580–587.
Reprinted, under the title "Fiction and Sir Walter Scott," in *Notes and Reviews*, 1921.

1865

D3 [HARRIET E. PRESCOTT SPOFFORD'S] AZARIAN: AN EPISODE (Unsigned review)

North American Review, C (January), 268–277.
Reprinted, under the title "Miss Prescott's 'Azarian,'" in *Notes and Reviews*, 1921.

D4 [T. ADOLPHUS TROLLOPE'S] LINDISFARN CHASE: A NOVEL (Unsigned review)

North American Review, C (January), 277–278.
Reprinted, under the title "Lindisfarn Chase," in *Notes and Reviews*, 1921.

D5 [MRS A. M. C. SEEMÜLLER'S] EMILY CHESTER: A NOVEL (Unsigned review)

North American Review, C (January), 279–284.
Reprinted in *Notes and Reviews*, 1921.

D6 THE STORY OF A YEAR

Atlantic Monthly, XV (March), 257–281.
Reprinted in *The American Novels and Stories of Henry James*, 1947.

D7 [MATTHEW ARNOLD'S] ESSAYS IN CRITICISM (Unsigned review)

North American Review, CI (July), 206–213.
Reprinted, under the title "Matthew Arnold's Essays," in *Views and Reviews*, 1908.

D8 [LOUISA M. ALCOTT'S] MOODS (Unsigned review)
North American Review, CI (July), 276–281.
Reprinted, under the title "Miss Alcott's 'Moods,'" in *Notes and Reviews*, 1921.

D9 [GOETHE'S] WILHELM MEISTER'S APPRENTICESHIP AND TRAVELS (Unsigned review)
North American Review, CI (July), 281–285.
Reprinted in *Literary Reviews and Essays*, 1957.

D10 THE NOBLE SCHOOL OF FICTION (Unsigned review of Henry Kingsley's *The Hillyars and the Burtons: A Story of Two Families*)
The Nation, I (6 July), 21–23.
Reprinted in *Notes and Reviews*, 1921.

D11 [ANTHONY TROLLOPE'S] MISS MACKENZIE (Unsigned review)
The Nation, I (13 July), 51–52.
Reprinted in *Notes and Reviews*, 1921.

D12 [MRS E. R. CHARLES'S] THE SCHÖNBERG-COTTA FAMILY (Unsigned critical notes on a series of novels)
The Nation, I (14 September), 344–345.
Reprinted in *Notes and Reviews*, 1921.

D13 [ANTHONY TROLLOPE'S] CAN YOU FORGIVE HER? (Unsigned review)
The Nation, I (28 September), 409–410.
Reprinted in *Notes and Reviews*, 1921.

D14 [MRS ADELINE DUTTON (TRAIN) WHITNEY'S] THE GAY-WORTHYS: A STORY OF THREADS AND THRUMS (Unsigned review)
North American Review, CI (October), 619–622.
Reprinted, under the title "The Gayworthys," in *Notes and Reviews*, 1921.

D14a A FRENCH CRITIC (Unsigned review of Edmond Schérer's *Nouvelles Études sur la Littérature Contemporaine*)
The Nation, I (12 October 1865), 468–470.
Reprinted in *Notes and Reviews*, 1921.
Daniel C. Haskell, in his *Nation* index (New York, 1951–53), ascribed this review to HJ Sr on the basis of an entry in the Garrison account books. In the first edition of our bibliography we accordingly noted that the review was not by James. However,

after a close examination of the text and a comparison with James's other published criticism of Schérer, we believe Haskell's ascription to have been in error. It is probable that here, as in other instances, payment was made to one member of the James family serving as agent for the work of another (see note, pp. 15–16).

D15 MISS BRADDON (Unsigned critical notes on M. E. Braddon's *Aurora Floyd* and other novels)
The *Nation*, I (9 November), 593–594.
Reprinted in *Notes and Reviews*, 1921.

D16 MR. WALT WHITMAN (Unsigned review of *Drum-Taps*)
The *Nation*, I (16 November), 625–626.
Reprinted in *Views and Reviews*, 1908.

D17 EUGÉNIE DE GUÉRIN (Unsigned review of G. S. Trébutien's *The Journal of Eugénie de Guérin*)
The *Nation*, I (14 December), 752–753.
Reprinted, under the title "Eugénie de Guérin's Journal," in *Notes and Reviews*, 1921.

D18 [CHARLES DICKENS'S] OUR MUTUAL FRIEND (Unsigned review)
The *Nation*, I (21 December), 786–787.
Reprinted, under the title "The Limitations of Dickens," in *Views and Reviews*, 1908.

1866

D19 [ANTHONY TROLLOPE'S] THE BELTON ESTATE (Unsigned review)
The *Nation*, II (4 January), 21–22.
Reprinted in *Notes and Reviews*, 1921.

D20 [A. C. SWINBURNE'S] CHASTELARD: A TRAGEDY (Unsigned review)
The *Nation*, II (18 January), 83–84.
Reprinted, under the title "Swinburne's 'Chastelard,' " in *Notes and Reviews*, 1921.

D21 [CHARLES KINGSLEY'S] HEREWARD, THE LAST OF THE ENGLISH (Unsigned review)
The *Nation*, II (25 January), 115–116.
Reprinted, under the title "Kingsley's 'Hereward,' " in *Notes and Reviews*, 1921.

D22 A LANDSCAPE PAINTER
Atlantic Monthly, XVII (February), 182–202.
The author's name appears as "Henry W. James" in the table of contents of Vol. XVII of the *Atlantic Monthly*.
Reprinted in *Stories Revived*, 1885.

D23 [MRS E. R. CHARLES'S] WINIFRED BERTRAM AND THE WORLD SHE LIVED IN (Unsigned review)
The *Nation*, II (1 February), 147–148.
Reprinted in *Notes and Reviews*, 1921.

D24 [MRS GASKELL'S] WIVES AND DAUGHTERS: A NOVEL (Unsigned review)
The *Nation*, II (22 February), 246–247.
Reprinted, under the title "Mrs. Gaskell," in *Notes and Reviews*, 1921.

D25 [HENRY D. SEDLEY'S] MARIAN ROOKE; OR THE QUEST FOR FORTUNE. A TALE OF THE YOUNGER WORLD (Unsigned review)
The *Nation*, II (22 February), 247–248.
Reprinted, under the title "Marian Rooke," in *Notes and Reviews*, 1921.

D26 [MRS D. M. M. CRAIK'S] A NOBLE LIFE (Unsigned review)
The *Nation*, II (1 March), 276.
Reprinted in *Notes and Reviews*, 1921.

D27 THE WORKS OF EPICTETUS. Edited by Thomas Wentworth Higginson from a translation by Elizabeth Carter. (Unsigned review)
North American Review, CII (April), 599–606.
Reprinted, under the title "Epictetus," in *Notes and Reviews*, 1921.

D28 VICTOR HUGO'S LAST NOVEL (Unsigned review of *Les Travailleurs de la Mer*)
The *Nation*, II (12 April), 466–468.
Reprinted in *Notes and Reviews*, 1921.

D29 A DAY OF DAYS
The *Galaxy*, I (15 June), 298–312.
Reprinted in *Stories Revived*, 1885.

D30 [GEORGE ELIOT'S] FELIX HOLT, THE RADICAL (Unsigned review)
The *Nation*, III (16 August), 127–128.
Reprinted in *Notes and Reviews*, 1921.

D. CONTRIBUTIONS TO PERIODICALS

D31 THE LETTERS OF EUGÉNIE DE GUÉRIN (Unsigned review)
The *Nation*, III (13 September), 206–207.
Reprinted in *Notes and Reviews*, 1921.

D32 THE NOVELS OF GEORGE ELIOT
Atlantic Monthly, XVIII (October), 479–492.
Reprinted in *Views and Reviews*, 1908.

D33 THE LAST FRENCH NOVEL (Unsigned review of Alexandre
Dumas, fils, *Affaire Clémenceau: Mémoire de l'Accusé*)
The *Nation*, III (11 October), 286–288.
Reprinted in *Notes and Reviews*, 1921.

1867

D34 MY FRIEND BINGHAM
Atlantic Monthly, XIX (March), 346–358.
Reprinted in *Eight Uncollected Tales of Henry James*, 1950.

D35 MAURICE DE GUÉRIN (Unsigned review of the English trans-
lation, by Edward Thornton Fisher, of the *Journal of Maurice de
Guérin*)
The *Nation*, IV (7 March), 187–189.
Reprinted in *Literary Reviews and Essays*, 1957.

D36 RECENT VOLUMES OF POEMS (Unsigned reviews of Julia Ward
Howe's *Later Lyrics*, Elizabeth Akers's [Florence Percy] *Poems*,
Amanda T. Jones's *Poems*, Mrs E. R. Charles's *The Women of
the Gospels, The Three Wakings, and Other Poems*)
North American Review, CIV (April), 644–646.
Reprinted in *Literary Reviews and Essays*, 1957.

D37 POOR RICHARD
Atlantic Monthly, XIX (June), 694–706; XX (July–August),
32–42, 166–178.
Reprinted in *Stories Revived*, 1885.

D38 [FRANCIS PARKMAN'S] THE JESUITS IN NORTH AMERICA
IN THE SEVENTEENTH CENTURY (Unsigned review)
The *Nation*, IV (6 June), 450–451.
Reprinted in *Literary Reviews and Essays*, 1957.

D39 HISTORICAL NOVELS (Unsigned reviews of Anne E. Manning's
The Household of Sir Thomas More and *Jacques Bonneval, or The
Days of the Dragonnades*)
The *Nation*, V (15 August), 126–127.
Reprinted in *Literary Reviews and Essays*, 1957.

D40 [WILLIAM MORRIS'S] THE LIFE AND DEATH OF JASON: A POEM (Unsigned review)
North American Review, CV (October), 688–692.
Reprinted, as Part I of "The Poetry of William Morris," in *Views and Reviews*, 1908.

D41 MR. FROUDE'S "SHORT STUDIES" (Unsigned review of James Anthony Froude's *Short Studies on Great Subjects*)
The *Nation*, V (31 October), 351.
Reprinted in *Literary Reviews and Essays*, 1957.

D42 [MRS R. H. DAVIS'S] WAITING FOR THE VERDICT (Unsigned review)
The *Nation*, V (21 November), 410–411.

D43 [MRS A. M. C. SEEMÜLLER'S] OPPORTUNITY: A NOVEL (Unsigned review)
The *Nation*, V (5 December), 449–450.

D44 [WILLIAM ROUNSEVILLE ALGER'S] THE FRIENDSHIPS OF WOMEN (Unsigned review)
The *Nation*, V (26 December), 522–523.

1868

D45 THE STORY OF A MASTERPIECE (With one illustration each by Gaston Fay and W. J. Hennessy)
The *Galaxy*, V (January–February), 5–21, 133–143.
Reprinted in *Eight Uncollected Tales of Henry James*, 1950.

D46 [WILLIAM DEAN HOWELLS'S] ITALIAN JOURNEYS (Unsigned review)
North American Review, CVI (January), 336–339.
Reprinted in *Literary Reviews and Essays*, 1957.

D47 THE HUGUENOTS IN ENGLAND (Unsigned reviews of Samuel Smiles's *The Huguenots: Their Settlements, Churches and Industries in England and Ireland* and Sarah Tytler's *The Huguenot Family in the English Village*)
The *Nation*, VI (9 January), 32–33.

D48 FATHER LACORDAIRE (Unsigned review of the English translation of Père Chocarne's *The Inner Life of the Very Reverend Père Lacordaire, of the Order of Preachers*)
The *Nation*, VI (16 January), 53–55.

D49 THE ROMANCE OF CERTAIN OLD CLOTHES
Atlantic Monthly, XXI (February), 209–220.
Reprinted in *A Passionate Pilgrim*, 1875.

D50 A MOST EXTRAORDINARY CASE
Atlantic Monthly, XXI (April), 461–485.
Reprinted in *Stories Revived*, 1885.

D51 [PHILIP GILBERT HAMERTON'S] CONTEMPORARY FRENCH
PAINTERS: AN ESSAY (Unsigned review)
North American Review, CVI (April), 716–723.
Reprinted, under the title "An English Critic of French Painting,
1868," in *The Painter's Eye*, 1956.

D52 TAINE'S ITALY (Unsigned review of the English translation of
H. Taine's *Italy: Rome and Naples*)
The *Nation*, VI (7 May), 373–375.
Reprinted in *Literary Reviews and Essays*, 1957.

D53 A PROBLEM (With a full-page illustration by W. J. Hennessy)
The *Galaxy*, V (June), 697–707.
Reprinted in *Eight Uncollected Tales of Henry James*, 1950.

D54 SAINTE-BEUVE'S PORTRAITS (Unsigned review of the
English translation of C. A. Sainte-Beuve's *Portraits of Celebrated
Women*)
The *Nation*, VI (4 June), 454–455.
Reprinted in *Literary Reviews and Essays*, 1957.

D55 [ANTHONY TROLLOPE'S] LINDA TRESSEL (Unsigned review)
The *Nation*, VI (18 June), 494–495.

D56 DE GREY: A ROMANCE
Atlantic Monthly, XXII (July), 57–78.
Reprinted in *Travelling Companions*, 1919.

D57 OSBORNE'S REVENGE (Illustration by W. J. Hennessy)
The *Galaxy*, VI (July), 5–31.
Reprinted in *Eight Uncollected Tales of Henry James*, 1950.

D58 [THE COUNT DE FALLOUX'S] LIFE AND LETTERS OF
MADAME SWETCHINE (Unsigned review of the English trans-
lation by H. W. Preston)
North American Review, CVII (July), 328–334.

D59 [WILLIAM MORRIS'S] THE EARTHLY PARADISE: A POEM
(Unsigned review)
North American Review, CVII (July), 358–361.

D60 [GEORGE ELIOT'S] THE SPANISH GYPSY (Unsigned review)
The *Nation*, VII (2 July), 12–14.
Reprinted in *Literary Reviews and Essays*, 1957.

D. CONTRIBUTIONS TO PERIODICALS

D61 [WILLIAM MORRIS'S] THE EARTHLY PARADISE (Unsigned review)
The *Nation*, VII (9 July), 33–34.
Reprinted, as Part II of "The Poetry of William Morris," in *Views and Reviews*, 1908.

D62 [GEORGE SAND'S] MADEMOISELLE MERQUEM (Unsigned review)
The *Nation*, VII (16 July), 52–53.
Reprinted in *Literary Reviews and Essays*, 1957.

D63 [OCTAVE FEUILLET'S] CAMORS: OR LIFE UNDER THE NEW EMPIRE (Unsigned review of the English translation)
The *Nation*, VII (30 July), 91–93.
Reprinted in *Literary Reviews and Essays*, 1957.

D64 [GEORGE ELIOT'S] THE SPANISH GYPSY: A POEM
North American Review, CVII (October), 620–635.
Reprinted, as Part I of "The Poetry of George Eliot," in *Views and Reviews*, 1908.

D65 [MRS R. H. DAVIS'S] DALLAS GALBRAITH (Unsigned review)
The *Nation*, VII (22 October), 330–331.

D66 MODERN WOMEN (Unsigned review of *Modern Women, and What is Said of Them*, a reprint of a series of articles in the *Saturday Review*)
The *Nation*, VII (22 October), 332–334.

1869

D67 PYRAMUS AND THISBE
The *Galaxy*, VII (April), 538–549.
Reprinted in *The Complete Plays of Henry James*, 1949.

D68 A LIGHT MAN
The *Galaxy*, VIII (July), 49–68.
Reprinted in *Stories by American Authors*, Vol. V, 1884, and in *Master Eustace*, 1920.

D69 GABRIELLE DE BERGERAC
Atlantic Monthly, XXIV (July–September), 55–71, 231–241, 352–361.
For first book publication, 1918, see A80.

1870

D70 [BENJAMIN DISRAELI'S] LOTHAIR (Unsigned review)
Atlantic Monthly, XXVI (August), 249–251
Reprinted in *Literary Reviews and Essays*, 1957.

D71 SARATOGA (Unsigned)
The *Nation*, XI (11 August), 87–89.
Reprinted in *Portraits of Places*, 1883.

D72 LAKE GEORGE (Unsigned)
The *Nation*, XI (25 August), 119–120.

D73 SELECTIONS FROM DE MUSSET (Unsigned review)
Atlantic Monthly, XXVI (September), 379–381.
Attribution made on the basis of the fact that Howells requested
a review of this book from HJ (1 July 1870) for James T. Fields
(unpublished letter, Houghton Library). The style and content
of the review suggests that it is from James's pen. But see Wayne
C. Paton, "Henry James and Alfred de Musset: A Possible Misattribution," *Long Room, Trinity College, Dublin*, No. 16 (1978).

D74 FROM LAKE GEORGE TO BURLINGTON (Unsigned)
The *Nation*, XI (1 September), 135–136.

D75 NEWPORT (Unsigned)
The *Nation*, XI (15 September), 170–172.
Reprinted in *Portraits of Places*, 1883.

D76 TRAVELLING COMPANIONS
Atlantic Monthly, XXVI (Nov–Dec), 600–614, 684–697.
Reprinted in *Travelling Companions*, 1919.

1871

D77 A PASSIONATE PILGRIM
Atlantic Monthly, XXVII (March–April), 352–371, 478–499.
Reprinted in *A Passionate Pilgrim*, 1875.

D78 STILL WATERS
Balloon Post, No. II (12 April), 8–10.
Six numbers of this publication were issued for sale at a Boston
Fair in aid of French Relief.
Reprinted in *The Dial of the Old South Clock* (Boston), edited by
Susan Hale, II, Nos. 4 and 5 (8 and 9 December 1879); and in *The
Complete Plays of Henry James*, 1949.

D79 WATCH AND WARD
Atlantic Monthly, XXVIII (August–December), 232–246, 320–
339, 415–431, 577–596, 689–710.
For first book publication, 1878, see A6.

D80 [GUSTAVE DROZ'S] AROUND A SPRING (Unsigned review of
the English translation by M.S.)
Atlantic Monthly, XXVIII (August), 248–251.

D. CONTRIBUTIONS TO PERIODICALS

D81 AT ISELLA
The *Galaxy*, XII (August), 241–255.
Reprinted in *Travelling Companions*, 1919.

D82 QUEBEC (Unsigned)
The *Nation*, XIII (28 September–5 October), 206–207, 223–224.
Reprinted in *Portraits of Places*, 1883.

D83 NIAGARA (Unsigned)
The *Nation*, XIII (12 and 19 October), 238–239, 254–255.
Reprinted in *Portraits of Places*, 1883.

D84 [JOHN TYNDALL'S] HOURS OF EXERCISE IN THE ALPS
(Unsigned review)
Atlantic Monthly, XXVIII (November), 634–636.
Reprinted in *Literary Reviews and Essays*, 1957.

D85 MASTER EUSTACE
The *Galaxy*, XII (November), 595–612.
Reprinted in *Stories Revived*, 1885.

1872

D86 A CHANGE OF HEART
Atlantic Monthly, XXIX (January), 49–60.
Reprinted in *The Complete Plays of Henry James*, 1949.

D87 ART [EXHIBITION OF FRENCH PICTURES IN BOSTON]
(Unsigned critical notes on LaFarge, Decamps, Rousseau,
Delacroix and others)
Atlantic Monthly, XXIX (January), 115–118.
Reprinted, under the title "French Pictures in Boston, 1872," in
The Painter's Eye, 1956.

D88 TAINE'S NOTES ON ENGLAND (Unsigned review of H. Taine's
Notes sur l'Angleterre)
The *Nation*, XIV (25 January), 58–60.
Reprinted in *Literary Reviews and Essays*, 1957.

D89 [THÉOPHILE GAUTIER'S] TABLEAUX DE SIÈGE (Unsigned
review)
The *Nation*, XIV (25 January), 61–62.

D90 ART [PICTURES BY HUNT, GÉRÔME, ZAMAÇOIS, AND
VIBERT] (Unsigned critical notes)
Atlantic Monthly, XXIX (February), 246–247.
Reprinted in part in *The Painter's Eye*, 1956.

D. CONTRIBUTIONS TO PERIODICALS

D91 ART: BOSTON [PICTURES BY COLE, DAUBIGNY, AND J. APPLETON BROWN] (Unsigned critical notes)
Atlantic Monthly, XXIX (March), 372–374.

D92 HAWTHORNE'S FRENCH AND ITALIAN JOURNALS (Unsigned review of *Passages from the French and Italian Notebooks of Nathaniel Hawthorne*)
The *Nation*, XIV (14 March), 172–173.
Reprinted in *The American Essays of Henry James*, 1956.

D93 [H. TAINE'S] ENGLISH LITERATURE (Review of H. Van Laun's translation of *Histoire de la Littérature Anglaise*)
Atlantic Monthly, XXIX (April), 469–472.
Reprinted in *Literary Reviews and Essays*, 1957.

D94 ART: THE DUTCH AND FLEMISH PICTURES IN NEW YORK (Unsigned critical notes)
Atlantic Monthly, XXIX (June), 757–763.
Reprinted, under the title "The Metropolitan Museum's '1871 Purchase,' 1872," in *The Painter's Eye*, 1956.

D95 A EUROPEAN SUMMER. I. CHESTER (Unsigned)
The *Nation*, XV (4 July), 7–9.
Reprinted in *Transatlantic Sketches*, 1875.

D96 A EUROPEAN SUMMER. II. LICHFIELD AND WARWICK (Unsigned)
The *Nation*, XV (25 July), 57–58.
Reprinted in *Transatlantic Sketches*, 1875.

D97 A SUMMER IN EUROPE. III. NORTH DEVON (Unsigned)
The *Nation*, XV (8 August), 86–87.
Reprinted in *Transatlantic Sketches*, 1875.

D98 A SUMMER IN EUROPE. IV. WELLS AND SALISBURY (Unsigned)
The *Nation*, XV (22 August), 117–119.
Reprinted in *Transatlantic Sketches*, 1875.

D99 A EUROPEAN SUMMER. V. SWISS NOTES (Unsigned)
The *Nation*, XV (19 September), 183–184.
Reprinted in *Transatlantic Sketches*, 1875.

D100 A EUROPEAN SUMMER. VI. FROM CHAMBERY TO MILAN (Unsigned)
The *Nation*, XV (21 November), 332–334.
Reprinted in *Transatlantic Sketches*, 1875.

D. CONTRIBUTIONS TO PERIODICALS

DIOI GUEST'S CONFESSION
  Atlantic Monthly, XXX (October–November), 385–403, 566–583.
  Reprinted in *Travelling Companions*, 1919.

1873

DIO2 THE BETHNAL GREEN MUSEUM
  Atlantic Monthly, XXXI (January), 69–75.
  Reprinted, under the title "The Wallace Collection in Bethnal Green," in *The Painter's Eye*, 1956.

DIO3 HENRI REGNAULT (Unsigned review of *Correspondance de Henri Regnault*)
  The *Nation*, XVI (2 January), 13–15.

DIO4 THE PARISIAN STAGE (Signed "From an occasional correspondent")
  The *Nation*, XVI (9 January), 23–24.
  Reprinted in *Transatlantic Sketches*, 1875.

DIO5 LAUGEL'S NOTES ON TRAVEL (Unsigned review of Auguste Laugel's *Italie, Sicile, Bohême: Notes de Voyage*)
  The *Nation*, XVI (27 February), 152.

DIO6 THE MADONNA OF THE FUTURE
  Atlantic Monthly, XXXI (March), 276–297.
  Reprinted in *A Passionate Pilgrim*, 1875.

DIO7 [GEORGE ELIOT'S] MIDDLEMARCH (Unsigned review)
  The *Galaxy*, XV (March), 424–428.
  Attribution made on the basis of unpublished correspondence between HJ and HJ Sr., in the Houghton Library.
  Reprinted in *The Future of the Novel*, 1956.

DIO8 A EUROPEAN SUMMER. VII. FROM VENICE TO STRASSBURG (Unsigned)
  The *Nation*, XVI (6 March), 163–165.
  Reprinted in *Transatlantic Sketches*, 1875. Also in *Italian Hours*, 1909, retitled "Venice: An Early Impression."

DIO9 THÉÂTRE DE THÉOPHILE GAUTIER: MYSTÈRES, COMÉDIES, ET BALLETS (Review)
  North American Review, CXVI (April), 310–329.
  Reprinted, under the title "Theophile Gautier," in *French Poets and Novelists*, 1878.

DIIO THE SWEETHEART OF M. BRISEUX
The *Galaxy*, XV (June), 760–779.
Reprinted in *Travelling Companions*, 1919.

DIII THE AFTER-SEASON AT ROME (Unsigned)
The *Nation*, XVI (12 June), 399–400.
Reprinted, under the title "The After-Season in Rome," in *Transatlantic Sketches*, 1875.

DII2 A ROMAN HOLIDAY
Atlantic Monthly, XXXII (July), 1–11.
Reprinted in *Transatlantic Sketches*, 1875.

DII3 ROMAN RIDES
Atlantic Monthly, XXXII (August), 190–198.
Reprinted in *Transatlantic Sketches*, 1875.

DII4 HOMBURG REFORMED (Unsigned)
The *Nation*, XVII (28 August), 142–144.
Reprinted in *Transatlantic Sketches*, 1875.

DII5 [VICTOR CHERBULIEZ'S] META HOLDENIS (Unsigned review)
North American Review, CXVII (October), 461–468.

DII6 AN EX-GRAND-DUCAL CAPITAL (Unsigned)
The *Nation*, XVII (9 October), 239–241.
Reprinted, under the title "Darmstadt," in *Transatlantic Sketches*, 1875.

DII7 DUMAS AND GOETHE (Unsigned review of Goethe's *Faust*, in a new translation by H. Bacharach, with a preface by Alexandre Dumas, fils)
The *Nation*, XVII (30 October), 292–294.
Reprinted in *Literary Reviews and Essays*, 1957.

DII8 FROM A ROMAN NOTE-BOOK
The *Galaxy*, XVI (November), 679–686.
Reprinted in *Transatlantic Sketches*, 1875.

DII9 ROMAN NEIGHBORHOODS
Atlantic Monthly, XXXII (December), 671–680.
Reprinted in *Transatlantic Sketches*, 1875.

1874

DI20 THE AUTUMN IN FLORENCE (Unsigned)
The *Nation*, XVIII (1 January), 6–7.
Reprinted in *Transatlantic Sketches*, 1875.

D. CONTRIBUTIONS TO PERIODICALS

D121 THE LAST OF THE VALERII
  Atlantic Monthly, XXXIII (January), 69–85.
  Reprinted in *A Passionate Pilgrim*, 1875.

D122 HOWELLS' POEMS
  The *Independent* (8 January), 9.
  Reprinted in *Literary Reviews and Essays*, 1957.

D123 A CHAIN OF ITALIAN CITIES
  Atlantic Monthly, XXXIII (February), 158–164.
  Reprinted, under the title "A Chain of Cities," in *Transatlantic Sketches*, 1875.

D124 MME. DE MAUVES
  The *Galaxy*, XVII (February–March), 216–233, 354–374.
  Reprinted, under the title "Madame de Mauves," in *A Passionate Pilgrim*, 1875.

D125 [JULES SANDEAU'S] JEAN DE THOMMERAY; LE COLONEL EVRARD (Unsigned reviews)
  The *Nation*, XVIII (5 February), 95.

D126 [PROSPER MÉRIMÉE'S] DERNIÈRES NOUVELLES (Unsigned review)
  The *Nation*, XVIII (12 February), 111.
  Reprinted in *Literary Reviews and Essays*, 1957.

D127 AN AUTUMN JOURNEY
  The *Galaxy*, XVII (April), 536–544.
  Reprinted, under the title "The St. Gothard," in *Transatlantic Sketches*, 1875, and under the title "The Old Saint-Gothard," in *Italian Hours*, 1909.

D128 FRÜHLINGSFLUTHEN. EIN KÖNIG LEAR DES DORFES. ZWEI NOVELLEN. VON IWAN TURGÉNIEW. (Review)
  North American Review, CXVIII (April), 326–356.
  Reprinted, under the title "Ivan Turgénieff," in *French Poets and Novelists*, 1878.

D129 THE LETTERS OF PROSPER MÉRIMÉE (Review of *Lettres à Une Inconnue*)
  The *Independent* (9 April), 9–10.
  Reprinted, under the title "Mérimée's Letters," in *French Poets and Novelists*, 1878.

D130 [VICTOR HUGO'S] NINETY-THREE (Unsigned review of *Quatrevingt-treize* and its English translation)
  The *Nation*, XVIII (9 April), 238–239.
  Reprinted in *Literary Reviews and Essays*, 1957.

D. CONTRIBUTIONS TO PERIODICALS

D131 FLORENTINE NOTES
The *Independent* (23 April), 2–3.
Reprinted, as Part II of an essay under the same title, in *Transatlantic Sketches*, 1875.

D132 FLORENTINE NOTES
The *Independent* (30 April), 2–3.
Reprinted, as Part I of an essay under the same title, in *Transatlantic Sketches*, 1875.

D133 ADINA
Scribner's Monthly, VIII (May–June), 33–43, 181–191.
Reprinted in *Travelling Companions*, 1919.

D134 A FLORENTINE GARDEN
The *Independent* (14 May), 3–4.
Reprinted, as Part VIII of "Florentine Notes," in *Transatlantic Sketches*, 1875.

D135 FLORENTINE NOTES
The *Independent* (21 May), 1–2.
Reprinted, as Part III of an essay under the same title, in *Transatlantic Sketches*, 1875.

D136 TUSCAN CITIES (Unsigned)
The *Nation*, XVIII (21 May), 329–330.
Reprinted in *Transatlantic Sketches*, 1875.

D137 SIENA
Atlantic Monthly, XXXIII (June), 664–669.
Reprinted in *Transatlantic Sketches*, 1875.

D138 [GUSTAVE] FLAUBERT'S *TEMPTATION OF ST. ANTHONY*
(Unsigned review of *La Tentation de Saint Antoine*)
The *Nation*, XVIII (4 June), 365–366.
Reprinted in *Literary Reviews and Essays*, 1957.

D139 OLD ITALIAN ART
The *Independent* (11 June), 2–3.
Reprinted, as Part IV of "Florentine Notes," in *Transatlantic Sketches*, 1875.

D140 FLORENTINE ARCHITECTURE
The *Independent* (18 June), 3–4.
Reprinted, as Part V of "Florentine Notes," in *Transatlantic Sketches*, 1875.

D141 AN ITALIAN CONVENT
The *Independent* (2 July), 3–4.
Reprinted, as Part VI of "Florentine Notes," in *Transatlantic Sketches*, 1875.

D. CONTRIBUTIONS TO PERIODICALS

D142 THE CHURCHES OF FLORENCE
   The *Independent* (9 July), 4.
   Reprinted, as part VII of "Florentine Notes," in *Transatlantic Sketches*, 1875.

D143 RAVENNA (Unsigned)
   The *Nation*, XIX (9 July), 23–25.
   Reprinted in *Transatlantic Sketches*, 1875.

D144 [EMILE MONTÉGUT'S] SOUVENIRS DE BOURGOGNE (Unsigned review)
   The *Nation*, XIX (23 July), 62.

D145 PROFESSOR FARGO
   The *Galaxy*, XVIII (August), 233–253.
   Reprinted in *Travelling Companions*, 1919.

D146 A NORTHWARD JOURNEY
   The *Independent* (20 August), 6; (27 August), 4.
   Reprinted, under the title "The Splügen," in *Transatlantic Sketches*, 1875.

D147 IN HOLLAND (Unsigned)
   The *Nation*, XIX (27 August), 136–137.
   Reprinted in *Transatlantic Sketches*, 1875.

D148 IN BELGIUM (Unsigned)
   The *Nation*, XIX (3 September), 151–152.
   Reprinted in *Transatlantic Sketches*, 1875.

D149 HENRY BEYLE (Unsigned review of Andrew A. Paton's *Henry Beyle (Otherwise De Stendhal): A Critical and Biographical Study*)
   The *Nation*, XIX (17 September), 187–189.
   Reprinted in *Literary Reviews and Essays*, 1957.

D150 [ERNEST FEYDEAU'S] THEOPHILE GAUTIER, SOUVENIRS INTIMES. [THÉOPHILE GAUTIER'S] HISTOIRE DU ROMANTISME, SUIVIE DE NOTICES ROMANTIQUES, ETC. (Reviews)
   North American Review, CXIX (October), 416–423.
   Reprinted in *Literary Reviews and Essays*, 1957.

D151 [GEORGE ELIOT'S] THE LEGEND OF JUBAL, AND OTHER POEMS (Unsigned review)
   North American Review, CXIX (October), 484–489.
   Reprinted, as Part II of "The Poetry of George Eliot," in *Views and Reviews*, 1908.

D152 EUGENE PICKERING
   Atlantic Monthly, XXXIV (October–November), 397–410, 513–526.
   Reprinted in *A Passionate Pilgrim*, 1875.

D. CONTRIBUTIONS TO PERIODICALS

D153 [FRANCIS PARKMAN'S] THE OLD RÉGIME IN CANADA (Unsigned review)
The *Nation*, XIX (15 October), 252–253.
Reprinted in *The American Essays of Henry James*, 1956.

D154 ART [THE DUKE OF MONTPENSIER'S PICTURES AT THE BOSTON ATHENAEUM] (Unsigned critical notes)
Atlantic Monthly, XXXIV (November), 633–637.
Reprinted, under the title "The Duke of Montpensier's Pictures in Boston," in *The Painter's Eye*, 1956.

D155 GAUTIER'S WINTER IN RUSSIA (Unsigned review of Théophile Gautier's *A Winter in Russia*)
The *Nation*, XIX (12 November), 321–322.
Reprinted in *Literary Reviews and Essays*, 1957.

D156 THE DRAMA ["THE SCHOOL FOR SCANDAL" AT THE BOSTON MUSEUM] (Unsigned critical notes)
Atlantic Monthly, XXXIV (December), 754–757.
Attributed to HJ by Phillips on the basis of its appearance in the *Index to the Atlantic Monthly, Volumes I–XXXVIII*, 1877. Although its attribution has been questioned on the ground that no record exists to show that James was in London during the British production of *The School for Scandal*, to which the critic makes allusion, it is beyond a shadow of doubt by James.
Reprinted in *The Scenic Art*, 1948.

D157 [JULIAN HAWTHORNE'S] IDOLATRY: A ROMANCE (Unsigned review)
Atlantic Monthly, XXXIV (December), 746–748.
Reprinted in *Literary Reviews and Essays*, 1957.

D158 [THOMAS HARDY'S] FAR FROM THE MADDING CROWD (Unsigned review)
The *Nation*, XIX (24 December), 423–424.
Reprinted in *The House of Fiction*, 1957.

D159 [J. W. DE FOREST'S] HONEST JOHN VANE: A STORY (Unsigned review)
The *Nation*, XIX (31 December), 441–442.
Reprinted in *Literary Reviews and Essays*, 1957.

1875

D160 [JAMES BAYARD TAYLOR'S] THE PROPHET: A TRAGEDY (Unsigned review)
North American Review, CXX (January), 188–194.
Reprinted in *Literary Reviews and Essays*, 1957.

D. CONTRIBUTIONS TO PERIODICALS

D161 [WILLIAM DEAN HOWELLS'S] A FOREGONE CONCLUSION (Unsigned review)
North American Review, CXX (January), 207–214.
Reprinted in *Literary Reviews and Essays*, 1957.

D162 ART [PICTURES BY WILDE, BOUGHTON, J. APPLETON BROWN, MRS. W. J. STILLMAN, AND EGUSQUIZA] (Unsigned critical notes)
Atlantic Monthly, XXXV (January), 117–119.

D163 RODERICK HUDSON
Atlantic Monthly, XXXV (January–June), 1–15, 145–160, 297–313, 422–436, 515–531, 644–658; XXXVI (July–December), 58–70, 129–140, 269–281, 385–406, 553–570, 641–665.
For first book publication, 1875, see A3.

D164 [WILLIAM DEAN HOWELLS'S] A FOREGONE CONCLUSION (Unsigned review)
The *Nation*, XX (7 January), 12–13.
Reprinted in *Literary Reviews and Essays*, 1957.

D165 NORDHOFF'S COMMUNISTIC SOCIETIES (Unsigned review of Charles Nordhoff's *The Communistic Societies of the United States from Personal Visit and Observation, Etc.*)
The *Nation*, XX (14 January), 26–28.
Reprinted in *Literary Reviews and Essays*, 1957.

D166 [STOPFORD A. BROOKE'S] THEOLOGY IN THE ENGLISH POETS (Unsigned review)
The *Nation*, XX (21 January), 41–42.
Reprinted in *Literary Reviews and Essays*, 1957.

D167 [CHARLES KINGSLEY] (Unsigned note)
The *Nation*, XX (28 January), 61.

D168 MR. GREVILLE'S JOURNAL (Unsigned review of Charles C. F. Greville's *A Journal of the Reigns of King George IV and King William IV*)
The *Nation*, XX (28 January), 62–63.

D169 [P. V. N. MYERS'S] REMAINS OF LOST EMPIRES: SKETCHES OF THE RUINS OF PALMYRA, NINEVEH, BABYLON, AND PERSEPOLIS, ETC. (Unsigned review)
The *Nation*, XX (28 January), 65–66.

D170 [SIR SAMUEL BAKER'S] ISMAILÏA: A NARRATIVE OF THE EXPEDITIONS TO CENTRAL AFRICA FOR THE SUPPRESSION OF THE SLAVE TRADE, ORGANIZED BY ISMAIL, KHEDIVE OF EGYPT (Unsigned review)
The *Nation*, XX (4 February), 81–82.

D. CONTRIBUTIONS TO PERIODICALS

D171 PROFESSOR MASSON'S ESSAYS (Unsigned review of David
Masson's *Three Devils: Luther's, Milton's, and Goethe's. With
other essays*)
The *Nation*, XX (18 February), 114–115.
Reprinted in *Literary Reviews and Essays*, 1957.

D172 SAINTE-BEUVE'S FIRST ARTICLES (Unsigned review of
C. A. Sainte-Beuve's *Premiers Lundis*)
The *Nation*, XX (18 February), 117–118.
Reprinted in *Literary Reviews and Essays*, 1957.

D173 CORRESPONDENCE OF WILLIAM ELLERY CHANNING,
D.D., AND LUCY AIKIN, FROM 1826 TO 1842. Edited by Anna
Letitia Le Breton (Unsigned review)
Atlantic Monthly, XXXV (March), 368–371.

D174 THE PRINCE CONSORT (Unsigned review of Theodore
Martin's *The Life of His Royal Highness the Prince Consort*, Vol. I)
The *Nation*, XX (4 March), 154–155.

D175 LIVINGSTONE'S LAST JOURNALS (Unsigned review of *The
Last Journals of David Livingstone in Central Africa, from 1866
to his Death*)
The *Nation*, XX (11 March), 175–176.

D176 NOTES ON THE THEATRES (Unsigned)
The *Nation*, XX (11 March), 178–179.
Reprinted in *The Scenic Art*, 1948.

D177 [SIR ARTHUR HELPS'S] SOCIAL PRESSURE (Unsigned review)
The *Nation*, XX (18 March), 193–194.

D178 MADAME RISTORI (Unsigned)
The *Nation*, XX (18 March), 194–195.
Reprinted in *The Scenic Art*, 1948.

D179 EZRA STILES GANNETT, UNITARIAN MINISTER IN BOS-
TON, 1824–1871. A MEMOIR, BY HIS SON, WILLIAM C.
GANNETT (Unsigned review)
The *Nation*, XX (1 April), 228–229.

D180 [AUGUSTUS J. C. HARE'S] DAYS NEAR ROME (Unsigned
review)
The *Nation*, XX (1 April), 229.
Attribution made on the basis of entry of payment to James in
the account book of Wendell Phillips Garrison.*

---

* For details of this account book see Introduction, pp. 15–16.

D. CONTRIBUTIONS TO PERIODICALS

D181 PERSONAL REMINISCENCES OF [THOMAS] MOORE AND [WILLIAM] JERDAN. EDITED BY R. H. STODDARD (Unsigned review)

The *Nation*, XX (1 April), 229.

Attribution made on the basis of entry of payment to James in the account book of Wendell Phillips Garrison.

D182 JOHN COLERIDGE PATTESON (Unsigned reviews of C. M. Yonge's *Life of John Coleridge Patteson* and Francis Awdry's *The Story of A Fellow-Soldier*)

The *Nation*, XX (8 April), 244–245.

D183 SAINTE-BEUVE'S ENGLISH PORTRAITS (Unsigned review of C. A. Sainte-Beuve's *Causeries du Lundi*, in English translation)

The *Nation*, XX (15 April), 261–262.

Reprinted in *Literary Reviews and Essays*, 1957.

D184 THOMSON'S INDO-CHINA AND CHINA (Unsigned review of J. Thomson's *The Straits of Malacca, Indo-China and China: or, Ten Years' Travels, Adventures, and Residence Abroad*)

The *Nation*, XX (22 April), 279–280.

D185 MACREADY'S REMINISCENCES (Unsigned review of *Macready's Reminiscences, and Selections from his Diaries and Letters*, edited by Sir Frederick Pollock)

The *Nation*, XX (29 April), 297–298.

D186 TAINE'S NOTES ON PARIS (Unsigned review of H. A. Taine's *Notes on Paris. The Life and Opinions of M. Frédéric-Thomas Graindorge, etc.*)

The *Nation*, XX (6 May), 318–319.

Reprinted in *Literary Reviews and Essays*, 1957.

D187 [H. WILLIS BAXLEY'S] SPAIN. ART REMAINS AND ART REALITIES: PAINTERS, PRIESTS, AND PRINCES, ETC. (Unsigned review)

The *Nation*, XX (20 May), 350–351.

D188 [MR GEORGE RIGNOLD AS MACBETH] (Unsigned note)

The *Nation*, XX (27 May), 362.

Reprinted in *The Scenic Art*, 1948.

D189 [MR FRANK DUVENECK] (Unsigned note)

The *Nation*, XX (3 June), 376–377.

D190 [VICTOR CHERBULIEZ'S] MISS ROVEL (Unsigned review of the English translation)

The *Nation*, XX (3 June), 381.

D191 [GEORGE H. CALVERT'S] ESSAYS-AESTHETICAL (Unsigned review)
The *Nation*, XX (3 June), 383.

D192 [JAMES ALBERT HARRISON'S] A GROUP OF POETS AND THEIR HAUNTS (Unsigned review)
The *Nation*, XX (10 June), 399–400.

D193 [MRS HENRY M. FIELD'S] HOME SKETCHES IN FRANCE, AND OTHER PAPERS (Unsigned review)
The *Nation*, XX (10 June), 400.

D194 [PAUL VERONESE AND JEAN-FRANÇOIS MILLET] (Unsigned notes)
The *Nation*, XX (17 June), 410.
Attribution made on the basis of entry of payment to James in the account book of Wendell Phillips Garrison.

D195 LADY DUFF GORDON'S LETTERS (Unsigned review of *Letters from Egypt, etc.*)
The *Nation*, XX (17 June), 412–413.

D196 [CAPTAIN J. A. LAWSON'S LITERARY FRAUD, *WANDERINGS IN THE INTERIOR OF NEW GUINEA*] (Unsigned note)
The *Nation*, XX (24 June), 425.

D197 PERSONAL REMINISCENCES OF CORNELIA KNIGHT AND THOMAS RAIKES. Edited by R. H. Stoddard (Unsigned review)
The *Nation*, XX (24 June), 428.

D198 ON SOME PICTURES LATELY EXHIBITED
The *Galaxy*, XX (July), 89–97.
Reprinted in *The Painter's Eye*, 1956.

D199 [OUIDA'S] SIGNA: A STORY (Unsigned review)
The *Nation*, XXI (1 July), 11.
Virginia Harlow erroneously ascribes this, the sixth of a group of recent novels reviewed, to T. S. Perry. The Garrison account book records payment to Perry for the first five reviews and to James for the sixth.

D200 [ANDREW WYNTER'S] FRUIT BETWEEN THE LEAVES (Unsigned review)
The *Nation*, XXI (1 July), 15–16.

D201 [GILBERT HAVEN'S] OUR NEXT-DOOR NEIGHBOR: A WINTER IN MEXICO (Unsigned review)
The *Nation*, XXI (8 July), 29–30.

D202 [THÉOPHILE GAUTIER'S] CONSTANTINOPLE (Unsigned review of Robert Howe Gould's translation)
The *Nation*, XXI (15 July), 45.
Reprinted in *Literary Reviews and Essays*, 1957.

D203 [HARRIET BEECHER STOWE'S] WE AND OUR NEIGHBORS: RECORDS OF AN UNFASHIONABLE STREET (Unsigned review)
The *Nation*, XXI (22 July), 61.
Reprinted in *Literary Reviews and Essays*, 1957.

D204 [A. C. SWINBURNE'S] ESSAYS AND STUDIES (Unsigned review)
The *Nation*, XXI (29 July), 73–74.
Reprinted, under the title "Swinburne's Essays," in *Views and Reviews*, 1908.

D205 BENVOLIO
The *Galaxy*, XX (August), 209–235.
Reprinted in *The Madonna of the Future*, 1879.

D206 THREE FRENCH BOOKS [VICOMTE HENRI DE BORNIER'S] LA FILLE DE ROLAND; [ALPHONSE DAUDET'S] FROMONT JEUNE ET RISLER AINE and [H. WALLON'S] JEANNE D'ARC (Unsigned reviews)
The *Galaxy*, XX (August), 276–280.
The three works are reviewed in a single essay. Attribution made on the basis of a comparison with the published review of notes and markings in James's copy of *Jeanne d'Arc*. The *Fromont Jeune* review parallels closely other of James's writings about Daudet. The review of Bornier's play contains HJ's well-known views on the theatre. The style throughout appears to be his.

D207 [ALBERT RHODES'S] THE FRENCH AT HOME (Unsigned review)
The *Nation*, XXI (5 August), 91–92.

D208 [FRANCES ELLIOT'S] THE ITALIANS: A NOVEL (Unsigned review)
The *Nation*, XXI (12 August), 107.
Virginia Harlow erroneously ascribes this, the sixth of a group of seven recent novels reviewed, to T. S. Perry. The Garrison account book records payment to James for this review and to Perry for the balance.

D. CONTRIBUTIONS TO PERIODICALS

D209 [MRS HENRIETTA L. (FARRER) LEAR'S] A CHRISTIAN PAINTER OF THE NINETEENTH CENTURY: BEING THE LIFE OF HYPPOLITE FLANDRIN (Unsigned review)
The *Nation*, XXI (26 August), 137–138.

D210 MR. TENNYSON'S DRAMA (Review of *Queen Mary*)
The *Galaxy*, XX (September), 393–402.
Reprinted, as Part I of "Tennyson's Drama," in *Views and Reviews*, 1908.

D211 [PORTRAITS BY MR FRANK DUVENECK] (Unsigned note)
The *Nation*, XXI (9 September), 165–166.
Reprinted with D212, under the title "Duveneck and Copley, 1875," in *The Painter's Eye*, 1956.

D212 [A PORTRAIT BY COPLEY] (Unsigned note)
The *Nation*, XXI (9 September), 166.
Reprinted with D211 in *The Painter's Eye*, 1956.

D213 NEW NOVELS (Unsigned reviews of Miss Thackeray's *Miss Angel*, Mrs Oliphant's *Whiteladies*, Mrs T. Erskine's *Wyncote*, Mrs C. Jenkin's *Within An Ace*, André Theuriet's *Le Mariage de Gérard*, Gustave Droz's *Les Etangs*, and L. B. Walford's *Mr. Smith*)
The *Nation*, XXI (23 September), 201–203.
Virginia Harlow erroneously ascribes these reviews to T. S. Perry. Garrison's account book records payment for the full set of reviews to James.

D214 [T. L. KINGTON-OLIPHANT'S] THE DUKE AND THE SCHOLAR, AND OTHER ESSAYS (Unsigned review)
The *Nation*, XXI (30 September), 216.

D215 THE LETTERS OF MADAME DE SABRAN
The *Galaxy*, XX (October), 536–546.
Reprinted, under the title "Madame de Sabran," in *French Poets and Novelists*, 1878.

D216 NADAL'S IMPRESSIONS OF ENGLAND (Unsigned review of E. S. Nadal's *Impressions of London Social Life, With Other Papers Suggested by An English Residence*)
The *Nation*, XXI (7 October), 232–233.

D217 [LOUISA M. ALCOTT'S] EIGHT COUSINS: OR THE AUNT-HILL (Unsigned review)
The *Nation*, XXI (14 October), 250–251.
Reprinted in *Literary Reviews and Essays*, 1957.

D. CONTRIBUTIONS TO PERIODICALS

D218 [JOHN LATOUCHE'S] TRAVELS IN PORTUGAL (Unsigned review)
The *Nation*, XXI (21 October), 264–265.

D219 THE TWO AMPERES (Reviews of *Journal et Correspondance de André-Marie Ampère* and *André-Marie Ampère et Jean-Jacques Ampère: Souvenirs et Correspondance*)
The *Galaxy*, XX (November), 662–674.
Reprinted in *French Poets and Novelists*, 1878.

D220 [ANDREW WILSON'S] THE ABODE OF SNOW: OBSERVATIONS ON A TOUR FROM CHINESE TIBET TO THE INDIAN CAUCASUS, ETC. (Unsigned review)
The *Nation*, XXI (11 November), 313–314.

D221 [MR HENRY IRVING'S MACBETH] (Unsigned note)
The *Nation*, XXI (25 November), 340.
Reprinted in *The Scenic Art*, 1948.

D222 [W. W. STORY'S] NERO: AN HISTORICAL PLAY (Unsigned review)
The *Nation*, XXI (25 November), 345.
Reprinted in *Literary Reviews and Essays*, 1957.

D223 HONORE DE BALZAC
The *Galaxy*, XX (December), 814–836.
Reprinted in *French Poets and Novelists*, 1878.

D224 [ALVAN S. SOUTHWORTH'S] FOUR THOUSAND MILES OF AFRICAN TRAVEL: A PERSONAL RECORD OF A JOURNEY UP THE NILE, ETC. (Unsigned review)
The *Nation*, XXI (2 December), 361.

D225 [WILLIAM MAKEPEACE THACKERAY'S] THACKERAYANA. NOTES AND ANECDOTES (Unsigned review)
The *Nation*, XXI (9 December), 376.
Reprinted in *Literary Reviews and Essays*, 1957.

D226 PARIS REVISITED (Dated 22 November)
(The Philosophy of Life in Paris—The American Quarter—The New Play by Alexandre Dumas—The Opera—Rossi in "Kean")
New York Tribune (11 December), 3:1–2.
Reprinted in part in *The Scenic Art*, 1948.
Reprinted in full in *Parisian Sketches*, 1957.

D227 LONDON SIGHTS (Unsigned)
The *Nation*, XXI (16 December), 387–388.

D228 PARIS AS IT IS (Dated 6 December)
(The Exhibition of Barye's Animal Statuary—The Story of the
Sculptor's Career—His Triumph Over Difficulties—Excellence
of His Figures—Carpeaux's Groups and Busts—The Deco-
rations of the Odeon Theater)
New York Tribune (25 December), 3:1–2.
Reprinted in *Parisian Sketches*, 1957.

D229 [CHARLES DE MAZADE ON FRENCH LITERATURE AND THE
EMPIRE] (Unsigned note)
The *Nation*, XXI (30 December), 419.

D230 [ERNEST RENAN AT ISCHIA] (Unsigned note)
The *Nation*, XXI (30 December), 419.

D231 [GEORGE BARNETT SMITH'S] POETS AND NOVELISTS: A
SERIES OF LITERARY STUDIES (Unsigned review)
The *Nation*, XXI (30 December), 422–423.
Reprinted in *Literary Reviews and Essays*, 1957.

1876

D232 [ROSAMOND AND FLORENCE HILL'S] WHAT WE SAW IN
AUSTRALIA (Unsigned review)
The *Nation*, XXII (6 January), 17.

D233 [A. P. RUSSELL'S] LIBRARY NOTES (Unsigned review)
The *Nation*, XXII (6 January), 17.

D234 VERSAILLES AS IT IS (Dated 16 December)
(The Election of Senators—Altered Aspect of Versailles—Pic-
turesqueness of the Place—The Prospects of the Republic—M.
Taine's New Book—Glimpses of the Old Regime)
New York Tribune (8 January), 2:1–2.
Reprinted in *Parisian Sketches*, 1957.

D235 RECENT NOVELS (Unsigned reviews of Frank Lee Benedict's
St. Simon's Niece, Charles H. Doe's *Buffets*, Mrs Annie Edwards's
Leah: A Woman of Fashion, George Sand's *Flamarande* and *Les
Deux Frères*, and Octave Feuillet's *Un Mariage dans le Monde*)
The *Nation*, XXII (13 January), 32–34.

D236 [ROBERT BROWNING'S] THE INN ALBUM (Unsigned review)
The *Nation*, XXII (20 January), 49–50.
Reprinted, under the title "On A Drama of Robert Browning,"
in *Views and Reviews*, 1908.

D237 PARISIAN SKETCHES (Dated 28 December)
(Meissonier's Battle of Friedland—Purchase of the Picture by
Mr. A. T. Stewart—Merits and Demerits of the Work—The
Holidays in Paris—Picturesqueness of the City at Eventide)
New York Tribune (22 January), 3 : 1–2.
Reprinted in part, under the title "The American Purchase of
Meissonier's 'Friedland,' 1876," in *The Painter's Eye*, 1956.
Reprinted in full in *Parisian Sketches*, 1957.

D238 [JOHN BURROUGHS'S] WINTER SUNSHINE (Unsigned re-
view)
The *Nation*, XXII (27 January), 66.
Reprinted, under the title "A Note on John Burroughs," in
Views and Reviews, 1908.

D239 [PROSPER MÉRIMÉE'S] LETTRES À UNE AUTRE INCONNUE
(Unsigned review)
The *Nation*, XXII (27 January), 67–68.
Reprinted in *Literary Reviews and Essays*, 1957.

D240 THE PARISIAN STAGE (Dated 7 January)
(The Drama As It is—Popularity of Opera Bouffe—Rossi as
Macbeth—Success of Sardou's Ferreol—Dearth of New Pieces)
New York Tribune (29 January), 3 : 1–2.
Reprinted in *The Scenic Art*, 1948.

D241 THE MINOR FRENCH NOVELISTS
The *Galaxy*, XXI (February), 219–233.
Reprinted in part, under the title "Charles de Bernard and
Gustave Flaubert," in *French Poets and Novelists*, 1878. The re-
mainder of the essay was reprinted in *Literary Reviews and Essays*,
1957.

D242 [PHILIP GILBERT HAMERTON'S] ROUND MY HOUSE: NOTES
OF A RURAL LIFE IN FRANCE IN PEACE AND WAR (Unsigned
review)
The *Nation*, XXII (3 February), 85–86.

D243 PARISIAN LIFE (Dated 18 January)
(Politics and the Drama—The Progress of the Electoral Cam-
paign—Minister Buffet's Dread of "Social Peril"—The New
Russian Drama—The Actor Rossi as Romeo)
New York Tribune (5 February), 3 : 1–2.
Reprinted in part, as Part 1 of "Notes From Paris," in *The Scenic
Art*, 1948.
Reprinted in full in *Parisian Sketches*, 1957.

D244 PARISIAN TOPICS (Dated 28 January)
(Victor Hugo's Address to the Communal Delegates—French National Vanity—The Lamartine Monument—Parisian "Conferences"—The Painter Pils's Career and Works)
New York Tribune (19 February), 3 : 1–2.
Reprinted in part, under the title "Two Pictures by Delacroix," in *The Painter's Eye*, 1956.
Reprinted in full in *Parisian Sketches*, 1957.

D245 [GEORGE ELIOT'S *DANIEL DERONDA*] (Unsigned note)
The *Nation*, XXII (24 February), 131.

D246 PARIS IN ELECTION TIME (Dated 11 February)
(The New Senate—M. Gambetta and Clerical Education—Ex-Minister Buffet's Personal Outlines—M. de Girardin on the Duty of France—Bonapartist Fancies—The Late Frederick Lemaitre)
New York Tribune (4 March), 3 : 4–5.
Reprinted in part, as Part 2 of "Notes From Paris," in *The Scenic Art*, 1948.
Reprinted in full in *Parisian Sketches*, 1957.

D247 [JULIUS RODENBERG'S] ENGLAND, LITERARY AND SOCIAL, FROM A GERMAN POINT OF VIEW (Unsigned review)
The *Nation*, XXII (16 March), 182.

D248 PARISIAN AFFAIRS (Dated 28 February)
(The Republic in the Hands of Republicans—Rapid Succession of Political Events—M. Gambetta's Sagacity—Dumas's New Play, "L'Etrangere"—Merits and Demerits of the Performance——The Carnival in Paris)
New York Tribune (25 March), 3 : 1–2.
Reprinted in part, as Part 3 of "Notes From Paris," in *The Scenic Art*, 1948.
Reprinted in full in *Parisian Sketches*, 1957.

D249 [JULIAN HAWTHORNE'S] SAXON STUDIES (Unsigned review)
The *Nation*, XXII (30 March), 214–215.
Reprinted in *Literary Reviews and Essays*, 1957.

D250 THE KING OF POLAND AND MADAME GEOFFRIN (Review of *Correspondance inédite du Roi Stanislas Auguste Poniatowski et de Mme. Geoffrin (1764–1797)* edited by Charles de Mouy)
The *Galaxy*, XXI (April), 548–550.

D251 PARISIAN TOPICS (Dated 10 March)
(The Reception of John Lemoinne at the Academy—His Characteristics as a Journalist—The Variable Merits of Academicians—

M. Gerome's "Chariot Race"—President Lincoln and Stonewall
Jackson Dramatized—Victor Tissot on the Prussians)
New York Tribune (1 April), 3 : 1–2.
Reprinted in part, as Part 4 of "Notes From Paris," in *The Scenic
Art*, 1948.
Reprinted in full in *Parisian Sketches*, 1957.

D252 SCHÉRER'S LITERARY STUDIES (Unsigned review of Ed-
mond Schérer's *Études Critiques de Littérature*)
The *Nation*, XXII (6 April), 233.
Reprinted in *Literary Reviews and Essays*, 1957.

D253 ART AND LETTERS IN PARIS (Dated 21 March)
(The Parisian Art Market—Decamp's [sic] Distinctive Merits—
Marilhat's Paintings—Oriental Sketches Abundant—Meissonier's
"Reader"—The Floods in the Seine—Current Literature)
New York Tribune (22 April), 3 : 1–2.
Reprinted in *Parisian Sketches*, 1957.

D254 CHARLES BAUDELAIRE (Unsigned retrospective review-
article of *Les Fleurs du Mal*)
The *Nation*, XXII (27 April), 279–281.
Reprinted in *French Poets and Novelists*, 1878.

D255 CHARTRES PORTRAYED (Dated 9 April)
(Brilliant Weather in Paris—Preliminaries of a Day's Excursion
—Impressiveness of the Cathedral at Chartres—General Aspect
of the Town—Quaintness of its Social Life)
New York Tribune (29 April), 3 : 1–2.
Reprinted, under the title "Chartres," in *Portraits of Places*,
1883.

D256 [AUGUSTUS J. C. HARE'S] CITIES OF NORTHERN AND CEN-
TRAL ITALY (Unsigned review)
The *Nation*, XXII (10 May), 325–326.

D257 PARISIAN FESTIVITY (Dated 22 April)
(Reappearance of the British Tourist—The Carrousel at the
Palais de L'Industrie—Cynical Artists—M. Mermet's Opera of
Jeanne d'Arc—Recent Books)
New York Tribune (13 May), 2 : 1–2.
Reprinted in part, under the title "The Impressionists," 1876, in
The Painter's Eye, 1956.
Reprinted in full in *Parisian Sketches*, 1957.

D258 ART IN FRANCE (Dated 5 May)
(The Salon of 1876—Greatness of the Display—Doré's Colossal
Canvas—Large Paintings by Montchabron [sic], Bin, and Blanc—

M. Sylvestre's Portrayal of Nero—Excellence of M. Detaille's
War Scene)
New York Tribune (27 May), 3 : 1–2.
Reprinted in *Parisian Sketches*, 1957.

D259 THE AMERICAN
Atlantic Monthly, XXXVII (June), 651–673; XXXVIII (July–
December), 15–31, 155–170, 310–329, 461–474, 535–550, 641–
657; XXXIX (January–May 1877), 1–18, 161–175, 295–311, 412–
425, 530–544.
For first book publication, 1877, see A4.

D260 ART IN PARIS (Dated 6 May)
(The Salon Revisited—Distinctive Merits of the Principal Por-
traits—Paintings by MM. Gérôme, Cabanel, Bouguereau, and
Vibert—M. Moreau's Artistic Vagaries—The Landscapes and the
Statuary)
New York Tribune (5 June), 2 : 1–2.
Reprinted in *Parisian Sketches*, 1957.

D261 PARISIAN TOPICS (Dated 27 May)
(M. Ernest Renan's New Volume—M. Michelet's Funeral— Poli-
tical Display Avoided—Mme. Plessy's Retirement from the Stage
—A Minor Art Exhibition—Plans for the Great Exhibition of
1878)
New York Tribune (17 June), 3 : 1–2.
Reprinted in part, as Part 5 of "Notes From Paris," in *The Scenic
Art*, 1948.
Reprinted in full in *Parisian Sketches*, 1957.

D262 [THE PARIS SALON OF 1876] (Unsigned note)
The *Nation*, XXII (22 June), 397–398.

D263 [M. VICTOR CHERBULIEZ ON THE PARIS SALON] (Unsigned
note)
The *Nation*, XXII (29 June), 415–416.

D264 PARISIAN TOPICS (Dated 9 June)
(The Late M. Doudan's Correspondence—M. Waddington's
University Bill—A Brilliant Season of Italian Opera—Verdi's
Aida and Requiem Performed—The Late George Sand)
New York Tribune (1 July), 3 : 1–2.
Reprinted in *Parisian Sketches*, 1957.

D265 A STUDY OF RUBENS AND REMBRANDT (Unsigned review of
Eugène Fromentin's *Les Maîtres d'Autrefois: Belgique-Holland*)
The *Nation*, XXIII (13 July), 29–30.

Reprinted, under the title "*Les Maîtres d'Autrefois*, 1876," in *The Painter's Eye*, 1956.

D266 GEORGE SAND (Dated 28 June)
(Incidents of Her Career—Her Tireless Industry—M. Renan's Tribute to Her Genius—Characteristics of Her Earlier and Later Works)
New York Tribune (22 July), 3 : 1–2.
Reprinted in *Parisian Sketches*, 1957.

D267 [M. TAINE'S LETTER ON GEORGE SAND] (Unsigned note)
The *Nation*, XXIII (27 July), 61.

D268 CRAWFORD'S CONSISTENCY
Scribner's Monthly, XII (August), 569–584.
Reprinted in *Eight Uncollected Tales of Henry James*, 1950.

D269 SUMMER IN FRANCE (Dated 22 July)
(Paris in Summer Time—Festive Aspect of the Boulevards—Dining at Auteuil and at the Bois—The Atlantic at Havre—The Cathedral in Rouen—The Church of St. Ouen)
New York Tribune (12 August), 3 : 3–4.
Reprinted, under the title "Rouen," in *Portraits of Places*, 1883.

D270 A FRENCH WATERING PLACE (Dated 4 August)
(Etretat on the Coast of Normandy—Its Simplicity and Attractions—Scenery—The Bluffs—Customs of Visitors—Jacques Offenbach)
New York Tribune (26 August), 3 : 1–2.
Reprinted, under the title "Etretat," in *Portraits of Places*, 1883.

D271 THE GHOSTLY RENTAL
Scribner's Monthly, XII (September), 664–679.
Reprinted in *The Ghostly Tales of Henry James*, 1949.

D272 [IVAN TURGENEV] (Unsigned note and translation of a prose poem from the French)
The *Nation*, XXIII (5 October), 213.
HJ to W. D. Howells, 24 October 1876: "Yes, I couldn't help translating those ... verses of Turgénieff, though I don't share the Russian eagerness for War." (*Letters*, II, 1975, p. 72.)

D273 [THE HENRI REGNAULT MONUMENT] (Unsigned note)
The *Nation*, XXIII (26 October), 258.

D274 [M. PARODI'S *ROME VAINCUE*] (Unsigned note)
The *Nation*, XXIII (16 November), 300–301.
Reprinted, as Part 6 of "Notes From Paris," in *The Scenic Art*, 1948.

D275 DANIEL DERONDA: A CONVERSATION
Atlantic Monthly, XXXVIII (December), 684–694.
Reprinted in *Partial Portraits*, 1888.

D276 [THE COUNT OF GOBINEAU'S] NOUVELLES ASIATIQUES
(Unsigned review)
The *Nation*, XXIII (7 December), 344–345.

D277 AN AMERICAN AND AN ENGLISH NOVEL (Unsigned reviews of Helen Hunt Jackson's *Mercy Philbrick's Choice* and Rhoda Broughton's *Joan*)
The *Nation*, XXIII (21 December), 372–373.

1877

D278 FROM NORMANDY TO THE PYRENEES
The *Galaxy*, XXIII (January), 95–109.
Reprinted in *Portraits of Places*, 1883.

D279 [MM. ERCKMANN-CHATRIAN'S *AMI FRITZ*] (Unsigned note)
The *Nation*, XXIV (4 January), 14.
Reprinted, as Part 7 of "Notes From Paris," in *The Scenic Art*, 1948.

D280 [SWINBURNE AND CARLYLE] (Unsigned note)
The *Nation*, XXIV (11 January), 29–30.

D281 MR. TENNYSON'S NEW DRAMA (Unsigned review of *Harold: A Drama*)
The *Nation*, XXIV (18 January), 43–44.
Reprinted, as Part II of "Tennyson's Drama," in *Views and Reviews*, 1908.

D282 [THE NATIONAL GALLERY] (Unsigned note)
The *Nation*, XXIV (25 January), 59.
Reprinted, under the title "The National Gallery, 1877," in *The Painter's Eye*, 1956.

D283 [CHARLES KINGSLEY'S] LIFE AND LETTERS (Unsigned review)
The *Nation*, XXIV (25 January), 60–61.
Reprinted in *Literary Reviews and Essays*, 1957.

D284 THE LETTERS OF HONORÉ DE BALZAC (Review of *Correspondance de H. de Balzac, 1819–1850*)
The *Galaxy*, XXIII (February), 183–195.
Reprinted, under the title "Balzac's Letters," in *French Poets and Novelists*, 1878.

D. CONTRIBUTIONS TO PERIODICALS

D285 THE OLD MASTERS AT BURLINGTON HOUSE (Unsigned)
The *Nation*, XXIV (1 February), 71–72.
Reprinted in *The Painter's Eye*, 1956.

D286 [*MAYFAIR* AND *TRUTH*] (Unsigned note on two new weekly journals)
The *Nation*, XXIV (1 February), 75.

D287 [DUTTON COOK'S] A BOOK OF THE PLAY: STUDIES AND ILLUSTRATIONS OF HISTRIONIC STORY, LIFE, AND CHARACTER (Unsigned review)
The *Nation*, XXIV (8 February), 91.

D288 MRS. BROWNING'S LETTERS (Unsigned review of *Letters of Elizabeth Barrett Browning, Addressed to R. H. Horne*, edited by S. R. Townshend Mayer)
The *Nation*, XXIV (15 February), 105–106.
Reprinted in *Literary Reviews and Essays*, 1957.

D289 [G. DE MOLINARI'S] LETTRES SUR LES ÉTATS-UNIS ET LE CANADA (Unsigned review)
The *Nation*, XXIV (22 February), 119–120.

D290 [BURLINGTON HOUSE] (Unsigned note on the John Gibson permanent exhibition of statuary)
The *Nation*, XXIV (15 March), 164.

D291 [D. MACKENZIE WALLACE'S] RUSSIA (Unsigned review)
The *Nation*, XXIV (15 March), 165–167.

D292 [*THE PORTRAIT: A WEEKLY PHOTOGRAPH AND MEMOIR*] (Unsigned note on William Black)
The *Nation*, XXIV (22 March), 177.

D293 [*THE NINETEENTH CENTURY*] (Unsigned note on a new periodical)
The *Nation*, XXIV (22 March), 177.

D294 [HORACE DE LAGARDIE'S "FRENCH NOVELS AND FRENCH LIFE"] (Unsigned note on article in March *Macmillan's Magazine*)
The *Nation*, XXIV (29 March), 194–195

D295 [FRED. BURNABY'S] A RIDE TO KHIVA: TRAVELS AND ADVENTURES IN CENTRAL ASIA (Unsigned review)
The *Nation*, XXIV (29 March), 196–197.

D296 THE THÉÂTRE FRANÇAIS
The *Galaxy*, XXIII (April), 437–449.
Reprinted in *French Poets and Novelists*, 1878.

D. CONTRIBUTIONS TO PERIODICALS

D297 [VERNEY LOVETT CAMERON'S] ACROSS AFRICA (Unsigned review)
The *Nation*, XXIV (5 April), 209–210.

D298 [THE OXFORD–CAMBRIDGE BOAT RACE] (Unsigned note)
The *Nation*, XXIV (12 April), 221–222.

D299 [MISS ELIZABETH THOMPSON'S PAINTINGS] (Unsigned note)
The *Nation*, XXIV (26 April), 250–251.

D300 [IVAN TURGENEV'S] TERRES VIERGES (Unsigned review of the French translation by E. Durand-Gréville)
The *Nation*, XXIV (26 April), 252–253.
Reprinted in *Literary Reviews and Essays*, 1957.

D301 THE LONDON THEATRES
The *Galaxy*, XXIII (May), 661–670.
Reprinted in *The Scenic Art*, 1948.

D302 [VICTOR HUGO'S *LÉGENDE DES SIÈCLES*] (Unsigned note)
The *Nation*, XXIV (3 May), 266.
Reprinted in *Literary Reviews and Essays*, 1957.

D303 [THEODORE MARTIN'S] THE LIFE OF H.R.H. THE PRINCE CONSORT, VOL. II (Unsigned review)
The *Nation*, XXIV (3 May), 269.

D304 [EDMOND DE GONCOURT'S *LA FILLE ELISA*] (Unsigned note)
The *Nation*, XXIV (10 May), 280.
Reprinted in *Literary Reviews and Essays*, 1957.

D305 [VICTOR TISSOT'S] VOYAGE AUX PAYS ANNEXÉS (Unsigned review)
The *Nation*, XXIV (17 May), 297.

D306 THE GROSVENOR GALLERY AND THE ROYAL ACADEMY (Unsigned)
The *Nation*, XXIV (31 May), 320–321.

D307 ALFRED DE MUSSET
The *Galaxy*, XXIII (June), 790–802.
Reprinted in *French Poets and Novelists*, 1878.

D308 [JULIA CONSTANCE FLETCHER'S] KISMET (Unsigned review)
The *Nation*, XXIV (7 June), 341.

D309 [JULIAN HAWTHORNE'S] GARTH (Unsigned review)
The *Nation*, XXIV (21 June), 369.
Reprinted in *Literary Reviews and Essays*, 1957.

D. CONTRIBUTIONS TO PERIODICALS

D310 GEORGE SAND
The *Galaxy*, XXIV (July), 45–61.
Reprinted in *French Poets and Novelists*, 1878.

D311 AN ENGLISH EASTER
Lippincott's Magazine, XX (July), 50–60.
Reprinted in *Portraits of Places*, 1883.

D312 THE PICTURE SEASON IN LONDON
The *Galaxy*, XXIV (August), 149–161.
Reprinted in *The Painter's Eye*, 1956.

D313 THREE EXCURSIONS
The *Galaxy*, XXIV (September), 346–356.
Reprinted in part, under the title "Two Excursions," in *Portraits of Places*, 1883.

D314 ABBEYS AND CASTLES
Lippincott's Magazine, XX (October), 434–442.
Reprinted in *Portraits of Places*, 1883.

D315 [M. THIERS'S ART COLLECTION] (Unsigned note)
The *Nation*, XXV (18 October), 243.

D316 [AUGUSTE LAUGEL'S] LA FRANCE POLITIQUE ET SOCIALE (Unsigned review)
The *Nation*, XXV (18 October), 244–245.

D317 [GEORGE SAND'S] DERNIÈRES PAGES (Unsigned review)
The *Nation*, XXV (25 October), 259–260.
Reprinted in *Literary Reviews and Essays*, 1957.

D318 LONDON AT MIDSUMMER
Lippincott's Magazine, XX (November), 603–611.
Reprinted in *Portraits of Places*, 1883.

D319 IN WARWICKSHIRE
The *Galaxy*, XXIV (November), 671–680.
Reprinted in *Portraits of Places*, 1883.

D320 FOUR MEETINGS
Scribner's Monthly, XV (November), 44–56.
Reprinted in *Daisy Miller* (English Edition), 1879.

D321 [OCTAVE FEUILLET'S] LES AMOURS DE PHILIPPE (Unsigned review)
The *Nation*, XXV (15 November), 306.
Reprinted in *Literary Reviews and Essays*, 1957.

D322 [CHARLES DE MAZADE'S] THE LIFE OF COUNT CAVOUR (Unsigned review of the English translation)
Lippincott's Magazine, XX (December), 772–774.

Attribution made on the basis of a comparison with the published review of notes and markings in James's copy of the French edition of the book.

D323 THE SUBURBS OF LONDON
The *Galaxy*, XXIV (December), 778–787.

1878

D324 PARIS REVISITED
The *Galaxy*, XXV (January), 5–13.
Reprinted, under the title "Occasional Paris," in *Portraits of Places*, 1883.

D325 A LITTLE TOUR IN FRANCE
Atlantic Monthly, XLI (January), 67–76.
Reprinted, under the title "Rheims and Laon: A Little Tour," in *Portraits of Places*, 1883.

D326 M. DOUDAN'S NEW VOLUMES (Unsigned review of X. Doudan's *Mélanges et Lettres*)
The *Nation*, XXVI (24 January), 64–65.

D327 THE OLD MASTERS AT BURLINGTON HOUSE (Signed "From An Occasional Correspondent")
The *Nation*, XXVI (31 January), 75–76.
Reprinted, under the title "The Norwich School," in *The Painter's Eye*, 1956.

D328 [GEORGE FLEMING'S] MIRAGE (Unsigned review of pseudonymously signed novel by Julia Constance Fletcher)
The *Nation*, XXVI (7 March), 172–173.

D329 ITALY REVISITED
Atlantic Monthly, XLI (April), 437–444.
Reprinted, as Parts I, II, and III of an essay under the same title, in *Portraits of Places*, 1883.

D330 [RUSKIN'S COLLECTION OF DRAWINGS BY TURNER] (Unsigned note)
The *Nation*, XXVI (18 April), 260.
Reprinted in *The Painter's Eye*, 1956.

D331 [GEORGE ELIOT'S NEWLY PUBLISHED TALES] (Unsigned notes on *The Lifted Veil* and *Brother Jacob*)
The *Nation*, XXVI (25 April), 277.
Reprinted in *Literary Reviews and Essays*, 1957.

D. CONTRIBUTIONS TO PERIODICALS

D332 RECENT FLORENCE
Atlantic Monthly, XLI (May), 586–593.
Reprinted, as Parts IV, V, and VI of "Italy Revisited," in *Portraits of Places*, 1883.

D333 THÉODOLINDE
Lippincott's Magazine, XXI (May), 553–563.
Reprinted, under the title "Rose-Agathe," in *Stories Revived*, 1885.

D334 [THE LONDON EXHIBITIONS—THE GROSVENOR GALLERY] (Unsigned note)
The *Nation*, XXVI (23 May), 338–339.
Reprinted, under the title "The Grosvenor Gallery, 1878," in *The Painter's Eye*, 1956.

D335 [LAURENCE OLIPHANT'S *THE TENDER RECOLLECTIONS OF IRENE MACGILLICUDDY*. ONE OF A SERIES OF TALES FROM *BLACKWOOD'S MAGAZINE*] (Unsigned note)
The *Nation*, XXVI (30 May), 357.

D336 [ÉMILE ZOLA'S] UNE PAGE D'AMOUR (Unsigned review)
The *Nation*, XXVI (30 May), 361–362.
Attribution made on the basis of entry of payment to James in the account book of Wendell Phillips Garrison.

D337 DAISY MILLER: A STUDY
Cornhill Magazine, XXXVII (June), 678–698; XXXVIII (July), 44–67. Also, in unauthorized appearances, in *Littell's Living Age*, CXXXVIII (6 and 27 July), 27–40, 226–241, and in the *Home Journal*, New York (subtitled "Americans Abroad"), 31 July, 7 and 14 August, p. 1 of each issue.
For first book publication, 1878, see A8.

D338 [THE LONDON EXHIBITIONS—THE ROYAL ACADEMY] (Unsigned note)
The *Nation*, XXVI (6 June), 371–372.
Reprinted, under the title "The Royal Academy, 1878," in *The Painter's Eye*, 1956.

D339 [THEODORE MARTIN'S] THE LIFE OF HIS ROYAL HIGHNESS THE PRINCE CONSORT, VOL. III (Unsigned review)
The *Nation*, XXVI (6 June), 377–378.

D340 [HENRY IRVING AS LOUIS XI; *OLIVIA* AT THE COURT THEATRE] (Unsigned note)
The *Nation*, XXVI (13 June), 389.
Reprinted in *The Scenic Art*, 1948.

D341 [AUGUSTUS J. C. HARE'S] WALKS IN LONDON (Unsigned review)
The *Nation*, XXVI (20 June), 407–408.

D342 [ÉMILE AUGIER'S *LES FOURCHAMBAULT*] (Unsigned note)
The *Nation*, XXVI (27 June), 419.
Reprinted, under the title "M. Émile Augier," in *The Scenic Art*, 1948.

D343 [PENSÉES OF JOUBERT, SELECTED BY HENRY ATTWELL] (Unsigned note)
The *Nation*, XXVI (27 June), 423–424.

D344 THE EUROPEANS
Atlantic Monthly, XLII (July–October), 52–72, 155–177, 262–283, 404–428.
For first book publication, 1878, see A7.

D345 THE BRITISH SOLDIER
Lippincott's Magazine, XXII (August), 214–221.

D346 LONGSTAFF'S MARRIAGE
Scribner's Monthly, XVI (August), 537–550.
Reprinted in *The Madonna of the Future*, 1879.

D347 LONDON IN THE DEAD SEASON (Unsigned)
The *Nation*, XXVII (26 September), 193–194.

D348 AMERICANS ABROAD (Unsigned)
The *Nation*, XXVII (3 October), 208–209.

D349 IN SCOTLAND (Unsigned)
The *Nation*, XXVII (10 and 24 October), 224–225, 254–256.

D350 THE AFGHAN DIFFICULTY (Unsigned)
The *Nation*, XXVII (14 November), 298–299.

D351 AN INTERNATIONAL EPISODE
Cornhill Magazine, XXXVIII (December), 687–713; XXXIX (January 1879), 61–90.
For first book publication, 1879, see A9.

D352 [FRANCES ANNE KEMBLE'S] RECORD OF A GIRLHOOD (Unsigned review)
The *Nation*, XXVII (12 December), 368–369.

D353 [MORITZ BUSCH'S *GRAF BISMARCK UND SEINE LEUTE WÄHREND DES KRIEGES MIT FRANKREICH*] (Unsigned note)
The *Nation*, XXVII (19 December), 384.

D354 [DR. BUSCH'S "AUTOBIOGRAPHIC" BISMARCK NOTES] (Unsigned note)
The *Nation*, XXVII (19 December), 384–385.

D355 [THE WHISTLER–RUSKIN LIBEL SUIT] (Unsigned note)
The *Nation*, XXVII (19 December), 385.
Reprinted, as Part I of "Contemporary Notes on Whistler vs. Ruskin," in *Views and Reviews*, 1908.

D356 [WILLIAM BLACK'S] MACLEOD OF DARE (Unsigned review)
The *Nation*, XXVII (19 December), 387–388.

D357 [GERALDINE MACPHERSON'S *MEMOIRS OF ANNA JAMESON*] (Unsigned note)
The *Nation*, XXVII (19 December), 388–389.
The Garrison account book records payment to HJ for the first two paragraphs of the note, and to Mary E. Parkman for the third.

D358 THE EARLY MEETING OF PARLIAMENT (Unsigned)
The *Nation*, XXVII (26 December), 397–398.

D359 HAYWARD'S ESSAYS (Unsigned review of A. Hayward's *Selected Essays*)
The *Nation*, XXVII (26 December), 402–403.

1879

D360 THE NEW YEAR IN ENGLAND (Unsigned)
The *Nation*, XXVIII (23 January), 65–66.
Reprinted, under the title "An English New Year," in *Portraits of Places*, 1883.

D361 THE WINTER EXHIBITIONS IN LONDON (Unsigned)
The *Nation*, XXVIII (13 February), 115–116.

D362 [WHISTLER AND ART CRITICISM] (Unsigned note)
The *Nation*, XXVIII (13 February), 119.
Reprinted, as Part II of "Contemporary Notes on Whistler vs. Ruskin," in *Views and Reviews*, 1908.

D363 THE REASSEMBLING OF PARLIAMENT (Unsigned)
The *Nation*, XXVIII (20 March), 197–199.

D364 ENGLISH VIGNETTES (Illustrated by C. P. Nichols and J. Sachs)
Lippincott's Magazine, XXIII (April), 407–418.
Reprinted in *Portraits of Places*, 1883.

D365 A FRIEND OF LORD BYRON (Review of *Memoir of the Rev. Francis Hodgson, B.D., with Numerous Letters From Lord Byron and Others*)
North American Review, CXXVIII (April), 388–392.
Reprinted in *Literary Reviews and Essays*, 1957.

D366 THE PENSION BEAUREPAS
Atlantic Monthly, XLIII (April), 388–392.
Reprinted in *Washington Square* (English Edition), 1881.

D367 AN ENGLISH WINTER WATERING-PLACE (Unsigned)
The *Nation*, XXVIII (3 April), 228–229.
Reprinted in *Portraits of Places*, 1883.

D368 THE ROYAL ACADEMY AND THE GROSVENOR GALLERY
(Unsigned)
The *Nation*, XXVIII (29 May), 366–368.
Reprinted in *The Painter's Eye*, 1956.

D369 THE LONDON THEATRES (Signed XX)
The *Nation*, XXVIII (12 June), 400–401.
Reprinted in *The Scenic Art*, 1948.

D370 THE DIARY OF A MAN OF FIFTY
Harper's New Monthly Magazine, LIX (July), 282–297; *Macmillan's Magazine*, XL (July), 205–223.
Reprinted in *The Madonna of the Future*, 1879.

D371 THE COMÉDIE-FRANÇAISE IN LONDON (Signed XX)
The *Nation*, XXIX (31 July), 72–73.
Reprinted in *The Scenic Art*, 1948.

D372 CONFIDENCE
Scribner's Monthly, XVIII (August–October), 507–519, 668–682, 849–864; XIX (November–January 1880), 65–80, 209–225, 393–411.
For first book publication, 1879, see A11.

D373 A BUNDLE OF LETTERS
The *Parisian* (Paris), No. 38 (18 December), 7–9.
Reprinted, in unauthorized editions, by Loring of Boston and by George Munro in The Seaside Library (see A13), 1880. For first authorized book publication, 1880, see A14.

1880

D374 SAINTE-BEUVE (Review of *Correspondance de C. A. Sainte-Beuve, 1822–69*)
North American Review, CXXX (January), 51–68.
Reprinted, with revisions by the author, in *American Literary Criticism*, 1904.

D375 [ÉMILE ZOLA'S] NANA
The *Parisian*, (Paris), No. 48 (26 February), 9.
Reprinted in part in Vizetelly's edition of *Nana*, 1884 (see B1);

reprinted in full in the *Colby Library Quarterly*, Series I, No. 3 (June 1943), 46–51, and in *The Future of the Novel*, 1956.

D376 THE LETTERS OF EUGÈNE DELACROIX (Review of *Lettres d'Eugène Delacroix (1815 à 1863)*, edited by Philippe Burty. *International Review*, VIII (April), 357–371.
Reprinted in *The Painter's Eye*, 1956.

D377 WASHINGTON SQUARE
Cornhill Magazine, XLI (June), 641–664; XLII (July–November), 107–128, 129–152, 364–384, 385–403, 616–640. Illustrated by George du Maurier.
Also in *Harper's New Monthly Magazine*, LXI (July–November), 287–301, 413–426, 593–607, 753–766, 907–918; LXII (December), 129–144. Not illustrated.
For first book publication, 1880, see A15.

D378 THE PORTRAIT OF A LADY
Macmillan's Magazine, XLII (October), 401–427; XLIII (November–April 1881), 1–27, 81–106, 161–189, 249–272, 329–356, 409–432; XLIV (May–October 1881), 1–26, 81–106, 171–198, 241–267, 320–341, 401–420; XLV (November 1881), 1–19.
Also in the *Atlantic Monthly*, XLVI (November–December), 585–611, 740–766; XLVII (January–June 1881), 1–27, 176–205, 335–359, 449–477, 623–647, 800–826; XLVIII (July–December 1881), 59–85, 213–240, 338–365, 479–499, 620–640, 751–770.
For first book publication, 1881, see A16.

1881

D379 THE LONDON THEATRES (Unsigned) (Illustrated by R. C. Woodville, H. Wolf, R. Blum, and others)
Scribner's Monthly, XXI (January), 354–369.
Reprinted in *The Scenic Art*, 1948.

1882

D380 ALPHONSE DAUDET (Review of Ernest Daudet's *Mon Frère et Moi: Souvenirs d'Enfance et de Jeunesse*)
Atlantic Monthly, XLIX (June), 846–851.
Reprinted in *Literary Reviews and Essays*, 1957.

D381 LONDON PICTURES AND LONDON PLAYS (Unsigned)
Atlantic Monthly, L (August), 253–263.
The first half of this essay was reprinted, under the title "London Pictures, 1882," in *The Painter's Eye*, 1956; the second half was reprinted, under the title "London Plays," in *The Scenic Art*, 1948.

D382 VENICE (Illustrated)
Century Magazine, XXV (November), 3–23.
Reprinted in *Portraits of Places*, 1883.

D383 THE POINT OF VIEW
Century Magazine, XXV (December), 248–268.
Reprinted in *The Siege of London*, 1883.

1883

D384 THE SIEGE OF LONDON (Woodcut illustration by W. Small)
Cornhill Magazine, XLVII (January–February), 1–34, 225–256.
Reprinted in *The Siege of London*, 1883.

D385 TOMMASO SALVINI
Atlantic Monthly, LI (March), 377–386.
Reprinted, as Part I ("In Boston, 1883") of an essay under the
same title, in *The Scenic Art*, 1948.

D386 DAISY MILLER: A COMEDY
Atlantic Monthly, LI (April–June), 433–456, 577–597, 721–740.
A privately printed edition, 1882, preceded serialization (see
A18a). For first published book edition, see A18b.

D387 DU MAURIER AND LONDON SOCIETY (With engraved por-
trait by T. Johnson and seven Du Maurier illustrations from
Punch)
Century Magazine, XXVI (May), 48–65.
Reprinted, without illustrations, under the title "George du
Maurier," in *Partial Portraits*, 1888.

D388 THE CORRESPONDENCE OF CARLYLE AND EMERSON (Re-
view)
Century Magazine, XXVI (June), 265–272.
Reprinted in *The American Essays of Henry James*, 1956.

D389 ANTHONY TROLLOPE (With portrait-sketch by R. Birch)
Century Magazine, XXVI (July), 384–395.
Reprinted in *Partial Portraits*, 1888.

D390 EN PROVINCE
Atlantic Monthly, LII (July–November), 24–38, 169–186, 303–
322, 453–469, 630–643; LIII (February, April–May 1884), 217–
228, 515–526, 623–631.
For first book publication, under the title *A Little Tour in France*,
1884, see A23.

D391 ALPHONSE DAUDET
Century Magazine, XXVI (August), 498–509.
Reprinted in *Partial Portraits*, 1888.

D392 THE REMINISCENCES OF ERNEST RENAN (Unsigned review
of Renan's *Souvenirs d'Enfance et de Jeunesse*)
Atlantic Monthly, LII (August), 274–281.
Reprinted in *Literary Reviews and Essays*, 1957.

D393 A POOR PLAY WELL ACTED (Signed "By a Casual Critic")
Pall Mall Gazette (24 October), 1–2; *Pall Mall Budget*, XXXI
(26 October), 6–7.
Reprinted in *The Scenic Art*, 1948.

D394 THE IMPRESSIONS OF A COUSIN
Century Magazine, XXVII (November–December), 116–129,
257–275.
Reprinted in *Tales of Three Cities*, 1884.

D395 TOURGÉNEFF IN PARIS: REMINISCENCES BY [ALPHONSE]
DAUDET (Anonymous translation)
Century Magazine, XXVII (November), 49–53.
The holograph manuscript of the Daudet essay in French,
together with the manuscript of James's translation in English,
bearing the compositor's markings, is in the collection of C.
Waller Barrett.

1884

D396 IVAN TURGÉNIEFF
Atlantic Monthly, LIII (January), 42–55.
Reprinted in *Partial Portraits*, 1888.

D397 MATTHEW ARNOLD (With portrait)
English Illustrated Magazine, I (January), 241–246.
Reprinted in *Literary Reviews and Essays*, 1957.

D398 A STUDY OF SALVINI (Signed "By a Casual Critic")
Pall Mall Gazette (27 March), 1–2; *Pall Mall Budget*, XXXI
(28 March), 9–10.
Reprinted, as Part II ("In London, 1884") of an essay under the
title "Tommaso Salvini," in *The Scenic Art*, 1948.

D399 LADY BARBERINA
Century Magazine, XXVIII (May–July), 18–31, 222–234, 336–
350.
Reprinted in *Tales of Three Cities*, 1884.

D400 THE AUTHOR OF *BELTRAFFIO*
English Illustrated Magazine, I (June–July), 563–573, 628–639.
Reprinted in *The Author of Beltraffio*, 1885.

D. CONTRIBUTIONS TO PERIODICALS

D401 PANDORA
  New York Sun (1 and 8 June), pp. 1:7 and 2 of each issue.
  Reprinted in *Stories Revived*, 1885.

D402 GEORGINA'S REASONS
  New York Sun (20 and 27 July, 3 August), pp. 1:7 and 2 of each issue.
  Reprinted in *Stories Revived*, 1885.

D403 A NEW ENGLAND WINTER
  Century Magazine, XXVIII (August–September), 573–587, 733–743.
  Reprinted in *Tales of Three Cities*, 1884.

D404 THE ART OF FICTION
  Longman's Magazine, IV (September), 502–521; reprinted in the *Writer*, XII (September 1899), 130–141 (presumably unauthorized).
  Reprinted without authorization in *The Art of Fiction*, 1884 (see A25). First authorized book publication in *Partial Portraits*, 1888.

D405 THE PATH OF DUTY
  English Illustrated Magazine, II (December), 240–256.
  Reprinted in *The Author of Beltraffio*, 1885.

1885

D406 THE BOSTONIANS
  Century Magazine, XXIX (February–April), 530–543, 686–700, 893–908; XXX (May–October), 58–66, 256–264, 423–437, 553–568, 692–708, 861–881; XXXI (November–December; January–February 1886), 85–98, 205–214, 337–351, 591–600.
  For first book publication, 1886, see A28.

D407 GEORGE ELIOT'S LIFE [by G. W. Cross]
  Atlantic Monthly, LV (May), 668–678.
  Reprinted, under the title "The Life of George Eliot," in *Partial Portraits*, 1888.

D408 THE PRINCESS CASAMASSIMA
  Atlantic Monthly, LVI (September–December), 289–311, 433–459, 577–602, 721–738; LVII (January–June 1886), 66–90, 145–178, 326–351, 485–507, 645–668, 789–813; LVIII (July–October 1886), 58–76, 209–228, 349–375, 433–448.
  For first book publication, 1886, see A29.

D409 WILLIAM DEAN HOWELLS (With portrait by R. Staudenbaur)
Harper's Weekly, XXX (19 June), 394–395.
Reprinted in *The Shock of Recognition*, edited by Edmund Wilson, 1943.

D410 EDWIN A. ABBEY (With portrait by Napoleon Sarony)
Harper's Weekly, XXX (4 December), 786–787.
Reprinted in part in *A Catalogue of the Drawings by Mr. Edwin A. Abbey for "She Stoops to Conquer"* . . ., 1886 (see B3). Reprinted in full in *Picture and Text*, 1893.

1887

D411 COQUELIN (With portrait by Van Bosch)
Century Magazine, XXXIII (January), 407–413.
Reprinted, with revisions by the author, as an introduction to Constant Coquelin's *Art and the Actor*, 1915.

D412 MISS CONSTANCE FENIMORE WOOLSON (With portrait)
Harper's Weekly, XXXI (12 February), 114–115.
Reprinted, under the title "Miss Woolson," in *Partial Portraits*, 1888.

D413 COUSIN MARIA (Illustrations by C. S. Reinhart)
Harper's Weekly, XXXI (6–20 August), 557–558, 577–578, 593–594.
Reprinted, under the title "Mrs. Temperly," in *A London Life*, 1889.

D414 JOHN S. SARGENT (With portrait and reproductions of three Sargent paintings)
Harper's New Monthly Magazine, LXXV (October), 683–691.
Reprinted, without illustrations, in *Picture and Text*, 1893.

D415 THE LIFE OF EMERSON (Review of James Elliot Cabot's *A Memoir of Ralph Waldo Emerson*)
Macmillan's Magazine, LVII (December), 86–98.
Reprinted, under the title "Emerson," in *Partial Portraits*, 1888.

D416 THE ACTING IN MR. IRVING'S *FAUST* (Unsigned)
Century Magazine, XXXV (December), 311–313.
Reprinted in *The Scenic Art*, 1948.

D417 INTERNATIONAL COPYRIGHT [A LETTER TO THE EXECUTIVE COMMITTEE OF THE AMERICAN COPYRIGHT LEAGUE

D. CONTRIBUTIONS TO PERIODICALS

ON THE OCCASION OF THE AUTHORS' READINGS IN
CHICKERING HALL, NOVEMBER 28, 29, 1887]
The *Critic*, n.s. VIII (10 December), 301–302. An excerpt from
this letter was reprinted in a pamphlet *What American Authors
Think About International Copyright*, New York, 1888. Reprinted
in full in *The Selected Letters of Henry James*, 1955.

1888

D418 LOUISA PALLANT (Illustrations by C. S. Reinhart)
Harper's New Monthly Magazine, LXXVI (February), 336–355.
Reprinted in *The Aspern Papers*, 1888.

D419 THE REVERBERATOR
Macmillan's Magazine, LVII (February–April), 263–275, 366–
378, 415–427; LVIII (May–July), 58–71, 81–94, 161–175.
For first book publication, 1888, see A31.

D420 GUY DE MAUPASSANT
Fortnightly Review, XLIX (March), 364–386.
Reprinted in *Partial Portraits*, 1888.

D421 THE ASPERN PAPERS
Atlantic Monthly, LXI (March–May), 296–315, 461–482, 577–
594.
Reprinted in *The Aspern Papers*, 1888.

D422 ROBERT LOUIS STEVENSON (With portrait by J. W. Alex-
ander)
Century Magazine, XXXV (April), 868–879.
Reprinted in *Partial Portraits*, 1888.

D423 PIERRE LOTI
Fortnightly Review, XLIX (May), 647–664.
Reprinted in *Essays in London and Elsewhere*, 1893.

D424 THE LIAR
Century Magazine, XXXVI (May–June), 123–135, 213–223.
Reprinted in *A London Life*, 1889.

D425 TWO COUNTRIES (Illustrations by C. S. Reinhart)
Harper's New Monthly Magazine, LXXVII (June), 83–116.
Reprinted, under the title "The Modern Warning," in *The Aspern
Papers*, 1888.

D426 A LONDON LIFE
Scribner's Magazine, III (June), 671–688; IV (July–September),
64–82, 238–249, 319–330.
Reprinted in *A London Life*, 1889.

D427 THE LESSON OF THE MASTER
Universal Review, I (16 July and 15 August), 342–365, 494–523.
Reprinted in *The Lesson of the Master*, 1892.

D428 THE PATAGONIA
English Illustrated Magazine, V (August–September), 707–718, 769–783.
Reprinted in *A London Life*, 1889.

D429 THE JOURNAL OF THE BROTHERS DE GONCOURT (Review)
Fortnightly Review, L (October), 501–520.
Reprinted in *Essays in London and Elsewhere*, 1893.

D430 LONDON (With 13 illustrations by Joseph Pennell)
Century Magazine, XXXVII (December), 219–239.
Reprinted, without illustrations, in *Essays in London and Elsewhere*, 1893.

1889

D431 THE TRAGIC MUSE
Atlantic Monthly, LXIII (January–June), 1–20, 184–205, 289–309, 509–528, 629–648, 764–785; LXIV (July–December), 44–64, 245–265, 389–410, 537–556, 652–669, 735–752; LXV (January–May 1890), 54–70, 208–224, 320–337, 444–465, 588–604.
For first book publication, 1890, see A34.

D432 AN ANIMATED CONVERSATION
Scribner's Magazine, V (March), 371–384.
Reprinted in *Essays in London and Elsewhere*, 1893.

D433 OUR ARTISTS IN EUROPE (With nine portraits and illustrations)
Harper's New Monthly Magazine, LXXIX (June), 50–66.
Reprinted, under the title "Black and White," in *Picture and Text*, 1893. Seven of the illustrations are reproduced in *Picture and Text*.

D434 AFTER THE PLAY
New Review, I (June), 30–46.
Reprinted in *Picture and Text*, 1893.

D435 [THE SUMMER SCHOOL AT DEERFIELD] (Letter)
New York Tribune (4 August), II, 10 : 3–4.
Reprinted, under the title "The Modern Novel," in *The Author*, I (15 August 1889), 116. Also reprinted, under the title "The Great Form," in Morton Dauwen Zabel's *Literary Opinion in America*, Revised Edition, 1951.

D436 GUY DE MAUPASSANT
Harper's Weekly, XXXIII (19 October), 834–835.
Reprinted as an introduction to *The Odd Number*, selected tales of De Maupassant, 1889.

D437 THE SOLUTION
New Review, I (December), 666–690; II (January–February 1890), 76–90, 161–171.
Reprinted in *The Lesson of the Master*, 1892.

D438 THE BRITISH THEATRE LIBRE (Letter)
The *Weekly Comedy* (London), I (21 December), 6.

1890

D439 DAUMIER, CARICATURIST (With uncredited portrait and 17 Daumier illustrations)
Century Magazine, XVII (January), 402–413.
Reprinted with minor revisions under the title "Honoré Daumier," in *Picture and Text*, 1893, without illustrations.
Serial text was reprinted as a book, 1954 (see A97).

D440 BROWNING IN WESTMINSTER ABBEY (Unsigned)
The *Speaker*, I (4 January), 10–12.
Reprinted in *Essays in London and Elsewhere*, 1893.

D441 CHARLES S. REINHART (With portrait by T. A. Butler)
Harper's Weekly, XXXIV (14 June), 471–472.
Reprinted in *Picture and Text*, 1893.

D442 PORT TARASCON: THE LAST ADVENTURES OF THE ILLUSTRIOUS TARTARIN. BY ALPHONSE DAUDET. [TRANSLATION AND TRANSLATOR'S PREFACE BY HENRY JAMES] (Illustrations by Rossi, Myrbach, Montégut, Bieler, and Montenard)
Harper's New Monthly Magazine, LXXXI (June–November), 3–25, 166–185, 327–340, 521–537, 683–699, 937–955.
For first book publication, 1890, see B6.

1891

D443 THE PUPIL
Longman's Magazine, XVII (March–April), 512–531, 611–632.
Reprinted in *The Lesson of the Master*, 1892.

D444 THE SCIENCE OF CRITICISM
New Review, IV (May), 398–402.
Also appeared, under the title "Literary Criticism, Valuable and Otherwise," in the *New York Herald* (10 May 1891), 14 : 5–6;

under the title "Honest Criticism," in the *Philadelphia Press* (10 May 1891), 22 : 1–4; and under the title "Literary Criticism," in the *Author*, III (15 May 1891), 67–69. These three appearances are believed to have been unauthorized.

Reprinted, under the title "Criticism," in *Essays in London and Elsewhere*, 1893.

D445 BROOKSMITH
Harper's Weekly, XXXV (2 May), 321–323. With illustrative title-sketch by Charles Howard Johnson. Also in *Black and White*, I (2 May), 417–420, 422. Illustrated by John H. Bacon.
Reprinted in *The Lesson of the Master*, 1892.

D446 ON THE OCCASION OF *HEDDA GABLER*
New Review, IV (June), 519–530.
Reprinted, as Part I of "Henrik Ibsen," in *Essays in London and Elsewhere*, 1893.

D447 THE MARRIAGES
Atlantic Monthly, LXVIII (August), 233–252.
Reprinted in *The Lesson of the Master*, 1892.

D448 THE CHAPERON
Atlantic Monthly, LXVIII (November–December), 659–670, 721–735.
Reprinted in *The Real Thing*, 1893.

D449 SIR EDMUND ORME (Illustrated by John H. Bacon)
Black and White, first Christmas issue (published 25 November), 8, 11–15.
Reprinted in *The Lesson of the Master*, 1892.

1892

D450 JAMES RUSSELL LOWELL
Atlantic Monthly, LXIX (January), 35–50.
Reprinted in *Essays in London and Elsewhere*, 1893.

D451 MRS. HUMPHRY WARD (With portrait by Julian Story) (Signed "H.J.")
English Illustrated Magazine, IX (February), 399–401.
Reprinted in *Essays in London and Elsewhere*, 1893.

D452 NONA VINCENT (Illustrations by W. J. Hennessy)
English Illustrated Magazine, IX (February–March), 365–376, 491–502.
Reprinted in *The Real Thing*, 1893.

D. CONTRIBUTIONS TO PERIODICALS

D453 THE PRIVATE LIFE
Atlantic Monthly, LXIX (April), 463–483.
Reprinted in *The Private Life*, 1893.

D454 THE REAL THING (Illustrated by Rudolf Blind)
Black and White, III (16 April), 502–507.
Reprinted in *The Real Thing*, 1893.

D455 LORD BEAUPREY
Macmillan's Magazine, LXV (April), 465–474; LXVI (May–June), 64–74, 133–144.
Reprinted, under the title "Lord Beaupré," in *The Private Life*, 1893.

D456 WOLCOTT BALESTIER (With photogravure portrait)
Cosmopolitan Magazine, XIII (May), 43–47.
Reprinted as an introduction to *The Average Woman* by Wolcott Balestier, 1892.

D457 THE VISIT (Illustrated by J. Finnemore)
Black and White, III (28 May), 696–700.
Reprinted, under the title "The Visits," in *The Private Life*, 1893.

D458 JERSEY VILLAS (Illustrations by Irving R. Wiles)
Cosmopolitan Magazine, XIII (July–August), 314–328, 433–449.
Reprinted, under the title "Sir Dominick Ferrand," in *The Real Thing*, 1893.

D459 COLLABORATION
English Illustrated Magazine, IX (September), 911–921.
Reprinted in *The Private Life* (English edition), 1893. Also in *The Wheel of Time*, 1893.

D460 GREVILLE FANE (Illustrated by A. Forestier)
Illustrated London News, CI (17 and 24 September), 361–363, 393–395.
Reprinted in *The Real Thing*, 1893.

D461 THE GRAND CANAL (Illustrated by Alexander Zezzos)
Scribner's Magazine, XII (November), 531–550.
Reprinted in *Great Streets of the World*, 1892, with the original illustrations.

D462 THE WHEEL OF TIME (Illustrated by A. B. Wenzell and George Wharton Edwards)
Cosmopolitan Magazine, XIV (December; January 1893), 215–228, 348–360.
Reprinted in *The Private Life* (English edition), 1893. Also in *The Wheel of Time*, 1893.

D463 OWEN WINGRAVE (Illustrated by Sahr)
The *Graphic*, Christmas number (published 28 November), 11,
14, 15, 18, 22, 26, 30.
Reprinted in *The Private Life* (English edition), 1893. Also in
The Wheel of Time, 1893.

1893

D464 IBSEN'S NEW PLAY (Critical notes on *The Master Builder*)
Pall Mall Gazette (17 February), 1–2.
Reprinted, as Part II of "Henrik Ibsen," in *Essays in London and
Elsewhere*, 1893, omitting one paragraph which was restored in
a reprinting of the article in *Theatre and Friendship*, 1932.

D465 GUSTAVE FLAUBERT (Review of *Correspondance de Gustave
Flaubert, Quatrième Série*)
Macmillan's Magazine, LXVII (March), 332–343.
Reprinted in *Essays in London and Elsewhere*, 1893.

D466 FRANCES ANNE KEMBLE
Temple Bar, XCVII (April), 503–525.
Reprinted in *Essays in London and Elsewhere*, 1893.

D467 THE MIDDLE YEARS
Scribner's Magazine, XIII (May), 609–620.
Reprinted in *Terminations*, 1895.

1894

D468 THE DEATH OF THE LION
The *Yellow Book*, I (April), 7–52.
Reprinted in *Terminations*, 1895.

D469 GEORGE DU MAURIER (With portrait)
Harper's Weekly, XXXVIII (14 April), 341–342.

D470 THE COXON FUND
The *Yellow Book*, II (July), 290–360.
Reprinted in *Terminations*, 1895.

1895

D471 THE NEXT TIME
The *Yellow Book*, VI (July), 11–59.
Reprinted in *Embarrassments*, 1896.

D. CONTRIBUTIONS TO PERIODICALS

1896

D472 THE FIGURE IN THE CARPET
Cosmopolis, I (January–February), 41–59, 373–392.
Reprinted in *Embarrassments*, 1896.

D473 GLASSES
Atlantic Monthly, LXXVII (February), 145–173.
Reprinted in *Embarrassments*, 1896.

D474 DUMAS THE YOUNGER
Boston Herald (23 February), III, 33 : 1–4; *New York Herald* (23 February), VI, 5 : 1–4. Also, under the title "On the Death of Dumas the Younger," in the *New Review*, XIV (March), 288–302. Reprinted, under the title "Dumas the Younger, 1895," in *Notes on Novelists*, 1914.

D475 THE OLD THINGS
Atlantic Monthly, LXXVII (April–June), 433–450, 631–640, 721–737; LXXVIII (July–October), 58–74, 201–218, 376–390, 518–530.
For first book publication, under the title *The Spoils of Poynton*, 1897, see A48.

D476 THE WAY IT CAME
The *Chap Book*, IV (1 May), 562–593; *Chapman's Magazine of Fiction*, IV (May), 95–120.
Reprinted in *Embarrassments*, 1896. Retitled "The Friends of the Friends," in *The Novels and Tales of Henry James* (New York Edition), 1907–09.

D477 THE OTHER HOUSE (Illustrated by Walter Paget)
Illustrated London News, CIX (4 July–26 September), 9–12, 41–43, 73–76, 105–108, 137–140, 169–172, 201–203, 233–235, 265–268, 297–299, 329–332, 361–363, 395–398.
For first book publication, 1896, see A47.

D478 MR. HENRY IRVING'S PRODUCTION OF *CYMBELINE* (With portraits of Ellen Terry)
Harper's Weekly, XL (21 November), 1150.
Reprinted in *The Scenic Art*, 1948.

1897

D479 SHE AND HE: RECENT DOCUMENTS [ON THE FRIENDSHIP OF GEORGE SAND AND ALFRED DE MUSSET]
The *Yellow Book*, XII (January), 15–38.
Reprinted, under the title "George Sand, 1897," in *Notes on Novelists*, 1914.

D480 WHAT MAISIE KNEW

The *Chap Book*, VI (15 January–1 May), 214–219, 253–260, 289–295, 326–331, 361–367, 395–401, 428–434, 478–485; VII (15 May–1 August), 16–25, 57–62, 90–97, 125–131, 162–168, 198–209.

Also in the *New Review*, XVI (February–June), 113–128, 241–263, 352–372, 469–490, 581–602; XVII (July–September), 1–20, 216–240, 334–356.

There are variations between the two serial texts, the last three parts of the *New Review* text being considerably abridged.

For first book publication, 1897, see A49.

D481 LONDON (Dated 1 January)

[Irving's *Richard III*—Elizabeth Robins's *Little Eyolf*—*John Gabriel Borkman*—*As You Like It* at the St. James's—The Art Show at the New Gallery: Watts, Leighton]

Harper's Weekly, XLI (23 January), 78.

Reprinted in part, under the title "Irving's *Richard III*; *Little Eyolf*," in *The Scenic Art*, 1948. Another section was reprinted, under the title "The New Gallery, 1897," in *The Painter's Eye*, 1956.

D482 LONDON (Dated 15 January)

[Archer's translation of *John Gabriel Borkman*—Lord Roberts's *Forty-one Years in India*—George Meredith's *Evan Harrington* in the Definitive Edition—Robert Louis Stevenson's Definitive Edition—Mrs Edward Ridley's *Story of Aline*—Mrs Meynell's *The Children*—Clement Shorter's *Charlotte Brontë and Her Circle*]

Harper's Weekly, XLI (6 February), 134–135.

Reprinted in part, under the title "London Notes, January 1897," in *Notes on Novelists*, 1914.

D483 LONDON (Dated 1 February)

[J. G. Marks's *Life and Letters of Frederick Walker*—Burlington House Exhibition: Leighton and Ford Madox Brown]

Harper's Weekly, XLI (20 February), 183.

Reprinted in part, under the title "Lord Leighton and Ford Madox Brown, 1897," in *The Painter's Eye*, 1956.

D484 LONDON (Dated 3 March)

[Lord Roberts's *Forty-one Years in India*—Sir William Hunter's *The Thackerays in India*—Mrs Steel's *On the Face of the Waters*—Gibbons's *Autobiography*—Meredith's *The Idea of Comedy*—Elizabeth Robins's production of *Mariana*]

Harper's Weekly, XLI (27 March), 315.

D485 LONDON (Dated 3 April)
[William Archer's article, "The Blight of the Drama"—Forbes-Robertson and Mrs Pat [Campbell] as Nelson and Lady Hamilton in *Nelson's Enchantress*—The Building of Her Majesty's Theatre—Charles Wyndham's production of Henry Arthur Jones's *The Physician*—Pinero's *Princess and the Butterfly*]
Harper's Weekly, XLI (24 April), 411.
Reprinted, under the title "The Blight of the Drama," in *The Scenic Art*, 1948.

D486 LONDON (Dated 5 May)
[The Art Exhibitions—Millais—Leighton—Abbey—Sargent—Anatole France's *L'Orme du Mail*]
Harper's Weekly, XLI (5 June), 562–563.
Reprinted in part, under the title "The Guildhall and the Royal Academy, 1897," in *The Painter's Eye*, 1956.

D487 LONDON (Dated 1 June)
[The Jubilee—Grafton Galleries—Whistler—Sargent—Severn's Keats—Watts's William Morris]
Harper's Weekly, XLI (26 June), 639–640.
Reprinted in part, under the title "London Notes, June 1897," in *Notes on Novelists*, 1914. Another section was reprinted under the title "The Grafton Galleries, 1897," in *The Painter's Eye*, 1956.

D488 LONDON (Dated 1 July)
[The English Novel and the Work of George Gissing—Pierre Loti]
Harper's Weekly, XLI (31 July), 754.
Reprinted, under the title "London Notes, July 1897," in *Notes on Novelists*, 1914.

D489 LONDON (Dated 31 July)
[The Jubilee—Bourget's Oxford Lecture on Flaubert—The Death of Mrs Oliphant—Mrs Oliphant's *Kirsteen*]
Harper's Weekly, XLI (21 August), 834.
Reprinted, under the title "London Notes, August 1897," in *Notes on Novelists*, 1914.

D490 GEORGE DU MAURIER
Harper's New Monthly Magazine, XCV (September), 594–609.

D491 OLD SUFFOLK
Harper's Weekly, XLI (25 September), 946.
Reprinted in *English Hours*, 1905.

D492 ALPHONSE DAUDET
Literature, I (25 December), 306–307.
Reprinted in *French Writers and American Women*, 1960.

1898

D493 JOHN DELAVOY
Cosmopolis, IX (January–February), 1–21, 317–332.
Reprinted in *The Soft Side*, 1900.

D494 THE TURN OF THE SCREW (Illustrated by John LaFarge and Eric Pape)
Collier's Weekly, XX (27 January–2 April); XXI (9–16 April).
Each issue is newly paginated; page ciphers are therefore eliminated to avoid confusion.
Reprinted in *The Two Magics*, 1898.

D495 AMERICAN LETTER: THE QUESTION OF THE OPPORTUNITIES
Literature, II (26 March), 356–358.
Reprinted in Morton Dauwen Zabel's *Literary Opinion in America*, Revised Edition, 1951.

D496 THE STORY-TELLER AT LARGE: MR. HENRY HARLAND
Fortnightly Review, LXIX (April), 650–654.
Reprinted in *The American Essays of Henry James*, 1956.

D497 THE LATE JAMES PAYN
Illustrated London News, CXII (9 April), 500.
A fragment of the final paragraph had appeared a week earlier, 2 April, in the same publication, under the title "A Tribute from Mr. Henry James to James Payn," with facsimile autograph (p. 465). The holograph manuscript, now in the Ashley Collection of the British Museum, reveals that editorial cuts were made in the published text.

D498 AMERICAN LETTER
(The Quantity of Fiction—The Noticeable—The International and the Local—Mr Hamlin Garland—Gertrude Atherton's *American Wives and English Husbands*—The Deviation of the Book)
Literature, II (9 April), 422–423.
Reprinted in *The American Essays of Henry James*, 1956.

D499 AMERICAN LETTER
(Published Letters of Ulysses S. Grant to E. B. Washburne—Walt Whitman's Letters to Peter Doyle (*Calamus*, edited by

R. M. Bucke)—Richard Harding Davis's *A Year from A Correspondent's Note-Book*)
Literature, II (16 April), 452–453.
The *Calamus* portion was reprinted in F. O. Matthiessen, *The James Family* (New York, 1947). Reprinted in full in *The American Essays of Henry James*, 1956.

D500 AMERICAN LETTER
(Theodore Roosevelt's *American Ideals and Other Essays Social and Political*—W. A. Dunning's *Essays on the Civil War and Reconstruction*—Walter Wyckoff's *The Workers*)
Literature, II (23 April), 483–484.
Reprinted in *The American Essays of Henry James*, 1956.

D501 AMERICAN LETTER
(Winston Churchill's *The Celebrity*—Gertrude Atherton's *His Fortunate Grace*—Bret Harte's *Tales of Trail and Town*)
Literature, II (30 April), 511–512.
Reprinted in *The American Essays of Henry James*, 1956.

D502 AMERICAN LETTER
(Walt Whitman's *The Wound Dresser*—George Cary Eggleston's *Southern Soldier Stories*—Paul Leicester Ford's *The Honorable Peter Stirling*)
Literature, II (7 May), 541–542.
Reprinted in *The American Essays of Henry James*, 1956.

D503 AMERICAN LETTER
(Sanford H. Cobb's *Story of the Palatines: An Episode in Colonial History*—Charles F. Dole's *The Coming People*—Norman Hapgood's *Literary Statesmen and Others*)
Literature, II (21 May), 593–594.
Reprinted in *The American Essays of Henry James*, 1956.

D504 AMERICAN LETTER
(Military Novels—Robert W. Chambers's *Lorraine, A Romance*—J. A. Altsheler's *A Soldier of Manhattan*—Capt. Charles King's *The General's Double*)
Literature, II (28 May), 620–621.
Reprinted in *The American Essays of Henry James*, 1956.

D505 AMERICAN LETTER
(American Magazines—Hugh L. Willoughby's *Across the Everglades*—Thomas W. Higginson's *Cheerful Yesterdays*—John Jay Chapman's *Emerson and Other Essays*)
Literature, II (11 June), 676–678.
Reprinted in *The American Essays of Henry James*, 1956.

D. CONTRIBUTIONS TO PERIODICALS

D506 AMERICAN LETTER
(E. L. Godkin's *Unforeseen Tendencies of Democracy*—Nicholas Murray Butler's *The Meaning of Education*—Three Interesting Articles on Education in the *Atlantic Monthly* for June)
Literature, II (25 June), 730–732.
Reprinted in *The American Essays of Henry James*, 1956.

D507 AMERICAN LETTER
(The Novel of Dialect—Charles E. Craddock's *The Juggler*—Miss Sarah Barnwell Elliott's *The Durket Sperret*—William Dean Howells's *The Story of A Play*—Mary E. Wilkins's *Silence*)
Literature, III (9 July), 17–19.
Reprinted in *The American Essays of Henry James*, 1956.

D508 PROSPER MÉRIMÉE
Literature, III (23 July), 66–68.
Reprinted in *French Writers and American Women*, 1960.

D509 THE AWKWARD AGE
Harper's Weekly, XLII (1 October–10 December, 24–31 December), 966–967, 990–991, 1011–1015, 1035–1039, 1059–1063, 1082–1087, 1106–1110, 1130–1135, 1154–1158, 1178–1183, 1202–1207, 1266–1271, 1290–1295; XLIII (7 Jan 1899), 13–18.
For first book publication, 1899, see A53.

D510 THE GIVEN CASE (Illustrated by Albert Herter)
Collier's Weekly, XXII (31 Dec), 14–16; XXII (7 Jan 1899), 14–16.
Reprinted in *The Soft Side*, 1900.

1899

D511 THE GREAT CONDITION
Anglo-Saxon Review, I (June), 7–38.
Reprinted in *The Soft Side*, 1900.

D512 "EUROPE"
Scribner's Magazine, XXV (June), 753–762.
Reprinted in *The Soft Side*, 1900.

D512a TWO OLD HOUSES AND THREE YOUNG WOMEN
The Independent, LI (7 September), 2406–2412.
Reprinted in *Italian Hours*, 1909.

D513 THE PRESENT LITERARY SITUATION IN FRANCE
North American Review, CLXIX (October), 488–500.
Reprinted in *French Writers and American Women*, 1960.

D514 PASTE (Illustrated by Howard Chandler Christy)
Frank Leslie's Popular Monthly, XLIX (December), 175–189.
Reprinted in *The Soft Side*, 1900.

D. CONTRIBUTIONS TO PERIODICALS

D515 THE REAL RIGHT THING (Illustrated by Howard Pyle)
Collier's Weekly, XXIV (16 December), 22, 24.
Reprinted in *The Soft Side*, 1900.

1900

D516 THE GREAT GOOD PLACE
Scribner's Magazine, XXVII (January), 99–112.
Reprinted in *The Soft Side*, 1900.

D517 THE LETTERS OF ROBERT LOUIS STEVENSON
North American Review, CLXX (January), 61–77.
Reprinted in *Notes on Novelists*, 1914.

D518 MAUD-EVELYN
Atlantic Monthly, LXXXV (April), 439–455.
Reprinted in *The Soft Side*, 1900.

D519 MISS GUNTON OF POUGHKEEPSIE
Cornhill Magazine, n.s. VIII (May), 603–615; *Truth* (N.Y.), XIX
(May–June), 116–118, 142–143. Illustrated by W. L. Jacobs in
Truth.
Reprinted in *The Soft Side*, 1900.

D520 THE SPECIAL TYPE (Illustrated by Charlotte Harding)
Collier's Weekly, XXV (16 June), 10–11, 14.
Reprinted in *The Better Sort*, 1903.

D521 THE TONE OF TIME
Scribner's Magazine, XXVIII (November), 624–634.
Reprinted in *The Better Sort*, 1903.

D522 BROKEN WINGS (Illustration by Maurice Greiffenhagen and
title decoration by F. C. Gordon)
Century Magazine, LXI (December), 194–203.
Reprinted in *The Better Sort*, 1903.

D523 THE FACES (Illustrated by Albert Herter)
Harper's Bazar, XXXIII (15 December), 2084–2092.
Reprinted, under the title "The Two Faces," in *Cornhill Magazine*,
n.s. X (June 1901), 767–780. Reprinted in *The Better Sort*, 1903.

1901

D524 WINCHELSEA, RYE, AND *DENIS DUVAL* (Illustrated by E. C.
Peixotto)
Scribner's Magazine, XXIX (January), 44–53.
Reprinted in *English Hours*, 1905.

D525 MATILDE SERAO
North American Review, CLXXII (March), 367–380.
Reprinted in *Notes on Novelists*, 1914.

D526 MRS. MEDWIN
Punch, CXXI (28 August–18 September), 160–161, 178–179,
196–197, 214–215.
Reprinted in *The Better Sort*, 1903.

D527 THE BELDONALD HOLBEIN (Illustrated by Lucius Hitchcock)
Harper's New Monthly Magazine, CIII (October), 807–821.
Reprinted in *The Better Sort*, 1903.

D528 EDMOND ROSTAND
Cornhill Magazine, n.s. XI (November), 577–598; the *Critic*,
XXXIX (November), 437–450.
Reprinted in *The Scenic Art*, 1948.

1902

D529 THE STORY IN IT
Anglo-American Magazine, VII (January), 1–13.
Reprinted in *The Better Sort*, 1903.

**D530 BROWNING IN VENICE. BEING RECOLLECTIONS BY THE
LATE MRS. KATHARINE DE KAY BRONSON, WITH A PREFA-
TORY NOTE BY HENRY JAMES**
Cornhill Magazine, n.s. XII (February), James's preface appearing
on pp. 145–149.
The preface appeared separately, under the title "The Late Mrs.
Arthur Bronson," in the *Critic*, XL (February 1902), 162–164.
Reprinted, under the title "Casa Alvisi," in *Italian Hours*, 1909.

D531 FLICKERBRIDGE
Scribner's Magazine, XXXI (February), 170–180.
Reprinted in *The Better Sort*, 1903.

D532 GEORGE SAND: THE NEW LIFE
North American Review, CLXXIV (April), 536–554.
Reprinted, under the title "George Sand, 1899," in *Notes on
Novelists*, 1914.

1903

D533 THE AMBASSADORS
North American Review, CLXXVI (January–June), 138–160,
297–320, 459–480, 634–656, 792–816, 945–968; CLXXVII (July–

December), 138–160, 297–320, 457–480, 615–640, 779–800, 947–968.

For first book publication, 1903, see A58.

D534 ÉMILE ZOLA
Atlantic Monthly, XCII (August), 193–210.
Reprinted in *Notes on Novelists*, 1914.

1904

D535 GABRIELE D'ANNUNZIO (Review of six English translations, 1898–1902)
Quarterly Review, CXCIX (April), 383–419.
Reprinted in *Notes on Novelists*, 1914.

D536 FORDHAM CASTLE
Harper's Magazine, CX (December), 147–158.
Reprinted in *The Novels and Tales of Henry James* (New York Edition), 1907–09, Vol. XVI.

1905

D537 NEW ENGLAND: AN AUTUMN IMPRESSION
North American Review, CLXXX (April–June), 481–501, 641–660, 800–816.
Reprinted in *The American Scene*, 1907.

D538 THE QUESTION OF OUR SPEECH
Appleton's Booklovers Magazine, VI (August), 199–210.
Reprinted in *The Question of Our Speech. The Lesson of Balzac. Two Lectures*, 1905.

D539 THE LESSON OF BALZAC
Atlantic Monthly, XCVI (August), 166–180.
Reprinted in *The Question of Our Speech. The Lesson of Balzac. Two Lectures*, 1905.

D540 NEW YORK AND THE HUDSON: A SPRING IMPRESSION
North American Review, CLXXXI (December), 801–833.
Reprinted in *The American Scene*, 1907.

1906

D541 NEW YORK: SOCIAL NOTES. I.
North American Review, CLXXXII (January), 19–31; *Fortnightly Review*, LXXXV (February), 250–261.
Reprinted in *The American Scene*, 1907.

D542 NEW YORK: SOCIAL NOTES. II.
North American Review, CLXXXII (February), 179–193.
Reprinted in *The American Scene*, 1907.

D543 NEW YORK REVISITED
Harper's Magazine, CXII (February–March, May), 400–406,
603–608, 900–907.
Reprinted in *The American Scene*, 1907.

D544 BOSTON
North American Review, CLXXXII (March), 333–355; *Fort-
nightly Review*, LXXXV (March), 439–459.
Reprinted in *The American Scene*, 1907.

D545 PHILADELPHIA
North American Review, CLXXXII (April), 542–564; *Fort-
nightly Review*, LXXXV (April), 751–771.
Reprinted in *The American Scene*, 1907.

D546 WASHINGTON
North American Review, CLXXXII (May–June), 660–675, 896–
905.
Reprinted in *The American Scene*, 1907.

D547 THE SENSE OF NEWPORT (Illustrated by Jules Guerin, H. D.
Nichols, and Marguerite Downing)
Harper's Magazine, CXIII (August), 343–354.
Reprinted in *The American Scene*, 1907.

D548 BALTIMORE
North American Review, CLXXXIII (August), 250–271.
Reprinted in *The American Scene*, 1907.

D549 RICHMOND, VIRGINIA
Fortnightly Review, LXXXV (November), 850–870.
Reprinted, under the title "Richmond," in *The American Scene*,
1907.

D550 THE SPEECH OF AMERICAN WOMEN
Harper's Bazar, XL (November–December), 979–982, 1103–
1106; XLI (January–February 1907), 17–21, 113–117.
Reprinted in *French Writers and American Women*, 1960.

1907

D551 THE MANNERS OF AMERICAN WOMEN
Harper's Bazar, XLI (April–July), 355–359, 453–458, 537–541,
646–651. Photographic portrait of James by Alice Boughton
illustrates p. 649 of the July issue.
Reprinted in *French Writers and American Women*, 1960.

1908

D552 JULIA BRIDE (Illustrated by W. T. Smedley)
Harper's Magazine, CXVI (March–April), 489–502, 705–713.
Reprinted in *The Novels and Tales of Henry James* (New York
Edition), 1907–09, Vol. XVII.
For first separate book publication, 1909, see A66.

D553 THE MARRIED SON (CHAPTER VII OF *THE WHOLE
FAMILY*) (Illustrated by Alice Barber Stephens)
Harper's Bazar, XLII (June), 530–544.
The serial version of *The Whole Family: A Novel by Twelve
Authors* ran from December 1907 to November 1908. The full
list of authors was given, but no identification was made of
authorship of the individual chapters as published, each serial
part being prefaced with the statement: "Each chapter of this
novel was written by one of the twelve authors whose names
appear above. The intelligent reader will experience no difficulty
in determining which author wrote each chapter—perhaps!"
For first book publication of *The Whole Family*, see B27.

D554 THE JOLLY CORNER
English Review, I (December), 5–35.
Reprinted in *The Novels and Tales of Henry James* (New York
Edition), 1907–09, Vol. XVII.

1909

D555 AN AMERICAN ART-SCHOLAR: CHARLES ELIOT NORTON
Burlington Magazine, XIV (January), 201–204.
Reprinted in *Notes on Novelists*, 1914.

D556 "THE VELVET GLOVE"
English Review, I (March), 625–649.
Reprinted, without quotation marks about title, in *The Finer
Grain*, 1910.

D557 MORA MONTRAVERS
English Review, III (August–September), 27–52, 214–238.
Reprinted in *The Finer Grain*, 1910.

D558 CRAPY CORNELIA
Harper's Magazine, CXIX (October), 690–704.
Reprinted in *The Finer Grain*, 1910.

D559 THE BENCH OF DESOLATION
Putnam's Magazine, VII (October–December; January 1910),
56–62, 151–160, 297–303, 487–494.
Reprinted in *The Finer Grain*, 1910.

1910

D560 IS THERE A LIFE AFTER DEATH?
Harper's Bazar, XLIV (January–February), 26, 128–129.
Reprinted in *In After Days*, 1910.

D561 A ROUND OF VISITS
English Review, V (April–May), 46–60, 246–260.
Reprinted in *The Finer Grain*, 1910.

1912

D562 THE LORD CHAMBERLAIN AND MR. PHILLPOTTS' PLAY
(Letter)
The Times (London), 14 February 1912, 10 : 3.
The letter, subtitled "A Protest From Authors," to the editor of
The Times is believed to have been drafted by William Archer;
twenty-three authors signed their names, including Henry James,
Bernard Shaw, George Moore, H. G. Wells, Arthur Pinero, John
Galsworthy, J. M. Barrie, Arthur Quiller-Couch, and Israel Zang-
will. The letter protested against the censoring of Phillpotts's
The Secret Woman.

So far as is known, Henry James signed his name to three other
public letters besides this one; one in *The Times* and the *Morning
Post* of 4 May 1904, signed by George Meredith and four others,
inviting subscriptions to a memorial to Leslie Stephen; another in
the *Manchester Guardian* on 23 December 1914, captioned "To
Russian Men of Letters: A Greeting from Their English Breth-
ren," with 34 signatories; and an "Address and Presentation to
Mr Robert Ross," which was published in the press on 29 March
1915 and later reprinted with a full list of the signatories in an
eight-page brochure by the Chiswick Press.

D563 A LETTER TO MR. HOWELLS
North American Review, CXCV (April), 558–562.
James's letter was written to be read at a dinner in New York,
on 2 March 1912, celebrating the seventy-fifth birthday of William
Dean Howells. It was published under the title "Literary Recol-
lections," with contributions by Howells and Frank B. Sanborn.
Reprinted in *The Letters of Henry James*, II, 1920.

D564 THE NOVEL IN *THE RING AND THE BOOK*
(An address delivered before the Academic Committee of the
Royal Society of Literature in Commemoration of the Centenary
of the Birth of Robert Browning, 7 May 1912)

D. CONTRIBUTIONS TO PERIODICALS

Transactions of the Royal Society of Literature, 2nd series: Vol. XXXI, Part IV, 1912, 269–298.
Reprinted in *Browning's Centenary*, 1912.
A revised text was published in the *Quarterly Review*, CCXVII (July 1912), 68–87, deleting some of the Browning quotations and adding a lengthy new paragraph (532 words). This text was reprinted in *Notes on Novelists*, 1914.

1913

D565 BALZAC (Unsigned review of Émile Faguet's *Balzac*)
The Times Literary Supplement, No. 597 (19 June), 261–263; *Living Age*, CCLXXVIII (9 August), 364–372.
Reprinted, under the title "Honoré de Balzac, 1913," in *Notes on Novelists*, 1914.

1914

D566 THE YOUNGER GENERATION
The Times Literary Supplement, No. 635 (19 March), 133–134; No. 637 (2 April), 157–158.
Reprinted, revised and enlarged, under the title "The New Novel," in *Notes on Novelists*, 1914. Original text reprinted in *Henry James and H. G. Wells*, 1958.

D567 [VLADIMIR KARÉNINE'S] GEORGE SAND, SA VIE ET SES OEUVRES, VOL. III (Review)
Quarterly Review, CCXX (April), 315–338; *Living Age*, CCLXXXI (13 June), 643–657.
Reprinted, under the title "George Sand, 1914," in *Notes on Novelists*, 1914.

1915

D568 FAMOUS NOVELIST DESCRIBES DEEDS OF U.S. MOTOR CORPS (Datelined London, December 23, [1914])
New York World (4 January), 2 : 5.
An abbreviated, extensively edited version of *The American Volunteer Motor-Ambulance Corps in France*, 1914 (see C2), printed as a news dispatch with the by-line of Henry James.

D569 HENRY JAMES'S FIRST INTERVIEW (With the by-line of Preston Lockwood)
New York Times Magazine (21 March), V, 3–4.

Although this interview bears the by-line of Preston Lockwood it is, as published, almost entirely from the pen of HJ. "No one would suspect," he remarked to his amanuensis (who reported the statement to Henry James, Jr., the author's nephew), "that the interviewed *dictated* the whole interview." The interview contains James's allusion to the English as "this decent and dauntless people." An extract was reprinted, under the title "Henry James on the War," in the *Suffragette*, IV (16 April), 5.

D570 MR. HENRY JAMES ON ENGLAND (A letter to the Editor)
The *Observer* (18 April), 14 : 3.

D571 MR. & MRS. FIELDS
Cornhill Magazine, n.s. XXXIX (July), 29–43. Also, with minor corrections, under the title "Mr. and Mrs. James T. Fields," in the *Atlantic Monthly*, CXVI (July), 21–31.
Reprinted in *The American Essays of Henry James*, 1956.

D572 THE FOUNDING OF THE *NATION*: RECOLLECTIONS OF THE "FAIRIES" THAT ATTENDED ITS BIRTH
The Nation, CI (8 July), 44–45.
Reprinted in *The American Essays of Henry James*, 1956.

D573 THE MIND OF ENGLAND AT WAR
New York Sun (1 August), V, 3; *Philadelphia Ledger Magazine Section* (1 August), 1.
First American appearance of the essay, *The Question of the Mind*, separately published in England, 1915 (see A75).

D574 [JAMES ON HIS NATURALIZATION]
The Times (London), 28 July, 6 : 6.
Quotation from a statement of reasons for requesting naturalization made by James in his application, supplied to *The Times* by J. B. Pinker at James's request. HJ to Pinker, 27 July 1915: "Here is the small passage, embodying my 'reasons,' extracted from my Application; I not only haven't, as I say, any objection at all to its being made public, but quite desire that this should be the case—for the sake of what I feel as the good example!" (Unpublished letter, Yale University Library.)
The published quotation was reprinted in Simon Nowell-Smith's *The Legend of the Master*, 1947.

D575 ALLEN D. LONEY—IN MEMORIAM ["A TRIBUTE BY HENRY JAMES: IN MEMORY OF ALLEN D. LONEY, WHO PERISHED ON THE LUSITANIA."]
New York Times (12 September), I, 4 : 2.

D576 NOVELIST WRITES OF REFUGEES IN ENGLAND

Boston Sunday Herald Supplement (17 October), 6, 8. Also, under the title "Henry James Writes of Refugees in England," in the *New York Times* (17 October), IV, 1–2.

Reprinted, under the title "Refugees in Chelsea," in *The Times Literary Supplement*, No. 740 (23 March 1916), 133–134, with textual changes, including the elimination of one long paragraph (250 words) and the insertion of a new passage (70 words). It is the latter text which was reprinted in *Within the Rim*, 1919. An unsigned prefatory note to the *Times Literary Supplement* publication was written by Logan Pearsall Smith.

1917

D577 WITHIN THE RIM (With an introduction by Elizabeth Asquith)
Fortnightly Review, CVIII (August), 161–171; *Living Age*, CCXCIV (8 September), 579–586; *Harper's Magazine*, CXXXVI (December), 55–61. The *Living Age* publication was probably unauthorized.
Reprinted in *Within the Rim*, 1919, and in *Harper Essays*, 1927.

D578 THE MIDDLE YEARS
Scribner's Magazine, LXII (October–November), 465–476, 608–615.
For first book publication, 1917, see A79.

1922

D579 THREE UNPUBLISHED LETTERS AND A MONOLOGUE BY HENRY JAMES
London Mercury, VI (September), 492–501.
The first two letters are addressed to H. M. Walbrook; the third, referring to the monologue written for her, is addressed to Ruth Draper. The monologue alone appeared also in *Vanity Fair* (December), 53, 108, 110, under the title "The Presentation at Court."
The monologue was reprinted in *The Complete Plays of Henry James*, 1949.

1934

D580 THE AMBASSADORS: PROJECT OF NOVEL (Edited, with introduction and comments, by Edna Kenton)
Hound and Horn, VII (April: June), 541–562.

About one-third of the full "project" was published here. The complete text was published in *The Notebooks of Henry James*, 1947.

1954

D581 'VERY MODERN ROME'—AN UNPUBLISHED ESSAY OF HENRY JAMES (Edited by Richard C. Harrier)
Harvard Library Bulletin, VIII (Spring 1954), 125–140.
The essay was found among the Aldrich papers now in the Houghton Library at Harvard.

1957

D582 AUTOBIOGRAPHY IN FICTION—AN UNPUBLISHED RE-VIEW BY HENRY JAMES (Edited with a prefatory note by Leon Edel) (Review of Bayard Taylor's *John Godfrey's Fortunes*, 1865), *Harvard Library Bulletin*, XI (Spring 1957), 252–257.
The review was discovered among *North American Review* papers presented by Charles Eliot Norton to the Harvard University Library.

1967

D583 AN UNPUBLISHED REVIEW BY HENRY JAMES (Review of Elizabeth Stoddard's *Two Men: A Novel*, 1865, edited with prefatory comments by James Kraft)
Studies in Bibliography (Papers of the Bibliographical Society of the University of Virginia), XX (1967), 270–273.

1968

D584 HENRY JAMES'S LAST DICTATION (Edited by Leon Edel)
Times Literary Supplement, No. 3453 (2 May), 459–460.
Also, under the title "The Deathbed Notes of Henry James," in the *Atlantic Monthly*, CCXXI (June), 103–105.

1970

D585 HENRY JAMES JUVENILIA: A POEM AND A LETTER (A juvenile poem ascribed by Richard Cary, and a letter, the earliest extant (*c*.1849–50), to Katharine Barber James Prince).
Colby Library Quarterly, Series IX (March), 58–63. (Since this publication new evidence shows the letter is misdated and was written by Henry James Jnr., the novelist's nephew.)

D. CONTRIBUTIONS TO PERIODICALS

ADDENDA

E. TRANSLATIONS

Henry James fiercely resisted translation during his writing career. He had, at the beginning, been badly translated; his texts were mutilated to such an extent that he could never reconcile himself to allowing his work to pass through hands other than his own, and in particular into a language for which it had not been designed. Proud of his craft, and having forged an inimitable style, he preferred not to submit to a process that robbed his work of much of its uniqueness.

The early tales which appeared in so flattering a fashion in the *Revue des Deux Mondes*, from the pen of a translator named Lucien Biart (and not, as some have supposed, in Henry James's own translation), were nearly all ruthlessly edited.

In Germany he fared no better. A translation of *The American* (E52) was published with the ending of the story altered. It followed inevitably that as Henry James developed a highly intricate means of expression, he should have felt that he was beyond any rendering into a foreign tongue. An article some years ago criticizing the French for their failure to translate James * brought an immediate rejoinder from French writers who had known him that the novelist did not want to be translated.

And this was expressed with vividness in James's letters to Auguste Monod, one translator who finally persuaded the novelist to allow him to render an earlier work, *The Siege of London*, into French. "Translation," wrote James, "is an effort—though a most flattering one!—to *tear* the hapless

---

* Leon Edel, "A Note on the Translations of H. James in France," *Revue Anglo-Américaine*, VII (August 1930), 539–540.

flesh, and in fact to get rid of so much of it that the living thing bleeds and faints away! forgive the violence of my figure." And he added that he was particularly pleased that his *A Small Boy and Others*, "while yet so tame and intrinsically safe a little animal, is locked fast in the golden cage of the *intraduisible* !"

Even before his death, however (and in spite of the novelist's objections), translation of James was more extensive than has hitherto been believed. Today he has found audiences in all corners of the world, in translations varying from effective renderings, such as *Le Tour d'Écrou* (*The Turn of the Screw*), which first served to present him to contemporary France, to wretched translations-of-translations in which, in some instances, old and corrupt texts have been used. Examples of this appear to be the rendering from the French into Hungarian and Danish of stories published in the *Revue des Deux Mondes*; the text in these instances is thus at two removes from the original.

BENGALI

BOOK:

E(pre-1) ... DAISY MILLER ... Krishnanagar, Homasikha Prakasani bibhag [1956]. Pp. xvi, 100. Translated by Gopal Bhaumik. No copy available for collation.

[SERBO-]CROATIAN

BOOKS:

EI [NASLJEDNICA]. Zagreb, "Zora," 1953. A translation, by Josip Torbarina, of *Washington Square*. No copy available for collation.

EIa ... AMBASADORI ... Beograd [Belgrade], Izdanje Nolit [1955]. ($7\frac{7}{8} \times 5\frac{1}{4}$): [1]⁸ 2–28⁸ 29⁴ [30]², pp. 460. A translation, by Slobodan Jovanović, of *The Ambassadors*.

CZECH

PERIODICAL:

E2 EUGEN PICKERING. *Světozor*, XVII (1883), 99, 111, 125, 137, 147, 158. Translated by Vaclav Černy. The Slovenská Akadémia Vied, Bratislava, has reported that the tale was also issued in book

E. TRANSLATIONS

form as Vol. 186 in the Ustredni Knihovna series, Prague, I. L. Kober [c.1887]. No copy available for collation, but it is believed that James's tale was one of a collected group of short stories.

DANISH

BOOKS:

E3 EUGENE PICKERINGS FØRSTE KJAERLIGHED ... Aalborg, Trykt I Stiftsbogtrykkeriet, 1876. ($6\frac{1}{8} \times 4$): [1]⁶ 2–4⁶ 5² [6]¹, pp. 54. A translation of "Eugene Pickering"; translator not recorded.

E4 FYRSTINDE CASAMASSIMA ... Kristiania, Forlagt af Alb. Cammermeyer, 1887. ($7\frac{15}{16} \times 5\frac{1}{16}$): [i]² 1–28⁸, pp. iv, 448. A translation, by Marie Krohg, of *The Princess Casamassima*.

E5 ... HVAD BARNET VIDSTE ... København & Kristiania, Martins Forlag, 1919. ($7\frac{5}{8} \times 5\frac{1}{4}$): [1]⁸ 2–18⁸, pp. 288. A translation, by Mag. Chr. Mathaeus Hansen, of *What Maisie Knew*.

E6 ... DAISY MILLER ... København & Kristiania, Martins Forlag, 1920. ($7\frac{11}{16} \times 5\frac{1}{4}$): [1]⁸ 2–12⁸, pp. 192. A translation, by Ellen Christensen, of "Daisy Miller," "An International Episode," and "Four Meetings."

E7 ... LØGNEREN OG ANDRE NOVELLER ... København, Thaning & Appels Forlag, 1948. ($8\frac{7}{8} \times 5\frac{15}{16}$): [1]⁸ 2–16⁸ 17² 18⁸ (inserted between 17₁,₂), pp. 276. A translation, by Ove Brusendorff, of "The Liar," "Brooksmith," "The Middle Years," "The Real Thing," "The Altar of the Dead," "The Beast in the Jungle," and "The Birthplace."

E8 ... SKRUEN STRAMMES ... [n.p.], Carit Andersens Forlag [1950]. ($8 \times 5\frac{1}{4}$): [1]⁸ 2–8⁸ 9⁴ 10⁸, pp. 152. A translation, by H. B. J. Cramer, of "The Turn of the Screw."

DUTCH

BOOK:

E9 ... IN DE GREEP ... Amsterdam, N. V. Em. Querido's Uitgeversmij, 1951. ($7\frac{1}{4} \times 4\frac{3}{8}$): 1⁶ [2]² 3–12⁸ [13]² 14⁸, pp. 196. A translation, by M. G. Binnendijk-Paauw, of "The Turn of the Screw."

FINNISH

BOOK:

E9a ... NAISEN MUOTOKUVA ... Porvov, Helsinki, Werner Söderström Osakeyhtiö [1955]. ($7\frac{3}{4} \times 5\frac{3}{8}$): [1]⁸ 2–19¹⁶ 20¹⁰, pp. 612. A translation, by J. A. Hollo, of *The Portrait of A Lady*.

E. TRANSLATIONS
FRENCH

BOOKS:

E10 LES DENTS D'UN TURCO PAR PAUL DE MUSSET. SUIVI DE
LE DERNIER DES VALÉRIUS ... Paris, G. Paetz, 1876. ($5\frac{7}{8}$ ×
$4\frac{1}{16}$): 1–9⁸ 10², pp. 148. A translation, by Lucien Biart, of "The
Last of the Valerii," reprinted from the *Revue des Deux Mondes*,
15 November 1875.

E11 UNE FEMME PHILOSOPHE—LE PREMIER AMOUR D'EUGÈNE
PICKERING ... Paris, G. Paetz, 1876. ($5\frac{7}{8}$ × $4\frac{1}{16}$): 1–9⁸, pp.
144. A translation, by Lucien Biart, of "Eugene Pickering,"
reprinted from the *Revue des Deux Mondes*, 1 January 1876. The
volume also includes tales by Bret Harte and Michel Masson.

E12 ... L'AMÉRICAIN A PARIS ... Paris, Librairie Hachette et Cie.,
1884. In two volumes. ($7\frac{5}{16}$ × $4\frac{5}{8}$): Vol. I, [i]² 1–16⁸, pp. iv, 256.
Vol. II, [i]² 1–16⁸ 17⁴, pp. iv, 264, followed by 8 pp. of advertisements. A translation, by Léon Bochet, of *The American*, reprinted
from *La République Française*, 12 February–6 May 1880.

E13 ... RODERICK HUDSON ... Paris, Librairie Hachette et Cie.,
1884. ($7\frac{5}{16}$ × $4\frac{5}{8}$): [i]² 1–19⁸ 20⁴, pp. iv, 312. Translated by Fr.
Bernard (pseud.).

E14 ... DAISY MILLER UN ÉPISODE INTERNATIONAL QUATRE
RENCONTRES ... Paris, Librairie Fischbacher, 1886. ($7\frac{1}{4}$ ×
$4\frac{11}{16}$): [i]² 1–18 gathered in alternate 12's and 6's (1¹² 2⁶ 3¹² etc.)
19⁴, pp. iv, 332. A translation, by Mme F. Pillon, of "Daisy
Miller," "An International Episode," and "Four Meetings."

E15 ... LE SORT DE POYNTON ... Paris, Calmann-Lévy, 1929.
($7\frac{1}{2}$ × $5\frac{1}{8}$): [i]² 1–15⁸ 16², pp. iv, 244. A translation, by Mme
[Simone] David, of *The Spoils of Poynton*, reprinted from *La
Revue de Paris*, 15 July–15 September 1928. Reissued, 1954,
under the title *Les Dépouilles de Poynton*.

E16 ... DANS LA CAGE SUIVI DE L'ÉLÈVE ET DE L'AUTEL DES
MORTS ... Paris, Librairie Stock, 1929. ($7\frac{3}{8}$ × 5): [i]⁶ 1–15⁸,
pp. xii, 240. A translation, by M. Lanoire and Denyse Clairouin,
of *In the Cage*; by L. Wehrlé and M. Lanoire, of "The Pupil,"
reprinted from *La Revue de Paris*, 1 and 15 June 1921; by Denyse
Clairouin, of "The Altar of the Dead," reprinted from *La Revue
de Paris*, 1 November 1925.

E17 ... LE TOUR D'ÉCROU SUIVI DE LES PAPIERS DE JEFFREY
ASPERN ... Paris, Librairie Stock, 1929. ($7\frac{7}{16}$ × 5): [i]⁶ 1–21⁸

22^4, pp. xii, 344. A translation, by M. Le Corbeiller, of "The Turn of the Screw" and "The Aspern Papers," the latter being reprinted from the *Journal des Débats*, 7 October–7 December 1920, at which time the translation was credited to Mme Le Corbeiller.

E18 ...LA BÊTE DANS LA JUNGLE...[Paris] Éditions Victor Attinger [1929]. $(7\frac{9}{16} \times 5\frac{7}{16})$: $[1]^8$ 2–8^8 9^6, pp. 140. A translation, by Marc Chadourne, of "The Beast in the Jungle," reprinted from the *Revue Hebdomadaire*, 8–22 September 1928.

E19 ...UN PORTRAIT DE FEMME... Paris, Librairie Stock, 1933. $(7 \times 4\frac{3}{4})$: $[1]^8$ 2–44^8, pp. 704. A translation, by Philippe Neel, of *The Portrait of A Lady*.

E20 ...CE QUE SAVAIT MAISIE...[Paris] Robert Laffont, 1947. $(7\frac{1}{8} \times 4\frac{5}{8})$: $[1]^8$ 2–22^8, pp. 352. A translation, by Marguerite Yourcenar, of *What Maisie Knew*. With a preface by André Maurois.

E21 ...LES AMBASSADEURS... Paris, Robert Laffont [1950]. $(7\frac{7}{8} \times 5\frac{3}{4})$: gathered in 16's, $[1–16]^{16}$; signed in 8's, $[1]^8$ 2–32^8, pp. 512. A translation, by Georges Belmont, of *The Ambassadors*. With a translated preface by Graham Greene, reprinted from *The English Novelists*, edited by Derek Verschoyle (London, 1936). The translation contains the reversed chapters of the American editions. (See A58b.)

E22 ...LES AILES DE LA COLOMBE... Paris, Robert Laffont [1953]. $(8 \times 5\frac{1}{2})$: $[1]^{16}$ 2–15^{16} 16^8, pp. 496. A translation, by Marie Tadié, of *The Wings of the Dove*.

E23 ...LES AMIS DES AMIS...[Paris] Editions Arcanes [1953]. $(7\frac{1}{2} \times 5\frac{1}{2})$: [unsigned: 1–$6^4$], pp. 48. A translation, by Marie Canavaggia, of "The Friends of the Friends."

E24 ...WASHINGTON SQUARE... Paris, Éditions Denoël [1953]. $(8\frac{3}{16} \times 5\frac{9}{16})$: $[1]^{16}$ 2–9^{16} 10^6, pp. 300. Translated by Camille Dutourd. With an introduction by Pierre Martory.

E25 ...CARNETS... Paris, Éditions Denoël [1954]. $(9 \times 5\frac{5}{8})$: $[1]^{16}$ 2–14^{16} 15^8, pp. 464. A translation, by Louise Servicen, of *The Notebooks of Henry James*, edited by F. O. Matthiessen and Kenneth B. Murdock.

E26 ...LA COUPE D'OR... Paris, Robert Laffont [1954]. $(8 \times 5\frac{5}{8})$: $[1]^8$ 2–38^8, pp. 608. A translation, by Marguerite Glotz, of *The Golden Bowl*.

E. TRANSLATIONS

E27 ... LES EUROPÉENS ... Paris, Éditions Albin Michel [1955]. $(7\frac{7}{16} \times 4\frac{11}{16})$: $[1]^8$ $2-15^8$, pp. 240. A translation, by Denise Von Moppès, of *The Europeans*.

E28 ... LES BOSTONIENNES ... Paris, Éditions Denoël [1955]. $(8\frac{1}{4} \times 5\frac{1}{2})$: $[1]^{16}$ $2-12^{16}$ 13^8 14^{16}, pp. 432. A translation, by Jeanne Collin-Lemercier, of *The Bostonians*.

E28a ... L'ÂGE DIFFICILE ... Paris, Éditions Denoël [1956]. $(8\frac{3}{16} \times 5\frac{1}{2})$: $[1]^8$ $2-23^8$ 24^4, pp. 376. A translation, by Michel Sager, of *The Awkward Age*.

E28b ... L'IMAGE DANS LE TAPIS ... Paris, Éditions Pierre Horay [1957]. $(7\frac{1}{2} \times 5\frac{1}{2})$: [unsigned: $1-14^8$ 15^6], pp. 236. A translation, by Marie Canavaggia, of "The Figure in the Carpet."

ANTHOLOGY:

E28c LES VINGT MEILLEURES NOUVELLES AMERICAINES ... textes choisis et présentés par Alain Bosquet. [Paris] Éditions Seghers [1957]. $(8\frac{1}{4} \times 5\frac{5}{16})$: $[1]^8$ $2-29^8$ ($[1_1]$ and 29_8 serve as paste-down end-papers); pp. 460. Contains "A Round of Visits" ("Une Série de Visites"), pp. [131]–163, translated by Arlette Rosenblum.

PERIODICALS:

E29 LE DERNIER DES VALERIUS. *Revue des Deux Mondes*, n.s. XII (15 November 1875), 431–455. Reprinted in the *Indépendance Belge*, 21–27 November, 1875. A translation, by Lucien Biart, of "The Last of the Valerii."

E30 LE PREMIER AMOUR D'EUGÈNE PICKERING—UNE FEMME PHILOSOPHE. *Revue des Deux Mondes*, n.s. XIII (1 January 1876), 153–179. A translation, by Lucien Biart, of "Eugene Pickering."

E31 LA MADONE DE L'AVENIR. *Revue des Deux Mondes*, n.s. XIV (1 April 1876), 590–617. A translation, by Lucien Biart, of "The Madonna of the Future."

E32 COUSIN ET COUSINE. *Revue des Deux Mondes*, n.s. XVII (1 October 1876), 512–553. A translation, by Lucien Biart, of "A Passionate Pilgrim."

E33 QUATRES RENCONTRES. *Revue des Deux Mondes*, n.s. XXX (15 December 1878), 904–928. Reprinted in *L'Union Libérale Democratique de Seine-et-Oise*, 27 April, 1, 4, 8, 11, 15, 18, 22, and 25 May 1879. A translation of "Four Meetings"; translator not recorded.

E34 PENSION BOURGEOISE. *Revue Britannique*, Vol. 5 for 1879 (September 1879), 97–152. A translation of "The Pension Beaurepas"; translator identified only by the initial "A."

E35 L'AMÉRICAIN À PARIS. *Le République Française*, 12 February– 6 May 1880, on p. 1 of each issue. Published in 70 parts (numbered 1–21 and 23–71; no text eliminated). A translation, by Léon Bochet, of *The American*.

E36 DAISY MILLER. *Revue Britannique*, Vol. 2 for 1883 (March– April 1883), 155–181, 441–475. Translated by Hephell (Pseudonym for several translators). This was the first of three translations of the tale (see also E14 and E48).

E37 ROMANS AMÉRICAINS: LES BOSTONNIENS DE HENRY JAMES. *Bibliothèque Universelle et Revue Suisse*, XXXI (August 1886), 363–386. One of a series of digests by Paul Gervais. The actual synopsis appears on pp. 366–386, and includes extensive direct quotation, in translation, of *The Bostonians*.

E38 PERLE FAUSSE. *Revue Bleue*, 5th Series, IX (18 January 1908), 73–81. A translation, by Auguste Monod, of "Paste."

E39 LA CONQUÊTE DE LONDRES. *Mercure de France*, C (16 November–1 December 1912), 303–348, 549–593. A translation, by Auguste Monod, of "The Siege of London."

E40 [LA DESTRUCTION DE LA CATHÉDRALE DE REIMS]. *Journal des Débats*, 10 October 1914, 2 : 3. Translation by Alfred de Sainte-André of an extract from a letter to Edith Wharton, read at a meeting of the Académie Française on 9 October 1914. Reprinted in Marie-Reine Garnier's *Henry James et la France* (Paris, 1927). The passage is the first paragraph of the letter to Mrs Wharton of 21 September 1914 (Lubbock, *Letters*, II).

E41 LES PAPIERS DE JEFFREY ASPERN. *Journal des Débats*, 7 October–7 December 1920. Published in 35 parts; erroneously numbered Part 28 on both 23 and 27 November. A translation, by Mme Le Corbeiller, of "The Aspern Papers."

E42 L'ÉLÈVE. *La Revue de Paris*, Vol. III for 1921 (1 and 15 June 1921), 472–490, 733–768. A translation by L. Wehrlé and M. Lanoire, of "The Pupil."

E43 LA LEÇON DU MAÎTRE. *Revue Hebdomadaire*, Vol. VIII for 1922 (5, 12, and 19 August 1922), 5–43, 155–185, 339–354. A translation, by Mme Charles Du Bos, of "The Lesson of the Master"; prefatory note by Charles Du Bos.

E. TRANSLATIONS

E44 LE MOTIF DANS LE TAPIS. *Revue de Genève*, Nos. 30–32 (December 1922–February 1923), 693–701; 42–65, 185–201. A translation, by S.-E. Laboureur, of "The Figure in the Carpet"; "Remarques" by Charles Du Bos, pp. 818–820 of the December issue.

E45 L'AUTEL DES MORTS. *La Revue de Paris*, Vol. VI for 1925 (1 November 1925), 83–125. A translation, by Denyse Clairouin, of "The Altar of the Dead."

E46 LE SORT DE POYNTON. *La Revue de Paris*, Vol. IV for 1928 (15 July–15 August 1928), 323–346, 654–692, 883–914; Vol. V for 1928 (1 and 15 September 1928), 168–192, 428–465. A translation, by Madame [Simone] David, of *The Spoils of Poynton*.

E47 LA BÊTE DANS LA JUNGLE. *Revue Hebdomadaire*, Vol. IX for 1928 (8–22 September 1928), 131–157, 306–322, 418–436. A translation, by Marc Chadourne, of "The Beast in the Jungle."

E48 DAISY MILLER. *Revue Bleue*, Nos. 17–19 for 1932 (3 and 17 September–1 October 1932), 513–523, 548–560, 588–597. Translated by Mme Fournier-Pargoire. For earlier French translations of *Daisy Miller*, see E14 and E36.

E49 L'EUROPE. *Mercure de France*, No. 1071 (1 November 1952), 385–410. A translation, by Jean Simon, of "Europe."

GERMAN

BOOKS:

E50 EIN LEIDENSCHAFTLICHER ERDENPILGER UND ANDERE ERZÄHLUNGEN ... Leipzig, Fr. Wilh. Grunow, 1876. (7 × 4⅞): [i]¹ 1–28⁸, pp. ii, 448. A translation, by Moritz Busch, of "A Passionate Pilgrim," "The Last of the Valerii," "Eugene Pickering," "The Madonna of the Future," "The Romance of Certain Old Clothes," and "Madame de Mauves."

E51 RODERICK HUDSON ... Leipzig, Fr. Wilh. Grunow, 1876. In two volumes. (7 × 4¾): Vol. I, [i]² 1–16⁸, pp. iv, 256. Vol. II, [i]² 1–17⁸ 18¹, pp. iv, 274. Translated by Moritz Busch.

E52 ... DER AMERIKANER ODER MARQUIS UND YANKEE ... Stuttgart, Verlag Von. Aug. Berth. Auerbach [1877]. In two volumes (6¼ × 4 1/16): Vol. I, [i]¹ 1–22⁸, pp. ii, 352. Vol. II, [i]¹ 1–22⁸ 23⁴, pp. ii, 360. A translation, by Heichen-Abenheim, of *The American*.

E53 DER AMERIKANER . . . Leipzig, Fr. Wilh. Grunow, 1877. In two volumes. ($7 \times 4\frac{3}{4}$): Vol. I, [i]^1 1–17^8 18^2, pp. ii, 276. Vol. II, [i]^1 1–18^8, pp. ii, 288. A translation, by Moritz Busch, of *The American.*

E54 DER AMERIKANER . . . Berlin, Verlag von Otto Janke [1878]. ($7 \times 4\frac{5}{8}$): [i]^2 1–20^8, pp. iv, 320. A translation of *The American;* translator not recorded.

E55 EUGEN PICKERING . . . Leipzig, Philipp Reclam Jun. [1878]. ($5\frac{3}{4} \times 3\frac{7}{8}$): 1–5^8, pp. 80. A translation, by Wilhelm Lange, of "Eugene Pickering." Issued uniform with series, No. 1058 in Reclam's *Universal-Bibliothek.*

E56 . . . DER ALTAR DER TOTEN . . . [Berlin] Müller & Kiepenheuer Verlag [1949]. ($7 \times 4\frac{5}{16}$): [unsigned: 1–4^8], pp. 64. A translation, by Karl Lerbs, of "The Altar of the Dead," reprinted from *Corona,* January 1932.

E57 . . . BILDNIS EINER DAME . . . Köln and Berlin, Verlag Gustav Kiepenheuer, 1950. ($8\frac{1}{4} \times 5\frac{5}{16}$): [1]^8 2–37^8, pp. 592. A translation, by Dr Hildegard Blomeyer, of *The Portrait of A Lady.*

E58 . . . EINE GEWISSE FRAU HEADWAY . . . München, Biederstein Verlag [1952]. ($7\frac{1}{2} \times 4\frac{5}{16}$): [1]^8 2–11^8, pp. 176. A translation, by Luise Laporte, of "The Siege of London."

E59 . . . MEISTERNOVELLEN: DIE DREHUNG DER SCHRAUBE ASPERNS NACHLASS . . . [Zürich] Manesse Verlag [1953]. ($5\frac{7}{8} \times 3\frac{9}{16}$): [1]^{16} 2–14^{16} 15^8, pp. 464. A translation, by Harry Kahn, of "The Turn of the Screw" and "The Aspern Papers." With an afterword by H. Lüdeke.

E60 . . . DIE SÜNDIGEN ENGEL . . . München, Biederstein Verlag [1954]. ($7\frac{7}{16} \times 4\frac{3}{8}$): [1]^6 2–13^8, pp. 208. A translation, by Luise Laporte and Peter Gan, of "The Turn of the Screw." With an afterword by Hans Hennecke.

E61 . . . PRINZESSIN CASAMASSIMA . . . Köln and Berlin, Kiepenheuer & Witsch [1954]. ($7\frac{7}{8} \times 4\frac{3}{4}$): [unsigned: 1–39^8 40^6], pp. 636. A translation, by Hans Hennecke, of *The Princess Casamassima,* including an afterword consisting of an abbreviated version of James's preface to Vol. V of the New York Edition.

E62 . . . MAISIE . . . Köln and Berlin, Kiepenheuer & Witsch [1955]. ($7\frac{15}{16} \times 4\frac{3}{4}$): [unsigned: 1–18^8 19^4], pp. 296. A translation, by Hans Hennecke, of *What Maisie Knew,* including an afterword consisting of the first eight paragraphs of James's preface to Vol. XI of the New York Edition.

E62a ... DIE ERBIN VON WASHINGTON SQUARE ... Zürich, Verlag Die Arche [1956]. ($7\frac{7}{16} \times 4\frac{3}{8}$): [unsigned: 1–15^8], pp. 240. A translation, by Alfred Kuoni, of *Washington Square*. In "A Literary Letter" from Germany (*New York Times Book Review*, 29 September 1957), Frederic Morton states that the translation was "recently" serialized in a number of German newspapers; no further information is available.

E62b ... DIE GESANDTEN ... Köln and Berlin, Kiepenheuer & Witsch [1956]. ($7\frac{7}{8} \times 4\frac{13}{16}$): [unsigned: 1–27^8 28^{10}], pp. 452. A translation, by Helmut M. Braem and Elisabeth Kaiser, of *The Ambassadors*. As the translation follows the text of the New York Edition, chapters I and II of Book Eleventh are in reverse order (see A58b).

E62c ... ERZÄHLUNGEN ... Köln and Berlin, Kiepenheuer & Witsch [1958]. ($7\frac{7}{8} \times 4\frac{5}{8}$): [unsigned: 1–33^8], pp. 528. A translation, by Helmut M. Braem and Elisabeth Kaiser, of "The Madonna of the Future," "Daisy Miller," "The Author of Beltraffio," "The Lesson of the Master," "The Real Thing," "The Figure in the Carpet," "The Tree of Knowledge," "The Real Right Thing," "The Beast in the Jungle," "The Two Faces," "Broken Wings," and "The Jolly Corner"; a translation, by Oswalt von Nostitz, of "The Solution."

E62d ... DAS TIER IM DSCHUNGEL ... Münschen, Piper Verlag [1959]. ($7\frac{1}{4} \times 4\frac{11}{16}$): [unsigned: 1–2^8 3^{10} 4^8], pp. 68. A translation, by Helmut M. Braem and Elisabeth Kaiser, of "The Beast in the Jungle." A separate printing of a translation which had previously appeared in *Die Neue Rundschau*, February 1958, and in *Erzählungen*, 1958 (see E62c).

E62e ... DAISY MILLER ... [Wiesbaden] Insel-Verlag [1959]. ($7\frac{1}{16} \times 4\frac{9}{16}$): [unsigned: 1–5^8], pp. 80. A separate printing of a translation, by Helmut M. Braem and Elisabeth Kaiser, which had previously appeared in *Erzählungen*, 1958 (see E62c).

ANTHOLOGIES:

E63 AMERIKANISCHE ERZÄHLER ... ausgewählt und eingeleitet von Fritz Güttinger. Zurich, Artemis-Verlag [1946]. ($7\frac{7}{8} \times 5\frac{1}{8}$): [1]^8 2–25^8, pp. xxxiv, 366. Contains "The Altar of the Dead" ("Der Totenaltar"), pp. [290]–349, translated by Ilse Leisi-Gugler.

E. TRANSLATIONS

E63a AMERIKANISCHE ERZÄHLER von Washington Irving bis Dorothy Parker. Zürich, Manesse Verlag [1957]. ($5\frac{7}{8} \times 3\frac{9}{16}$): $[1]^{16}$ 2–16^{16} 17^{10} 18^{16}, pp. 564. Contains "The Altar of the Dead" ("Der Altar der Toten"), pp. 282–350, translated by Elizabeth Schnack.

E63b DIE SCHÖNSTEN LIEBESGESCHICHTEN DER WELT. München, Kurt Desch Verlag [1957]. Pp. 876. Contains "The Tone of Time" ("Patina"), pp. 843–862, translated by Hansi Bochow-Blütghen. Previously serialised in *Der Monat* (Berlin); no additional information available.

PERIODICALS:

E63c DIE EUROPÄER. *Die Romanwelt* (Stuttgart), I, Nos. 48–52 (1894), 680–695, 722–733, 757–768, 783–800, 818–836. A translation, by Fel. Bench, of *The Europeans*.

E64 DER ALTAR DER TOTEN. *Corona*, II (January 1932), 426–475. A translation, by Karl Lerbs, of "The Altar of the Dead."

E64a DAS TIER IM DSCHUNGEL. *Die Neue Rundschau*, LXIX (February 1958), 213–257. A translation, by Helmut M. Braem and Elisabeth Kaiser, of "The Beast in the Jungle."

GREEK
BOOK:

E65 ... I KLIRONOMOS ... [Athens] Ikaros, [c1953]. ($7\frac{1}{2} \times 5\frac{1}{4}$): $[1]^{8}$ 2–14^{8} 15^{2}, pp. 228. A translation, by Ninilas Papajanni, of *Washington Square*.

HEBREW
BOOK:

E66 ... HA-YORESHET ... Tel-Aviv, S. Friedman, 5712 [i.e., 1952]. ($8\frac{1}{4} \times 5\frac{3}{8}$): [unsigned: 1–11^{8}], pp. 176. A translation, by Arye Anavi, of *Washington Square*.

HUNGARIAN
BOOK:

E67 [UNOKATESTVÉREK]. Budapest, Athenaeum, 1877. The first of three tales (the others are by L. Collas and Nathaniel Hawthorne) in the second of a two volume collection of short stories, in the Novellák, Külföldi series. A translation, by Sasvári Ármin, of "A Passionate Pilgrim." No copy available for collation.

E. TRANSLATIONS

ITALIAN

BOOKS:

E68 ... DAISY MILLER ED ALTRI RACCONTI ... Milano, Fratelli Treves Editori, 1930. ($7\frac{1}{4} \times 4\frac{3}{4}$): [i]^6 1–14^8 15^{10}, pp. xii, 244. A translation, by Jessica, of "Daisy Miller," "The Diary of A Man of Fifty," and "The Velvet Glove."

E69 ... IL SEGRETO DELL' ISTITUTRICE ... Firenze, R. Bemporad & Figlio [1932]. ($8 \times 5\frac{3}{4}$): [1]^8 2–7^8 8^6, pp. 124. A translation, by Laura Padovano, of "The Turn of the Screw."

E70 UNA FANCIULLA NELL' OMBRA ... Milano, S.A. Elit, 1933. ($7\frac{9}{16} \times 4\frac{7}{8}$): [unsigned: 1–14^8], pp. 224. A translation of *In the Cage*; translator not recorded.

E71 ... L'AMERICANO ... Milano, A. Mondadori [1934]. ($6\frac{5}{8} \times 3\frac{7}{8}$): [1]^8 2–35^8, pp. 560. A translation, by Carlo Linati, of *The American*.

E72 ... GIRO DI VITE ... Milano, Rizzoli & C., 1934. ($6 \times 4\frac{1}{16}$): [1]^{16} 2–6^{16} 7^{12}, 8^{16}, pp. 248. A translation, by Gerolamo Lazzeri, of "The Turn of the Screw" and "The Altar of the Dead."

E73 ... L'ALTARE DEI MORTI ... Firenze, G. C. Sansoni Editore [1943]. ($6\frac{5}{16} \times 4\frac{3}{16}$): [1]^8 2^8 3^6 4^8 [5]^1, pp. 62. A translation, by Viviana Praz, of "The Altar of the Dead."

E74 ... RITRATTO DI SIGNORA ... Torino, Giulio Einaudi, Editore, 1943. ($8\frac{7}{16} \times 6\frac{1}{8}$): [i]^6 1–36^8, pp. x, 578. A translation, by Carlo and Silvia Linati, of *The Portrait of A Lady*.

E75 ... UNA TERZA PERSONA ... Roma, Documento, Libraio Editore, 1944. ($4\frac{5}{8} \times 3\frac{1}{16}$): [1]^4 2–11^4 12^6, pp. 100. A translation, by Suso Cecchi d'Amico, of "The Third Person."

E76 ... I DOCUMENTI ASPERN ... Milano–Roma, Jandi-Editore [1944]. ($7\frac{7}{16} \times 4\frac{5}{8}$): [1]^8 2–9^8, pp. 144. A translation, by Eugenio Giovannetti, of "The Aspern Papers."

E77 .... DUE DONNE ... Milano, Rosa e Ballo Editori [1945]. ($7\frac{1}{4} \times 4\frac{3}{4}$): [1]^4 2–15^8, pp. viii, 224. A translation, by Bruno Maffi, of "Madame de Mauves" and "Daisy Miller."

E78 ... ROMANZI BREVI ... [Milano] Bompiani [1946]. ($7\frac{7}{8} \times 4\frac{5}{8}$): [1]^8 2–5^8 6^6 7–9^8 10–41 signed in 6's and 8's, consistently, in a ratio of one gathering of 6 to three of 8, 42–43^6, pp. xx, 624. A translation, by Carlo Izzo, of "The Pension Beaurepas," "Four Meetings," "The Aspern Papers," "The Liar," "Sir Edmund Orme", "The Chaperon," "The Private Life," "Owen Wingrave," "The Middle Years," "The Pupil," "The Abasement of the Northmores," "The Two Faces," "The Beast in the Jungle," "Mrs. Medwin," and "The Bench of Desolation."

E79 ... FIDUCIA ... [Milano] I[stituto] E[ditoriale] I[taliano] [1946]. ($7\frac{7}{16} \times 4\frac{3}{4}$): [1]⁸ 2–23⁸ 24¹⁰, pp. 388. A translation, by Giorgio Manganelli, of *Confidence*.

E80 ... LA TIGRA NELLA JUNGLA ... Milano, Enrico Cederna [1947]. ($8\frac{1}{16} \times 5\frac{1}{8}$): [unsigned: 1–6⁸ 7⁶], pp. 108. A translation, by Giansiro Ferrata, of "The Beast in the Jungle," reprinted from the anthology *Americana* (see E83).

E81 ... L'EREDITIERA. Milano, Baldini & Castoldi [1950]. ($7\frac{7}{8} \times 5\frac{3}{8}$): [1]⁸ 2–20⁸, pp. 320. A translation, by Marianna Battistella and Emanuele Moca, of *Washington Square*.

E82 PIAZZA WASHINGTON ... [Parma] Guanda [1950]. ($6\frac{5}{8} \times 4$): [i]⁸ [1]⁸ 2–14⁸ 15¹⁰, pp. xvi, 244. A translation, by Carla Miggiano, of *Washington Square*. With an unauthorized translation of the preface by Graham Greene which appears in the French translation of *The Ambassadors* (see E21).

E82a ... LE PREFAZIONI ... Venezia, Neri Pozza [1956]. Pp. 400. A translation of *The Prefaces* to the New York Edition (see A64).

E82b ... L'ARTE DEL ROMANZO ... Milano, C. M. Lerici Editore [1959]. ($8\frac{7}{16} \times 5\frac{5}{8}$): [unsigned: 1–21⁸ 22⁶], pp. 348. A translation, by Alberta Fabris, of "The Art of Fiction," "Ivan Turgénieff," "Guy de Maupassant," and "Emerson," from *Partial Portraits*; "Honoré de Balzac," "Emile Zola," "Gustave Flaubert," and "The New Novel," from *Notes on Novelists*; "Criticism," from *Essays in London*; "Ivan Turgenieff," from *The Library of the World's Best Literature*.

ANTHOLOGY:

E83 AMERICANA, a cura di Elio Vittorini. [Milano] Bompiani, 1943. ($8\frac{1}{8} \times 5\frac{1}{4}$): [i]⁴ 1–65⁸ 66¹⁰, pp. xxiv, 1044. Illustrated. Contains a translation, by Giansiro Ferrata, of "The Beast in the Jungle," pp. 366–412. For first separate edition, 1947, see E80.

PERIODICAL:

E83a L'ANGOLO ALLEGRO. *Il Mondo* (1953). A serialised translation, by Paola Bompard, of "The Jolly Corner."

JAPANESE

BOOKS:

E84 A DAY OF DAYS ... Tokyo, The Ars Press [1926]. $(7\frac{1}{4} \times 4\frac{7}{8})$:
[unsigned: $1^1\ 2^1\ 3-10^8\ 11^4\ 12^2$], pp. iv, 140. Translated by Tokuboku Hirata. English and Japanese texts on facing pages.

E85 [DAISY MILLER]. Tokyo, Kawade shobo [1941]. $(7\frac{1}{16} \times 5)$:
[unsigned: $1^1\ 2-16^{16}\ 17^8\ 18^4$], pp. [ii], 1–26, 1–478. Translated
by Masami Nishikawa. Included in one volume with translations
(by Tomoji Abe and others) of *Moby Dick*, "Rip Van Winkle,"
and "Ligeia." Reissued as a separate volume: Tokyo, Shinchô-
sha [1957].

E86 ONNA SOZOKUNIN ... Tokyo, Kadokawa Shoten [1950].
$(5\frac{7}{8} \times 4\frac{3}{16})$: $1-18^8\ [19]^4\ [20-21]^1$, pp. 300. Signed in Japanese
characters, paginated in arabic numerals. A translation, by Tadae
Fukizawa, of *Washington Square*.

E86a KOKUSAI EPISÔDO. Tokyo, Iwanami shoten [1956]. Pp. 134.
A translation, by Tsutomu Ueda, of "An International Episode."
No copy available for collation.

E86b YONDO NO DEAI; SHORÔ. Tokyo, Eihô-sha [1956]. Pp. 242.
A translation, by Hajime Okita and Ariyoshi Mizunoe, of "Four
Meetings," "The Middle Years," and "An International Episode."
No copy available for collation.

E86c [THE AMERICAN and THE TURN OF THE SCREW]. Tokyo,
Kochi Publishing Co. Ltd. [1958]. $(7\frac{7}{16} \times 5\frac{1}{16})$: [unsigned: 1^1
$2-28^8\ 29^4\ 30^1$], pp. [2], 442. Vol. 6 of the *Collection of Contemporary American Literature*. *The American* was translated by Mrs
Fumi Takano, "The Turn of the Screw" by Shoichi Sako.

ANTHOLOGY:

E87 EIKOKU KINDAI KESSAKU SHU [MASTERPIECES OF MODERN
ENGLISH LITERATURE]. Edited by Tokuboku Hirata. Tokyo,
Kokumin bunko [1915]. In two volumes, Vol. II. $(8\frac{5}{8} \times 5\frac{7}{8})$:
$[1]^1\ 2^8\ 3^4\ [4]^1\ 5-55^8\ [56]^1$, pp. 846. Signatures and pagination in
Japanese characters. Contains translations, by Tokuboku
Hirata, of "An International Episode," pp. 1–154, and "The
Pension Beaurepas," pp. 155–262.

PERIODICALS:

E88 TEMMATSU. *Waseda-Bungaku*, No. 38 (January 1909), 50–74;
No. 39 (February 1909), 13–41. A translation, by Tengen Kata-
gami, of "The Friends of the Friends."

E. TRANSLATIONS

E89 GOJUOTOKO NO NIKKI. *Sekai-Bungaku*, No. 29 (February 1949), 3–13; No. 30 (March 1949), 71–96. A translation, by Saburō Yamaya, of "The Diary of A Man of Fifty."

E89a THE ART OF FICTION. *Eigo Seinen* (*The Rising Generation*), CV (January–March 1959), 15–17, 81–84, 131–133. Abridged text in English and in a translation by Yoshinori Yoshitake. Reprinted in *The Art of Fiction and Other Essays* (the "other essays" are all by Frank Norris). Tokyo, Eihô-sha, 1959.

KOREAN

BOOKS:

E89b AMERICAIN. Seoul, Seog Gu Go [1957]. Pp. 616. A translation, by Jung-Angmunhwasa, of *The American*.

E89c MANG-YEONG. Seoul, Seong Mug Choe [1957]. Pp. 360. A translation, by Baegjosa, of "The Turn of the Screw" and "Daisy Miller."

POLISH

BOOK:

E90 ... AMERYKANIN ... Lwów, Gubrynowicza i Schmidta, 1879. In two volumes. $(8\frac{3}{8} \times 5\frac{1}{2})$: Vol. I, $[1]^8$ $2–14^8$, pp. 224. Vol. II, $[1]^8$ $2–14^8$ 15^4 $[16]^1$, pp. 234. A translation, by A. Callier, of *The American*.

PORTUGUESE

BOOKS:

E91 ... CALAFRIO ... Lisboa, Portugália Editora [1943]. $(7\frac{5}{8} \times 4\frac{3}{4})$: $[1]^8$ $2–18^8$ $[19]^2$, pp. 292. A translation, by João Gaspar Simões, of "The Turn of the Screw."

E92 ... O MENTIROSO ... Lisboa, Portugália Editora [1944]. $(6\frac{3}{8} \times 4\frac{7}{16})$: $[1]^8$ $2–8^8$, pp. 128. A translation, by Januário Leite, of "The Liar."

E93 ... RETRATO DUMA SENHORA ... Lisboa, Portugália Editora [1944]. $(8\frac{9}{16} \times 5\frac{5}{8})$: $[1]^8$ $2–40^8$ 41^2, pp. 644. A translation, by Cabral Do Nascimento, of *The Portrait of A Lady*.

E93a [A HERDEIRA]. São Paulo, Saraiva [c. 1956]. A translation, by Ondina Ferreira, of *Washington Square*.

ANTHOLOGIES:

E94 OS MELHORES CONTOS AMERICANOS. First Series. Edited by João Gaspar Simões. Lisboa, Portugália Editora [1943].

E. TRANSLATIONS

$(7\frac{1}{2} \times 4\frac{3}{4})$: $[1]^8$ 2–26^8, pp. 416. Contains a translation, by João De Oliveira, of "Four Meetings," pp. 203–242.

E95 OS MELHORES CONTOS INGLESES. First Series. Edited by João Gaspar Simões. Lisboa, Portugália Editora [c1943]. $(7\frac{1}{2} \times 4\frac{3}{4})$: $[1]^8$ 2–27^8 28^4, pp. 440. Contains a translation, by Cabral Do Nascimento, of "The Middle Years," pp. 95–125.

E96 COLEÇÃO CONTOS DO MUNDO. Vol. 3: OS NORTE AMERI-CANOS ANTIGOS E MODERNOS. Edited by Vinicius de Morais, with a preface by Morton Dauwen Zabel. Rio de Janeiro, Companhia Editôra Leitura, 1945. $(9 \times 6\frac{1}{4})$: [unsigned: 1^4 2–30^8 31^4], pp. 480. Contains a translation, by Vinicius de Morais, of "Four Meetings," pp. 123–143.

RUSSIAN

ANTHOLOGIES:

E97 AMERIKANSKAYA NOVELLA XX VEKA. Edited by A. Gavrilov, I. Kashkin, N. Eishiskina and A. Yelistratova. Moscow, Goslitizdat, 1934. $(7\frac{5}{8} \times 5)$, pp. 372. Contains a translation, by Nina Leonidovna Daruzes, of "The Real Right Thing" ("Biografiya Pisatelya"), pp. 51–68.

E98 AMERIKANSKAYA NOVELLA XIX VEKA. Edited by A. Startsev. Moscow, OGIZ (State Publishing House for Artistic Literature), 1946. $(7\frac{5}{8} \times 5)$: 1–30^8, pp. 480. Contains a translation, by H. Volzhina, of "Daisy Miller," pp. 296–360.

PERIODICALS:

E98a POSLEDNII IZ VALERIYEV. *Modnyi Magazine*, Nos. 1–6 for 1876 (January–June 1876), pagination unavailable. A translation, by S. Rekhnevskoy, of "The Last of the Valerii."

E98b MADONNA BUDUSHCHEVO. *Pchela* (1876), No. 24, pp. 1–6; No. 25, pp. 1–7. A translation of "The Madonna of the Future"; translator not recorded. Also appeared (new translation?) in *Khudozhestvennyi Journal* (January 1887), pp. 21–56.

E99 AMERIKANKI. *Weekly Novoe Vremya*, V (14 and 28 February, 20 and 27 March 1880), cols. 401–419, 528–548, 718–735, 806–817. A translation of *An International Episode*; translator not recorded.

E100 VASHINGTONSKI SKVĖR. *Zagranichnyi Vestnik*, I (October, December 1881), 93–133, 461–529. A translation of *Washington Square*; translator not recorded.

E. TRANSLATIONS

E101 SVIAZKA PISYEM. *Vestnik Yevropy*, Vol. 4 for 1882 (August 1882), 608–641. A translation of "A Bundle of Letters"; translator identified only by the initials "O.P."

E102 OSADA LONDONA. *Vestnik Yevropy*, Vol. 1 for 1884 (January–February 1884), 277–321, 659–701. A translation of "The Siege of London"; translator identified only by the initials "A.E."

E103 LONDONSKAYA ZHIZN'. *Vestnik Yevropy*, Vol. 4 for 1889 (August 1889), 729–768; Vol. 5 for 1889 (September 1889), 189–234. A translation of "A London Life"; translator identified only by the initials "A.E."

E104 LGOON. *Vestnik Yevropy*, Vol. 6 for 1889 (November 1889), 230–280. A translation of "The Liar"; translator identified only by the initials "A.E."

E104a NASTOYASHCHIYE GOSPODA. *Vestnik Yevropy*, Vol. 5 for 1893 (September 1893), 244–266. A translation of "The Real Thing"; translator identified by the initials "A.E."

E105 MAT' I DOCH. *Vestnik Yevropy*, Vol. 6 for 1896 (December 1896), 676–716. A translation of "The Chaperon"; translator not recorded.

E105a DAISY MILLER. *Zhivopisnoye Obozreniye* (1898), Nos. 20–25, pp. 395–398, 418–422, 434–436, 454–458, 478–483, 494–499. Translated by E. Solovieff.

E105aa K BIOGRAFII I. S. TURGENEVA: II. VOSPOMINIYA O TURGENEVE AMERIKANSKOVO BELLE-TRISTA GENRI DZHEIMSA. *Minuvshie Gody*, No. 8 (1908), 48–60. A translation of "Ivan Turgénieff" (D396); translator not recorded.

SERBO[-CROATIAN]

BOOK:

E105b [PORTRET YEDNE LEDI]. Beograd (Belgrade), Serbian Book Co-Operative, 1956. ($7\frac{7}{16} \times 5\frac{1}{4}$): $[1]^8$ 2–45^8 46^1, pp. 722. A translation, by Predrag Milojević, of *The Portrait of A Lady*.

SLOVENE

BOOK:

E105c [AMERIČAN]. Ljubljana, Slovenski knjižni Zavod [c. 1956]. A translation, by Božidar Pahor, of *The American*. No copy available for collation.

SPANISH

BOOKS:

E106 Nathaniel Hawthorne: LA LETRA ESCARLATA. Buenos Aires, Editorial Nova [1944]. ($8 \times 5\frac{1}{2}$): [unsigned: 1–39^4], pp. 312.

Contains a translation, by M. Loyzaga de Romero and José E. Romero, of an extract from the fifth chapter of Henry James's *Hawthorne* (1879), which serves here as "Prologo."

E107 RETRATO DE UNA DAMA ... Buenos Aires, Emecé Editores [1944]. ($7\frac{11}{16} \times 4\frac{11}{16}$): [unsigned: 1–49⁸], pp. 784. A translation, by Mariano de Alarcón, of *The Portrait of A Lady*.

E108 ...LA HUMILLACIÓN DE LOS NORTHMORE ... Buenos Aires, Emecé Editores [1945]. ($7\frac{1}{4} \times 4\frac{15}{16}$): [unsigned: 1–4⁸], pp. 64. A translation, by Haydée Lange, of "The Abasement of the Northmores." With a preface by Jorge Luis Borges.

E109 OTRA VUELTA DE TUERCA ... Buenos Aires, Emecé Editores [1945]. ($7\frac{5}{8} \times 4\frac{5}{8}$): [unsigned: 1–13⁸ 14⁴], pp. 216. A translation, by José Bianco, of "The Turn of the Screw."

E110 ...LOS PAPELES DE JEFFREY ASPERN ... [Barcelona] Ediciones Lauro, 1944 [1946]. ($7\frac{7}{16} \times 5\frac{9}{16}$): [i]² [1]⁸ 2⁸ 3⁶ 4–5⁸ 6⁶ 7–8⁸ 9⁶ [10]², pp. 140. A translation, by Juan Antonio Antequera, of "The Aspern Papers."

E111 ...LOS FANTASMAS DEL CASTILLO ("LA VUELTA DEL TORNILLO") ... Barcelona, "Victoria" [1946]. ($6\frac{7}{16} \times 4\frac{5}{8}$): [1]⁸ 2–12⁸ 13⁴, pp. 200. A translation, by Juan Antonio Antequera, of "The Turn of the Screw." With a translated preface by T. S. Eliot, which originally appeared in *La Nouvelle Revue Française*, XIV (1 May 1927), 669–675.

E112 LOS PAPELES DE ASPERN ... Buenos Aires, Emecé Editores [1947]. ($7\frac{5}{16} \times 4\frac{1}{4}$): [unsigned: 1–11⁸], pp. 176. A translation, by María Antonia Oyuela, of "The Aspern Papers."

E113 ...LA LECCIÓN DEL MAESTRO Y OTROS CUENTOS... Buenos Aires, Emecé Editores [1949]. ($7\frac{3}{16} \times 5$): [unsigned: 1–22⁸ 23¹⁰], pp. 372. A translation, by María Antonia Oyuela, of "The Lesson of the Master," "The Velvet Glove," "The Death of the Lion," "The Middle Years," "The Altar of the Dead," "The Tree of Knowledge," and "The Jolly Corner."

E114 [EL SITIO DE LONDRES and LOS PAPELES DE ASPERN]. Buenos Aires, Losada, 1950. A translation, by Aida Aisenson and J. Kogan Albert, of "The Siege of London" and "The Aspern Papers." No copy available for collation.

E115 ...LA HEREDERA. Buenos Aires, Ediciones Siglo Veinte [1951]. ($9\frac{1}{16} \times 6\frac{1}{8}$): [unsigned: 1–11⁸], pp. 176. A translation, by J. Martinez Alinari, of *Washington Square*.

E116 ... LA HEREDERA ... Barcelona, Editorial Surco [1952]. ($7\frac{5}{16} \times 5\frac{1}{4}$): [1]^8 2–23^8, pp. 368. A translation, by María Luz Morales, of *Washington Square*.

ANTHOLOGY:

E117 COLECCION PANAMERICANA. Vol. 15: CUENTISTAS NORTEAMERICANOS. Edited by Herschel Brickell, Dudley Poore, and Harry Warfel. Buenos Aires, etc., W. M. Jackson Inc. [1946]. ($7\frac{1}{2} \times 5$): [unsigned: 1–38^8 39^4], pp. xxvi, 590. Contains a translation, by J. R. Wilcock, of "Four Meetings," pp. [179]–210.

SWEDISH

BOOKS:

E118 [EN FILOSOFISK QVINNA. EUGÈNE PICKERINGS FÖRSTA KÄRLEK]. Stockholm, M. Sahlstrom, 1876. A translation of "Eugene Pickering." Translator not determined. No copy deposited for copyright in any of the four Swedish libraries of deposit. Not located.

E119 RODERICK HUDSON ... Stockholm, Viktor Böhlmarks Förlag [1877]. ($7\frac{3}{16} \times 4\frac{5}{8}$): [1]^8 2–26^8, pp. 416. Translator identified only by the initials "G–N."

E120 FYRA BERÄTTELSER ... Jönköping, Nordströmska Bokhandeln [1880]. ($6\frac{7}{16} \times 4\frac{5}{8}$): [i]^1 [1]^8 2–22^8 23^4 , pp. ii, 360. A translation of "Longstaff's Marriage," "Eugene Pickering," "Benvolio," and "Madame de Mauves." Translator not recorded.

E121 AMERIKANEN ... Stockholm, Fahlcrantz & Co. [1884]. ($7 \times 4\frac{3}{4}$): [i]^1 1–23^8 24^6 [25]^1, pp. ii, 382. A translation, by Erik G. Folcker, of *The American*.

E122 FRU DE MAUVES FRAMTIDENS MADONNA FYRA SAMMANTRÄFFANDEN TRE BERÄTTELSER ... Stockholm, Wahlström & Widstrand [1893]. ($7\frac{3}{16} \times 4\frac{3}{4}$): [i]^1 1–12^8 13^4(—13$_4$), pp. ii, 198. A translation of "Madame de Mauves," "The Madonna of the Future," and "Four Meetings." Translator not recorded.

E123 ... AMERIKAN I PARIS ... [Stockholm] Bokförlaget Natur och Kultur [1944]. ($7\frac{1}{4} \times 4\frac{7}{8}$): [1]^8 2–28^8, pp. 448. The text is based on the 1884 translation of *The American* by Erik G. Folcker (see E121), newly revised and modernized by Per Kellberg.

E. TRANSLATIONS

E124 ETT KVINNOPORTRÄTT . . . Stockholm, Ljus [1947]. $(8\frac{1}{16} \times 5\frac{11}{16})$: $[1-2]^8$ $3-42^8$ 43^6, pp. 684. A translation, by Lisbeth and Louis Renner, of *The Portrait of A Lady*. With a foreword by Kenneth B. Murdock.

E125 . . . TVÅ BERÄTTELSER. [Stockholm] Forum [1951]. $(7\frac{5}{8} \times 5)$: $[1]^8$ $2-16^8$ 17^4, pp. 264. A translation, by Herbert Karlsson, of "The Aspern Papers" and "The Turn of the Screw."

E. TRANSLATIONS

ADDENDA

F. MISCELLANEA

F. MISCELLANEA

I. ENGLISH-LANGUAGE FOREIGN EDITIONS

F1 *English Library* (Leipzig)

($6\frac{5}{16} \times 4\frac{9}{16}$): 16mo. M. 1,60 or 2 francs.

Light buff paper wrappers, cut flush, uniformly lettered and ruled in brown.

a. *A London Life* (1891), Vol. 30. Lacks "The Patagonia," included in first edition (A33).

b. Rudyard Kipling, *Soldiers Three*, with preface by Henry James (1891), Vol. 59. For full collation, see B9.

c. Wolcott Balestier, *The Average Woman*, with preface by Henry James (1892), Vol. 100.

d. *The Lesson of the Master* (1892), Vol. 135. Contents uniform with first edition (A36).

F2 *Keibunkan* (Tokyo)

a. *Ten Short Stories by Henry James*, 2 vols., with an introduction, prefaces, and notes by Gregg M. Sinclair. Dark blue cloth, lettered in gilt. Published June 1926.

Vol. I: *The Madonna of the Future; The Author of Beltraffio; Four Meetings; The Middle Years; The Altar of the Dead.*

Vol. II: *The Liar; The Death of the Lion; Sir Edmund Orme; Brooksmith; The Lesson of the Master.*

F3 *Kenkyusha English Classics* (Tokyo)

($7\frac{3}{8} \times 4\frac{3}{4}$): 8vo. May have been intended for school use only, as colophon reads "Not For Sale."

Cherry-red cloth, lettered and blocked in gilt on front cover and spine, blocked in blind on back cover.

a. *Daisy Miller, An International Episode*, and *The Death of the Lion* (1924). Reissued 1935.

F4 *Kenkyusha Pocket English Series* (Tokyo)

($6\frac{3}{4} \times 4\frac{1}{2}$): 16mo. Y. 100.

Pale blue-green paper wrappers, cut flush, uniformly lettered and decorated in black.

a. *An International Episode* (1952).

F. MISCELLANEA

F5 *Nan' Un-Do* (Tokyo)

(7 × 5): 8vo. Y. 120.

Dark red lacquered paper boards, lettered and decorated in gilt.

a. *Daisy Miller* (1951).

F6 *The Rainbow Library* (Paris)

($6\frac{15}{16}$ × $4\frac{1}{2}$): 16mo. 120 francs.

Tan paper wrappers, cut flush, lettered and decorated in black and white.

a. *Daisy Miller* (1948), Vol. 21.

Issued with separate study pamphlet of "Introduction, Notes and Exercises" for school use.

F7 *Tauchnitz "Collection of British Authors"* (Leipzig)

($6\frac{7}{16}$ × $4\frac{5}{8}$): 16mo. M. 1.60. (After 1907, wrappers M. 2.20, cloth, M. 3.–).

Pale buff paper wrappers, cut flush, uniformly lettered and decorated in black. Catalogue of advertisements included at back of most volumes.

a. *The American* (1878), Vols. 1713–1714.

b. *The Europeans* (1878), Vol. 1792.

c. *Daisy Miller: A Study. An International Episode. Four Meetings* (1879), Vol. 1819.

d. *Roderick Hudson* (1879), Vols. 1842–1843.

e. *The Madonna of the Future. Longstaff's Marriage. Madame de Mauves* (1880), Vol. 1881.

f. *Eugene Pickering. The Diary of A Man of Fifty. Benvolio* (1880), Vol. 1888.

g. *Confidence* (1880), Vol. 1901.

h. *Washington Square. The Pension Beaurepas. A Bundle of Letters* (1881), Vols. 1977–1978.

i. *The Portrait of A Lady* (1882), Vols. 2042–2044.

j. *Foreign Parts* (1883), Vol. 2164. See A2b for full collation and description of contents.

k. *French Poets and Novelists* (1883), Vol. 2181. See A5b for full collation. Specially revised by James for this edition.

l. *The Siege of London. The Point of View. A Passionate Pilgrim* (1884), Vol. 2234.

m. *Portraits of Places* (1884), Vol. 2276. See A21c for note on contents.

n. *A Little Tour in France* (1885), Vol. 2334.

o. *The Finer Grain* (1910), Vol. 4224.

p. *The Outcry* (1912), Vol. 4308.

F. MISCELLANEA

F8 *Zephyr Books: A Library of British and American Authors* (Stockholm)
($7\frac{3}{16} \times 4\frac{5}{8}$): 8vo. S.kr. 2.75.
White stiff paper wrappers, cut flush, lettered in black and ruled
in orange; red-brown dust-jacket, lettered and decorated in
yellow and white, uniform for Modern American Authors
volumes.
a. *The Aspern Papers* (1947), Vol. 158.
b. *The Turn of the Screw* (1947), Vol. 159.

II. BRAILLE EDITIONS

F9 *The Death of the Lion* and *The Figure in the Carpet* (London,
National Institute for the Blind, 1926).

F10 *The Lesson of the Master* (London, National Institute for the
Blind, 1926).

F11 *The Next Time* and *The Coxon Fund* (London, National Institute
for the Blind, 1926).

F12 *The Story In It*, together with Dreiser's *The Lost Phoebe*, one
volume in the series *Selections from "Great Short Stories of the
World"* (London, National Institute for the Blind, 1927).

F13 *The Turn of the Screw* (Louisville, Ky., American Printing House
for the Blind, 1936). Reprinted from the American plates by the
Royal National Institute for the Blind, London, 1937.

F14 *Daisy Miller* and *An International Episode*, 2 vols. (Cincinnati,
Ohio, Clovernook Printing House for the Blind, 1938).

F15 *Short Stories of Henry James*, 7 vols. (Louisville, Ky., American
Printing House for the Blind, 1947). The text is that of the Random House edition, selected and edited by Clifton Fadiman, 1945.

F16 *The Aspern Papers*, in *Short Novels of the Masters*, edited by
Charles Neider, 9 vols. (Louisville, Ky., American Printing
House for the Blind, 1950).

F17 *The Portrait of A Lady*, 7 vols. (Louisville, Ky., American Printing House for the Blind, 1950).

F18 *The Ambassadors*, 4 vols. (Boston, Howe Press of the Perkins
Institution, 1951).

III. TALKING BOOKS FOR THE BLIND

F19 *The Turn of the Screw*, read by John Brewster, 9 records (New
York, American Foundation for the Blind, 1943).

F20 *Washington Square*, read by John Brewster, 13 records (New York, American Foundation for the Blind, 1948).

F21 *The American*, read by Alvar Lidell, 41 records (London, Royal National Institute for the Blind, 1951).

F22 *The Portrait of A Lady*, read by John Knight, 41 records (New York, American Foundation for the Blind, 1951).

IV. TIMES BOOK CLUB ISSUES

To an older generation of bookmen, and to biblio-graphers, the history of the venture of *The Times* (London) into book distribution is well known. It has been, moreover, documented in detail in *The History of the Book War*, London, 1907, and in *The History of The Times*, Vol. III, 1947. Founded in 1905, the Times Book Club sought to offer free library services to its subscribers and also discount purchases of well-known titles. The Club dealt largely in remainders, and its publicity methods and drastic price-cuts created considerable hostility among publishers with attendant disputes and litigation. After a two-years' "war" a satisfactory *modus vivendi* was arrived at in which the Club agreed to a time-lapse before secondhand or remaindered copies were distributed and recognized limitations to its role as bookseller.

Henry James loomed large in the various *Times* issues during this book war. The publishers of his works had large quantities of unbound sheets which they readily sold. The result was the issue by the Times Book Club, almost from its inception, of more titles of James than of any other single author in its catalogue—thirty-four of his works plus five volumes containing his prefaces or introductions were advertised in the Club's first catalogue of 1905. Eleven more titles were added in the catalogues of 1908 and 1911.

Many of these were sold in their original bindings, and may be recognized as *Times* issue only by the small brown label pasted at the bottom of the inner back cover. Some were inexpensively bound for the Club by the publishers; others were especially bound in the Club's standard remainder binding. Only those volumes noted by us which varied in binding from primary issue have been included in this bibliography. They are identified by the following code letters:

A: Publisher's binding and brasses in cheap format, with Times Book Club device in place of publisher's imprint at foot of spine. All edges trimmed.

B: Hybrid issue, combining original brasses and Times Book Club remainder binding.

C: Times Book Club standard remainder binding, in varying pastel shades. Linen-grain cloth, single-rule border in black on front cover, lettering and single-rule at top and bottom in black on spine; white end-papers; all edges trimmed. Times Book Club device on spine.

D: Uniform with C, but without Times Book Club device at foot of spine.

———

F23 *The Aspern Papers* (Second edition, English issue, 1890) C: orange cloth. Also D: pale rose cloth.

F24 *Daisy Miller* (Second English edition, 1880) A: lettered and blocked in black; biscuit or orange-brown cloth.

F25 *The Europeans* (Second English edition, 1879) A: lettered and blocked in black; biscuit cloth. Also C: orange cloth.

F26 *In the Cage* (First edition, 1898) C: blue cloth; lacks advertisements at back.

F27 *The Lesson of the Master* (First edition, Colonial issue, 1892) C: cerise cloth.

F28 *A London Life* (Second edition, English issue, 1889) C: light green cloth.

F29 *The Madonna of the Future* (Second edition, 1880) A: lettered and blocked in black; lemon-yellow or yellow-green cloth.

F30 *The Real Thing* (First edition, English issue, 1893) C: salmon cloth.

F31 *The Reverberator* (Second edition, English issue, 1888) C: salmon or pale orange cloth.

F32 *Stories Revived,* 2 vols. (Second edition, 1885) A: lettered and blocked in black; lemon-yellow, biscuit, or dark burgundy cloth.

F33 *Tales of Three Cities* (First English edition, 1884) D: rust-brown cloth.

F34 *The Tragic Muse* (Second English edition, 1891) C: rose cloth. Also D: lettered and blocked in dark blue; light blue cloth.

Miscellaneous

F35 Alphonse Daudet, *Port Tarascon,* translated by Henry James (First English edition, 1890) B: lettered in black (original brasses) on front cover and spine, single-rule in black at and bottom of spine; brown cloth; also seen lettered in blue on grey-blue cloth; all edges trimmed. No date on title-page, verso of title blank. $7\frac{1}{4} \times 5\frac{1}{2}$.
Also noted in "de luxe" binding: blue calf, lettered and ruled as above in gilt, with single-rule border in gilt added to front and back covers; top edge gilt.

F36 Pierre Loti, *Impressions,* with an introduction by Henry James (First edition, 1898) A: decorative blocking eliminated from front cover; light green cloth.

V. COLONIAL ISSUES

It was standard procedure in the nineteenth and early twentieth centuries for British publishers to issue colonial editions of their books simultaneously with the domestic edition and printed from the same plates, in both wrappers and cloth, or sell sheets to Empire distributors. Many James titles appeared in this fashion; they are, in effect, a part of the first edition, but we have preferred to treat them as being in the nature of reprints, since they have only a relative bibliographical importance. They were invariably printed from plates of the first one-volume English or American edition and they contain, to our knowledge, no added material or textual revision. The only difference is that they have new prelims.

F. MISCELLANEA

		PUBLISHER	SERIES NUMBER	PRICE (wrappers; cloth)
F37	*The Ambassadors* (1903)	Methuen	—	1s. 6d.; 1s. 9d.
F38	*The American Scene* (1907)	George Bell	—	7s. 6d. (cloth only)
F39	*The Awkward Age* (1899)	Heinemann	165	2s. 6d.; 3s. 6d.
F40	*The Better Sort* (1903)	Methuen	—	1s. 6d.; 1s. 9d.
F41	*Embarrassments* (1896 [1897])	Heinemann	74	2s. 6d.; 3s. 6d.
F42	*The Finer Grain* (1910)	Methuen	—	1s. 6d.; 2s.
F43	*The Golden Bowl* (1905)	Methuen	—	1s. 6d.; 2s.
F44	*The Lesson of the Master* (1892)	Macmillan	148	(undetermined)

Some copies remaindered domestically through the Times Book Club; see F27.

F45	*The Other House* (1897)	Heinemann	85	2s. 6d.; 3s. 6d.
F46	*The Outcry* (1911)	Methuen	—	1s. 6d.; 2s.
F47	*The Real Thing* (1893)	Macmillan	149	(undetermined)
F48	*The Sacred Fount* (1901)	Methuen	—	1s. 6d.; 1s. 9d.
F49	*The Soft Side* (1900)	Methuen	—	1s. 6d.; 1s. 9d.
F50	*The Spoils of Poynton* (1897)	Heinemann	90	2s. 6d.; 3s. 6d.
F51	*Tales of Three Cities* (1888)	Macmillan	14	(undetermined)
F52	*Terminations* (1895)	Heinemann	41	2s. 6d.; 3s. 6d.
F53	*The Tragic Muse* (1890)	Macmillan	109	(undetermined)
F54	*The Two Magics* (1898)	Heinemann	149	2s. 6d.; 3s. 6d.
F55	*What Maisie Knew* (1897 [1898])	Heinemann	120	2s. 6d.; 3s. 6d.

Miscellaneous

F56	Guy de Maupassant, *The Odd Number*, with an introduction by Henry James (1891)	E. A. Petherick	15	(undetermined)

F. MISCELLANEA

VI. MANUSCRIPTS

When one considers the number of Henry James's letters preserved by his correspondents, it is a matter of some surprise to discover that so few of his holograph manuscripts have turned up. Of these the most important are the notebooks, published almost in their entirety in 1947 (A92). They are to be found in the James Collection of the Houghton Library at Harvard. There are nine notebooks, most of them ordinary old-fashioned scribblers, in which James sketched in his rapid hand the ideas he later fashioned into novels and tales.

It is difficult to say why more holograph manuscripts are not extant, particularly since James achieved fame early. Those which may have been in the novelist's possession do not appear to have survived the fire in which he burned a large part of his personal papers. The paucity of manuscripts may be attributed in part to the fact that most of James's novels were serialized; his books were set up from the instalments on which James made revisions. The magazines of that era were less conscious of the "value" of the manuscript than we are today and many archives appear to have perished. One editor of the *Atlantic Monthly*, Thomas Bailey Aldrich, however, had a strong sense of the uses for posterity of manuscripts. Among the Aldrich papers, now in the Houghton Library at Harvard, are a number of the holograph instalments of *The Princess Casamassima*. Chapter 38, which was owned by the Providence, R.I., public library, has now been presented to Harvard, but Chapters 41–47 remain unlocated. Aldrich also preserved the instalments of *En Province*, published in the *Atlantic*, which became *A Little Tour in France*. Also found among the Aldrich papers was an unpublished essay of James's entitled "Very Modern Rome," which has since been printed in the *Harvard Library Bulletin* (D581).

For the rest, the surviving manuscripts are few indeed.

Only one other novel, and a minor one at that, has been found in James's hand. This is *Confidence*, which is also at Harvard. Apparently someone at *Scribner's Monthly* collected James's manuscripts, for not only was this novel preserved—but also the tales "Longstaff's Marriage," "Crawford's Consistency" (now in the library of the National Institute of Arts and Letters, New York), and "Four Meetings" (the last in the Huntington Library), all published in that magazine. Since James, however, contributed to *Scribner's* during the 1870's and 1880's largely such work as he deemed unsuited to the *Atlantic Monthly*, it is to be regretted that the collecting spirit was not applied as zealously in the latter journal. Time may yet disclose, among further papers of various *Atlantic* editors, manuscripts of the major works, but for the present there is little more to report. The Houghton Library also has the typewritten MS. of "The Jolly Corner" as well as the monologue written by James for Ruth Draper.

The Yale University Library owns leaves 14–95 of *The Europeans* bound together with the first 13 leaves of "The Pension Beaurepas." Additional fragments of *The Europeans* are owned by Robert H. Taylor, W. Jones, Wayzata, Minn., and the Barrett collection of the University of Virginia. The Morgan Library owns the signed holograph manuscript of one of James's American tales, "The Impressions of A Cousin," as well as a ninety-page typewritten scenario or outline of *The Ambassadors*, dated 1 September 1900. Book Third of *The Other House* came, via Clement Shorter and the *Illustrated London News*, to the library of Sir Hugh Walpole, who bequeathed it to the King's School, Canterbury.

Among the posthumous papers at the Houghton Library are the various typescript drafts of the unfinished novels *The Sense of the Past* and *The Ivory Tower* and the fragment *The Middle Years*—which would have been Henry James's third part of his autobiographies. Typescripts are extant also in the library of part of a short story barely begun, the war articles on France and "The Long Wards," and James's translation of Barrès's "The Saints of France," as well as the anniversary article for the *Nation*, the essay on Mr and Mrs J. T. Fields, which contains about 700 words of notes for the article, and the original draft and redictated version of the introduction to Rupert Brooke's *Letters from America*.

An account of the manuscripts (holograph and typescript) of Henry James's plays is given in *The Complete Plays of Henry James* (1949). This was amplified in a bibliographical article published in the *Harvard Library Bulletin* (III 3, 395–406, Autumn 1949) by Leon Edel entitled "The Texts of Henry James's Unpublished Plays."

Few of James's non-fictional writings have been preserved in holograph. The Houghton Library has his essay on Trollope (it was owned by Amy Lowell) and the paper on Alphonse Daudet which appeared in June 1882 in the *Atlantic* (this again among the Aldrich papers), as well as the unsigned review of Renan's reminiscences (*Atlantic*, August 1883). More recently, in a collection of papers written for the *North American Review* between 1864 and 1868 and presented to Harvard many years ago by Charles Eliot Norton, holographs of four early reviews by Henry James were found: of T. W. Higginson's *Epictetus*, Morris's *Life and Death of Jason*, P. G. Hamerton's *Contemporary French Painters* and Bayard Taylor's *John Godfrey's Fortunes*, the last not published and believed to be of 1865. (See D582.)

In the Berg Collection at the New York Public Library will be found the essay on Coquelin, the review of Howells's *Italian Journeys*, and "Venice." The Buffalo Public Library has James's second essay on Turgenev (*Atlantic*, January 1884), and the Huntington Library has James's review of the Carlyle–Emerson correspondence (*Century*, June 1883). In the Ashley Library in the British Museum there is the tribute to James Payn which originally appeared in the *Illustrated London News* of 9 April 1898. The manuscript contains some material eliminated from the published text. Yale has the manuscript of "The Present Literary Situation in France" (*North American Review*, October 1899), which shows that he originally titled it "The Century's End: The Literary Situation in France."

The manuscripts of the essay on Alphonse Daudet (*Century*, August 1883) and the reviews of the life and letters of Madame Swetchine (*North American Review*, July 1868) and of "Recent Volumes of Poems" (*North American Review*, April 1867) have been noted in sale catalogues. A review of the novel *Two Men* by Elizabeth Stoddard (1865) and James's translation of Daudet's essay on Turgenev (D395) are in the Barrett collection at Virginia.

Harvard has the revised pages of *The American* and *The Portrait of a Lady* prepared for the New York Edition. In the Scribner archives there exist signed typescripts of "Flickerbridge" and "The Great Good Place" containing the printer's markings. The original *Galaxy* magazine pages of "A Light Man" extensively corrected by James for re-publication in the Scribner series (Vol. V) of *Stories by American Authors* are also in the Barrett collection. The typescript of the 1900 essay on the letters of Robert Louis Stevenson is owned by the Century Association in New York. A fragment of the corrected typescript of *What Maisie Knew* (Chapter XVII, pages 184–201) is in the Estelle Doheny collection of the Doheny Memorial Library, St John's Seminary, Camarillo, California.

The Humanities Research Center of the University of Texas at Austin has the final portion of *What Maisie Knew*, a typed manuscript with holograph revisions, numbered pp. 308–14. It also has a typed manuscript with holograph revisions of the essay "The Long Wards," and a typed manuscript, signed, of the one-act play "Summersoft."

ACKNOWLEDGMENT

In a work of such amplitude as this bibliography we have
been indebted to many persons in many lands, as well as to
a large number of libraries, publishing and printing houses
and other institutions—including the National Libraries of
most of the Western countries and some of the East. We
found everywhere the greatest interest in our project and
were given the fullest co-operation. It would take too much
space to begin specifying the extent of our indebtedness in
each instance; it will be apparent, to a degree, in the sources
of some of our materials. Here we can only confine our-
selves to listing gratefully, in alphabetical order, the in-
dividuals and institutions in whose debt we stand:

Prof. Nelson F. Adkins; Mrs Frances M. Gale, of the
American Foundation for the Blind; Miss Helen Cohan of
Appleton-Century-Crofts Inc.; Prof. George W. Arms;
Mr C. Waller Barrett; Dr Middendorf of the Bayerische
Staatsbibliothek, München; G. Bell & Sons Ltd.; Miss Clare
Benedict; the late E. F. Benson; Mr John D. Gordan,
Curator of the Henry W. and Albert A. Berg Collection
(New York Public Library); the Biblioteca Nacional,
Madrid; the Biblioteca Narodowa, Warsaw; the Biblioteca
Nazionale Centrale, Florence; the Biblioteca Nazionale di
Brera, Milan; the Biblioteca Vittorio Emanuele, Rome; the
Bibliothèque de Documentation Internationale Contempor-
aine, Paris; Prof. Leo Olivenbaum of the Slavic Section and
staff of the Bibliothèque Nationale, Paris; the Birmingham
Public Library (England); Mr Jacob Blanck; Mr Andrew
Block; the Bodleian Library; Bokförlaget Natur och Kultur,
Stockholm; Mr Albert Boni; Miss Theodora Bosanquet;
Mr James J. Dromey, Librarian of the *Boston Herald*; Mr
John M. Carroll of the Boston Public Library; Mr Donald

ACKNOWLEDGMENT

G. Brien; Mr F. C. Francis, Keeper, Mr A. V. Hull, Super-intendent of the Newspaper Library, and staff of the British Museum; Mr Deming Brown; Brown University Library; Mr I. R. Brussel; *Burlington Magazine*.

William Andrews Clark Memorial Library, University of California; Cambridge University Library; Jonathan Cape Ltd.; Prof. Oscar Cargill; Mr John Carter; Chapman & Hall Ltd.; Chatto and Windus; University of Chicago Library; The Chiswick Press; Richard Clay & Co.; Cleveland Public Library; William Clowes & Sons; William E. Colburn of Central Michigan University; Mr Benton L. Hatch of the Colby College Library; Mr H. Bacon Colla-more; *Collier's Magazine*; Columbia University Library; the late Michael Sadleir of Constable & Co. Ltd.; T. & A. Constable Ltd.; Corlies, Macy & Co.; Cornell University Library; the late Oliver Simon of the Curwen Press; Mr Horvell Daniels; J. M. Dent & Sons; Mr E. Porter Dickinson, Amherst College Library; Ethel Lady Dilke; Doubleday & Co.; James F. Drake Inc.; Duckworth & Co.; Miss Mattie Russell of the Duke University Library; Mr Philip C. Duschnes; the Rt. Hon. David Eccles, and his secretary, Miss Mary Bulloch; Editorial Nova, Buenos Aires; The Essex Institute; Mr Albert C. Gerould and staff of the Free Library of Philadelphia; Mr Gilbert Fabes; the Fine Arts Society; Mr Maurice Firuski; Prof. Kathleen Fitzpatrick, Melbourne; the Fitzwilliam Museum, Cambridge; Mr Richard Foley; the late Alice Fullerton.

The late Henry Gerson; Prof. William M. Gibson; Mr James Gilvarry; Mr George T. Goodspeed; Mr Donald Gutstein; Miss Erica Marx of the Hand and Flower Press; Prof. Virginia Harlow; Miss Dorothy B. Fiske of Harper & Brothers; George G. Harrap & Co.; Mr Rupert Hart-Davis and staff of Rupert Hart-Davis Ltd.; Mr John Hayward; Mr Arnold Gyde of William Heinemann Ltd.; Mr G. Heywood Hill; Mrs Charles Hoeing; Miss Elizabeth Seanor of the

Hofstra College Library; Prof. William A. Jackson, Librarian, Mr W. H. Bond, Miss Carolyn Jakeman and Mrs Mary Goulart of the Houghton Library; Miss Christina Carlow of the Houghton Mifflin Company; Mr M. A. DeWolfe Howe; the Henry E. Huntington Library; Iowa State University Library; the late Henry James; Mr William James; Johns Hopkins University Library; the late Edna Kenton; Mr George Kirgo; Kyushu Imperial University Library, Fukuoka, Japan; M. Robert Laffont of Editions Robert Laffont, Paris; Mr Harold M. Landon; Mr H. Lauritzen, Copenhagen; Mr J. B. Boxley of the Copyright Office, Library of Congress; the Hispanic Foundation, Library of Congress; Mr Frederick Goff, Director, and staff of the Rare Books Division, Library of Congress; the late Paul Lemperly; Mr Sidney E. Lind; Livraria Sá Da Costa, Lisbon; The London Library; Longmans Green & Co.; Sampson Low, Marston & Co.; Mr Percy Lubbock.

Sir Compton Mackenzie; Robert Maclehose & Co. Ltd.; Macmillan & Co. Ltd., London; The Macmillan Company, New York; Mr Laurence Marr; Mr Dudley Massey; M. André Maurois; Mr John Cullen of Methuen & Co.; Mr Albert Mordell; the Pierpont Morgan Library; Mr Malcolm Morley; Sir John Murray of John Murray Ltd.; Miss Anne Petrides of the National Book League; the National Institute for the Blind, London; the New York Public Library; Mr Simon Nowell-Smith; Miss Judith Nussbaum; Mr Lennart Nylander, Royal Consul-General of Sweden; the late P. S. O'Hegarty; the late William Dana Orcutt; Oxford University Press; Parke-Bernet Galleries; University of Pennsylvania Library; the late Le Roy Phillips; Polish University College Library, London; Portugalia Editora, Lisbon; Mr Howard C. Rice and staff of the Princeton University Library; G. P. Putnam's Sons; Mr David Randall; the late Dr Moses Ratner; the Rodale Press; Mr Bertram Rota; Mr W. N. Roughead; the Royal Bibliothek, Copen-

ACKNOWLEDGMENT

hagen; the Royal Society of Literature; Mrs Sara F. Ruben-
stein; Rutgers University Press; Mrs Herta Ryder; Prof.
Makoto Sangu, Tokyo; Mr J. W. Robertson Scott; Mrs Vera
Scriabine; Miss Elizabeth Youngstrom of Charles Scribner's
Sons; Mr Martin Secker; Mr John G. Pattisson of Secker
& Warburg Ltd.; Mr John S. Van E. Kohn, Mr Michael
Papantonio, and Mrs Alexandra Schultz of the Seven Gables
Bookshop; Sidgwick & Jackson Ltd.; Dr Gregg M. Sin-
clair.

Slovenská Akadémia Vied, Bratislava; Mr Herbert S.
Stone, Jr.; the late Sir Ronald Storrs; Mr John L. Sweeney;
Mr Robert H. Taylor; *Town & Country Magazine*;
Trinity College Library, Dublin; U.S. Information Ser-
vice; University Press, Cambridge, Mass.; the late Mary
James Vaux; Viesseux's Library, Florence; the late Allan
Wade; Miss Dorothy M. Ward; Washington Square Col-
lege Library; A. P. Watt & Son Ltd.; Prof. Carl J.
Weber; Westdeutsche Bibliothek, Marburg/Lahn; Western
Reserve University Library; Mr Edmund Wilson; Mr Ed-
ward Brett of The Windmill Press; Wyman & Sons; Yale
University Library; Mr Morton Dauwen Zabel; Zentral-
bibliothek, Zurich; Zentralkatalog der Wissenschaftlichen
Bibliotheken Nordrhein-Westfalen, Cologne.

L. E.

D. H. L.

INDEX

INDEX

Works by Henry James, including short stories and articles which serve as titles of volumes, titles chosen by editors of James's writings, as well as serials whose titles were altered for book publication, are in uniform capitals. All other book titles are italicized. Short stories, articles, reviews and notes (by James or others) are in quotation marks. Where James used identical, or similar, titles for two or more works, the date of first appearance is inserted. Numerals of collations of the principal works as well as posthumous compilations are set in bold face. Where there is reference to portions of the text of this book not covered by the bibliographical serial numbers, page numbers are given in brackets.

INDEX

Altsheler, J. A., D504

Alvin Langdon Coburn Photographer: An Autobiography, C191

AMBASSADORS, THE, [12]; A**58**, 64, 86, 92a; C44a, 49a; D533, 580; E1a, 21, 62b, 82; F18, 37; [391]

AMERICAN, THE, [13]; A**4**, 20, 64, 86, **106**; C4, 141a; D259; [349]; E12, 35, 52–54, 71, 86c, 89b, 90, 99, 105b, 121, 123; F7a, 21; [393]

AMERICAN, THE (play), A35, 95; B14

"American and An English Novel," D277

American Art Association, C3

American Art Galleries, B13

"American Art-Scholar: Charles Eliot Norton," A73, 98; D555

"American Criticism," A98

"American Democracy and American Education," A98

AMERICAN ESSAYS OF HENRY JAMES, THE, A**98**; B10a, 15, 40; C50

American First Editions (ed. M. Johnson), A57b

American Ideals, D500

"American Letter," A98; D495, 498–507

"American Letter: The Question of the Opportunities," A98; B42; D495

American Literary Criticism, B24

American Literature (journal), A58b; C179

"American Magazines," A98

American Notes and Queries, C199

"American Novel, The," A98

AMERICAN NOVELS AND STORIES OF HENRY JAMES, THE, A**90**, 91

"American Purchase of Meissonier's *Friedland*," A100; D237

AMERICAN SCENE, THE, A**63**; C195; F38

American Theatre as Seen by Its Critics, A93a; B34, **39**

AMERICAN VOLUNTEER MOTOR-AMBULANCE CORPS IN FRANCE, THE, A81; C2; D568

American Wives and English Husbands, D498

"Americans Abroad," D348

Ami Fritz, L', A93a; D279

Amours de Philippe, Les, A103; D321

Ampère, André-Marie and Jean-Jacques, A5a; D219

Anavi, Arye, E66

Andersen, Hendrik Christian, C161

Anderson, Mary, C4a, 11a, 42

André-Marie Ampère et Jean-Jacques

Ampère: Souvenirs et Correspondance, D219

Andrews, Mary R. Shipman, B27

Anglo-American First Editions: West to East, [16]

Anglo-American Magazine, D529

Anglo-Saxon Review, D511

"Animated Conversation, An," A40; D432

Antequera, Juan Antonio, E100–111

Anteus, C189a

"Anthony Trollope," A30, 99; D389

Appleton & Co., B5b, 21a, 22a

Appleton's Booklovers Magazine, D538

Archer, Charles, C12

Archer, William, C12, 40; D482, 485, 562

Aria, Eliza, B20

Ármin, Sasvári, E67

Arms, George, [10]; A38, 69a

Arnim, Countess von ("Elizabeth"), C52

Arnold, George, B2

Arnold, Matthew, A65, 103; D7, 397

Around A Spring, D80

"Art," A100a; D87, 90, 154, 162

"Art: Boston," D91

"Art: The Dutch and Flemish Pictures in New York," A100a; D94

"Art and Letters in Paris," A101; D253

Art and the Actor, B**34**, 39

"Art in France," A101; D258

"Art in Paris," A101; D260

Art of Authorship, The, B5; C16

ART OF FICTION, THE (1884), A**25**, 30, 99; B41; D404; E82b, 89a; (1948), B15

ART OF THE NOVEL, THE, A**89**

As You Like It, D481

Ashendene Press, A84

ASPERN PAPERS, THE, A**32**, 64, 74, 86; D421; E17, 41, 59, 76, 78, 110, 112, 114; 125; F8a, 16, 23

Asquith, Elizabeth, D577

Asquith, H. H., C13

Asquith, Margot, C14

"At Isella," A82, 88; D81

Athenaeum, The, A4c, 10, 15b, 16a, 23d, 31a, 32a, 33a, 34b, c, 36b, 37b, 42a, 44a, 49a, 52a; B1a, 6b, 14, 17a, 20a, 27b, 32

Atherton, Gertrude, C15; D498, 501

Atlantic Monthly, [14], [16]; D6, 22, 32, 34, 37, 49–50, 56, 69–70, 73, 76–77, 79–80, 84, 86–87, 90–91, 93–94, 101–102, 106, 112–113, 119, 121, 123, 137, 152, 154, 156–157, 162–163, 173, 259, 275, 325, 329, 332,

INDEX

Caine, Hall, A47a
Calamus, A98; D499
Callender, L., C31
Callier, A., E90
Calvert, George H., D191
Cambon, Paul, B33
Cameron, Verney L., D297
Camors, A103; D63
Campbell, Mrs. Patrick, D485
Can You Forgive Her? A87; D13
Canavaggia, Marie, E23, 28b
Canby, Henry Seidel, B37
Capadose, Anton E., C37
Cape (Jonathan), Ltd., C10a
Carlyle, Thomas, A98, 103; D280, 388; [392]
"Carlyle's Translation of Goethe's Wilhelm Meister," A103
Carpeaux, Jean Baptiste, D228
Carrington, C. E., C32
Carter, Elizabeth, D27
Carter, John, [10]; A68b
Carter, Morris, C33
Cary, Richard, D585
"Casa Alvisi," A67; D530
Catalogue of Collection of Drawings by Alfred Parsons, A38; B7
Catalogue of Drawings by Mr. Edwin A. Abbey, A38; B3
Cather, Willa, C150
Causeries du Lundi, A103; D183
Cavour, Camillo Bensodi, D322
Caxton Publishing Co., B26b
Celebrity, The, D501
Censorship and Licensing, B28
Central Committee for National Patriotic Organisations, A75
Century Co., B19
Century Magazine, D382-383, 387-389, 391, 394-395, 399, 403, 406, 411, 416, 422, 424, 430, 439, 522; [393]
Century of French Romance series, A99; B21-22
"Century's End, The," [393]
Černy, Vaclav, E2
Chadourne, Marc, E18, 47
"Chain of [Italian] Cities," A2, 67; D123
Chambers, Robert W., D504
"Change of Heart, A," A95; D86
Channing, William Ellery, D173
Chap Book, The (journal), D476, 480
"Chaperon, The," A37, 64, 86; D448; E78, 105
Chapman, John Jay, A98; D505
Chapman & Hall, A63a
Chapman's Magazine of Fiction, D476

"Characteristic Manuscripts," B12
Charles, Mrs. E. R., A87; D12, 23, 36
"Charles Baudelaire," A5
"Charles de Bernard and Gustave Flaubert," A5; D241
"Charles Kingsley's Life and Letters," A103
"Charles Nordhoff's Communistic Societies," A103
"Charles S. Reinhart," A38; D441
"Charleston," A63
Charlotte Brontë and Her Circle, D482
Charnwood, Lady, C34
"Chartres [Portrayed]," A21, 101; D255
Chastelard, A87; D20
Chatto & Windus, A11a, c, 76a; C51
Chaundy & Co., A62a
Cheerful Yesterdays, D505
Cherbuliez, Victor, D115, 190, 263
"Chester," A2, 62; D95
Children, The, D482
Childs, Mrs. Francis, C181
Chiswick Press, C1; D562
Chocarne, Père Bernard, D48
Christensen, Ellen, E6
Christian Painter of the Nineteenth Century, D209
Christy, Howard Chandler, D514
Chronicles of the Schönberg-Cotta Family, A87; D12
Church, Francis, C126a
Church, William, C126a
"Churches of Florence," A2a; D142
Churchill, Winston, A98; D501
Cities of Northern and Central Italy, D256
Clairin, Georges, B1a
Clairouin, Denyse, E16, 45
Clarke (J.) & Co., B5a
Clarke Co., Ltd., B18b
Clifford, Lucy (Mrs W. K.), C40, 185
Clodd, Edward, C35
Clowes (William) & Sons, B6b
Clutton-Brock, A., A75
Cobb, Sanford H., D503
Coburn, Alvin Langdon, A64a; C191
Cockerell, Sydney, C117
Cohen, B. Bernard, C35a
Colby Library Quarterly, D375, 585
Cole, J. Foxcroft, [16]; D91
"Collaboration," A39a, 41, 86; D459
Collamore, H. B., [10], [17]; A17, 37a; B13
Collas, L., E67
COLLECTIVE EDITION OF 1883, A20
Collier (P. F.) & Son, B21a, 22a
Collier's Weekly, D494, 510, 515, 520

INDEX

INDEX

"Guildhall and the Royal Academy,"
A100; D486

"Gustave Flaubert" (1893), A40;
D465; (1902), A73, 99; B22; E82b

Güttinger, Fritz, E64

"Guy de Maupassant" (1888), A30, 99;
E82b; D420; (1889), B4; D436

GUY DOMVILLE, A43, 95; B14, 23;
C204

Haldeman-Julius, E., A88

Hale, Susan, D78

Hamerton, Philip G., A100a; D51,
242; [392]

Hamilton, Lady, D485

Hammersley, Violet, C141

Hammerton, J. A., C73

Hammond, Gertrude D., B26a

Hand & Flower Press, A52c

Hansen, Mag. Chr. Mathaeus, E5

Hapgood, Isabel F., B11

Hapgood, Norman, D503

Harding, Charlotte, D520

Hardy, Arthur Sherburne, C67

Hardy, Thomas, A102, 103; C3; D158

"Hardy's Far from the Madding
Crowd," A103

Hare, Augustus J. C., D180, 256, 341

Harland, Henry, A98; D496

Harlow, Virginia, [10]; C68–69; D199,
208, 213

Harold: A Drama, A65a; D281

Harper, J. Henry, B6a

Harper & Brothers, A8a, c, 9, 12b, 14,
15a, 38, 39b, 40b, 41, 42b, 44b, 45b,
53b, 58b, 63b, 66; B4a, 6a, 11b, 26a,
27, 29, 37, 38b, 42

Harper Essays, A81; B**37**

Harper's Bazar, C51b; D523, 550–551,
553, 560

Harper's [New Monthly] Magazine,
D370, 377, 414, 418, 425, 433, 442,
490, 527, 536, 543, 547, 552, 558, 577

Harper's Weekly, B15; D410, 412–
413, 436, 441, 445, 469, 478, 481–
489, 491, 509

Harrap (George G.) & Co., B26b

Harrier, Richard C., C70; D581

Harris, Marie P., C71

Harrison, James Albert, D192

Hart-Davis, Rupert, [21]; B1; C72, 177

Hart-Davis (Rupert), Ltd., A93b, 95b,
100a, 101b, 102, 105; B41; C11b

Harte, Bret, A98; D501; E11

Harvard Library Bulletin, A58b; D581–
582; [390], [392]

Harvard University Press, A100b;
C175

Harvey, George, C92, 181, 195

Hasler, Jörg, C192

Hassall, Christopher, C72a

Haven, Gilbert, D201

Havens, Raymond D., C73

HAWTHORNE, A**12**, 60b; B40; E106

Hawthorne, Julian, A103; D157, 249,
309

Hawthorne, Nathaniel, A12, 60b, 98,
102, B15, 25, 40; C35a, 135; D92;
E67, 106

"Hawthorne's French and Italian
Journals," A98; D92

Hay, Clara Stone, C201

Hay, John, C181, 199, 201

Hay, Mrs., C201

Hayward, Abraham, D359

"Hayward's Essays," D359

Head, Ruth, A76; C74

Hearthstone Series, A87

Hedda Gabler, A40, 93; D446

Heffer (W.) & Sons, A67a; B41

Heichen-Abenheim (Heichen, Paul
Hermann), E52

Heinemann, William, B10b; C91

Heinemann (William), Ltd., A23d, e,
35, 45a, 46a, 47a, c, 48a, 49a, 52a,
53a, 62a, 67, 74a; B10a, 16, 21, 22a

Heinemann & Balestier, A33d; B9

Helps, Arthur, D177

Henderson, Isaac Austen, C204

Henley, W. E., B1

Hennecke, Hans, E60–62

Hennessy, W. J., D45, 53, 57, 452

"Henri Regnault," D103

"Henrik Ibsen," A40, 93; D446, 464

"Henry Beyle," A103

*Henry Beyle (Otherwise De Stendhal):
A Critical and Biographical Study*,
D149

"Henry Irving as Louis XI," A93;
D340

HENRY JAMES AND H. G. WELLS, B**43**

"Henry James and Alfred de Musset:
A Possible Misattribution," D73

*Henry James and John Hay: The
Record of a Friendship*, C201

*Henry James and Robert Louis Steven-
son*, B**41**; C156

"Henry James and the Struggle for
International Copyright," C179

Henry James at Home, C194

"Henry James, Daudet, and Oxford,"
C198

Henry James et la France, E40

"Henry James haggles over Terms for
'Guy Domville,'" C204

Henry James in Cambridge, C94a

INDEX

INDEX

INDEX

INDEX

PRIVATE LIFE, THE, A**39**, 41, 64, 86, 94; D453; E78
"Problem, A," A96; D53
Proceedings in Commemoration of 100th Anniversary of Birth of Hawthorne, A98; B**25**; C135
"Professor Fargo," A82, 88; D145
"Professor [David] Masson's Essays," A103; D171
"Progress of Anthropology," [15]
Prophet, The, A103; D160
"Prosper Mérimée," A104; D508
Prothero, Fanny, Lady, C127a
Publishers' Circular, A34b
Publishers' Weekly, A3a, 16b, 46b, 51b, 52b, 69a, 76b, 85a; B8, 13, 17b, 18b, 21a, 26a, 34; C9
Punch, D526
"Pupil, The," A36, 64, 74a, b, 86; B12; D443; E16, 42, 78
Purdy, Richard, C3
Putnam's Magazine, D559
Putnam's (G.P.) Sons, C10b
Putt, S. Gorley, C204
Pyle, Howard, D515
"Pyramus and Thisbe," A95; D67

Quarterly Review, D535, 564, 547
Quatrevingt-treize, D130
"Quebec," A21; D82
Queen Mary, A65a; D210
QUEER PEOPLE AND A DAMNING PASSION, A**88**
Quest of the Holy Grail, The, B**13**
QUESTION OF OUR SPEECH, THE, A**61**, 99, 104; D538
QUESTION OF THE MIND, THE, A**75**; D573
"Question of the Opportunities, The," A98; B42; D495
Quiller-Couch, Arthur, D562

Raikes, Thomas, D197
Rainbow Library, F6
Rambeau, James, [22]
"Rambler, The," C205
Randall, David, [10]; A16b, 56a
Ransom, Will, [10]; C6
Rantoul, Robert S., A98; B25; C35a
"Ravenna," A2, 67; D143
Ray, Gordon N., B43; C136
Reading, Writing and Remembering, A68b; B**38**
"Real Right Thing, The," A54, 64, 86, **94**; D515; E62c
REAL THING, THE, A**37**; 64, 86; D454; E7, 62c, 104a; F30, 47
"Reassembling of Parliament," D363

"Recent Florence," A21a; D332
"Recent Novels," D235
"Recent Volumes of Poems," A103; D36; [393]
Record of a Girlhood, D352
REFUGEES IN CHELSEA, A81, **84**; D576
"Refugees in England," A81
Regnault, Henri, D103, 273
Reid, Forrest, C137
Reid, Wemyss, C123a
Reid, Whitelaw, A101a; C36, 51a, 105
Reinhart, Charles S., A38; D413, 418, 425, 441
Rekhnevskoy, S., E98a
Remains of Lost Empires, D169
Rembrandt, A100a; D265
"Reminiscences of Ernest Renan," A103; D392
Renaissance Press, B26a
Renan, Ernest, A103; D230, 261, 266, 392; [392]
"Renan's Dialogues and Philosophic Fragments," A103
Renner, Lisbeth and Louis, E124
Répin, Ilya E., B11
Report from the Joint Select Committee . . . on the Stage Plays (Censorship), B28; C138
Repplier, Agnes, C139
"Reprobate, The," A44, 95
République Française (newspaper), E12, 35
Reubell, Henrietta, C40
"Rev. Francis Hodgson, A Friend of Lord Byron," A103
REVERBERATOR, THE, A**31**, 64, 74a, b, 86; D419; F31
Review of English Studies, C209
"Review of Zola's Novel *Nana*," A99
Revue Anglo-Américaine, [359]
Revue Bleue, E38, 48
Revue Britannique, E34, 36
Revue des Deux Mondes, [359-360]; E10-11, 29-33
Revue de Genève, E44
Revue des langues vivantes, C190
Revue de littérature comparée, C180
Revue de Paris, E15—16, 42, 45-46
Revue Hebdomadaire, E18, 43, 47
Reynolds, Paul R., A70b
"Rheims and Laon: A Little Tour," A21, 23a; D325
Rhodes, Albert, D207
Rice, James, A13b
Richard III, A93; D481
"Richmond [, Virginia]," A63; D549
Ride to Khiva, D295

INDEX

INDEX